MW01641155

# Stock Market Investing for Beginner

***The Bible 6 books in 1**: Stock Trading Strategies, Technical Analysis, Options Trading, Pricing and Volatility Strategies, Swing Trading with Options and Day Trading*

William L. Anderson

# Table of content

**Fast with Options Trading. How to Trade to Get Your Financial Freedom**

## Swing Trading

**A beginner's guide with proven strategies on how to trade with options, stocks, futures and make profits fast. Tools, time and money management, rules and routine of a trader.**

## Swing Trading with Options

**A Crash Course for Beginners to Highly Profitable Day and Swing Trade**
**Proven Strategies & Techniques to Trade Options, Stocks, Forex and Day Trading**

# Stock Trading Strategies

*A Guide for Beginners on How to Trade in the Stock Market with Options and Make Big Profit Fast; Psychology, Basics and Tips to Create Your Financial Freedom*

William L. Anderson

# Table of Contents

# Introduction

Welcome to stock trading strategies! In the first book of this series, we will introduce you to the world of stock trading. Taking control over your own financial future as an active trader and investor can be exciting. However, it can also be an intimidating prospect. In this series, we hope to teach you the information you need to begin successfully managing your own investment accounts.

As I write this book, the stock market continues an unprecedented rise that has lasted since the end of the last recession. There have been ups and downs, but every time it seems like the market is pulling back, it rebounds and continues its steady climb.

That certainly won't last forever, and someday the inevitable bear market will arrive. However, the first lesson that you should learn when you start managing your own trading and investing is this one. Bear markets are always temporary. There is no need to panic during recessions. When it comes to the long-term trend in the stock market, increasing asset prices are the rule.

Of course, there are ways that you can profit from the short-term gyrations of the stock market, and even make money from declining share prices. This is the world of trading and speculation. Traders are less interested in the fundamentals of the companies they invest in and seek to earn profits from the up or down trends in the markets. Incorporating some trading into your overall strategy can actually help you beat average market returns. The good news is that there are ways to earn profits even when the market is going down. When you learn how to implement them, you can profit from the market at all times.

In this book, we will learn about traditional stock investing. We'll show you how to manage it yourself, and teach you about the strategies that the big and successful investors use. We'll also teach you about the solid strategies that millionaire traders use to make profits every year that outperform leading market indicators. This will help you build wealth faster than what's possible following the traditional path of pure buy and hold investing or buying mutual funds.

Stock market investing can be fun, interesting, and exciting! Remember that knowledge is power. By reading this book, you are taking the first step on your journey to becoming a successful investor. Nearly every single time on the markets, those who are educated on how the markets operate are the winners.

# Chapter 1
## The Keys to Stock investing

If you've been watching on the sidelines, you're probably a bit concerned. Over the last 10 years, the stock market has enjoyed an unprecedented rise. In one of the biggest bull markets in history, stocks fully recovered from the 2008 recession. Not only that, but the gains keep coming. Over the past six years, the markets have surpassed everyone's expectations, continuing to rise higher and higher.

If you feel like you've missed out, my message to you is don't worry. The best time to get into the stock market is *always* right now. The key to doing it successfully is by having the knowledge that you need to do well in all situations.

I'm going to let you in on a little secret. Even though the news media hypes up downturns in the stock market, using the negative news to create an alarm that sells to the worried public, professional investors know a bear market is no time to panic. First of all, bear markets are always short-lived. Did you know that even during the Great Depression, the stock market had massive gains during most years? Seeing a bear market as an indication that the future is bleak for all time is naïve. The market always recovers. While it might take time, eventually it ends up higher than it had been before the crash. Successful long-term investors like Warren Buffett know that bear markets are buying opportunities. Big blue chip companies like Walmart and Apple are still there and conducting business. When their stock is cheap during a downturn, that's a buying opportunity.

But there is more. Traders have ways to profit from the movements in share prices no matter what the situation is. When prices move down, they can earn profits. When prices move up, they can earn profits. The key is learning how they do it. The secret techniques they use aren't well known by the general public. But I am going to teach them to you in this book series so that you will be fully armed and ready the next time the market experiences a downward trend.

## An Overview of the Basics

Let's begin by focusing on the keys to successful stock investing. You will be surprised that there really isn't any mystery. Successful investing revolves around two key ideas.

- The overall market trend is rising. Over time, the stock market always increases. Although it's easy to panic in the heat of the moment, history shows that sudden drops in share prices – even when they are prolonged – are always followed by gains that take the market to new heights. For long-term investors looking to build wealth, the trend in the market is always up.
- The stock market is volatile, and some stocks are more volatile than others. That means that share prices can move up and down rapidly for some stocks, while prices are more stable for others. Learning to recognize volatility and use it to your advantage is one of the keys to successful investing. Many new investors don't realize that it's easy to get hard data on a stock's volatility, and you can use that to your advantage.

- Picking individual stocks isn't that hard. Many new investors are intimidated by having to pick their own stocks. For some people, it's too much, and they'd rather have a professional money manager do it for them. However, it's not really that complicated. We'll teach you some key characteristics a company should have before you invest. That will make picking stocks to grow your portfolio much easier.
- Diversification is easy. A strategy called diversification can be overwhelming when you consider the prospect of having to pick a large number of companies to invest in. However, exchange-traded funds make that easier than ever. They are like mutual funds, but trade on the stock market. That means you can invest in a wide array of assets and indices without having to hire an expensive money manager. Since they trade like stocks, they have more liquidity, meaning that you can get into and out of your positions fast, if need be. We'll show you how to increase the diversity of your portfolio using these wonderful and profitable tools.
- Income investing is easier than you think. Many investors like the idea of having a large portfolio that generates income in the here and now for them. If you are just getting started, that can seem like a faraway dream. However, we'll show you fun and exciting ways that you can generate income in the here and now.

## What Is Stock and What Types of Stock Are Available

People like to throw around the word *stock*. But most people don't really understand what it means. For the record, let's clarify the meaning of the word so that you really understand what you're getting into.

Stock is an ownership stake in a company. When a company issues stock, it divides up the ownership into portions called *shares*. You buy an ownership stake in a company by purchasing shares of stock. So if you purchase shares of Exxon, which means that you are one of the owners of Exxon that entitles you too many things, including a share of the company profits. As the fortunes of the company improve, the value of the shares increases because there will be more demand for ownership. If the company experiences bad times, or the economy starts doing badly, investors will start selling off their ownership stakes. That means supply will exceed demand, causing prices to drop. Since owning shares in the company may not be seen as profitable, the prices have to drop to attract new buyers.

Publicly traded companies issue large numbers of shares, and they are traded on regulated public markets called stock exchanges. There are two general classes of stock. These are:

- Common stock: This is what most people are referring to when they use the word *stock*. A common stock gives you an ownership stake and voting rights in the company. Voting will occasionally take place when shareholders have the opportunity to vote on important company decisions. Shares of common stock entitle the holder to receive dividends. But not all companies pay dividends, as we'll explain in a moment. Something to keep in mind is that common stockholders are last in line if a company decides to liquidate or declare bankruptcy.
- Preferred stock: These are special shares that are, in a sense, more like bonds. Preferred stock does not confer

voting rights, but there are other advantages to owning the preferred stock. In some cases, companies will guarantee the yield paid with dividends. Preferred stock also confers some rights not available to common stockholders, such as being ahead of them in line when a company goes bankrupt. If a company goes under, creditors and bondholders will get paid first. Then preferred shareholders will get paid, and finally, if anything is left over, common stockholders get paid. Most companies don't issue preferred stock. Some companies in the financial sector, like Bank of America, offer preferred stock.

## What is a Dividend

Many people invest in the stock market, hoping to earn income from dividends. However, it's important to know that not all companies pay dividends. Let's explore how this works.

When a company earns profits, they have some choices. They can pay out all the profits to the owners, which are the shareholders. Or they can reinvest some of the money back into the company. That means they will build new plants, invest in research and development, or hire more employees. They may put a large sum of money behind efforts to break into a new market, such as entering a developing market for the first time.

Companies that are experiencing a rapid growth phase may choose to reinvest all of their profits back into the company. These companies do not pay dividends because all of their profits have been reinvested. Even though these stocks don't pay dividends, they may be highly prized. Examples include Amazon, Netflix, and Google. Investors seek out these stocks because they appreciate or gain value over time.

If a company pays dividends, it's more likely to be an older, more stable company. Examples include IBM and GE. That doesn't mean the company isn't growing; Walmart also pays dividends and continues to experience growth. But the company is more mature than a new company like Tesla, which is poised for rapid growth. The amount paid in dividends varies widely. Deciding what stocks to buy depends on what your investment goals are.

## Preparation

Before quickly opening an account and starting to load up on stocks, an investor needs to put some effort into preparation. This will include three phases, and to be honest, preparation is a long-term effort. The first stage in preparation is to thoroughly review your own personal situation. You'll need to determine if you are really ready for investing, and how much you need to invest. Simply knowing what your financial goals are is a large part of the process of preparation. These issues will be discussed in the following chapter.

The preparation process will be ongoing. Before you invest in any stock, you will need to thoroughly analyze the company and its past performance. You'll need to determine how well any given stock fits in with your own financial goals, and square this with the prospects of the stock going forward. While you don't have to be a financial expert, it's important to determine the prospects of any given company going forward. Sometimes you will make the wrong bets, but using the right strategies can help minimize your overall risk.

Preparation continues after you've invested in a company. You'll need to keep track of the stock and periodically evaluate its performance. At times, you may have to decide whether or not to keep a company in your portfolio. And you'll be picking new stocks to include in your investments. As an active investor, preparation is a process that is ongoing. People who enjoy financial analysis and business are the best suited for active investing.

## Picking Winning Stocks

The million-dollar question is: knowing how to select winning stocks. While there are no guarantees in life, there are guidelines you can follow that will increase your odds of success. The fact is knowledge is power, and having some knowledge about how the stock market behaves and about the companies that you invest in will help you grow wealth over time.

There are several factors to consider when picking winning stocks. It's important to realize that you aren't always going to get it 100% right. Even the best investors make mistakes. The key to success is picking yourself up and moving on when mistakes happen and focusing on your overall portfolio rather than on individual wins and losses. Thinking long-term always helps as well.

Let's go over some of the key points that are important when picking winning stocks.

### *Understanding Company Value*

New investors may have a gut-level understanding that Apple and Google are valuable stocks. But it's important to really understand what makes a stock valuable. Investing in hunches can produce profits sometimes, but in most cases, it will lead investors sideways or even toward losses. It's important to combine your gut-level feelings about different investments with the cold, hard facts that we can derive from doing analysis.

There are two types of analysis used by professional investors, fundamental analysis and technical analysis. Over the long-term, fundamental analysis is more important. This involves studying the company's "fundamentals" – profit margins, cash on hand, assets, liabilities, trends in revenue, products, and services the company is offering, and management. The company's plans and potential for the future also play a role in fundamental analysis. Companies that may not be profitable now may be strong investments because of the potential. For years Amazon didn't earn any profits, but investors knew it was disrupting the marketplace and was likely to become a giant. A disruptive technology might make a company well placed for future gains. An example of this is Tesla, which is currently going through some rough spots. But it may still be a good investment because over time the technologies the company is developing might turn it into tomorrow's Amazon.

The first way to assess company value is to look at its *market capitalization*. This is the number of outstanding shares multiplied by the current share price. So if a company has 1,000 outstanding shares and they are trading at $20 a share, the market capitalization is $20,000. Companies with a high level of market capitalization tend to be more mature, stable, and dominant. They are poised to enjoy a solid long-term future that will bring investors good returns. Examples of companies with large market capitalization include Apple, Netflix, Walmart, and Google.

However, young companies that have lower market capitalization can be great investments as well. Smaller market capitalization is often a trade-off between risk and the possibility of substantial growth in the future. In the late 1990s, people who made that bet on Amazon when it was a relatively small and growing company have been paid handsomely for their decision. However, the risk can be high. There were many “dot com” companies around in the 1990s which seemed as appealing or more appealing than Amazon that don’t even exist anymore. It’s hard to know with any reasonable degree of certainty which smaller company is going to break out over time. That’s one reason why diversity is important, and we’ll show you ways that you can take advantage of the growth that young and smaller companies may offer without putting your investments at risk.

Investors will group companies into different categories, based on market capitalization. Values for each category are approximate.

These include:

- Mega cap (also ultra-cap): These are companies with a market capitalization that is $100 billion or more. Amazon has a market capitalization of $932 billion. Other examples include Google, Apple, Netflix, and Facebook.
- Large cap: A large cap company has a market capitalization that ranges between $10 billion and $100 billion. These are stocks that are often sought out by risk-averse investors who are looking for a relatively safe place to put their money and grow it slowly. Large cap companies can represent slow but steady growth over the long term but probably won’t provide the same returns that the dominant mega cap companies provide. Examples include General Electric, Duke Energy, and IBM.
- Mid cap: Companies in this category have a market capitalization that ranges in value between $1 billion and $10 billion. These are attractive investments if you are looking for relatively safe investments that still have a lot

of growth potential. To get to this size, a company has to be relatively stable with a solid outlook. Depending on other factors, the company may have the potential to grow so that it becomes a large cap stock, which means a lot of appreciation over time.

- Small cap: These are companies with a market capitalization less than $1 billion, but more than $250 million. Their smaller size means they have strong potential for growth, but they are also more risky investments. These companies are not large enough to be considered safe. These companies not only have the potential for growth, but they also have the potential for failure. Investors will put their money into small caps to take advantage of the growth potential, but the best way to do that is using an index fund. Tying yourself to a small number of small cap companies could leave you in a position of losing your investment capital.
- Micro cap: Finally, we have the smallest publicly traded companies. These are companies that have a market capitalization under $250 million. Investing in a micro-cap company carries significant risk. Of course, the higher the risk, the higher the potential reward. Micro cap stocks are going to be low priced, and if you bet right, you might realize huge profits. The problem is knowing which micro-cap company is going to be the diamond in the rough is pretty difficult to figure out, even for experienced traders. If you want to develop a solid investment plan, putting money into these types of companies is probably not something you should consider.

The best investment strategy involves a mixture of Ultra/Large cap, mid cap, and some small cap companies. The investments should be diversified, and the smaller the market capitalization, the more diversity. Your tolerance for risk, age, and investment goals will determine how much risk you should assume.

## *Aside: Penny Stocks*

While we are on the subject of market capitalization, it's important to have a precise definition of penny stocks. The name comes from the old days when you could actually buy something for a dime, and small and risky stocks really traded for pennies. Today, the Securities and Exchange Commission defines a penny stock as any stock that is $5 a share or less. Some penny stocks actually trade on the major exchanges, others trade "over the counter" and are called *pink sheets*. The bottom line is that you should stay away from penny stocks. It's certainly possible that a company with stock prices this low can turn things around and experience tremendous growth, but that is a rare event. Many hucksters promote "investing" in penny stocks by peddling fake promises of riches. Don't fall for their sales pitches. Most people that try investing in penny stocks end up broke. Professional day traders might be able to make profits from penny stocks, but that is not most people and its high risk. What they do is load up on large numbers of shares and attempt to profit from very short-term price movements, or they will short the stock. Beginning and everyday investors should stay away from penny stocks. They don't provide a way to build wealth over time and trying to earn profits from short-term price movements using penny stocks is a very high-risk activity.

## *Company Fundamentals*

The next factor to consider when picking a winning stock is to look at company fundamentals. This will include having a look at the financial statements of the company, which they are required to make available if they are a publicly traded company on a major stock exchange. These reports will help you analyze the cash flow, assets, liabilities, and revenue of the company. You'll want to use them to determine the company's profitability and outlook going forward. This is something that we will explore in detail in a later chapter.

Company fundamentals don't just involve financial details. You will also want to study the products and services the company offers. This means not only knowing how the company makes money now, but also how it plans to grow in the future. You'll want to know what the company's plans are for new product development and expansion into new markets.

Another aspect of company fundamentals is less tangible but equally important: management. Who is on the management team and what their backgrounds are is an important factor in determining the future potential of a company. You'll want to know their history, experience, and what role if any they played in founding the company. You'll also want to know how the team has performed in the past. Are there members of the management team that played leading roles at other successful companies? That can be a factor that increases your overall confidence in the company.

In short, there are many factors that need to be evaluated when studying company fundamentals. The complete picture is more important than one factor taken in isolation. Part of this process can be education; you can help develop your skills by reading how experienced investors like Warren Buffett evaluate fundamentals.

## *Price to Earnings Ratio*

Price to earnings ratio compares the price of a share to the earnings per share. If a company has solid fundamentals and a high level of earnings per share, a low price to earnings ratio is a signal that the stock is available at a discount. Sometimes investors are behind the times in finding good value, and so the stock will be low priced because of lack of demand. That situation won't last forever, so if you find a stock that fits this description, it can be a good addition to your portfolio. A stock with a low price to earnings ratio is probably well-placed to appreciate in value over time.

Of course, at times the opposite can occur as well. A stock might be overvalued, and this will be indicated by an unusually high price to earnings ratio. We will discuss this in more detail later.

## *Aligning Stock Picks With Your Investment Goals*

As we'll see, it's important to develop an investment strategy that helps you realize your financial goals. You might be late getting in on investing, and so aggressive growth through strong stock appreciation will be more important. Alternatively, you might be looking to build a safe investment income portfolio, preserving wealth and earning an income from it rather than seeking out rapid growth. No matter what your investment goals are, picking stocks that align with your goals is as important as looking at fundamentals and other characteristics like market capitalization.

## *Do Your Research*

Doing your research is important. It will help you pick good companies that are going to help you build wealth. Doing research will also help you determine the best times to enter a position or to exit a position that isn't helping you meet your goals. A winning investor studies the companies they invest in as well as the markets. They also pay close attention to financial, economic, and political news. You need to know how the overall economy and political situation is doing as well because the overall market is often impacted by external events.

### *Timing Buying and Selling*

Keeping an eye on short term trends can help you time your buying and selling the right way to ensure you get the most out of your financial gains. There are different ways to do that, depending on the situation, and we'll be talking about those through the book.

### *Become Familiar with the Tax Laws*

You don't have to become a tax expert to become a successful investor, but you should learn the basic structure of the tax laws. It's going to be important to know how you are going to be hit with taxes and how that impacts your gross profits. We'll be giving you an overview of this topic in a future chapter.

In the next chapter, we will discuss the first step in becoming an individual, self-directed investor. That is determining where you stand in your personal financial situation and figuring out what your investment goals should be. Knowing that will be key to your future investment strategies.

# Chapter 2
# Evaluating your Personal Financial

## Situation

There are many ways to go about investing, and knowing which path to take can be a daunting process. You can narrow down the possibilities to a strategy that works for you by evaluating your current financial situation. This should be done before you enter into your first trade. To be successful, an investor needs a clear picture of where they are going. Keep in mind this is not a one-time event. You should reevaluate your financial situation on an annual basis since it's going to be changing. When you find yourself in a different financial situation, your investment strategies will change over time.

## Where are you now?

Establishing a starting point is the first step. You don't have to be a financial wizard, but you need to be aware of your present situation before jumping in and buying stocks. Consider the following scenario. An investor with a large personal debt that has an interest rate of 17% keeps putting money in the stock market, hoping to build wealth over time. That sounds reasonable, but most market returns are, going to be in the range of 5-10%. That means that someone in this situation is actually *losing money*.

## Seek Liquidity

We are going to recommend that you look for assets you can sell. The money can be used to pay debts, back taxes, or to seed investment capital. You'll want to list all of your assets by liquidity, which means how easily they can be converted into cash. You'll also want to consider how much cash you can raise by selling each item if you were to sell it. A house might have a lot more value than a television set, but you might sell the television set in 24 hours while you'd have to wait months to sell the house.

## Dealing With Debts

Taking care of debts is one of the first things that a budding investor needs to do. While you might be anxious to get started with a large-scale investment plan if you have debts to take care of you might want to put it off. So the first step in preparing your investment plan is to create a simple balance sheet. You don't have to be an accountant, and you're only doing this for yourself, but it needs to be honest and accurate.

You're going to want to put together a listing of all of your assets and liabilities. When compiling assets, include everything of value that you could possibly sell. This could be a computer that you're not using, a dusty TV in a room nobody goes into very often, or an old guitar. Selling things you don't need can help you pay off debts faster and raise investment capital. You might object that you wouldn't raise much money, but imagine having an extra $500 to $1,000 to start off with.

When listing your liabilities, you're going to want to know how much debt you have, what the interest rates are, and what your monthly payments are. Monthly payments are less important than interest rates. Once you've listed all of your debts, you'll want to develop a plan to pay them off in a reasonable amount of time. There are many calculators available online, and you can also read many books on how to pay off debt. The series of books by debt guru Dave Ramsey is highly recommended. Here is an example of a good debt calculator:

https://www.creditkarma.com/calculators/debt_repayment/

You can use this calculator to figure out how long it will take to pay off a debt, for a given monthly payment. You can enter the interest rate, and the time frame you would like along with the monthly payment you're willing to make. Start off with the current minimum payment in order to determine the time required to pay off the debt, and work up from there.

In this example, we considered a $21,000 debt with a high 11% interest rate. Paying $450 a month would take five years to pay off the debt.

Additional Debt Repayment Information

Full Payoff

| Balance | Interest Rate | Expected Monthly Payment | Expected Payoff Time |
|---|---|---|---|
| $21,000 | 11% | $450 | 62 months |

Debt Repayment Chart

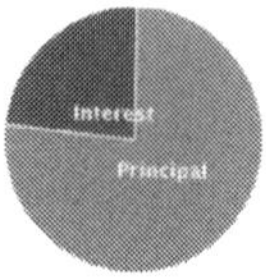

Interest
Principal

| Principal: | $21,370 |
|---|---|
| Interest: | $6,530 |

Click on the chart to see how much interest you will pay over the life of the debt.

That isn't a good situation to be in – do you want to saddle yourself with a $21,000 debt for five years?

When you have listed all of your debts, then you can prioritize them. In order to make the most progress in the shortest amount of time, it can be helpful to tackle the smallest debts first. This not only helps you get rid of your debt faster, but it will also have psychological benefits as you improve your financial situation.

If you have back taxes, you should make these a priority. The reason is that the government tacks on lots of fees and penalties, and if the tax debt is allowed to sit around, it can grow substantially in size. Get payment plans arranged to take care of these debts before they become unmanageable.

Take a look at your spending habits. Having material goods now isn't important if you plan to become a successful investor. You will be able to buy that BMW or Mercedes you want later when you can really afford it. For now, your focus should be on being able to direct your financial resources into your investments, so that you can grow your wealth over time. Expensive toys, like a new car, can be a large financial drain. If you have car loans, consider getting out of the car and into a used car that is reliable but costs a lot less. From this point forward, don't use debt to finance purchases. Keep a credit card on hand for emergencies, but don't use it to buy things like books or groceries that should be paid for using cash. If you can't pay for something with cash, it can wait.

## Having an Emergency Fund

Life is never fair, and we are all going to encounter emergencies. Recent studies have shown that most Americans don't have enough cash on hand to pay a $500 bill. If you are in that situation, you need to rectify it before you jump in with a large-scale investment plan. Remember that paying off debt first is always the priority. Debt is a sink that sucks important financial resources down the drain that could be used for other purposes. However, it's important to start putting money away for an emergency fund to be prepared for the unexpected – and being able to pay for it without having to take on more debt. Or worse, getting into a situation where you can't get credit but still need to find money to pay emergency bills. Set aside a small amount of money that you can start depositing into a savings account that you won't touch unless there is an emergency. Over time, the goal should be to have enough cash on hand to take care of emergency bills ranging up to $5,000 and to have funds on hand to cover times when you might be unemployed.

## Consider Additional Sources of Income

If you have a large amount of debt or find yourself in a situation where coming up with a significant amount of money to invest is difficult, you should consider taking action to increase your income. There are many paths to consider. You can start by looking for a higher paying job. Alternatively, you can look into taking a second job, at least until you are in a better financial situation. Another approach that can be used is to either take on "gigs" or short-term contract work. This can be done online or by doing some side work with companies like Uber. You can even look into starting your own online business to generate more income. This doesn't have to be a permanent situation, but you are going to want to get to a place where you are debt free and can put $1,000 or more into the stock market every month.

## Convert Debts from High Interest to Low Interest

If possible, you should refinance your debts to get lower interest rates. Consider the previous example, a high interest $21,000 debt that would take five years to pay off. If you could get a lower interest rate, you could shave off months or even years from the debt, while requiring you to put in less overall capital. Getting a secured debt can help as well. A secured debt is a lower risk for the lender, so they will offer lower interest rates. That means you will be able to get out of debt faster.

## Net Worth and Changes Over Time

When you've gathered everything together, you'll want to determine your net worth. You are doing this for yourself, so don't be embarrassed if it's in a bad position right now. Simply add up the total current value of your assets and liabilities, and subtract the total value of the liabilities from the total value of your assets. This is your net worth. If you can compare the value of each asset now to the value it had at the beginning of the year; you can also calculate the change in your net worth in percentage terms.

## Are You Ready to Invest

If you are debt free or have a plan in place to take care of your debts and to build an emergency fund, you are ready to begin investing. The first rule of investing is to never invest more than you can afford to lose. If you go about your investment plan carefully, the chances of losing everything are slim to none. That said it's a wise approach to invest as if that could really happen. So you shouldn't be investing next months house payment or your kid's college funds in the hopes of gaining returns. After you have taken care of your debts and emergency fund, add up all of your basic living expenses, so you know how much you actually need per month. Anything left over above that is the amount of money you can invest for now.

## Determining Your Financial Goals

Once you are in a position to invest something – even if you can only put in $100 a month now because you're paying off large debts – it's time to sit down and figure out your financial goals. There are several things to keep in mind:

- Age: Generally speaking, the older you are, the more conservative you should be in your investment approach. The reason for this is simple. When things go badly, it takes time to recover and get back on the road to profitability. The older you are, the less time you have to grow your wealth in the future. That means a market crash or a bad investment has larger consequences than it would have if you had thirty years to recover. Financial advisors generally recommend that older investors put their money in safer investments, which means putting some money into bonds and safe investments like US Treasuries that preserve capital. In the stock market, the older investor will seek out more stable companies that are larger, and while they may be growing, they have slow and steady growth with lower levels of risk. Of course, age can cut both ways. Many people reach their fifties with little to no savings or investment. If that describes your situation, you're going to want to invest more aggressively to seek rapid growth. Younger people also want to invest more aggressively, as they have a time horizon that permits taking on more risk. But time horizon isn't the only factor if you have no capital to protect; you definitely want to be more aggressive.

- Your financial situation: Are you broke? If so, you might need to think small, investing a little bit at a time. At the same time, you might want to take an aggressive approach, buying high growth stocks that can help you build wealth faster. On the other extreme, if you have a large amount of cash available, you're probably going to want to seek out investments that provide returns while protecting your capital.
- Seeking income or growth: Are you seeking to generate income? This question doesn't have to mean right now. You might be seeking to generate income in ten or twenty years. If so, then you're going to be looking at dividend and value stocks rather than stocks that are going to give you more return from appreciation. If you want growth, then you're going to want to target companies that are growing rapidly and taking market share that will give you a larger appreciation in share value.
- Rapid generation of cash: Are you looking to generate cash now, either for income or to invest? If so, you might be more of a speculator or trader than an investor. Trading stocks looking for short-term gains in price and profiting from them in the here and now is one way to generate cash over the short term. Another possibility is trading options,

which can lead to quick profits. Both approaches can help you generate income in the immediate future, but both carry a high risk of losing money as well.

Not every investor is going to fit neatly into a box. You might want to take an approach that utilizes all three goals. You can do that, but remember that doing it successfully requires a high level of discipline.

# Chapter 3
# Common Approaches to Investing

Once you've figured out your financial situation and defined your goals, the next step is to find an investment style and stocks that most closely align with your goals. While everyone has different goals, the best way to invest is the same today as it's always been. You should invest with an eye toward a long-time horizon. The reality is that speculating with day trading or swing trading leads to losses for most people, probably up to 90% or more of traders. Trading options is also very risky, it's a bet on the directional move of a stock over a short time period, and guess what most people bet wrong. About 85% of options expire worthlessly. Chances are you don't have the free time necessary to stay on top of your trades anyway. Rule#1 is to buy and hold for at least a year. At the end of each year, you can evaluate your holdings and determine whether or not they are profitable and still aligned with your goals, and you might decide to replace some of them. In most cases, you will simply *rebalance* your portfolio, so that the overall structure of your investments helps to keep you on track for meeting your goals.

## Seeking Stocks to Meet Your Goals

There is a wide range of stocks available, and it's important to have some guidelines that you can use to make your picks. Over the decades, investment experts have developed rules of thumb that can be used to decide what stocks to pick. The first factor in determining what stocks to pick is taking a look at your time horizon. Are you looking to reach your goals soon, like by the end of the year? Or are you looking at a time frame that is two years or longer? These are important questions that can be used as general guidelines. Remember that there are no absolute rules here. For example, you could buy a large/ultra-cap stock like Apple, and profit from a short-term swing in price. But Apple would also be an excellent investment for a buy and hold investor who is looking to build up a solid portfolio for retirement. But let's look at the general rules that financial advisors tend to stick by.

General investment strategies:

- Conservative: This means that you have a low tolerance for risk. The amount of money you've accumulated can be a reason for being conservative if you already have a large amount of capital; you probably aren't willing to risk losing it. Some people are conservative investors by nature. A conservative investor is going to stick to investing in large/mega cap and mid cap stocks. Depending on age, a conservative investor may also seek to protect capital by moving some of it out of the stock market and into bonds, treasuries, and money market funds (we'll see later that you can invest in bonds through the stock market, using exchange-traded funds). Conservative investors seek steady growth but aren't necessarily looking for large capital appreciation. The targets for a conservative strategy include a mix of more mature and established companies and some companies that are already quite established, but that may be on the smaller end and poised for some growth. If you are looking to earn income from dividends, you're also going to take a conservative investment strategy. Most conservative investors have a time frame of five years or longer.

- Long-term, but high tolerance of risk: This is a more aggressive approach to investing. You may be willing to hold your assets for 2-5 years or even longer, but you seek rapid growth and appreciation in stock price. In this case, you are going to be seeking to include more small cap and mid cap stocks in your portfolio. You might also devote a large portion of your investments to companies that might be larger, but poised for rapid growth or market dominance. Tesla could be an example. It's a risky investment because the company can't seem to get its act together. But at the same time, they have a technology that is potentially disruptive. That means Tesla might be worth a lot more five or ten years from now. A conservative investor might not be willing to take that bet, a more aggressive investor probably is. Aggressive investors might also be interested in investing in developing markets. That carries a high risk, but also offers the possibility of greater returns.
- Aggressive but short-term time horizon: If you are looking to make profits over a time span of months to 1-2 years maximum, then you are going to be more interested in speculative moves. That means you'll take positions in stocks hoping to see asset appreciation over the lifetime of your trade. But it's a trade, not an investment. You'll be looking to exit the trade as soon as you can sell your shares to meet your financial goals. This type of investor would be a swing or position trader. You'll be seeking out low priced stocks (relatively speaking) and hoping to buy-low and sell-high if gains in the near-term are expected. The risk is higher but may help people who are cash poor

generate funds that can be used for income or to put into long-term investments.

- Purely speculative: If you have a time horizon of less than a year, and seek to generate cash now, then you are a trader and not an investor. This category includes swing traders, who hold positions for a few days to months, and day traders who seek to profit off random movements in share price throughout the day. This category also includes options traders that make money on time frames of one week to a month from price movements of stocks. Day trading is certainly not recommended. It's very high risk. Swing trading and options trading can be incorporated into an overall investment strategy if you need to raise actual cash. Some people are also seeking a way to get rid of their day job and devote full-time to the stock market. Trading can help you generate a regular income. However, keep in mind that trading is high risk, and doing it successfully requires studying and research. Options trading, in particular, can be quite complicated.

## Investing for the Future

Remember that over the long term, the stock market always rises. There are downturns, bear markets, and recessions. Sometimes they might last awhile. But the long-term trend is always in favor of increasing asset prices.

Investing is a method of securing your financial future by taking advantage of long-term gains. The primary goal of this book is to teach you what you need to know in order to build your financial future. We want to head to a place where you achieve financial independence, and you can retire and have a good income. Building large amounts of wealth may or may not be part of your goals. The main focus should be on financial security. Therefore, long-term investing is preferred over trading and speculating. People who are speculators are looking to make a regular income each month and may be looking to "get rich quick." This is a different mindset than investing.

This doesn't mean you can't use investing to meet short-term financial goals. In fact, you can use a buy-low and sell-high strategy over any time period from a few months out to two years in order to raise capital. This can be done for any reason. Maybe you're hoping to raise money to purchase a home, or to send the kids to college. Working to meet these goals can be a part of a larger investment strategy.

## Matching Investments and Goals

Once you have figured out your investment goals, start doing some research on different stocks. Group stocks you are interested in by market capitalization. Look to see whether or not the company pays dividends, and how long it's been around. You're also going to want to study the past behavior of the stock. Take a look at the value of the stock at the start and end of each of the past three years, and write down its growth rate. If you are an aggressive investor, you can use this procedure to find high-growth stocks that can help you meet your goals. You should also look into exchange-traded funds that invest in high-risk but high-reward companies, like small and mid-cap funds and emerging market funds. The diversity that these funds offer can help you manage your risk while also helping you get exposure to the types of companies that you are interested in. Aggressive investors might want to keep up with technology news and find out what companies are developing technology that might be extremely impactful five and ten years down the road.

If you are conservative, then you'll want to, seek out older and more established companies. They should also show some growth; you don't want an older company that is stagnant or in decline. Some innovative and cutting-edge companies might be in between, such as Apple. While it's a very large cap company that pays dividends, as the past decade has shown it's also capable of rapid growth.

Conservative investors will also be interested in looking at dividends. Rank companies by yields and check to see that their dividends grow with time so that you don't get eaten alive by inflation. Finally, index funds might be of special interest to conservative investors. Investing in index funds will let you minimize risk while tracking the overall returns of the stock market.

## Different Approaches for Different Personality Types

Not everyone is the same. Some people like high-pressure environments, and they are drawn to risk. Others prefer a safe approach and are concerned about saving money and really worried about losing it. Aggressive people might be confident about their ability to make money in the future, so they may have a high tolerance for risk.

You need to determine where you fit on the scale of personality types when it comes to the stock market. At one extreme, you have day traders who are aggressive and thrive under high-pressure. A day trader may be willing to lose thousands of dollars in a single day as they strive to meet their goals. They like pouring over financial data and paying close attention to the stock market all day long.

That kind of approach might send waves of terror through others, who are more conservative. At the other end of the spectrum, you have investors who don't want to risk a cent of their capital, or at least they are very conservative when it comes to risk. They may not want to even manage their own investments and hire a financial advisor to do it for them. Mutual funds hold special appeal to these folks, so they can adopt an attitude set-it and forget-it. They might only check their investments periodically, to make sure they are slowly growing.

Most of us fit in between these two extremes. The first question to ask yourself, once you've established your financial goals, is how much devotion do you have to the stock market itself. Are you interested in being an active participant? Are you willing to devote yourself to keeping a close eye on financial news? If so, you are better suited to being an active investor.

A conservative investor who wants to guard their capital is looking for proven investments. If this is your mindset, then you're looking for stable companies that practically guarantee the safety of capital and results, even if the appreciation isn't as high as you could get through other investments. While you are looking to slowly withdraw your money from investments in retirement to fund your lifestyle, you might also be strongly inclined to dividend stocks for income. Conservative investors generally want to spend less time paying close attention to the markets and are willing to hold their investments through thick and thin. They are not concerned with short-term fluctuations and see recessions as buying opportunities.

Aggressive investors are looking for breakouts. They may or may not drift into the realm of speculation. At the very least, an aggressive investor is looking for rapid and strong growth over short time periods. You're probably more interested in keeping daily tabs on the markets. You might closely follow individual stocks and hope to profit from price swings. While you may hold investments for the long term, you're looking for a rapid growth small cap or mid cap stock, or a company with disruptive technology. The innovations your favorite picks have may or may not work out, but the hope is the pay off of one or more of them will be handsome over the long-term if successful. You're willing to take a risk on a small, unknown company that might be the next Google or Facebook. So being an aggressive investor can be a short-term or a long-term mindset.

# Chapter 4
# Risk and Volatility

Understanding risk and volatility are two of the most important things to keep in mind with the stock market. In this chapter, we are going to cover the main types of risk that you need to be aware of when investing. We will also talk about ways to manage risk. Finally, we'll talk about volatility, which is a natural part of the stock market. Any investor in the stock market needs to understand volatility and be able to quantify it. Fortunately, it's pretty simple.

## Risk

There are many different types of risk in the stock market. Some are direct, such as a small company that has the *potential* to make gains because of innovative products. Others are indirect and external. You can't manage all types of risks. Some come out of the blue, like the 9/11 terrorist attacks or the 2008 financial crash. So if you think that you can control every form of risk, take a deep breath and realize you can't. In this chapter, we are going to try and describe every major category of risk investors face, and if possible, we'll suggest ways to deal with them.

### *Emotional and Person Risk*

First and foremost, you can control the risks to your investments that come from personal factors. These include fear, impatience, and greed. Emotions like these can be hard to control, but learning to take charge of them is essential if you are going to be a successful investor. When real money is on the line, these emotions can become strong and overpowering. You must not let that happen.

The most common problem when it comes to emotions and personal risk is fear. When a stock market starts looking bearish, many investors immediately jump ship. They are making a huge mistake. A good investor is not getting in and out of the market at the slightest sign of a problem. In fact, selling off when everyone else is could be one of the biggest mistakes individual investors make. By the way, that doesn't exempt large investors. Many professional traders are subject to the same emotions and exhibit the same behavior during downturns. Massive selloffs are what cause bear markets to develop.

First of all, remember that you are looking to hold your investments over the long term. So ups and downs of the market and even recessions are not a reason to sell them. Over the past 50 years, by far the worst stock market contraction happened in the 2008 financial crisis. However, even that was short-lived. People that sold off their investments were either faced with being out of the markets altogether or having to get back in the markets when prices were appreciating. The lifetimes of other major bear markets were similar or even more short-lived. The first lesson in managing personal risk is to hold your investments through downturns.

The second lesson is that rather than giving into fear, you should start to see market downturns as opportunities. When prices are rapidly dropping due to a market sell-off, you should be buying shares. It's impossible to know where the bottom of a market is, and you shouldn't concern yourself with that. At any time that share prices are declining, it's an opportunity, and so you should be making regular stock purchases. In one year, two years, or five years down the road, on average, the stocks that you purchased in a downturn are going to be worth quite a bit more.

The second problem that arises as a part of personal risk is greed. Many people start seeing dollar signs when they begin investing. Having a get rich quick mentality is not compatible with successful investing. Your approach should be centered on slowly and steadily accumulating wealth and not making a quick buck. As you invest, you're going to be coming across claims that certain trades or stocks are the next best thing, but you're better off ignoring such claims. More often than not, they turn out to be false. The stock market is not a gambling casino, even though many people treat it that way. You can avoid succumbing to greed by maintaining a regular investment program and not being taken in by the temptation that you can profit from short-term swings or "penny stocks" that are going to supposedly take off.

Finally, there is the related problem of impatience. After the Great Depression, people developed a more reasonable and cautious approach to the stock market. They realized that you're not going to get rich in six months or a year. The idea of long-term investing became dominant.

Unfortunately, in recent years, this lesson seems to be getting lost. More people are behaving like traders rather than as investors. Far too many investors are being taken in by the seduction of being able to beat market returns. Instead of being impatient, you should realize that you're in it for the long haul. Rather than trying to make a few extra bucks now, you're seeking to build wealth.

## *Risk of Loss of Capital*

Obviously, financial risk is something you face when investing. Theoretically, there is a chance that you will lose all the money you invest in the stock market. This can happen if you tie your fate to a small number of companies. Several well-known companies like Lumber Liquidators, Bear-Stearns, and GM have either had major problems or gone completely under. Investors may have lost large sums in the process. The way to deal with this is to avoid investing in a small number of companies. Later in the chapter, we will investigate diversification as an investment strategy.

You'll also want to pay attention to the types of companies you invest in. Putting all of your money into small cap stocks, for example, is probably a bad idea. So is putting all of your money into emerging markets, or into one sector of the stock market. Again, the key message is diversification. It's the way to protect you from financial risk.

## *Market and Economic Risk*

Some factors are beyond your control, and the economy inevitably cycles through slowdowns and downturns. The market will cycle along with the economy, and also experiences crashes when the economy may be doing fine overall. This happened in 1987, for example.

While these factors are not under your control, how you react to them is under your control. As we discussed in the section on emotional risk, you should not panic when there is a downturn. Remain level headed, and use downturns as a buying opportunity. They are always followed by a brighter day; your job is to have the patience to wait for it to arrive.

## *Interest Rate Risk*

Changing interest rates can impact the markets. Although this is a book about stock market investing, you should have some awareness of how bond markets work. You should also be aware that investor money can flow back and forth between bond and stock markets depending on conditions.

One thing that bond markets offer is the safety of capital, especially when we are talking about U.S. government bonds. When interest rates are high, U.S. government bonds (and other types of bonds, including corporate and municipal bonds) become very attractive.

Interest rate changes have risks for bond investors, however. Bonds are traded on secondary markets. When interest rates rise, bond prices fall, because older bonds that offer lower interest rates become less attractive. Conversely, when interest rates fall, older bonds that pay higher interest rates have more value than new bonds being issued that pay relatively low rates.

This doesn't directly affect a stock market investor, but if demand for bonds rises, that can mean less capital flowing into the stock market. Less demand means lower prices, so the market may see declines.

Also, as we'll see, you can invest in bonds through the stock market using exchange-traded funds. If you are using this method, you'll want to keep close tabs on interest rates. That means paying closer attention to the Federal Reserve and their quarterly announcements. You should be doing so even if you are not going to invest in bonds in any way. Announcements on interest rate changes can have a large impact on stock prices. But as always, keep your eye on the long ball. If the markets react negatively to an increase in interest rates that can be an opportunity to buy undervalued stocks.

## *Political Risk and Government*

Government and politics can create big risks in the stock market. International events can cause market crashes, and these days even a tweet from the President can cause markets to rise and fall. Lately, some politicians have also been discussing breaking up the big tech companies. Others are talking about investigating them. Such talk – and worse actions – can have a negative impact on the markets. Part of your job as an investor is to keep a close eye on the news. You're going to want to know what's happening so that you can adjust if necessary.

## *Inflation Risk*

Inflation hasn't been high in decades. However, in the late 1970s inflation rates were routinely in the double digits. Hopefully, that isn't going to be something that happens anytime soon, because high inflation rates can eat your returns alive. If the stock market is appreciating at 7% per year, but inflation is 14%, you can see that it's like having debt but investing in stocks – it's a losing proposition. Right now, inflation risk is very low, but you'll want to have some awareness of it and always keep tabs on it. High inflation rates also tend to go hand-in-hand with high-interest rates, since the Federal Reserve will raise rates to try and slow down inflation. That means that bonds might become more attractive when inflation gets out of control.

## *Taxes and Commissions*

Finally, we have the risk imposed by taxes. Of course, we are all going to be hit with taxes no matter where our money comes from. However, you need to take into account the taxes that you are going to pay when it comes to any gains you realize on the stock market. Part of being a successful investor is having an understanding of how much your taxes are cutting into your profits. If you are investing for the long-term, it will be less of an issue. But keep in mind that taxes can really eat into short-term trades. Frequent, short-term traders also face risk from commissions and fees. If you execute a lot of trades, the commissions can add up. This is not an issue for long term investors.

## *Risk vs. Return*

One of the fundamental trade-offs that an investor will make is a risk vs. return. Generally speaking, the higher the risk, the greater the *possibility* of good returns. In 1998, Amazon was a pretty high-risk investment. While it had potential, major bookstores like Borders and Barnes & Noble dominated the space. Amazon was on shaky ground at the time, and another company could have come in and competed successfully for online book sales. That never happened, and Amazon ended up dominating book sales and expanding widely across retail and into cloud computing. That risk has translated into massive returns. A $10,000 investment in 1998 would be worth more than $1 million today.

But hindsight is 20/20. Today, there are similar opportunities all around us, but it's hard to know which ones are going to end up being successful over the long term. If you are an aggressive investor, part of your job is going to be estimating which companies are the best bets for the future.

Risk vs. return also plays a role in emerging markets. These countries may experience massive GDP growth year after year since they have lots of room to grow. Domestic companies that are growing with their economies can offer remarkable returns.

However, there are many risks. Rapid growth can often evaporate with major downturns. Stability is lower in emerging markets; you could face complete loss of capital.

These examples serve to illustrate why a diversified portfolio is essential.

## Managing Risk

There are a few time-tested strategies that have been developed that help manage risk. They even minimize, as much as possible, the kinds of risk that you will face that are completely out of control. That could include anything from a terrorist attack to interest rate changes.

These strategies are simple and easy to understand. The problem is that in practice, many investors fail to follow them, and instead let their decision making be guided by emotions. You might end up following that path as well. However, we are going to give you the tools you need to avoid it. It's up to you whether you utilize them or not.

### *Dollar Cost Averaging*

The first strategy seeks to avoid being impacted by the ups and downs of the market. You don't know when you are buying at the top of a market or the bottom. None of us has a crystal ball, but what we can do is average out our investments over the long-term. You can do this using a technique called dollar cost averaging, which is simply buying shares at regular intervals – completely ignoring price fluctuations. Most ups and downs in the stock market are actually noise. So you should avoid worrying about them as much as possible. And we've already noted that stock goes up and down with bull and bear markets. Using dollar cost averaging, you remove the stress (and hence the emotion) that is associated with these fluctuations. The costs are averaged out because sometimes you are going to be buying when prices are low, even though at other times you will be buying when prices are relatively high.

Speaking of rising share prices, this technique also helps you avoid another emotional problem. If share prices are rising, many investors panic. The reason they panic is they are worried that share prices will rise to new heights and never come back down again. They will "miss an opportunity" of gains, and also be forced into a position of having to buy shares at higher prices.

Those short-term ups and downs don't matter over the long-

term. Whether Amazon had a

long gain 4 years ago or not won't matter to the investor using dollar cost averaging. All that matters is the long-term trend – and regularly purchasing shares along the way. Looking at the chart below, we've used an arrow to show Amazon's long-term trend and circled a few of the short-term fluctuations that at the time, caused a great deal of angst and anxiety. Traders probably tried to profit from them. But look how small they are, compared to the overall picture.

## *Diversification*

A lot of people don't like to hear about this one since financial advisors are constantly shoving it down people's throats. But diversification remains one of the most important strategies in stock market investing. The problem is most investors don't diversify enough.

Having investments in 5-7 or even ten companies is not true diversification. When it comes to individual companies, having investments in 15-20 companies is probably the range you want to shoot for. The problem with investing in individual companies is that you have to strike a balance. On the one hand, you want to invest in a wide range of companies to lower risk, in case one or more of them take a tumble. On the other hand, as an individual investor, you also need to closely study the companies you invest in. There simply isn't time for one individual to closely study dozens of companies and keep up with them as time goes on. So twenty companies is considered the maximum limit for individual investors.

However, you should take things a step further. First of all, you need to look at sectors, not just companies. If you invest in twenty social media companies, you aren't diversified. The sector itself could take a hit, causing all the companies in the sector to go into a tailspin. When they do, your investments sink with the sector.

The best way to diversify your portfolio is to utilize fund investing. Mutual funds aren't a personal favorite, but you can use them as part of an overall strategy if you would like to. Most individual investors are interested in a more active role in their portfolios, so don't typically do that.

Instead, you should consider using exchange-traded funds. They trade like stocks and give you a large amount of diverse exposure. We will discuss them in detail in the next chapter.

## Volatility

The next topic we are going to address in this chapter is volatility. You probably have an intuitive understanding of what this means. Graphically, it's represented by the jagged appearance of stock market charts. Prices are moving up and down, dramatically swinging between highs and lows. That's what volatility is. It can be measured in terms of the frequency of price changes and the magnitude. The higher the differences between the highs and lows, and the more frequently stock prices fluctuate, the higher the volatility.

Traders like high volatility. That means there are more opportunities for stock prices to trend in their favor. An options trader, for example, likes a high volatility stock because, over the lifetime of the option, the probability is increased that the share price will move to a favorable position, even if it's just for a short time.

Conservative investors either don't like volatility or if the fundamentals are good, they don't care about it. The thing about volatility is that it's usually a short-term measure. For example, Amazon has a high level of volatility. But does that matter to a long-term investor? Not really. The overall trend within which that volatility is taking place is what matters.

For a long-term investor, worrying about volatility is something that should be occupying a relatively low position on your list. And by long-term, we mean anything more than a 1-year time frame. Consider Microsoft, which has relatively low volatility, much less than Amazon. Looking at its five-year chart, it has a similar trend. So did the volatility matter?

To quantify the volatility of a stock, you will want to take a look at a quantity investors call *Beta*. This compares the volatility of any given stock to the entire market. The volatility of the market is 1.0. Any number above this indicates that the stock is more volatile than the market. Any number below this indicates that the stock is less volatile than the market.

Amazon has a beta of 1.75. That means its 75% more volatile than the market (note these numbers are subject to change). Microsoft has a volatility of 1.05. That means it's slightly more volatile than the market – 5 % more. However, it's much less volatile than Amazon.

General Electric has a volatility of 0.90. That's a low volatility stock. It's 10% less volatile as the entire market. But does that make it attractive? Probably not – the share price is only 1/3 what it was just a few years ago.

Volatility can also be negative. If volatility is positive, that means the share price tends to rise when the overall stock market rises. And when stock prices fall, the market is probably falling as well. Amazon and Microsoft both rise and fall, on average, with the overall market.

If volatility is negative, that means that on average, the stock moves against the market. So when share prices are rising, the stock market is declining, and vice versa.

Volatility has been rising. But that isn't necessarily something to be afraid of. One of the reasons that it's rising is technology. Since it's easier to place trades, decisions by large investors that can buy and sell massive amounts of shares quickly can cause stock prices to fluctuate by larger amounts over shorter time periods. It's also a lot easier for individual investors and traders to make moves on the market. While as an individual, you practically have zero influence, when you sum up the decisions of large numbers of investors that fit together in herd behavior, this can have an impact as well.

# Chapter 5
# Investing through Funds

A *fund* is pooled money that has been gathered together from investors. Then it's used to purchase securities on behalf of the investors. For example, we could create a fund that bought shares in Amazon, Apple, and Facebook and call it AAF. Then we could gather $10,000 from our friends, and buy shares in each of the stocks. Since the fund owns underlying shares of stock, and its value will fluctuate with the prices of Amazon, Apple, and Facebook, the fund itself has value. We could divide it up into shares. Say it was split up so that each share was worth $50. Then our friends would have a number of shares proportionate to the amount of money they put in the fund. A year from now, depending on how the stock for the three companies performs, the fund may be worth more or less than $50 a share. The people who had shares in the fund could sell their shares back or trade them with others. We could put more money in the fund and buy more shares, and let others buy into the fund.

## The Advantages of Funds

We will get into the specifics of funds in a minute, but let's talk about some of the advantages of funds. As the above example illustrates, funds allow you to invest in multiple companies at once. As such, funds give the investor automatic diversification. For this reason, funds are generally considered a safer way to invest. If Facebook gets investigated by Congress and sees a large drop in share prices, the investor is somewhat protected because they also have investments in Amazon and Apple. In practice, funds will have investments in dozens or even hundreds or thousands of companies.

This also saves the investor a great deal of time. While an individual doesn't have the time to thoroughly evaluate a large number of companies to invest in at once, funds are created and managed by large financial companies. They have the time to determine which companies are good to invest in, and they can also create funds that have lower or higher risk profiles. This allows the individual investor to focus on the level of risk they would like to assume, rather than having to dive into the details of financial statements and stock prices and try to estimate which companies are best to invest in. Many funds, for example, track the S & P 500, which means they invest in all 500 companies. Most individuals don't have the time or resources to do something like that. You will also find that many funds beat the market on returns, allowing you to earn 10% returns or higher in many cases.

Funds also make it easier to invest across sectors and even markets. As we'll see, you can invest in funds that track everything from U.S. government bonds to stock indexes to precious metals. You can also invest in real estate trusts or energy companies. Many funds pay dividends. In short, there is a fund that will appeal to any investor.

Funds are also available with different share prices, allowing investors to pick a pricing point that fits their budget.

Keep in mind that fund investing is not mutually exclusive with doing your own stock picks. While you can create a portfolio that is exclusively made up of funds, you can also break your portfolio down into different proportions. That is, you could take a certain fraction of your investment money and use it to buy stock in individual companies that you like, and use the rest to invest in funds. Depending on individual preferences, different people can take different approaches. You could invest 75% of your money in funds and 25% in individual stocks, or do a 50/50 split. How you do it is up to you if you invest in funds at all.

## What Kinds of Investments Are Available with Funds

There are several classes of funds that are available to invest in. The most popular types track the performance of stock indexes. These types of funds will own shares in stocks that are on some index such as the Dow Jones Industrial Average or the S & P 500. In this case, selecting the companies to invest in would be a straightforward process, so any costs associated with the fund will be lower because it requires less professional management. However, different funds might have different weighting. To understand how that would work, let's return to our fictitious example we used at the beginning of the chapter. Suppose that two funds, fund A and fund B, tracked the three stocks. Fund A might own 34 shares of Amazon, 33 shares of Apple, and 33 shares of Facebook. Fund B might own 40 shares of Amazon, 40 shares of Apple, and 20 shares of Facebook. Depending on how the individual stocks performed, fund A and fund B will have different returns over the course of time. If you are interested in investing in a specific fund, be sure to check offerings from different companies and compare their historical performance. Some will provide better results than others.

The second type of fund tracks *equity*, but not some specific index. Equity is simply another way of saying stocks, and it's usually used to distinguish stock investing from buying income-generating instruments like bonds. An equity fund will invest in multiple companies with some goal in mind. For example, you can invest in a growth fund. That fund would invest in a large number of companies that are undergoing rapid growth but don't pay dividends. The goal of investing in a growth fund would be to get rapid appreciation in the value of your shares. A growth fund might focus more on small and mid-cap companies or large high-tech companies that are large but experiencing continued growth, such as Google.

Other types of funds might seek to invest only in large-cap stocks. Others might advertise themselves as investing in value stocks, which means they will seek out slow growing but undervalued stocks in large companies (Warren Buffett style investing). Still, others might be equity investments but be advertised as income funds, because they invest in companies that pay dividends so that you can earn an income from your investments. When investing in these types of funds, sit down and figure out what your goals are (growth, income, more aggressive or conservative), and then you can find funds that meet your goals.

The next kind of fund is called a fixed income fund. These types of funds invest in bonds, which pay interest. Someone who invests in the fund, therefore, will receive income from the interest. There will be a wide variety of fixed income funds available. For example, you could invest in U.S. government bonds. There are many types of U.S. government bonds, and a fund might allow you to invest in a mixture of them. Other fixed income funds invest in other types of bonds. One might invest in municipal bonds, which are bonds issued by state and local governments. Still, others would invest in corporate bonds. Junk bond funds invest in bonds issued by companies with bad credit histories. As a result of their bad credit, they pay higher interest rates. Using a fund to invest in junk bonds rather than doing it yourself can reduce your exposure to risk because the fund will invest in a large number of junk bonds. That way if one or more of them don't make payments, the fund isn't impacted that much because the rest of the companies in the fund probably are making payments. A fund manager might also actively manage the fund, and so replace companies that aren't paying with other companies that are. Fixed income investing really isn't a topic of this book; however, due to the existence of funds that do fixed income investing on your behalf, you can invest in them like stocks. This can help diversify your portfolio even more. However, if you invest in these types of funds, you will need to pay attention to interest rate risk.

Money market funds invest in fixed income securities. These tend to be short-term securities like certificates of deposits offered by banks and certain types of short-term government bonds. These will have lower returns than other types of funds. People invest in these types of funds if they are conservative, and they seek a very low-risk investment. The advantage of fixed-income and money market funds is that they offer protection of capital. However, both are subject to interest rate and inflation risk. If the return on the fund is not beating inflation, then your principal is losing value. You will also need to consider any commissions and fees of the fund, so it actually has to beat inflation added up with commissions and fees.

The next type of fund that you can invest in is called a *balanced* fund. These include a mixture of equity and fixed income investments in different proportions. The fund can be more aggressive, which means investing more in equities, or it might aim to be low risk, investing more heavily in fixed income and money market investments. The advantage of balanced funds is an investor can readily seek a level of risk that meets their own personal investment goals.

Next, we have specialty funds. They may invest in a certain sector, like real estate. Or they may invest in commodities of various types. You can find funds that invest in precious metals like gold, silver, and platinum. In recent years, funds that invest in the cryptocurrency have emerged. These types of funds, like the others, described here, work like stock investing (in fact as we'll see they are stocks or mutual funds). So you can focus your entire portfolio on stock investing, but get exposure to a wide range of investments.

## Mutual Funds

The type of fund that most people are familiar with is the *mutual fund*. The name mutual fund conveys the central idea behind funds, which is the fund is a pool of money gathered from a large number of people (so it's "mutual"). Mutual funds are the safest type of investment, and most people that invest in them are looking to build wealth for retirement. Mutual funds are not stocks, so you need to learn a little bit about the specifics before investing in one. We will see below that exchange-traded funds are a better choice while offering many of the same benefits.

Mutual funds are divided into "units" rather than shares, although the two terms can be used interchangeably. Rather than having a share price, each unit or share is given a *net asset value*. In practice, it works like share price. So if the net asset value were $50 per unit, if you buy 10 units, it would cost $500 (plus fees).

The first thing an investor needs to note about mutual funds is they can be actively managed or passively managed. If a fund is actively managed, then a professional money manager will be actively buying and selling shares regularly in an effort to enhance the funds' performance. Since the fund requires the attention of professional money managers, there are additional fees associated with the fund. You can determine how well a fund is performing by comparing its 3-5 year returns with the S & P 500. If the performance is beating the S & P 500, the fund might be worth investing in. However, remember that you need to account for any commissions and fees associated with the fund.

Passively managed funds will have lower commissions and fees. These are not actively managed, so they cost less to invest in. In either case, mutual funds may have minimum investment requirements. The amounts required vary, but you may have to invest several thousand dollars into the fund, so you can't show up and just buy one share (but the details will vary by fund offering and company).

Mutual funds also trade differently than stocks. While stocks are trading throughout the day, mutual funds only trade once per day. You won't know the change in the cost of a share until after the market closes. So if an index or stock is highly volatile over the course of a day, you won't know how much it would cost to buy more shares until after the mutual fund has traded, after market close.

Another consideration when considering mutual funds is the fees. Funds can be "load" or "no-load" mutual funds. A "load" is a fee that is charged every time you buy or sell shares. These expenses can add up and diminish the value of investing in mutual funds.

## Exchange-traded Funds

As a result of many of the negative characteristics of mutual funds, exchange-traded funds, also known as ETFs, emerged. There are a few differences between exchange-traded funds and mutual funds, and they are very important. The first is that the fees associated with exchange-traded funds are much lower. So with exchange-traded funds, you're not going to see as much of your income eaten up by transaction costs and commissions. With an exchange-traded fund, you're not paying handsome fees to help pay a professional money manager.

The second advantage of exchange-traded funds is that they trade exactly like stocks. You buy and sell shares in an exchange-traded fund at will any time the stock markets are open. Their price fluctuates throughout the day, rather than being fixed like a mutual fund. To see why this is important, let's consider the S & P 500.

Often a news event or some big development in the economy can have a large impact on the S & P 500. So it might rise rapidly on the news of a good jobs report, or it might crash because of a trade feud or some other bad economic news. If you had invested in a mutual fund that tracked the S & P 500, you would have to wait until the end of the day, when the fund made its only trade, to see how the price of the fund changed. That could make investment decisions difficult.

In contrast, for an exchange-traded fund that was tracking the S & P 500, you would be able to see prices changing in real time. That would make it easy for you to determine the right time to get into the fund or sell your shares. You can even day or swing trade exchange-traded funds if that is your inclination. Moreover, you can buy options on exchange-traded funds.

To summarize in comparison to mutual funds, exchange-traded funds have much lower costs, and they trade like stocks. That makes them very easy to manage, and your gains are not going to be constantly eaten into by commissions. There is no mutual fund company to deal with and nobody to pay. The funds to have small fees, but they are tiny in comparison.

Another difference between exchange-traded funds and many mutual funds is that exchange-traded funds don't have minimum investment requirements. You can buy as little as a single share if you want to. So you can get started now investing in mutual funds without having to invest thousands of dollars immediately.

Furthermore, exchange-traded funds have all of the advantages of mutual funds. They offer investors the same diversification that mutual funds do. There are also exchange-traded funds designed to meet different investment goals, like fixed income or equity, or tracking an index. In fact, the types of exchange-traded funds that are available are the same as the types of mutual funds available. Think of exchange-traded funds as mutual funds without all the baggage.

If you are the type of person who would prefer making arrangements with a money manager, and meeting them in their offices and having the input from a financial professional, then you are better suited to mutual fund investing. Of course, if that describes your outlook, you probably wouldn't be reading this book. Exchange-traded funds are better suited for investors that want to manage their own investing. So if you want to take an active role in investing, exchange-traded funds can definitely be a part of that.

## How to Buy Exchange-traded Funds

You buy exchange-traded funds the same way that you buy stocks. You simply look up the ticker and find one you want to invest in, and then buy shares. It's that simple, and there is nothing more to it. You don't have to become associated with any company like Fidelity of Vanguard. Also, if you need to sell your shares, you can do so. Exchange-traded funds have a little more liquidity than mutual funds. To take an example, if Joe has invested in exchange-traded funds and he wants to liquidate his investment at 11 AM because the market is dropping rapidly, he can simply put in a sell order for his shares. If Sally wants to do the same thing, she has to wait until closing to actually get it done. As a result, Sally might suffer a lot more than Joe from the stock market drop. Joe got out early and won't be impacted by what happens for the rest of the day.

## Exchange-traded Funds Offerings

Exchange-traded funds are offered by several companies. When you find something you want to invest in, you will want to visit the different company websites or look up the stock tickers on Yahoo Finance to compare performance.

### *iShares*

Barclays created these exchange-traded funds in 1996. A few years ago, they were acquired by a company called BlackRock. The offerings by iShares are some of the most popular ETFs on the market. They offer hundreds of funds investing in everything from silver to the S & P 500, and they hold more than $3.5 trillion in assets. Complete diversity is available from iShares, including by investment goals, region, and asset class. Let's look at a few offerings so that you can understand the types of investments you can make by purchasing shares of exchange-traded funds.

IVV tracks the S & P 500. It's a 20-year-old fund, and it's currently trading at $297 a share. The expense ratio is only 0.04%, which compares very favorably with mutual funds. It has an astounding year-to-date return of nearly 19%. This shows the advantages of investing in an exchange-traded fund.

IWY tracks the Russell top 200, which is an index of large cap growth stocks. You can invest in this one for just $86 a share (as we are writing this). It has an even better return, at more than 20%.

If you're looking for higher returns, you could consider investing in JKK, at $204 a share. It has a return of 23%. This fund invests in stocks that are on the Morningstar small cap list.

It's also possible to invest in several commodity funds. There are offerings that invest in gold, silver, and other commodities. You can use iShares to invest in real estate and fixed income investments as well.

## Other offerings

We aren't seeking to encourage you to buy iShares but only use it as an example to illustrate the possibilities. There are many other very good offerings from different companies. State Street SPDRs are some of the most popular offerings. Their exchange-traded fund SPY that tracks the S & P 500 is one of the most popular investments on the stock market. It's also very popular for trading options. Vanguard is another large company that not only offers mutual funds but provides several exchange-traded funds as well. Another company that has many offerings is Proshares.

Keep in mind that you don't invest in exchange-traded funds by going directly to the company; you simply buy shares on the stock market. So to find the funds you want, study the offerings from the different websites, and make comparisons as to what they invest in and what the returns are. While people have different tastes, chances are you will find that one company offers all the funds you need. But you can go through your broker and buy shares on the stock market that are offered by the company you like best or a mix of funds offered by several companies.

## Shorting Stock

There are also bearish ETFs, which basically allow you to short stock. That is you're betting against the stock and hoping to profit off declines in the share price. The advantage of using an ETF is you can do this without being a big player with a margin account. An example is ProShares SH, which bets against the S & P 500. At the time of writing it's trading at $26 a share. During the 2008 financial crisis, however, it was trading at $188 a share. So to be clear, this fund shorts the market. That means it gains value when stock prices fall, and it loses value when stock prices rise.

A fund like ProShares SH offers some interesting possibilities. When the stock market is booming, the shares are cheap. So you can load up on them without having to spend much money. Then you can keep them in your portfolio as a kind of insurance. If the stock market crashes or enters any kind of bear market, the value of your shares will increase a great deal. Then you can sell them and take the cash. The cash could then be used to purchase shares of stock you are interested in owning, which would be available for bargain prices. Alternatively, if you just want to take out the cash that would be a possibility as well.

This is a good example of the types of investing that are available using exchange-traded funds that you can't get by simply buying shares of stock in individual companies, especially if you don't have a large amount of capital to invest.

## Tracking Indexes

For diversification purposes, you can use ETFs to invest in index funds. You are probably already familiar with the two main stock market indexes, the Dow Jones Industrial Average and the S & P 500. There are also a few others you can consider investing in, but the main indices are:

- S & P 500: the vaunted Standard and Poors Company on Wall Street compile this index. It includes the 500 largest publicly traded companies on the stock market. The kinds of companies in the S & P 500 include Apple, Exxon-Mobile, Amazon, and JP Morgan. It's a good way to track the market, and there are many exchange-traded funds that track it.
- Dow Jones Industrial Average: This index is the one usually quoted by news organizations. It's taken as a barometer of the overall performance of the stock market. It focuses on the 30 biggest large cap stocks. These days, most people consider the S & P 500 more representative of the market as a whole.
- NASDAQ Composite: This stock market became famous during the dot com boom, because it's where most tech stocks are traded, although it's not exclusively made up of tech stocks. The stocks on this index tend to be high-growth stocks, so it's a good index to track if you are looking to be more aggressive.
- Wilshire 5000: This index tracks a large number of companies (5000) of varied sizes, and so it gives you more diverse exposure to the market.
- Russell 2000: This index tracks 2,000 small cap companies. An ETF that tracked this index would give you exposure to the small cap arena with lower risk since you'd

have the diversification that you can get from investing in 2,000 companies.

## Ownership

Just an aside – it's important to realize that when you buy shares of an exchange-traded fund or mutual fund, you don't actually own shares in any of the underlying companies that make up the fund. Rather you own shares of the fund, which owns shares in the companies that are in the fund. In the end, it's a distinction without a difference, but it's important to be clear about that point, so there is no misunderstanding.

## Mutual Fund vs. Exchange-traded Fund

You can't really go wrong either way. Although there are a lot more expenses associated with mutual funds and some other downsides, nobody that took a buy and hold approach to mutual funds found themselves in poverty by the time they retired. Exchange-traded funds are more suitable to personality types that want to take an active role in investing, but who want the advantages that fund investing provides over investing in individual stocks. If you would prefer to let someone handle things for you, and possibly take advantage of the situation where a professional who devotes their entire life to the stock market is managing the fund, then mutual funds might be to your liking.

# Chapter 6
# Choosing a Broker

Once you've done all your preparation, the next step is to choose a broker so that you can start trading. In the old days, choosing a broker meant going to an office where an actual stockbroker worked. Today, a "broker" is usually an online website or even a mobile app, and everything is run by computer. The role of a broker is to buy and sell shares for you and manage your account. Brokers can also lend you money that you can use to buy shares or options, or they can lend you shares. There are various factors to consider when selecting a broker, including commissions and fees, features, and tools offered by their websites and the level of personal service provided. Choosing a broker is a personal decision and motivated largely by taste, so we cannot tell you which broker to select. You can go online and search for brokers or brokerages and find one that works best for you. In this chapter, we'll consider the factors that you should use when making your selection.

## The Role of a Broker

The broker plays the role of a middleman. You will place your orders with the broker to buy or sell stocks, and the broker will actually carry out the transaction for you. They will also maintain your account and keep records for you, including anything you'll need related to your investing for tax purposes.

Brokers also provide many investment tools, although the offerings will vary. Some brokers provide a complete suite of tools that let you chart stocks, study past behavior, and review financial statements. Many brokers even offer simulators that people interested in trading can use to hone their skills. Whether or not you actually need these tools in your account is questionable, since there are many free resources available online. However, some people like to have all of their tools in one location.

Brokers can also play the role of a lender. You can borrow money or even borrow shares. The money can't be used for any purpose, the money would remain in your brokerage account, and you can use it to purchase shares of stock and other financial securities. Borrowing money from the broker to buy shares is known as "trading on the margin."

## Full Service vs. Discount Brokers

Generally, brokers can be classified as either being full service or discount brokers. A full-service broker goes beyond simply providing the tools and computer interface to trade stocks. They will actually make investment advice available to their clients. A full-service broker is more in line with what you probably think of when you say the word "stockbroker." An example would be Charles Schwab or Fidelity.

Discount brokers, on the other hand, are largely automated and found online. These firms only provide the mechanics you will use in order to buy your shares and maintain your account. Some may provide educational information, and in the case of tasty works (to use one example) that information can be quite extensive, including full video suites of tutorials. Others, like Robinhood, provide minimal sets of tools and limited information, but the trade off is they are very simple to use.

The bottom line with your choice here is that if you want access to a financial advisor to help you make your investment decisions, then you're going to want to go with a full-service broker. If you are comfortable being an independent investor and are completely comfortable going it alone, then you can use a discount broker. Of course, nothing is free, so you should expect higher fees from a full-service broker.

## Commissions and Fees

Commissions and fees are tacked on to your trades, and depending on how much you trade, they can add up. If you're a frequent trader, that means they can be a consideration when thinking about your profitability. Some brokerages charge small or even zero commissions. An example of this is Robinhood, which has become popular among amateur options traders for that reason along with its simplicity of use. Options only last from one week to a month in most cases, so people who trade options will be making frequent trades, and they don't want commissions eating into their profits.

An organization like Charles Schwab or Fidelity that may make professional financial advisors available to you is probably going to charge higher commissions, in order to pay for the service.

## Account Minimums

Different brokerages are going to have different account minimums. Some will even let you open an account without depositing any money. But others may require that you deposit a significant amount of funds just to get started. If you are starting out small and this is an issue for you, then you need to shop around and make sure you open an account with a brokerage that has no account minimums.

## Broker Recommendations

If you decide to go with a full-service broker, you might utilize them to help you with your stock picks. For people that feel more comfortable having a trained professional assist you with this task, it may be worth the higher commissions. You might want to read reviews on firms that you are considering in order to determine whether or not they have a good track record. A minimal requirement would be to see if their recommendations meet the S & P 500 benchmark, but you will probably want advisement from someone who can actually beat it. If you decide to discuss your investments with an advisor, you should have your financial goals clearly set in your mind before doing so. That means being able to tell them your time horizon and investment goals (growing wealth rapidly, income investing, etc.). You will also need to have some idea about how much you plan to invest and what your plans are for a future investment schedule. If you find that their recommendations are not to your liking, you are not required to follow them. But they may attempt to pressure you to do so.

## Asset Classes and Types of Brokerage Accounts

Different brokerages may allow investment in different asset classes or markets. If you are interested in going beyond simple stock investing, and engaging in activities like trading options or investing directly in bonds, you are going to need to investigate what your broker does and does not allow. To get exactly what you need, you may have to open more than one brokerage account. For example, some people may be interested in investing in stocks but also engaging in Forex or crypto trading. Finding one broker that does all you want may be possible, but you might have to open other accounts for more specialized trading.

There are two major types of brokerage accounts. A cash account is a standard account. That is, you deposit cash from your bank, and then you buy shares using the cash in the account. If you want to buy more shares, you have to deposit more money.

The other type of brokerage account is a margin account. This type of account still requires you to make a cash deposit, and federal law requires that you deposit at least $2,000 to open a margin account. However, you can borrow money and shares using a margin account. Typically, you can use 2:1 leverage. For example, if you have $5,000 in your margin account, you can purchase $10,000 worth of stock. Each account will have its own buying power, which is the amount you can fund. That is buying power is the amount of cash you have plus the amount you can borrow.

## Company List

There are a large number of available brokers, and the best thing for you to do is go online and search for one to your liking. That said, here is a partial listing of brokerages:

- Ally Invest
- Charles Schwab
- E-Trade
- Fidelity Investments
- Interactive brokers
- Merrill Edge
- Robinhood
- Tasty Works/Tasty Trade
- TD Ameritrade

- Trade Station
- Vanguard

The best brokers for beginners include E-Trade, Robinhood, and TD Ameritrade. Each has its advantages and disadvantages. You will want to consider features available for analysis as well as commissions. Robinhood is a zero-commission broker.

## Types of Orders

It's important for beginners to understand the different types of orders that they can place. People think that you can just buy and sell shares, but it's a little more involved than that.

The first type of order you can place is called a market order. This is what most people think about when considering buying and selling the stock. It's simply placing an order where you will buy or sell at the prevailing market price at that moment in time. You are telling the broker that you will accept whatever price they come up with, but it's going to be at or near the market price or "mark" that you see when you place the order in most cases.

Something you will want to look at when placing your orders is *bid* and *ask*. A bid is an amount that traders who want to buy a given stock are offering. Ask is the asking price sellers currently want. These figures change by the moment, but if there is a large bid-ask spread, it might take longer to find a buyer.

A limit order, in contrast, is an order that specifies a price that you are willing to accept when selling or a price you're willing to pay if you want to buy shares. If you are looking to get out of a stock quickly, a limit order can help you do that, since instead of selling at the market price you could sell at the bid price, which would mean a quick sale. Alternatively, you can use a limit order to hold out for a price that you are willing to accept even if you have to wait. A limit order could be placed as a buy order to only buy shares if the priced dropped to a certain level, or alternatively while selling you could decide only to sell when the price reached a certain point. Traders use limit orders in order to set pre-determined profit levels. You can create a limit order that expires at the end of the trading day, or use a good until canceled order that will sit out there until it's executed. It will be executed when a bid or ask matches your price.

A stop loss order is a type of limit order that is used to sell your shares automatically if the price drops to a certain level. Traders use this to protect themselves from large losses. As a long-term investor, you are probably not interested in stop-loss orders, because a long-term investor should keep their shares through downturns as well as rising stock markets if the shares help them meet their long-term goals.

84

# Chapter 7
# Fundamentals

In this chapter, we will go over some of the characteristics of stocks that you should be looking at when picking your investments. This will help you get some familiarity with the stock market and make wiser investment decisions. We will also take a look at a few things you should consider when looking over company financial statements, and where you can get them.

## Pricing

The first thing you will want to look at is the price per share and data on previous prices. The price per share is the main thing quoted for any stock, so it's hard to miss. You will also see the Open, Close, 52-week High, and 52-week Low. The Open is the most recent price of the stock at market open. Close is the most recent closing price, so if it's Tuesday at Noon, the Close will be Monday's closing price.

You can also look at the price range for the current or most recent trading day, which will give you the most recent high and low prices. You will also want to look at the 52-week high and low as well. Most websites will include an analyst recommendation and a hot bar indicating whether or not the stock is overvalued, priced just right, or undervalued. Use these as guidelines rather than as absolutes.

## Chart

The stock market chart for each stock gives you a graphical representation of price changes with time. This allows you to get a visual on price changes over any time range that you like, from a few hours out to 5 years or even the entire lifetime of the stock. Using this tool will help you decide whether or not a stock is a good investment and whether or not it's showing a solid history of increasing in value, something that you want to consider when investing in a stock for a long-term portfolio. Charts also allow you to add various tools and indicators used for trend analysis.

## Price to Earnings Ratio, Earnings Per Share

For any stock you are investing in, you want to look at the earnings per share and price to earnings ratio. There are not really absolutes that you can use to evaluate these quantities; what you should do is make comparisons between companies in the same industry. If a company has a very high price to earnings ratio compared to its competitors in the same industry, it might mean that the stock is significantly overvalued and likely to decline in price in the near future. *Earnings per share* gives you a measure of the profitability of a company. If a company is relatively new and in a growth face, they may not have profits but still be a worthwhile investment – but that assumes more risk. Conservative investors are going to shy away from such companies and focus on those that make steady profits.

## Volume

Volume is the amount of trading going on for a given stock. You will want to compare volume to average volume, to see if there is an unusual amount of trading going on at the time you are looking at the stock. A high level of trading compared to the average can indicate that traders are either extremely bullish (expecting rising prices) or bearish (trying to get out of the stock) at the moment. Keep in mind that these considerations are more important for traders, rather than for investors. As an investor, you are not really interested in the short-term gyrations of the stock; you want to invest in stocks that you intend to keep in your portfolio for extended periods of time.

## Beta

As discussed earlier, beta is a measure of the stock's volatility relative to the volatility of the entire stock market. Let's quickly review. If beta is 1.0, it's average with respect to volatility. If it's greater than 1.0, that means it's more volatile than the stock market. If it's less than 1.0, then it's less volatile than the stock market. Finally, if the beta is negative, that means its trends against the stock market, so has rising prices when the major stock indices are dropping, and vice versa.

## Earnings Date

The earnings date is the date when the company will report its earnings and profits for the previous quarter. This is often done in an "earnings call." Earnings dates are important; you should follow the earnings calls for any companies that you invest in. This will help you keep up with the company's fortunes and future plans.

## Dividend Yield, Dividend, and Ex-Dividend Date

If a company pays dividends, these quantities will be listed. If it does not, they will not be listed. The reason that a company doesn't pay dividends is usually that it's in a growth phase and reinvesting its profits back in the company. For people looking for high growth companies whose stock will appreciate at rates far above the market average, companies that don't pay dividends will be of more interest.

On the other hand, if you are looking into income investing, then you are going to be interested in companies that pay dividends. The first thing to look at is the dividend itself. This is quoted as an absolute dollar value, and it gives the dollar amount paid annually. However, these payments are broken up by a quarter, and so you will receive ¼ of the dividend payment each quarter. Normally the forward dividend is quoted, which means the expected dividend that is going to be paid in upcoming quarters.

The dividend yield is the amount of the dividend per share. So if a company pays a $4 dividend and its share price is $100, the yield is $4/$100 x 100 = 4%. Yield gives you a measure of the dividend taken together with what you have to pay per share to own stock in the company. Looking at yield, you can compare one dividend paying stock to another independently of the price per share, and you can also compare to other income-generating investments that pay interest, and compare yields directly. Keep in mind, however, that only stocks appreciate with time. Dividend stocks often see large amounts of appreciation, just like other stocks, and many high growth companies like Apple also pay dividends.

Next, you will want to look at the ex-dividend date. This gives you a marker when the dividend will be paid. You need to own the stock before this date in order to receive the next dividend payment. Companies will announce when the actual dividend is paid, and this is after the ex-dividend date.

Keep in mind that exchange-traded funds that specialize in dividends will pay dividends as well. They may have lower absolute dividend payments per share but have high yields. The dividends for all the stocks in the fund are collected, and then divided up on a per share basis (as compared to the ETF) and paid out to people who own shares in the fund.

## Financial statements

You are going to want to carefully evaluate the financial statements of any individual stocks that you invest in. You can find these online, but the most important documents you will want to read are the 10K and the prospectus. These are quarterly and annual reports made to shareholders that give detailed accounting statements for the company. The prospectus will also include detailed plans for the company, an overview of its management team, and an analysis of its competition.

For the financials themselves, you will want to look at the income statement, the balance sheet, and cash flow. You should go back five years if possible, looking closely to see if the company is making progress in gaining profitability and increasing revenues. You can look at the data annually and quarterly. Remember that many companies are seasonal, so compare like quarters.

Income statements will include total revenue, gross profit, and operating expenses. You will see operating income or loss, along with income from continuing operations. Two important things you will want to look at are net income and net income applicable to common shares (to help you gauge profitability and if applicable, money available for dividend payments). A company may not be profitable now but be a wise investment for the future, but if it's not profitable, you'll want to understand why and see that it's making progress each year.

The balance sheet will give you an overview of assets and liabilities. You will be able to review the inventory of each company, as well as a long-term investment and plant and equipment spending. This report also includes information on long-term debt. It's important to have some awareness if a company is accumulating a large amount of debt. If you are looking for companies that pay dividends, this can be particularly important because large amounts of debt can eat into future dividend payments. Remember that when a company takes on a large amount of debt (often by issuing bonds), it has to make interest payments – and those take priority.

Finally, you can review shareholder equity on this report, and see how many shares of different classes of stock the company has, including preferred and common stock. You can also see treasury stock, which are shares the company is holding in reserve.

The last statement that you will want to review is the cash flow statement. This statement gives net income, depreciation, changes in inventory, and other important information. You will also see the amount paid in dividends and capital expenditures.

## Financial News

Besides looking at the stock prices to see how it's changing with time, evaluating metrics like the price to earnings ratio and going over financial reports, you will also want to pay attention to financial news about the company. This can include learning about the company and watching for any news about the company. This will include new product development, construction of plants, hiring plans, or expansions into foreign markets. You will also want to pay attention to news about important management changes. If a key person leaves the company, you'll want to find out why.

Other financial news will be information related directly to the stock. When looking to invest in the company, you will want to see if analysts are giving buy or sell recommendations, and how they see the stock playing out in the near future or the coming year.

However, you will want to take this information with a grain of salt. A long-term investor should be focusing on the long-term growth and health of the company, not worrying about whether the stock will go up or down over the next week or month. You should also be focused on long term trends more so that quarterly earnings report. Also keep a focus on new product development and how much the company spends on R & D. Those are indicators that are important for what is coming down the road, which will determine how much the stock appreciates with time.

# Chapter 8
# Investment Strategies

In this chapter, we will review strategies that you can use for long term growth or income investing, and also look at aggressive investment in small caps and other assets.

## Investing to Achieve Long-Term Growth

The top reason to invest in stocks over the long term is to grow and build your wealth. People primarily invest in having a comfortable retirement, but you can get rich in the process if it's done correctly. If you want to adopt this type of investment strategy, you are looking for the share price to appreciate with time, so that at some future date you'll be able to sell the shares in order to get cash. Financial advisors suggest holding your investments until retirement and then taking out a fixed percentage per year as cash that you can use to live on, make large purchases, or enjoy travel and other activities. The general recommendation is to cash out about 4-5% of your portfolio per year. If you stay invested, it can keep growing, but as investors get closer to retirement, they tend to seek capital preservation more than growth.

Growth stocks are those that grow faster than the market average. To determine whether or not a stock you are interested in is a growth stock, get the percentage gain of the stock over the previous year and compare that to the gain in the S & P 500. If you find a stock that is growing at 10% per year, but the S & P

500 is only growing at 6% per year, that's a growth stock. If the stock is only growing at 4% a year, it's not a growth stock.

Some stocks grow steadily over time while some are in a rapid growth phase. Obviously, rapid growth has its limits, but as Apple has shown, a company can be relatively mature and still be growing rapidly if it develops new products and aggressively enters new markets.

If you are a growth-oriented investor, you are going to be looking for rapid appreciation in the share price. Amazon is a good example; another one is Netflix. High price to earnings ratios are not only not something to be concerned about, but you might also even seek them out. You're looking for the value of your shares to increase rapidly if you are a growth investor.

Growth investing is generally suited for younger investors under the age of 45, and for older investors who haven't been saving and investing and who need to build up retirement funds quickly.

## Value Investing

Warren Buffett is the most famous value investor. In short, value companies tend to be more mature but have steady growth. But the term "value investment" comes from the fact that the stock is undervalued, and so it can be purchased at a bargain price. This is indicated by a low price to earnings ratio when the company has solid fundamentals. One key you could look for is a company that has relatively high earnings per share, but a relatively low price to earnings ratio. A value stock isn't necessarily one that isn't going to grow a lot in the future. The perception is that value stocks are stuck, that they are going to grow but grow slowly over time forever. These are more appealing to conservative investors. However, that isn't necessarily the case, and you should be looking out for value stocks that also have a high potential for growth in the future.

## Choosing the Right Industries

When choosing your investments, you will want to look at industries and sectors as well as individual companies. Over time, sectors that are likely to see the most robust growth may change. So when you are investing, you'll want to put some research in to find out what sectors are seeing the best growth prospects at the present time. This can help you find value stocks that have the potential for future growth.

## Following Trends

Traders talk about trends all the time, meaning the short-term ups and downs in stock prices. However, right now, we are going to think about trends outside the stock market. It's important to think about and examine what's going on in society at large to identify trends. The kinds of trends we are thinking about are those that will have a direct impact on the stock market. Over the past ten years, the development and rise of social media were one of those trends. Had you been paying attention, you would have been observing this trend and the rise of the new companies associated with it like Facebook and Twitter. Following that larger trend could be used as a guide for investing. As with anything, you don't want to put all of your eggs in one basket. However, recognizing the trends is an important factor in spotting coming growth opportunities. Had you realized this years ago, you would have made ground-floor investments in these companies, and you would have been able to take advantage of their rapid growth to build your wealth.

There are many types of trends to look for. Changes in demographics are an important trend. The population is becoming older and more Hispanic. Companies that provide products and services for specific demographic groups might have bright futures. In particular, pharmaceutical companies might be something you can look at with an eye to the future because as people age, they tend to need more prescription drugs to stay healthy. Another trend of late is obesity. One side effect of this is more people are becoming diabetic, so investing in companies that have or are developing new treatments for diabetes is something that might be lucrative going forward.

## Research and Development

If you are looking for growth, companies that have a strong investment in research and development can be good investments. Apple is a good example – they are always spending large sums of money on developing new products and improving old ones. That ensures that they will have a leading market position, at least for the coming five years. If the company is also in a sector that would be hard for new companies to enter, that is also a plus. It would be hard for a new company to duplicate Apple's overall product line at this time. They would have to have desktop computers, laptops, tablets, and smartphones, among other things like an extensive selection of software products to compete with Apple. That is unlikely to happen, which makes Apple's position more secure than it would be otherwise.

## Small caps and Emerging Markets for Aggressive Growth

It's possible to get solid and even very high returns investing in established companies. As we've seen, some exchange-traded funds that invest in major stock indexes can provide very high growth rates. However, if you are seeking the most aggressive type growth possible, you'll be interested in small cap stocks as well as looking into emerging markets.

Let's take the latter first. If you are interested in emerging markets, it's strongly recommended that you utilize exchange-traded funds. This will save you from a lot of hassle. Doing it directly and on your own can create a lot of problems. First of all, you need to realize that in other countries you won't have the same protections that you have in the United States or a country like Great Britain. There are also other issues to worry about, such as currency exchange. You can avoid these problems by seeking out exchange-traded funds that invest in the countries you are interested in – and let the company managing the fund deal with all the headaches.

Remember that high returns usually correlate with increased risk. That said, you can find funds investing in emerging markets that have remarkable returns. For example, an iShares fund that invests in Russian companies sees 30% returns – at least for now. When an economy is still developing, it has more room to grow. But things are also less stable, and you never know when political developments could cause things to crash. Results vary. Some funds for developing markets don't even perform as well as funds investing in the S & P 500, and some even have negative returns. But if you need some rapid growth, it's something to consider.

Small caps provide the opportunity to get in early on a younger company with a lot of potential for growth. At one time, Netflix, Amazon, and Microsoft were small, unheard of companies. People who got in on these companies early were able to generate amazing amounts of wealth.

However, if you find small caps intriguing, keep in mind that the risk is high. A small proportion of small caps will grow large and be tomorrow's dominant companies. Most, however, won't do anything more than stay where they are. In fact, many of them are going to end up liquidating and going out of business. Others will do OK but never really take off.

This leaves us with two choices. We can try picking the winners ourselves, or we can invest in small cap exchange-traded funds to get some exposure to the growth without tying ourselves to an individual company. The fact is, investing in small caps is more speculative. Nobody has a crystal ball, and while it's easy to see the inevitability of a Microsoft or Apple in hindsight, at the time knowing which companies would go on to be tomorrows giants is nothing more than making educated guesses. You also might be a little disappointed by the returns available from small cap funds, because another cold truth is that most small cap companies are not growing rapidly. If you do decide to invest yourself, be sure to carefully pick your companies, and invest in several of them so that your boat is not anchored to a single company that may turn out to be a bust. To be perfectly honest, the odds that you are going to pick a winner for tomorrows markets are pretty slim.

## IPOS

People are also excited about investing in IPOs. That’s a bad idea as well. You can keep an eye on companies that have IPOs, but more often than not company IPOs start on a high note and then sink. It’s better to let things settle out for a year or two before deciding to invest in a company that recently went public. Remember that as a long-term investor, you are looking at five, ten, and twenty-year time horizons. So it’s not in your interest to be seeking out get rich quick opportunities.

## Diversity

When it comes down to it, whether or not you are aggressive or conservative, the old rules of diversification and dollar cost averaging are the best rules for you to follow. If you stick to these rules, and invest consistently, over time, you are going to build wealth.

## Rebalancing

At the end of each year, many investors engage in rebalancing. At the start of the year, you might have a portfolio with specific asset allocations to meet your goals. Say, for the sake of example, you had 65% in growth stocks, 25% in value stocks, and 10% in income securities. At the end of the year, the proportions might have changed because some stocks grew faster than expected, and some grew more slowly than expected. You might find at the end of the year you have 70% in growth stocks, 20% in valuc stocks, and 10% in income stocks. Maybe you will be satisfied with the change, but if you are set on keeping your portfolio within certain bounds, you will engage in rebalancing at the end of the year. This means buying and selling shares of different asset classes to maintain the percentages you seek. So in the example that we've specified, you would sell some of your shares in growth stocks, and use the proceeds to buy more value stocks so that you kept your overall portfolio at 65% in growth stocks, 25% in value stocks, and 10% in income.

# Chapter 9
# Income Investing

Income investing is a little bit of a different ballgame than growth investing. In this case, we are seeking out companies that pay dividends. That means ignoring a lot of high growth stocks like Amazon and Netflix. It also means ignoring disruptive companies with potential like Tesla. When you are an income investor, you are looking to make a certain level of income from your stock holdings. That may be now, or it may be in the future. But your portfolio is going to look quite different from a growth investor, and even a value-oriented growth investor.

## Yield

Start compiling a diverse list of companies that pay dividends that you find interesting. In each case, track the yield, which is the dividend divided by the share price. That will help you compare apples-to-apples when judging one dividend stock against another. Keep in mind that you are going to be seeking some kind of balance, so buying up stocks with the highest yields isn't the best philosophy. To see why to consider a company called consolidated communications. They pay a yield of 32%. The problem is, it's a penny stock. That means it's only $4 or so a share. Most analysts are rating it a SELL. A glance at the chart indicates it has dropped from a $29 share price over the past couple of years, and yet it's still rated as being overvalued. These are major red flags.

## Dividend

You may also be interested in the actual dividend payment, and not just the yield. IBM pays $6 a share, but Apple only pays $1.55 a share. So you'd have to own more than three Apple shares for every share of IBM you could buy in order to get the same annual income from your stocks. Since IBM is cheaper on a per share basis, that is something to take into consideration.

## Dividend Growth

For any stock that you invest in, you're going to want to look at the history of their dividend payments. The ideal dividend stock is one that pays higher dividends over time. IBM is a great example because they paid consistent dividends through the 2008 financial crisis, and they have been increasing their dividends since then. Dividend growth ensures that your dividend payments will keep up with or exceed inflation.

## DRIPS and Reinvesting

If you have a large amount of capital available right now, you can buy up shares of stock and start living off the dividend payments. However, if you are looking at a long-term investment program, you are going to want to reinvest your dividends. In the future, you're going to want to have as many shares as possible, so taking cash out now simply doesn't make sense. Instead, the payments from dividends should be used to purchase additional shares. Some companies even allow you to purchase fractional shares with the money.

A DRIP is a Dividend Reinvestment Program. In this case, the company will automatically take any dividends you earn and use them to buy additional shares. This will help enforce discipline, in case you get tempted to cash out your dividends and waste the money on a trip or new car. Instead, the company will force you to save for the future.

## Exchange-traded funds

The possibility of using exchange-traded funds to meet your investment goals always exists. In this case, you can seek out an ETF that invests in dividend stocks. You will still receive dividend payments, and the fund will have built-in diversification. When looking at ETFs to use for dividend investing, be sure to focus on yield, and pick funds that have the highest yields. Many investors can do a mixture of both; you could invest in ETFs while also investing in specific companies like IBM.

## Alternative Investments

The world of dividend investing isn't restricted to traditional stock investing. You can also invest in the following:

- REITS
- MLPs
- BDCs

A REIT is a real estate trust. This is a company that owns hard property assets and rents them out. The types of property are quite varied. For example, you can invest in REITs that own rental homes, apartments, or commercial real estate. There are also REITs that own hotels and resorts. In fact, any type of property that you can think of is represented by at least one REIT. But interestingly there are REITs that have great prospects for the future because they are technology related. For example, some REITs own cell phone towers, and there are others than own cloud computing.

REITs pay high dividends, and they trade like stocks on the stock market. Investing in REITs is a good way to get some exposure to real estate, and other types of property ownership.

An MLP is a master limited partnership. These companies are midstream energy companies, that transport oil and gas, own pipelines, or own refinement facilities. These are great investments to consider, and they also pay high dividends. You also invest in them by purchasing shares on the stock market. These types of investments are particularly noteworthy because the companies are partnerships and not corporations. When you invest, you become a limited partner. This means that you can deduct company expenses on your tax returns. Essentially, a large share of the income from an MLP is tax-free.

The final alternative investment that we are looking at is called a BDC, or Business Development Corporation. They also trade on stock exchanges and pay dividends. These are financial companies that invest in small to mid-sized companies that need cash. They can provide loans to companies or take an ownership stake.

## When to Cash Out

Cashing out is a personal decision. By cashing out, in this case, we don't mean selling off your shares. What we mean is when should you stop reinvesting and start taking dividends as cash income. The answer is you start doing this when the level of dividend payments you receive starts matching your desired income.

Don't be afraid to shake up your portfolio. If you find an investment that suits your needs better than stocks you are currently invested in, then you should be ready to sell some of your shares and invest in the other stock. There is no reason for you to be locked into a particular stock, you can buy shares in other companies and then start getting dividend payments from them in the next upcoming cycle.

## Fundamentals Always Matter

No matter which path you choose, when dividend investing, you want to pay close attention to the fundamentals. In the end, fundamentals are what matters. A company with good fundamentals is going to be a good investment. So you'll want some trade-off between solid fundamentals, yield, and dividend payment that suits your goals. Remember to always think long-term.

## Bond Investing

Finally, if you are looking for an income investing portfolio, consider buying exchange-traded funds that invest in bonds. As we discussed earlier, there is a wide array of choices, allowing you to find the right amount of risk and the right interest payments. You'll want to look at the yields of the bond funds. Some have high rates of growth and high yields. That is, you can achieve growth as well as income by investing in bond funds too. The advantage of using ETFs is that you can avoid the hassle of trying to invest in bond markets.

# Chapter 10
# Technical Analysis

Technical analysis is a method of looking at stock charts and data in order to spot price trends. It is a method primarily used by traders who are interested in short term profits, but it can be helpful for long-term investors as well. Long-term investors can use technical analysis to determine (estimate) the best entry points into their positions. Note that technical analysis certainly isn't required, and most long-term investors ignore short-term trends and use dollar cost averaging. Nonetheless, it's a good idea to become familiar with technical analysis in case you decide you want to use it in the future.

## Technical vs. Fundamental Analysis

Technical analysis is different than fundamental analysis. They could be but aren't necessarily related. Fundamental analysis is focused on the underlying fundamentals of the company. These can include earnings, price to earnings ratio for the stock, and profit margins. The technical analysis ignores all of these things and is simply focused on the trades of the moment. It seeks to discover upcoming trends in buying behavior. So whether or not a company was profitable in the previous quarter – it doesn't necessarily matter. Of course, profitability can drive more stock purchases, and so drive up the price. But many things can drive the price up or down over the short term. Simple emotion can do it, and so traders that use technical analysis study the charts themselves and pay far less attention to external factors or fundamentals.

## Trend Seeking

The first thing that technical analysis seeks to discover is the trend. Simply put, a trend is a prevailing price movement in one direction or the other. The time period isn't specific and will depend on the trader's needs and goals. For example, day traders are looking for a trend that might only last two hours. Swing traders may hope to ride a trend that last weeks or months. Position traders are looking for longer-term changes, and simply want to enter a position at a low price and exit that position months or between 1-2 years later at a higher price to take a profit.

Trends are easy to estimate, but your estimations have no guarantee of being correct. For an uptrend, traders typically draw straight lines through the low points of the gyrations of the stock on the graph. This will help you estimate where the trend will end up at some future point in time. You can use this to set a selling point when you will exit your position.

In the following chart, we see the trend in JNK from April through October.

## Support and Resistance

Over relatively short time periods, stocks will stay confined between a range of prices. The low pricing point of this range is called *support*. The upper price point of the range is called *resistance*. The trader seeks to enter their position at a point of support. They can also place a stop loss order slightly below support so that they will exit the position if they bet wrong and share prices drop substantially. Then they can sell their stocks when the share price gets close to resistance levels, on the theory that it's more likely than not to drop back down after reaching resistance. The chart below illustrates this concept. Notice, however, that the stock eventually breaks out of the range. In this case, it's the support on the right side of the chart, and the price drops significantly.

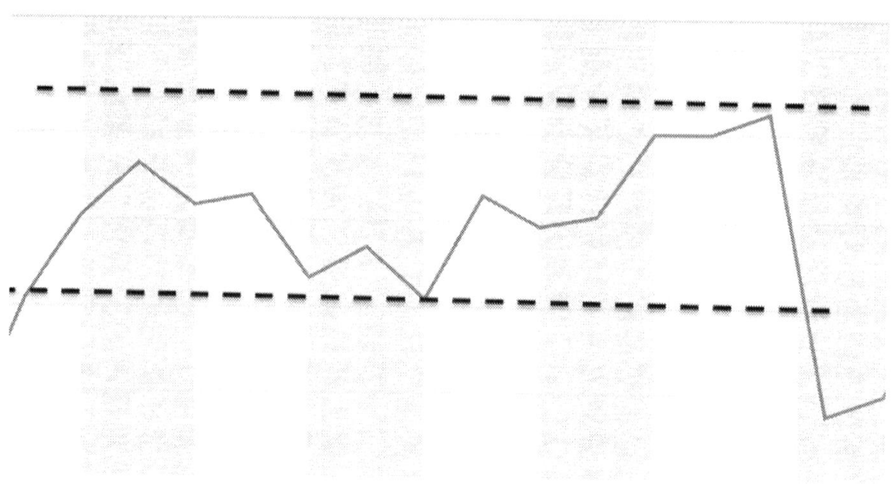

## Candlesticks

A *candlestick* is a graphical representation of price and trading that occurred over a specified time period. Candlesticks have a body, and "wicks" sticking out of the ends. On most stock charts candlesticks are in color, with green representing a "bullish" candlestick and red representing a "bearish" candlestick. A bullish candlestick is a time period where buyers were moving into the market buying up shares. The bottom of the body indicates the opening price for the period, and the top of the body indicates the closing price.

A bearish candlestick represents a time period of decline in price. In this case, the top of the candlestick body is the opening price, and the bottom of the body is the closing price.

In either case, the top wick of a candlestick represents the high price throughout the time period. The bottom wick represents the low price for the time period. You can choose what time period you want to be represented, from one-minute out to one year. In the example below, we view the JNK chart but using candlesticks instead of a line. This is with one-day intervals. So the chart tells us whether or not it was a bullish or bearish day, and the sizes of the candlesticks indicate the spread in opening and closing prices for the day.

Traders will look for certain patterns in candlestick charts that indicate changing trends. For example, if the share price has been dropping for a long period, and a large bullish candlestick suddenly appears, that can indicate that buyers are now entering the market, pushing up prices. The trader will confirm the signal by looking up the volume of trading and comparing that to the average. A high-volume trading day is a strong indicator that the price will probably move up.
Alternatively, if the price is at peak value, and there is a bearish

candlestick with higher than average volume, that tells us that

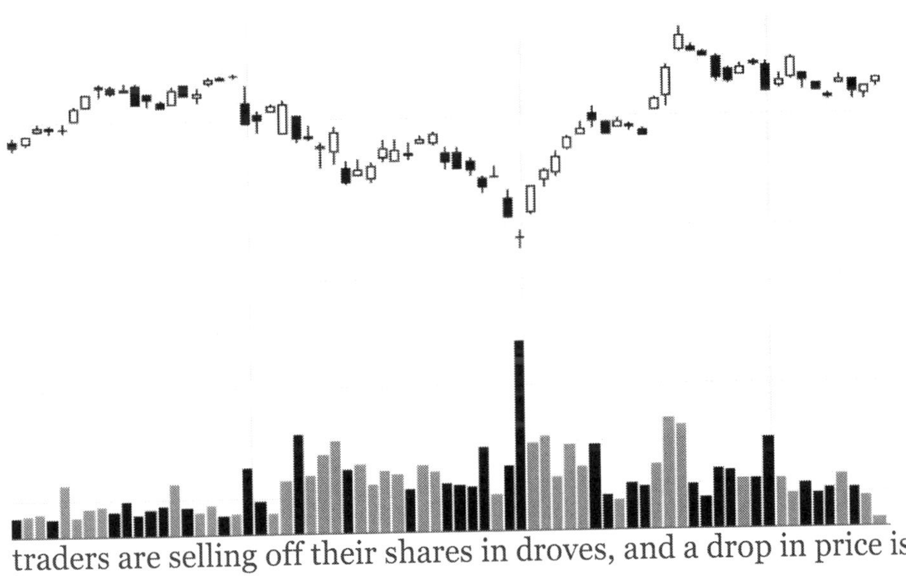

traders are selling off their shares in droves, and a drop in price is probably coming.

## Moving Averages

Another tool used in technical analysis is the moving average. A moving average is defined by the number of periods. So if we were using a chart that is framed in terms of days, a 9-period moving average would be a 9-day moving average. To plot points on the chart, the moving average would take the 9 previous days and average them. This helps eliminate noise from the stock charts and can be useful in spotting trends.

This example shows how a moving average (the purple line) generates a smooth curve for Apple, allowing us to focus more clearly on the trend in price.

The real benefit comes from comparing moving averages with different time periods. When a short period moving average crosses above a long period moving average, this indicates that an upward trend in pricing can be expected. That's because it indicates that buyers are moving into the market more recently. Conversely, when a short period moving average crosses below a long period moving average, that indicates a coming downward trend in the market.

A simple moving average, one that simply calculates the average of the past given number of days, is going to give equal weight to prices days ago and prices more recently. This is an undesirable feature, and so traders prefer to use exponential moving averages to get more accurate data. Exponential moving averages weight the data, giving more weight to recent prices and less weight to more distant prices. Here is the Apple chart with a 9-day exponential moving average and a 20-day exponential moving average. The 20-day moving average is in red. Notice that when the 9-day moving average crosses above the 20-day moving average, the price enters an upward trend. Conversely, when the 9-day moving average passes below the 20-day moving average, the price enters a downward trend.

We also see signals in the candlesticks on the chart as well. Notice that at the low point in June, a larger green candlestick follows the red candlestick. That is a bearish day of selling Apple off was followed by a bullish day of rising prices. When a candlestick of one type is larger than the previous candlestick ofthe opposite type, we say that it engulfs the other candlestick. Usually, this is a sign of a trend reversal.

## Chart Patterns

Traders also look for specific chart patterns that can indicate coming trend reversals. For example, you might be looking for signs that a stick is unable to move any higher in price after having undergone a large and long-lasting uptrend. What happens in these cases, is that the stock price will touch or reach a certain price level that is slightly higher than where it is at the present time, and do so two or more times. But each time it reaches the peak value, it will drop back down in price. That indicates that the stock has been bought up as much as it's going to be bought up at the present time.

Traders also look for signals in the chart that a breakout is going to occur. A breakout can happen to the upside, that is, stock prices can increase a great deal, or it can happen to the downside, in which case a strong downward trend in share price will follow.

In this case, you will see the price rise (or fall) and then for a short period of time, the trend will reverse. Then it reverts back to the same price rise (or decrease). This is a sign that the stock is "reverting to the mean," where the mean is the overall upward (or downward) trend. If you spot such a pattern early, it's possible to buy shares and be ready to profit from selling them when they reach the peak value.

## Bollinger Bands

It's possible to utilize a wide array of more sophisticated tools. Bollinger bands attempt to combine the idea of a moving average with moving zones of support and resistance. The levels of support and resistance for a stock are calculated at any given time using the standard deviation. Bollinger bands will include a simple moving average curve in the center to represent the mean stock price. There will be upper and lower level curves, which show two-standard deviations from the mean. Here we see a chart of Apple using Bollinger bands:

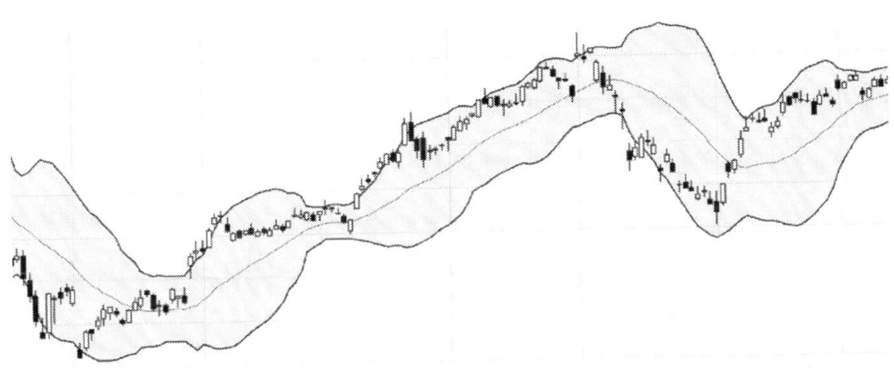

For the time period shown, Bollinger bands provide a great deal of information. The mean share price for the period was $194.38, while the upper line, two standard deviations above the mean, was $206.05. The lower line, which is two standard deviations below the mean, is $182.71.

Knowing these values can be useful to some traders. For example, options traders that sell put options can use the values of the standard deviation to select their prices.

## An Overview and Summary of Technical Analysis for the Stock Investor

Technical analysis does have its uses. However, unless you are a speculator, the use of technical analysis is questionable. Over the long term, the price movements shown on charts like these are not very important. If you are investing for the long term, dollar cost averaging is a more useful strategy. Think about the time horizons of your investments. If you are looking at 1-2 years, five years, or ten years, the momentary fluctuations shown here aren't very relevant. So focusing on the exact right moment to buy shares to save a penny is overkill. These charts are really only useful for speculators, that hope to profit for the sake of earning fast money rather than by investing in the companies themselves.

A second concern is a time spent doing this kind of analysis. Any time that you are spending doing technical analysis is the time that you are not spending doing fundamental analysis. That means that you're not learning about the companies that you are investing in over the long term. The financial statements and news about the company are far more relevant than a few short-term gyrations on the chart. If this sort of analysis interests you, then maybe you are more suited to becoming a swing or day trader instead.

# Chapter 11
# The Corporate and Government Insider Actions

An investor should always be on the lookout for signals that might be clues about their investments. One signal you should be keeping an eye on is the actions taken by the insiders with a company. Are they sticking by the company and investing in it? Or do they seem to be running away from it despite amazing stock prices? These can be important clues as to the health and intermediate future of the company. One thing you need to keep tabs on is whether or not the insiders are buying or selling shares of the company. You'll also want to note major departures from the company. Of course, the company is going to make up some pleasant story about why some major figure is leaving. You know, they want to spend more time with their grandmother. But is that really what's going on? If other news or more signals are indicating otherwise, including insider moves, you might view such news with a negative eye. People often leave a sinking ship.

## Insider Trading

Here we aren't talking about criminal activity, but rather company members themselves who own shares of the company that they are associated with. A good indication that people are confident in the future of their company is finding out that they own and are buying more shares of stock in their own company. On the other hand, if they are selling off their shares, that can be a sign that the people actually running the company or involved with it don't have that much confidence in its future.

It's actually possible to find out what company insiders are doing when it comes to shares of stock in their own company. The Securities and Exchange Commission requires them to file publicly available reports. You can find publicly filed reports on a government website known as "edgar." It can be found here:

https://www.sec.gov/edgar.shtml

"Insiders" will file various forms, including an initial form that they have to submit to the government indicating their insider status with the company. This is called form 3.

If you are researching this data, you're going to want to pay special attention to form 4 and form 144. On form 4, any transactions involving a large number of shares are recorded. So if the insider bought a large number of shares, it would be recorded on form 4. Also, if they sold a large number of shares, it's going to be reported on form 4.

If a single insider is selling shares, that doesn't necessarily mean anything. However, if you notice that multiple insiders are off-loading their shares, pay attention. That might be an indication that a large number of people who are in the know about the company's prospects aren't confident about the company's future.

Form 144 is related to a special class of stock called restricted stock. This is stock that the insider was provided as compensation for employment. If they decide to unload it after a required holding period, this will be noted with a form 144.

In summary, if insiders are confident that the company is doing well and has solid long-term prospects, they are probably going to be buying shares in the company, not trying to get rid of them. You will want to take this kind of information and incorporate it into the larger picture of course. It's important to consider all the indicators for the company and not get lost in the details of focusing on one sign. So if you notice that there is a large sell-off, you'll want to check other information like the company's latest earnings reports.

## Quantity also Matters

Don't get alarmed if people sell a small number of shares. When they are trying to divest their own portfolio of any interest in the company, that is when you should take notice.

## Congressional Insiders

A few years ago, the news program 60 Minutes did an interesting investigation. They found that members of Congress were playing the role of insiders at many companies, and getting advantageous stock buys as a result. Unfortunately, there isn't much we can do about that, but it's good to have awareness about it.

## Stock Buybacks

Stock buybacks can be a good sign or a bad sign. If a company is doing well, a stock buyback can be used as a way for a company to pass on profits to investors. However, stock buybacks can also be an indicator that a company is heading for trouble. The first thing to consider is that the company has lower than expected earnings. In that case, a company might use a stock buyback in order to artificially boost their indicators on the stock market. Buying back shares of stock, if done on a large enough scale, can alter important metrics like the price per earnings ratio and earnings per share. If you have fewer shares but the same earnings, earnings per share are going to look more favorable. They can do this in the hopes of artificially boosting the value of the stock and hence it's the market price. Consider an example. Suppose that a company has $500 in earnings and 100 shares. The earnings per share are $5. If they buy back 50 shares, then you still have $500 in earnings, but with 50 shares, so now the earnings per share are $10. That looks better to investors taking a cursory look at the stock, but in reality, the company's prospects haven't changed.

Another negative possibility is that the company has stagnated. If companies are out of ideas and not pursuing new ones, they aren't investing a large amount of money into research and development. That means they have cash sitting around, and using a stock buyback could be a simple way to unload the cash.

You'll also want to check the price to earnings ratio and look up to see if the stock is overvalued. It can be a bad sign when a company is buying back overvalued shares.

Another question to ask is, where is the company getting the cash used for the buyback? Hopefully, they have enough money on hand to do it. But if they are borrowing money for the share buyback, that is definitely a sign that the company is unhealthy.

If you have invested in a company and they engage in a share buyback, you'll want to investigate further to find out what's behind it. In many cases, it's not something to worry about. However, sometimes it's an indicator that the future with this company is not so bright.

## Stock Splits

Another corporate action you will need to be aware of is a stock split. Companies can do stock splits or reverse stock splits. In a stock split, a share is converted from 1 share to 2 or 3 or more shares. That immediately changes the price per share and impacts metrics like earnings per share. Imagine that a company has a share trading at $100, and it has 100 shares outstanding, and earnings per share of $5, meaning they have a price to earnings ratio of $20. If they do a 2-1 split, now there are 200 shares. The amount of money invested in the company hasn't changed, so the share price immediately drops to $50 a share. Now you have twice the number of shares in your portfolio, so the value of your investment hasn't changed. Earnings per share would be cut in half and would be reported as $2.50. Price to earnings ratio would remain at $20.

One reason a company might do a stock split is to reduce the price of a share, in order to attract more investors. A stock trading at $1,000 a share might be unaffordable for a lot of small investors. If a company was interested in attracting more small investors, they might to a 4-1 stock split and drop the share price to $250 per share. A stock split for a high-priced stock can also increase liquidity. That is, it will increase the ease with which you can sell your shares. Very high-priced stocks will have large bid-ask spreads, which can make them harder to sell. Doing a split and bringing the price back down to a lower level can reduce the bid-ask spread and make it easier for investors to sell their shares.

A reverse stock split is going to reduce the number of shares that you own. So if you own 100 shares and they did a 1-2 reverse split, you would only own 50 shares after that. If the share price had been $100, it would rise to $200 after the split. Remember that the amount of money invested remains the same before and after the split, so the share price also has to change if the number of shares changes.

# Chapter 12
# Taxes

Ah, we come to our favorite subject, taxes! The objective in the stock market is to make money, and every time that you make money, you are going to find yourself in a position of having to pay taxes on it. Unfortunately, it's a reality we can't escape. You might delay it, but at some point, you're going to have to pay.

There are many different issues you need to be aware of when it comes to taxes. This isn't a tax advisory book, and you should consult an accountant to make sure you're doing everything right. However, we'll take a brief look at some of the main issues.

## Capital Gains

Suppose that you hold an asset and the price appreciates. If you sell it, you'll realize a capital gain – in other words, you made money. When you make money by selling appreciating assets, you owe capital gains tax. The important thing to consider is how long you held the asset.

If you held the asset for one year or less, this is a short-term capital gain. The bad news about this is short-term capital gains are considered ordinary income. That means you'll pay the regular income tax rate on your gain.

If you hold the asset for longer than a year, even if it's just a day, then it becomes a long-term capital gain. For some reason, Congress has decided that they know that holding assets for an arbitrary period that they made up is better, and so long-term capital gains have very favorable tax rates. These are much lower than income tax rates.

The bottom line here is that you'll want to take into account how long you have held an asset (aka stocks) when selling. If you are a long-term investor and planning to hold your investments until retirement, this means that you will be paying long-term capital gains taxes on your investments when you sell them off to get the money. Of course, if your retirement is in the distant future (more than ten years away), it's hard to say what the laws are going to be.

## Dividend Income

The important thing to note about dividend income when considering taxes is that it's considered to be ordinary income. There isn't anything special to consider dividend income. The one exception is dividends paid by an MLP. That's because they aren't technically dividends and you're considered a "partner" in the business. In that case, you are able to deduct depreciation from your taxes. The company passes it on to the "partners." This has huge implications. Many investors in MLPs are able to enjoy their income from the investments virtually tax-free. It's a little complicated, so if you start putting money into MLPs, you'll want to consult an accountant. The company will be sending you the appropriate forms.

## Individual Retirement Accounts

One of the advantages of individual retirement accounts or IRAs is that they allow investments to grow inside of them tax-free. You can utilize this to your advantage. One way to do so is to buy dividend stocks inside the IRA and then reinvest the dividends.

That way, you can continually grow your account and grow it beyond the usual limitations.

## Expenses

Deducting expenses related to your investing might be problematic. The IRS isn't too friendly when it comes to deducting expenses related to investing. There is one exception, and that is if you are a day trader. Then a day trader can deduct expenses like publications they read, and all the computer equipment and software services that they sign up for. But if you are doing ordinary investing, that might be a hard sell.

One way to get around it is to set up a business to run your investing. Then have the business buy all the equipment and so forth. Of course, this will inject other complications into the situation, so you'll have to weigh the pros and cons in order to determine whether or not it's really worth the extra hassle. Quite frankly, in most cases, it's not going to be.

# Chapter 12
# Ten Indicators of a Great Investment

There aren't any guarantees in the stock market, but one thing we can say is there are a set of *necessary* conditions that must be met by any potential investment in order to label it as a good buy. We'll give an overview of some of the most important indicators in this chapter.

## Increasing Revenue

In most cases, you aren't going to want to invest in a company with stagnant or declining revenues. Look for companies that have shown increasing revenues over the past three years. Of course, there are no hard and fast rules, there may be reasons why a company is not showing increasing revenues now, but it's a good investment for the future. Each case has to be evaluated individually.

## Increasing Profit

A good company to invest in is one that has increasing profits as well. More aggressive investors can be more flexible here; some companies that are in their early growth phases are good investments even though they are not making profits right now. They can be poised to make solid profits in the future. However, that is a risk. So conservative investors are probably going to want to avoid those types of companies, and stick with those that are already earning profits.

## Growing Dividend Payments

If a company is paying dividends, a company with growing dividends is preferred over a company that has stagnant or declining dividends. The latter cases might indicate a company is becoming less profitable or making bad moves like taking on too much debt. If the company has been around for a while, you'll want to see how it behaves in bear markets. If they cheat shareholders by cutting dividends, that might not be a company you want to hitch your wagon too. Look for companies that try and stand by their investors and keep them happy.

## Growing Markets

A company that is in a growing market is preferable to one in a shrinking market. For example, would you rather invest in coal companies or natural gas companies? The prospects for the latter are probably much better.

## The Company Doesn't Carry Excessive Debt

If a company is loading up on excessive debt, that can lead to future problems. They might have problems paying it back, or one simple but important problem is interest payments can start cutting into profits. As we mentioned earlier, this can leave less money to pay for dividends in the future.

## Trends Favor the Company's Future

Companies that are positioned to capitalize on large trends have better long-term prospects. For example, the population is aging. This trend favors two industries. One is the pharmaceutical industry since as we mentioned earlier, people need more medications as they age. Another industry that might benefit is nursing homes. You can invest in REITs that own nursing homes – something to consider.

## Price to Earnings Ratio is Relatively Low

If possible, always invest in value stocks. So you'll want to seek out companies that have solid earnings and cash flow, but low price to earnings ratio when possible. That doesn't mean you should always buy value stocks; you should stick to the types of companies that you need in order to meet your investment goals. But when all other things are equal, you're going to want to buy value stocks if possible. Remember that stocks can be growth and value, so it's not necessarily an either-or choice.

## The Company is Innovative

Innovative companies that are releasing new, groundbreaking products are preferable to stagnant companies that have lost their edge. At least until recently, Apple fit that bill perfectly. Think of Apple under Steve Jobs, and you have the ideal company.

## You Can Buy and Sell Options on the Stock

Being able to buy options on the stock is an important benefit. Fortunately, most major companies also have options. Two ways you can utilize options as a long-term investor include selling call options to generate some monthly income, and buying put options for some insurance if you are concerned that the stock price might drop by a large amount and wipe out the value of your investment.

## The Stock is Liquid

All things being equal, a more liquid stock is better. Look for narrow bid-ask spreads. That can be important if you are thinking about selling off your shares, you want to be sure that you can get rid of them quickly if you need to.

# Chapter 13
## Ten Tips for a Bear Market

We haven't had a real bear market for some time. The stock market continues its seemingly permanent and inevitable march upwards. However, one thing we know for sure is that bear markets always arrive at some point. There is no reason to panic in a bear market, and having some tips to help you get through it will help you reduce the pain.

### Don't Panic

The first thing to do is don't panic. If you panic, this might lead you into a position where you're going to make bad moves. For example, many people sell off all their stocks. It doesn't matter if the markets are going up or down, you don't want to follow the herd. Running off the cliff with the lemmings is the worst thing you can do. Avoid making major selling moves during a bear market, especially in the early phases when plummeting prices cause the most panic. Take a deep breath and relax, and avoid watching too much financial news for a while. Also, don't keep looking at your shares to see how they are doing.

### Invest in Short ETFs

Earlier in the book, we showed an illustration where you can buy shares in short ETFs. These are great to invest in during good times. The share prices will be low, and they will rise high in a downturn, allowing you to pocket a large cash profit when they are in high demand. You need to invest in those types of funds now, rather than waiting for a crash to happen. Suppose that you could buy 100 shares for $25 each. That would require an upfront investment of $2,500. In a major bear market, the price might rise high to $100 or $200 a share. If it went to $200 a share, you should sell your shares for $20,000, making a profit of $17,500 fewer commissions.

## Buy Stocks

Remember that downturns are always buying opportunities. You should be looking to buy any time there are major price drops in the stock market. This holds true for individual stocks as well as for bear markets. Those extra shares that you can pick up at bargain prices will benefit you a great deal later, so you can see that instead of panic when a bear market hits, excitement might be more appropriate.

## Sell Call Options

Call options rise in value when share prices rise, but you can still make some money by selling call options in bear markets. The good thing about selling call options in bear markets is that since the price is dropping, you can pick an appropriate strike price such that the chance of the option being exercised is slim to none. You can sell a covered call for every 100 shares of stock that you own. The money can then be reinvested to buy more shares.

## Buy Put Options

Put options rise in value in response to declining share prices. When share prices start dropping, you can start buying put options to make some extra money. Options can be tricky because they expire and suffer from a phenomenon known as "time decay," so you should learn how to do it properly before just jumping in. But if you do it right when there is a clear trend in the market, you can make solid profits by selling the put options before they expire. You can then either cash out the money or reinvest it by purchasing more shares. The latter is preferred, after all over the long term having more shares is going to be more beneficial than some short-term cash.

## Get Into Bonds

Money has to go somewhere, and if it's fleeing the stock market, you might find it in the bond markets. You might watch bond ETFs and see if they are increasing in value during a major bear market. If so, this could provide a good short-term opportunity.

## Look for Sectors Weathering the Storm

One thing to keep in mind is that not all sectors feel the impact of a bear market in the same way. In fact, some sectors go forward at full-speed as if nothing bad is happening. We saw this in the 2008 financial crisis. Apple introduced the iPhone right in the midst of the recession and made huge profits from it. Google also introduced Android and continued its growth. Meanwhile, the banking sector was on the verge of collapse. When a recession is being driven by a particular sector, you can take advantage of looking for investments in other sectors better positioned to thrive.

## Stick with Dividend Stocks

Many companies continue to pay good dividends even during bear markets. That is extra money that can be used to invest by purchasing more stock that is available at discount prices.

## Remember it Shall Pass

The main thing about bear markets is to remember that bear markets are temporary. No bear market has lasted forever. They only last at most a couple of years. Even in the great depression, the market downturn was short-lived. By 1933 the stock market was experiencing large gains, even though it wasn't growing as much as it had during the "roaring 20s". The important thing is to keep a realistic attitude. Don't follow everyone else into hysteria.

# Chapter 14
# Secret Investment Strategies

Now we'll review 10 secret investment strategies that the pros use to earn even more money on the stock market. These can be used in conjunction with your regular investing.

## Options Trading Using Spreads

Options trading can be lucrative, but it also carries high risk. The way you will want to go about it using spreads. Do some research and learn how to utilize spreads to do low-risk options trading. While the risk is capped, when you do spreads, your potential profit is capped as well. However, spreads usually tip the odds in your favor if you do it right. The extra income can be taken out as cash or reinvested to buy more shares of stock.

## Selling Put Options

If you have enough money in your account to cover it, selling put options can be a way to earn profits off the stock market. To do it properly, the first thing you should look into is selling naked put options. That means that you are selling put options without the full amount of cash required that would cover the option. However, you will need a margin account and have some cash in it to act as insurance. If done correctly, you can earn a good income every week.

## Sector Funds

You should look into buying exchange-traded funds that cover different sectors. This is a good way to increase the diversification that is in your account. There are funds available for many different sectors, like healthcare related stocks, or energy stocks. When you add in some sector diversification, this will help you grow your investments during good times and have an added layer of protection during bad times.

## I Bonds

The Federal government offers inflation-protected securities or TIPS. These can be very lucrative, especially in an era of low interest rates. In many cases, the low interest rates mean that investing in bonds is not desirable. With TIPS, you get an added boost since the inflation rate is incorporated to make sure your investments are not losing value.

## Consumer Staples

Consider investing in consumer staples. These include things people need no matter what, such as nondurable products like toilet paper and Kleenex, or food. These are the things that people need in order to make it through each day. Having some investments in consumer staples isn't necessarily going to bring you the greatest return. However, it's going to have some appreciation in value, and more importantly, it can provide an insurance policy for your portfolio in bad times. Remember, these are things that people ALWAYS need to buy.

## LEAPs

LEAPS are long-term options. Some people have referred to LEAPs as the poor-man's way of owning additional stocks. They allow you to control shares of stock at lower prices than you'd have to pay in order to actually buy the shares. You can do interesting things with them like sell covered call options against them. In addition, you can profit from price moves of the stock while you own the LEAP. You can sell it at any time and take your profits.

## Funds of Funds

Another interesting way to invest that can help you diversify your portfolio is to invest in funds of funds. These are mutual funds that invest in other mutual funds. You might be asking why do this – the reason is it can give you a high level of diversification. It's not necessarily for everyone but it's something to consider.

## Mix things up

People tend to think of an investor in either-or terms. That is, are you a trader or an investor? Are you a day trader, or an investor? Are you a bond investor, or a stock investor? You get the picture.

Why not wear multiple hats? The best thing to do is to be a long-term stock investor – but that doesn't mean you have to do that exclusively. That should be your central focus, of course. But you can also pursue other avenues. These can include swing trading, or options trading. You might also want to get into other markets like Forex. You don't have to be constrained by one approach. Of course, that is entirely up to each individual. Many people are not interested in getting involved with every little market, and many people find the intense attention that has to be paid to the markets when you're trading Forex or Options to be more than they care to involve themselves with. But, if it interests you, it's something to consider in order to accelerate your wealth building program.

## EE Savings Bonds

This is a special type of bond issued by the government that is guaranteed to double in value. You need to hold them for a long time. The term is 20 years. This is a secure way to diversify your investments because at the present time, at least, capital is considered completely secure when invested with the U.S. government.

# Conclusion

Well, you have made it to the end of the book! I would like to offer my thanks. I am glad that you took the time to read the book to the end, and I hope that you have found it educational and informative.

Becoming a self-directed investor is an exciting way to take charge of your finances. It is great to take ownership and begin to control your own financial future. This can help you in many ways, not the least of which is getting to a position of financial independence. Unfortunately, most people never get there. But now that you've begun educating yourself, you have also begun to acquire the knowledge and tools you need to achieve it yourself. Before we leave, I want to reiterate the most important lessons of the book.

Just remember to say in the markets for the long-term. That is the first rule of success. Traders are trying to sell people on the promise of quick cash, but long-term investing remains the best way to build wealth for the future.

Second, you should build a highly diversified portfolio. It can include some individual stocks, but it should also include exchange-traded funds. They should be diverse as well, so you should have funds in your account that track major stock market indices, but also funds that track sectors, real estate, and energy. Also, be sure to do some bond investing through your exchange-traded funds. A diversified portfolio is a winning portfolio — every time.

And finally, make sure to follow the principles of dollar cost averaging. This not only helps you with averaging out your costs so that you're not mistakenly buying stocks always at price peaks. Dollar cost averaging also keeps you in the habit of investing regularly. Many people fail to keep up, and then years later, they find their investments are not as large as they had hoped. By following a program of regularly investing, you can ensure that you get to a place where you want to go.

Again, thank you for taking the time to read the book! If you have found the book helpful please go to Amazon and be sure to leave a review! We always like to hear from our readers.

# Stock Trading Strategies

## ***Technical Analysis to Master the Financial Market.***

*A Crash Course for Beginners to Make Big Profits Fast! Psychology about How to Start, Trends and Strategy*

William L. Anderson

# Table of Contents

# Introduction

In this book, which is the second in my series, we are going to take a new turn in our look at the stock market. In book 1 we discussed the long-term buy and hold approach to investing. While that works for many people, others prefer to take a more active and short-term approach. Instead of investing for the long term,
they seek to make profits from short term price movements in the markets.

There are actually many ways you can do this, depending on the time frame over which the trader hopes to earn money, among other things. While it's a more action packed and stress filled approach to the markets, some people find it exciting. And the most exciting part about it is that you can build your own successful trading business, and earn big profits in the process. As we'll see, you can do that on a full-time, or a part-time basis.

Despite stereotypes, traders don't earn profits on the market based on guessing or gut-level hunches. Instead, you need to know how to carefully analyze stock market data so that you can estimate what future trends in pricing will be. There are many tools that are used to do this, and we will be exploring them in this book.

We will begin by going over the idea of trading versus investing, and then explore the different paths that exist for trading. Normally, people think about *day trading* when the word *trading* is used, but not all traders are day traders. There are many variations in trading style. So if the high pressure and high risk world of day trading is not to your liking, there are other ways to trade. They require less time commitment and are not as risky.

The main focus of this book will be exploring the tools and techniques that are used to earn big profits. Surprisingly, they are actually relatively simple to learn despite their technical nature. Applying them in practice may be more of an art form than a science.

When it comes down to it, the only way you'll be able to find out if you're really suited for trading is to try it. We'll explore ways that you can do it without risking much money, so that you can experience the process and figure out whether or not you really have the talent necessary to become a winning trader. And the first step is acquiring the knowledge you need to get started – which you have done by downloading this book!

# Chapter 1
# An Introduction to Trading

In this chapter we are going to introduce the concept of trading, and explain how it's different from traditional stock market investing. Then we will explore the different types or styles of trading that are available. One thing to keep your eye on is what the requirements for entry are. The good news is there is a style of trading that fits many personality types, and while you might not be able to get started with the capital required for one style, you can find others that will suit your situation.

Finally we will discuss the profit potential of trading, and selecting a broker.

## Trading defined – and how it differs from investing

The goal of trading is to earn profits over the short-term from price movements that occur with financial securities. So rather than investing over the course of years and decades to build wealth, trading is a for-profit business approach to the markets. Investors are happy getting an annual average return, traders seek to beat the markets over short time periods that can last anywhere from minutes to day, or weeks to a few months.

There are some trading styles that will even hold positions for more than a year, but they never hold them any longer than 2 years. The goal in all cases is to get in and get out. Not every trade is going to be a winner, you're looking to build a track record where you have more winning trades than losing trades, which adds up to profit.

That's what trading is, it's a for-profit business, and many traders make seven figure incomes. You can do it part-time or full-time. Some traders only spend a couple of hours a day on a part-time business, while others quit their day jobs and devote full-time effort to trading.

While investors are hoping to build a portfolio of stocks that they hold for long time periods, traders often don't hold positions at all. When they do hold positions, it might be one or two stocks at a time that they will exit quickly once there is a good price move.

By studying charts and using the tools of analysis, traders identify relatively low risk price levels when they should enter a position. Then when a price movement occurs giving an opportunity to earn profits by exiting the position, they do so rather than holding onto the investment.

Most investors put a lot less thought into the right time to enter a position, and instead use techniques like dollar cost averaging. This is done in the belief that years from now the ups and downs of prices will have averaged because they have used methodical, regular stock purchases. Compared to the price swings of today, the value of their portfolio years and decades from now will be overwhelming. Many investors never think about exiting a position, and those that do, only do so over longer time frames, of at least one year. That can be done when rebalancing a portfolio, for example. And even then, they may only sell part of a position, but stay with the company.

Investing is more of a commitment to specific companies, or to the market through index funds. There are many reasons that people will invest in a company. They may do so simply because they believe they'll be able to build their wealth through the company's stock. In other cases, a belief in the mission of the company or a love of its products and management might be a factor. Examples include Apple, Amazon, or Tesla.

Investors are putting their money into a stock for the purposes of taking an ownership stake in the company. They may exercise their voting rights as part of the investment, and feel they are really a part of the company.

Contrast these views and approaches to those of a trader. A trader has no intention of taking an ownership stake in the company, but only wants to control the shares for a short time frame in order to make a profit. They don't directly care about the products a company is offering or its mission, they are only interested in upcoming potential for price movements. So if a company releases a new product, great. The trader will seek to profit from the large price movements that occur shortly after the product is released, but they aren't going to ride it out over the long term.

One of the biggest differences between investors and traders is that some people are risk averse, while others are willing to take risks. The investor often won't invest in specific companies, because they seek security for their capital. Wanting to build a retirement nest egg, they invest in a diversified array of stocks and funds. They look for relative safety, and they get it through diversification. The hope here is that you can ride the long term tide of the market. That's a good bet over the course of several years to decades, history shows the trend is always upward. Recessions may come and go, but over time they pass and the markets recover. The goal in this case is to have a large number of stocks in your possession by the time you retire, so that you can cash them out gradually and enjoy the benefits of a passive income.

Another approach investors use is to seek out stocks that pay dividends. This often requires settling for slow growing, but steady companies that are mature and not seeking aggressive growth. Investors accumulate large numbers of shares in these companies so that they can enjoy passive income from the dividends. It's unlikely that a trader would be interested in those types of companies. Traders are looking for stocks with high levels of volatility.

As you can see, the approaches and goals when it comes to trading and investing are quite different. We have summarized the major differences in the table below.

| | **Trading** | **Investing** |
|---|---|---|
| Time Horizon | Day to Months | Years to Decades |
| Holdings | Short-term<br>often no holding | Growing portfolio<br>often 100% invested |
| Types of Investment | Any stock that is likely to<br>see large price swings | Solid company fundamentals<br>Value stocks<br>Dividends |
| Price Movements | Fluctuations in price over a day, weeks, or at most over months | Gradual and consistent growth and ignores short-term fluctuations |

| Goals for Returns | 10% or more per Month | 10% a year |
|---|---|---|

## Trading as a business

Trading is an entirely different approach to the markets. Rather than thinking of it as a short-term method of investing, it should the thought of as a for-profit business. But it's not gambling. Since the stock market is inherently random, there is going to be some probability involved. But a trader doesn't randomly pick stocks to trade and hope for lady luck to smile. Trading involves using study and methodical analysis to choose stocks that are likely to have large price moves over specific time periods. So to be a trader, you need to have an analytical mind.

As you can see by looking at any stock chart, prices gyrate up and down all the time. Some stocks often undergo wild price swings over short time periods (they have a lot of volatility). Highly volatile stocks can make big moves in a single day, often changing price rapidly over the course of a few hours. Other less volatile stocks undergo large price movements over longer time frames, over the course of days or weeks. And any stock can do both, from time to time.

One interesting contrast between trading and investing is that investors always hope for price appreciation of a stock. Not so for traders. As a trader, you make money from price movements, not appreciation. So while you're accustomed to seeking out investments that appreciate with time, a trader can make just as much money from declines in prices as they can from gains. You just have to know what steps to take in order to do it. So it's a more flexible way of being in the markets.

Let's take an example to see how this can work in practice. Over the course of the first month of 2019, General Motors increased in price by about $5 a share. If you had purchased 1,000 shares when the stock was in the low range of prices, and then you sold them near the high point, that would have enabled you to walk away with a $5,000 profit. And that's the goal of trading. Run it like a business, and earn profits. Where GM would be in six months, a year, or five years, would not be of any concern to the trader that made that profit. If GM wasn't around anymore, there are plenty of other stocks to trade.

It's important to understand that such trades are not made randomly. So, its not a "what if" scenario picked out of thin air. There are technical reasons for choosing when to enter and exit a stock, and we will help you begin your training to learn how to recognize these opportunities.

The interesting thing is that a few months later, GM dropped in price again – going all the way down to $33 a share. While investors would find this upsetting, or at the most see it as a buying opportunity while they wait for the next upturn in stock prices – for traders it's another chance to make profits. A trader can make profits by shorting the stock.

Here's how it works. After peaking a bit, GM started dropping, and it was trading at about $38 a share. At this point, after doing some technical analysis indicating a downturn, the trader can borrow 1,000 shares from the broker. Then they can sell them on the open market immediately, holding the case proceeds in reserve. A few weeks later, GM drops to about $33 a share. Now the trader springs into action.

Now they buy 1,000 shares of GM at the lower price, using the money they obtained from the first transaction. Since it's $5 cheaper per share, they have made a $5 profit per share and earned $5,000. The trader then simply returns the borrowed shares back to the broker.

## Trading Style

There are three major styles of trading stocks. The primary differentiating characteristic between them is the time frame over which they invest. That is, some traders will enter and exit positions over shorter time frames than others. There are specific reasons why this is important, and it's actually a crucially important distinction.

There are some other differences too, such as what types of companies that you'll invest in. The central goal of any trader, regardless of style, is to profit from price swings in the market. They will use the same tools in their analysis. These include many of the topics covered in this book, such as candlesticks, chart patterns, and technical analysis. The time frame used will dictate which stocks are the best to use for your trades.

The main types of stock traders are day traders, swing traders, and position traders.

## Day Trading

*Day trading* is what most people think of when you mention the word "trading". This is a style of trading that involves getting in and out of a position on the same trading day. In many cases, positions are only held for a couple of hours.

A day trader never holds their positions overnight, and there are reasons for this that go well beyond style. Day traders seek out highly volatile stocks, and small movements in these stocks mean large amounts of capital. Any gaps in the ability of the trader to exit a position (such as during after hours trading) could completely wipe out an account. So day traders must get out of their positions by market closing because of the type of positions they hold, and that isn't a matter of taste.

You can day trade any stock, but the focus is usually on penny stocks and small caps. These types of stock typically have high volatility, so they are good candidates for day trading. Large price moves over the course of hours are the bread and butter of the day trader.

A *penny stock* is any stock with a share price of $5 or less. Some trade over the counter, and are known as "pink sheets". However, there are many penny stocks on the major stock markets.

Penny stocks can be liquid enough to enter into and exit out of trades quickly. They can also fluctuate wildly in price. In the chart below, we have a near and sometimes penny stock, from a company called *Consolidated Communications Holdings* (CNSL).

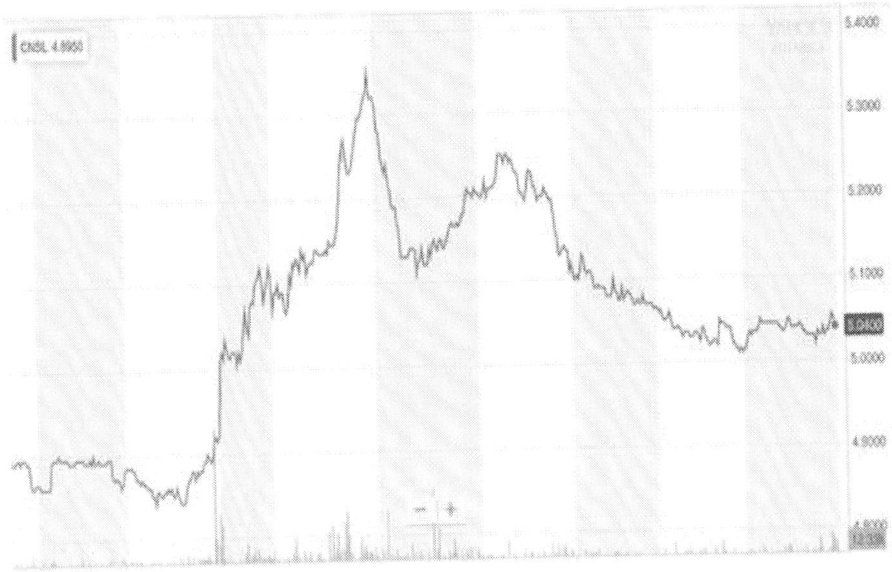

Over a short time period, the share price jumped from about $4.84 a share to $5.35 a share. That might not seem like much, but that is a 10% jump in price. Try and imagine Apple making that kind of move in a couple of hours. In the morning it would be trading at $200 a share, and then by noon it would be trading for $220 a share. So this is a pretty significant move.

To see the kind of profit this kind of move can generate, let's suppose that we purchased a number of shares of CNSL.

If we bought $10,000 worth of shares in Consolidated Communications Holdings at $4.84 a share, we would have been able to purchase 2,066 shares. Seeing the signs pointing to the upward trend shown in the chart, we would enter the position at the beginning of the day with plans to get out in a matter of hours.

There were plenty of opportunities to exit the trade and make a profit. If we sold them at the right moment, we'd have earned about $0.51 per share.

Again, that may not sound like much. But with 2,066 shares, we would have earned a profit of $1056. And that is over the course of two hours, to be precise. I am sure most readers would be happy making $1,000 a day in profits.

This is an example of the types of trades that day traders are looking for.

The key to success in day trading is to be a master of the charts. You need to have a thorough understanding of the stock you are getting into and how it behaves, so that you can enter and exit the trade at the right moments. Day trading is a game of probabilities, and so you're not going to have winning trades all the time. You'll need to hone your skills so that the more trades you make, the better you get at analyzing the markets.

Day trading is not for everyone. It's high risk. It's also high pressure, and it requires you to be at your computer paying very close attention to the stocks you've taken positions in. A successful day trader needs to be someone who doesn't panic under pressure and who can focus like a laser beam.

Moreover, it requires capital. In the United States you must deposit a minimum of $25,000 in order to start day trading. Many experts recommend that you have at least $30,000 before you start. You shouldn't make that kind of commitment unless you are in a situation where you could lose the entire account and still go on in your life. In other words, never invest more than you can afford to lose.

There are also legal and technical definitions of what constitutes a day trader. In order to be labeled a "pattern day trader" by a broker, you must make 4 day trades within a 5-trading day period. Weekends don't count. So if you make 4 day trades between Thursday and the following Tuesday, that makes you a pattern day trader, and you'll be required to fund the account to $25,000.

On the flip side, day traders are able to treat their trading activities as a business for tax purposes. They are able to make a large number of deductions that investors can't make, such as deducting expenses for computer equipment and subscriptions to financial publications.

To summarize, Day Traders:

- Tend to trade smaller, highly volatile stocks.
- Must enter and exit trades very quickly.
- Never hold positions overnight.
- Need $25,000 in capital to start.
- It's a full-time commitment, requiring hours at the computer during the daytime. You will need a few hours to trade and hours spent studying charts and indicators.

## Swing Trading

Swing trading is a more relaxed alternative for those who don't want the high pressure, or lack the ability to meet the high capital requirements. Swing trading seeks to take advantage of similar price moves in a stock as well. However, positions are held for days, weeks, or even a couple of months. Swing traders definitely hold their positions over night. If you are impatient, swing trading might not be to your liking. Although it can't be viewed as a form of investing, it will involve a bit of waiting. You might have to wait weeks until the right moment to get out of a trade arrives.

Swing trading is more involved than investing, but it's pretty relaxed compared to day trading. A swing trader can build a flexible trading business that can be part-time or full-time. If you are only entering a few trades at a time, you don't have to be sitting at your computer all day. Many swing traders keep full-time jobs while they swing trade on the side. Some swing traders also have long-term investment accounts, and some are even retired. But they use swing trading as a means to generate extra cash over the short-term.

Since swing trading extends over a relatively long time period, there is a great deal more of flexibility in the type of stocks you can trade. A swing trader doesn't need large volatility over the course of hours, and almost any stock – even indexes – have enough volatility to make large profits from price movements over the course of weeks.

While charting and technical analysis play central roles in swing trading, fundamental analysis is also important, due to the longer time frames involved. I

There are many differences between swing trading and day trading, but the two trading styles rely on the same tools and technical analysis. Both require a great deal of research, studying chart patterns and the like. They are also activities that are run as a for-profit business. That doesn't mean you have to run out and form a company, but the activity is geared to making cash.

Here is an example of a swing trade. On January 8, 2019 you could buy shares of Apple at $150 per share. With a 52-week range of $142 - $233.47, that would be a reasonable entry point for the trade. We're assuming that you'd make the trade based on other indicators and possibly external factors. My March, the stock price had risen to $170 and higher. We could have exited the trade on March 18, selling our shares for $188.02. That would give us a profit of $38 per share. This trade is the essence of swing trading, but you'll look to trade swings on different time scales.

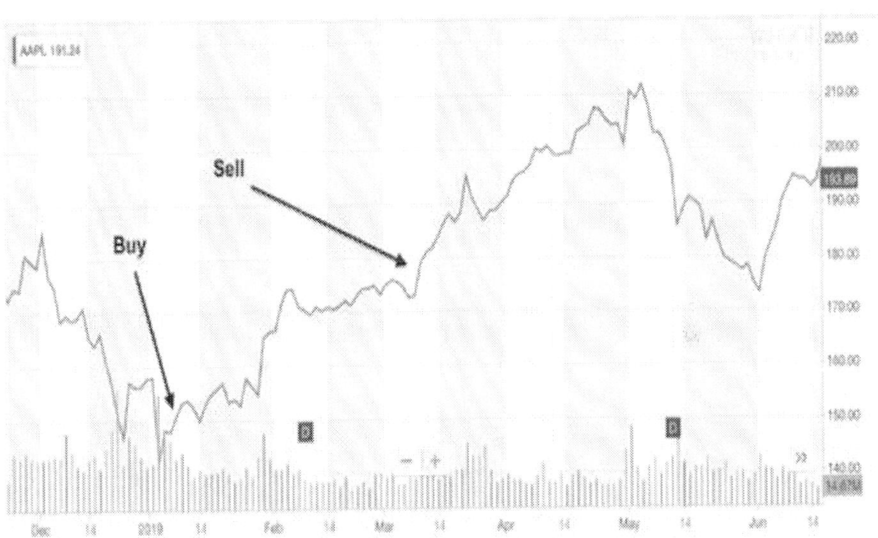


## Position Trading

Position trading takes the time frames involved even further out, but the goals are basically the same. Think of a position trader as a longer term swing trader. Rather than looking to profit over days or weeks, position trading means making a smaller number of trades, seeking to make profits over months and usually over the course of a year or more. A position trader might make 10-12 trades per year. At the most, a position would be held 1-2 years.

As an example of a position trade, consider Netflix. Over the past five years its popularity has skyrocketed, so it's not a surprise that its stock has done well. A reasonable position trade would have been to acquire the stock as the company was gaining in popularity, and simply wait for the share price to rise to a level such that you could book a desired profit.

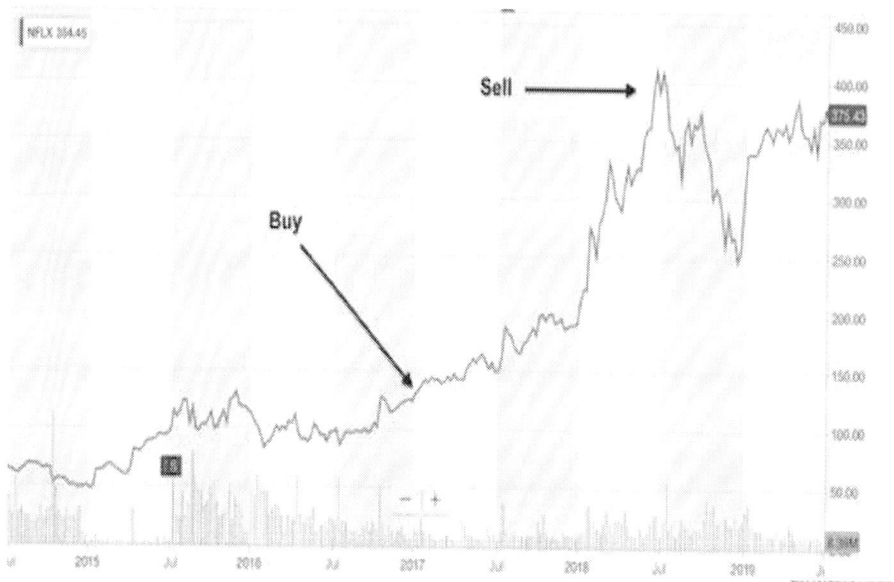


In the example above, we show a trade that could have been used by a position trader, entering the position in mid-2017, and holding it for about a year. The signs of a sustained uptrend were already in place in mid-2017. The trader could have entered the position in June of 2017 at $165 a share, and then sold their shares a year later for about $365 a share, taking a $200 per share profit.

## You can be any type of trader

While these different styles are presented as if they are exclusive categories, there is no rule that says you can't swing trade if you are a day trader, and position trading on some securities can fit in well with an overall swing trading approach. As a trader you should look for opportunities to profit as they arise rather than follow some textbook definitions. If you bought Apple stock in the morning planning to profit from a price movement you were expecting over the course of a week, but it went up by $10 a share that day, it would be reasonable to exit your position and take the profits. The only caveat here if you seek to be a swing trader is that you need to keep an eye on your activities and make sure you don't fall under the pattern day trader rule.

## Choosing a Broker

You can't just show up on the trading floor and start making deals. You need a middleman to execute trades for you. That is what a brokerage does.

A broker can be an individual, but it's usually a company. They maintain an account for you and when you place buy and sell orders for stock, they actually execute the trades on your behalf. In return for these services, you usually pay commissions and fees on your trades. However there are some commission free brokers.

### *Types of Accounts*

There are two general types of accounts that you can open with a broker. The first type is a straightforward cash account. You deposit cash from your bank into the brokerage account, and then you can buy shares of stock with it.

The other type of account is called a margin account. This is an account that utilizes leverage to buy more stock than you can with the cash you have on hand. To open a margin account, you must deposit $2,000. Most brokerages offer 2-1 margin on stocks. So the more money you deposit, the more margin you can access in absolute terms. The amount of stock you can buy at any given time is called buying power. If you deposit $3,000, the 2-1 margin rule means that you could buy $6,000 worth of stock, borrowing $3,000 from the broker. Before you've purchased any shares, your buying power is $6,000. If you buy $500 worth of stock, your buying power drops to $5,500.

Margin accounts also let you borrow shares. As we will see, the ability to borrow shares is a useful tool that can be used to profit when stock prices are declining.

## *Account Minimums*

Some brokers require a minimum deposit to open an account. It might be $500, or it might be several thousand dollars. Not all brokers have this requirement. For many, you can open an account without making a deposit, and then only deposit the amount of money you want to use in order to enter a trade. When it comes to margin accounts, however, all brokers require that you deposit at least $2,000. This is required by law.

## *Tools and Analysis*

When it comes to trading, having access to the tools used in the business is essential. You can actually get these anywhere. Free stock charting tools that are available online usually provide access to all of the tools described in this book. However some brokerages go above and beyond the typical offerings, and provide exceptional user interfaces that are required by traders. The level of insight that you need for trading activities will depend on how deeply you get involved and what trading style you use. If you seek to become a day trader, this is going to be a more important issue than it will be for swing or position trading. The stereotypical view of a day trader with a bank of computer screens showing charts and prices is somewhat accurate.

An interesting feature that some brokers offer is the ability to simulate trades. This can be helpful if you are just starting, so that you can practice and test your ability to make profitable trades without risking any real money. Of course you can just write down your trading ideas in a notebook or spreadsheet and then follow the stock prices to see what happens, but a simulator is advantageous because it brings you through the process of actually making trades and following them in a simulated account.

## *Commissions and Fees*

Commissions and fees can be important for traders. If you are trading frequently, they can add up to significant amounts if you are using a broker that charges high commissions. No matter where you trade, you'll have to take them into account when figuring out your actual profits. There are some commission free brokers, but you will have to determine whether or not they meet the other needs you have for your trading business.

## *Choosing a broker is not a lifetime or absolute commitment*

It's important to realize that the broker you select is not going to permanently seal your position as a trader. You can start with a simple trading platform and change to a broker that offers more tools later on. In the early stages, you can utilize free tools in the internet to perform your analysis, so having a full fledged broker aimed at day trading isn't necessary. The ability to get your feet wet and easily execute trades is more important.

## *Full service vs. discount brokers*

A broker can be *full service*, or it can be *discount*. A full service brokerage will give you access to professional financial advisors. If you want to seek their counsel, this might be something to consider. However, that type of expertise costs money, so the commissions and fees charged by a full service brokerage may be higher.

A discount broker simply maintains an account for you and executes your trades. They may have tools and information available online, but it will be automated and amount to reading some articles. So with a discount broker, you're truly running a self-directed account.

### *Settling on a broker*

In the end you will have to weigh all the factors that are important to you and then get online and do research to find an offering that best suits your needs. Most brokers are quite suitable for trading activities, so the main issues are going to be whether or not you can fund the account minimum and any special requirements a given broker will have, along with how their commissions and fees compare to others.

## Funding to Start

The number one rule in trading is to never risk more capital than you can afford to lose. We will discuss strategies you can use to limit your losses on bad trades. However, you should go into trading assuming that you could lose your entire investment. Therefore to start only invest an amount you can afford, even if it's only a few hundred dollars. Although you can't day trade with any amount less than $25,000, you can start swing trading using small amounts of capital. You can use that to practice or to actually start building your revenues, if you are able to make successful trades.

## Education

It's important for traders to become as educated as possible about their craft. Don't hesitate to read books or take courses. However, be careful about enrolling in expensive online courses that make promises of wealth.

# Chapter 2
# Analysis and Herd Behavior

Before we get into the details of charting and technical analysis, we are going to describe what it's all about in general terms. It basically involves crowd behavior. One of the most famous sayings among traders is "the trend is your friend". That means the goal is to simply do what other people are doing – to a point.

## Supply and Demand

Over the short-term, changes in stock prices are due to changes in supply and demand. When there are more people interested in buying a stock, sellers can hold out for higher prices. The prices that traders are willing to pay for a stock that is seen as more valuable can rise rapidly. On the other hand, when sellers are trying to get out quickly, they have to lower their asking prices. If a stock is seen in a negative light, people aren't willing to pay as much money in order to own it. In short, the basic rules of economics apply to stock prices.

## Bid and Ask

This is reflected in two metrics used in pricing stocks, *bid* and *ask*. The current stock price that you see quoted on the market is called the market price, or mark. However, that doesn't mean you can buy or sell your shares for that price by the time you place your order. The bid for a given stock is the price that bidders are willing to pay for the stock. Ask is the price that sellers are asking for it. In order for a share of stock to sell, the bid and ask must come together. The difference in the bid and ask at any given moment is called the *bid-ask spread.*

In modern markets, things are happening at a quick pace. In most circumstances when you place a buy or sell order at the market price, you'll find another trader willing to accept your terms relatively quickly. On the other hand, if a stock is rapidly increasing or decreasing in value, it might be difficult to close a transaction. Prices can move fast, and by the time you place your order the price you need to move to in order to close the deal may have moved. If you need to sell a stock quick and the price is rapidly dropping, consider placing your trade as a limit order using the current bid price as your limit price. This will ensure a quick sale.

## The role of emotion on the market

When money is involved, especially the prospect of losing or gaining a lot of money, emotions can become overwhelming. Fear and panic can set in when asset prices decline, leading people to sell off in large numbers. This deepens and speeds up the rate of decline. When prices are rising, people often become irrationally exuberant. With increasing enthusiasm and the appearance of greed, people

# Chapter 3
# Charts, Trends, and Ranging

We begin our examination of the tools used by traders to seek out significant price movements by looking at trend analysis and ranging. The techniques described in this chapter are better described as *craft* rather than technical analysis, but they form the foundation of all that follows. Moreover, all traders use them from time to time. In short, you need to be able to eyeball charts to spot trends and pricing levels, and then use them to project ahead to determine future price points. Spotting trends is often the first step in analysis, with deeper examination using more sophisticated tools to confirm or reject the trend.

## Trend lines

As a starting point, we use the simplest type of analysis you can do. That is, simply draw trend lines on your charts. In practice, you shouldn't rely on this alone, but it's a simple method that can be used in order to determine where a stock price *might* end up in the future. Other indicators will have to be used to confirm the appearance that a trend is in the making or will continue.

The procedure used to draw trend lines relies on the wavy shape of stock prices when they are graphed on a chart – that is they go up and down like an oscillator. There are three rules for trend lines:

- Look for an up and down swing in price that is moving in one direction or the other. It needs to revert or move back in the opposite direction to the main trend at least twice. If there are more of these points the trend line will be more accurate, but you have to use what you have.

- If the price is increasing, use the low points to anchor your trend line. Simply draw a straight line through each of the low points. Projecting out to the future will give you an estimate of where prices are going to end up.
- If the price is decreasing, draw your line through the peaks in the graph as the price declines. This will give you an estimate to the future, lower price of the stock.

In the example below, we have used an uptrend in a stock price to show you how to draw a trend line. Notice that had we drawn the line at an earlier time when we only had the two low points in the price oscillation, the end point of the line would have been fairly accurate in meeting the future price.

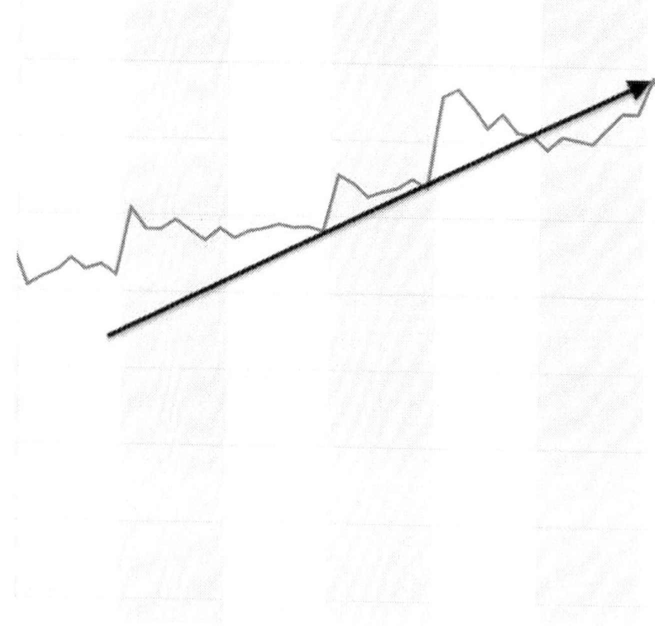

In the example below, we use the technique on a downward trend. Notice that the line is drawn through the peaks in the graph.

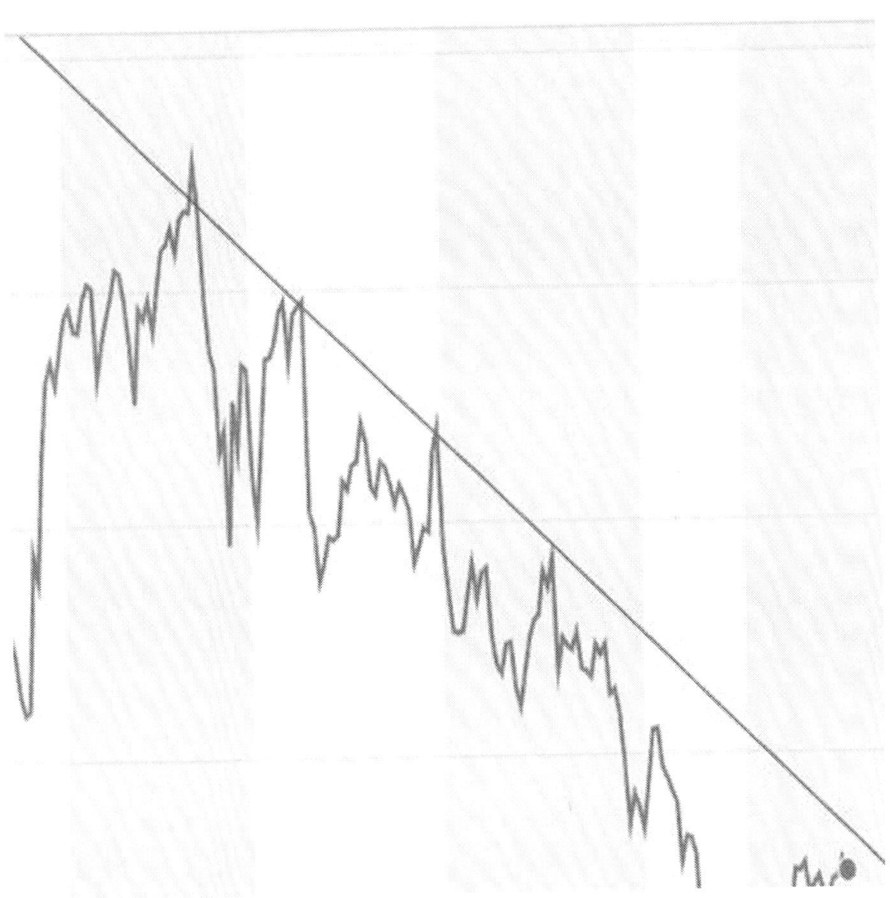

While trend lines can often be fairly accurate, they should only be used as a guideline in your decision making. A trend point is nothing more than eyeballing the chart. Many traders swear by trend lines, and those who master them can actually utilize them to enter into many successful trades. However the best approach is to use a trend line as a starting point for further analysis. Most stock charts that are available online allow you to draw lines directly on the charts.

## Trading with the Trend

The simplest trading strategy is to simply follow the trend, and follow it for as long as you can. Once you've used a trend line to estimate where the stock price can go if it continues following the trend, you enter your position. Then place a limit order to sell your shares when the price reaches the point that you've determined the stock is going to reach if it continues rising.

Alternatively, you can short the stock when it's bearish. This is a technique that will be available for more advanced traders with margin accounts. In order to short the stock, you'll borrow the shares from the broker and sell them at the current market price. Of course you will need to keep close tabs on this kind of move – it could work against you.

After selling the shares, you wait for the stock price to drop to the level that you are expecting. Then you buy the shares on the market at the lower price. The difference in prices paid for the shares is your profit. You simply return the shares to the broker at that point.

You could simply trade with trends, and win some trades and lose some. But you can improve your odds by learning the tools of technical analysis to use in conjunction with your trend analysis. We will be discussing those in coming chapters.

## Support

The next concept you need to be aware of is *support*. This is a pricing level that sets a lower boundary for the stock over a short time period. It's a low price that the stock won't drop beneath. So bulls and bears are balanced at this pricing level. Keep in mind that while zones of support can be useful to spot, that you'll need to look at other metrics to determine where price is going. In many cases, the stock price will keep touching the support pricing level and it simply won't drop below. It will bounce off the support price and go higher. However, that doesn't mean that at some point in the future the support level won't be breached. In the next chapter we'll start looking at candlesticks that will help you decide whether or not a breach is coming, or whether the stock is going to break to the upside instead. Moving averages can also help analyze these situations.

To find a level of support, draw a line through the lows of the stock price over a given time period. The level of support is taken to be the low price for the stock, for the present analysis.

In the chart below, we've drawn a line of support, shown as the horizontal line.

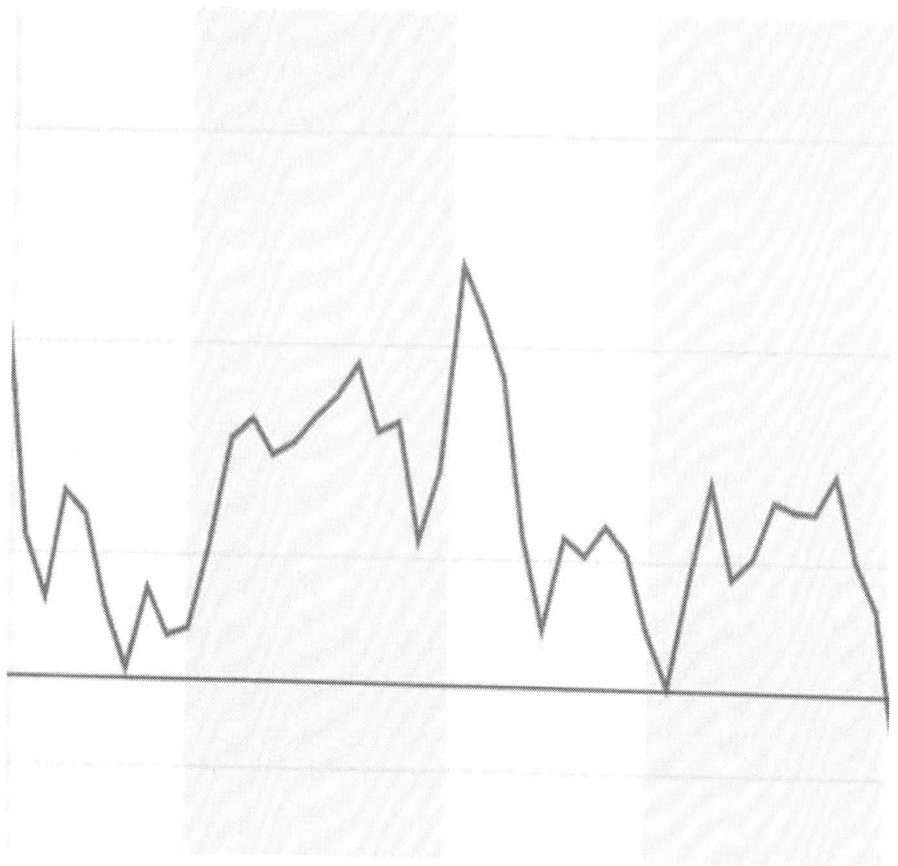

Notice that the stock touched the line twice. At a minimum, when deciding where a level of support is located, you must be able to see the stock price touch the line at least two times. It's better if it touches it more frequently. On the far right of the chart the price went slightly below the support line, but quickly returned to the support level. Remember that stock market data is incredibly noisy, so you'll have to look at data like that and ask yourself if the drip was statistically significant or not. To be a breach, it's got to be significant. Of course there will be other tools you can use to estimate the next move of the stock.

## Resistance

Resistance is the flip-side of support. This is an upper boundary in pricing that the stock price can't cross. Bulls are able to bid up the price to the resistance level, but there isn't enough bullish sentiment to push prices higher. Resistance involves drawing a line through the peaks of the curve over a given time period. Again, the peaks of the price must touch the line at a minimum of two times.

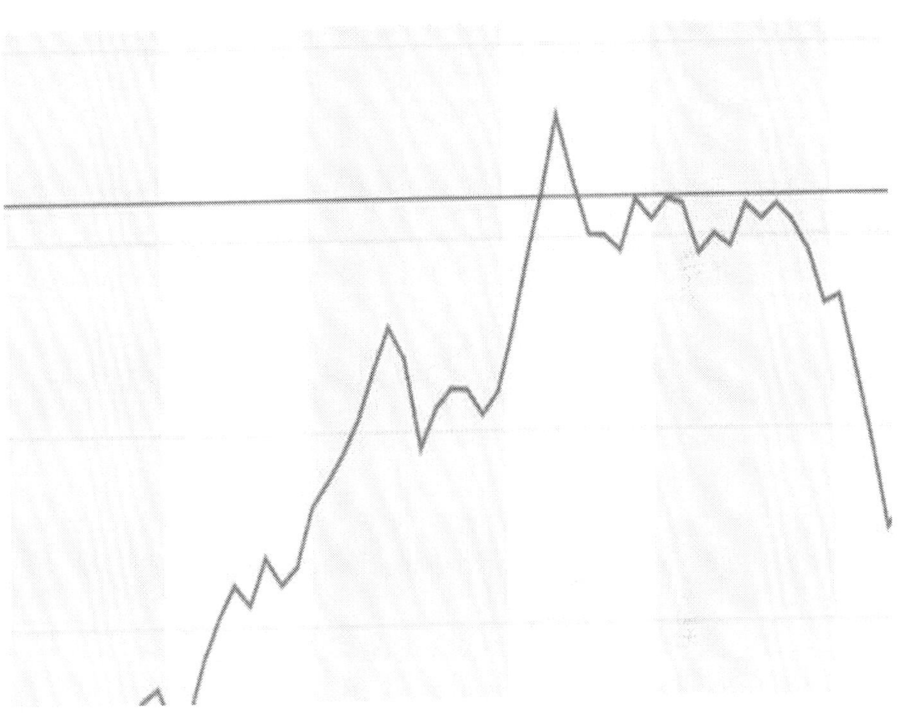

## How to use support and resistance

Support is used to determine the low price of a stock over a given time period. Then, this can be used in different ways depending on how you are trading. First let's assume you are "long", so hoping to buy the shares in anticipation of a price increase. In that case, after you have determined the level of support, you wait until the stock price returns back to that price level. When it does, you enter your position. Then you'll wait for the stock to rise.

Support level can also be used to set a stop-loss order, to protect yourself if your estimate was wrong. The stop-loss can be set slightly below the support level. Remember because of random behavior the price might dip a little bit below the support level without really indicating that further drops in price are about to occur. To take an example, suppose that we determine the level of support is $50 a share. You could set your stop loss order at $49 a share. This means that if the stock dips to that price, our shares will be sold automatically. If the stock dipped to the downside then the stop-loss order will protect us from large losses.

Assuming that for our trade the stock stays in the trading range over a time period of interest, then we set a limit order to sell the shares a little bit below the resistance level. That means setting a level of profit when we enter the trade. Remember, you don't want to get greedy, and your entire life doesn't ride on the results of a single trade.

So the goal here is to set a decent level of profit on *this* trade. You don't let emotion come in and get you upset if the price happens to continue rising. You book your profits and then move forward to the next trade. A business that gets sustainable, regular profits is the one that survives. You want to keep that thought in mind as you proceed with your trades.

## Ranges

Sometimes a stock will repeatedly swing between two pricing levels for a relatively extended period of time. That is, it is trading within a range. The range can be estimated by drawing levels of support and resistance on the same chart.

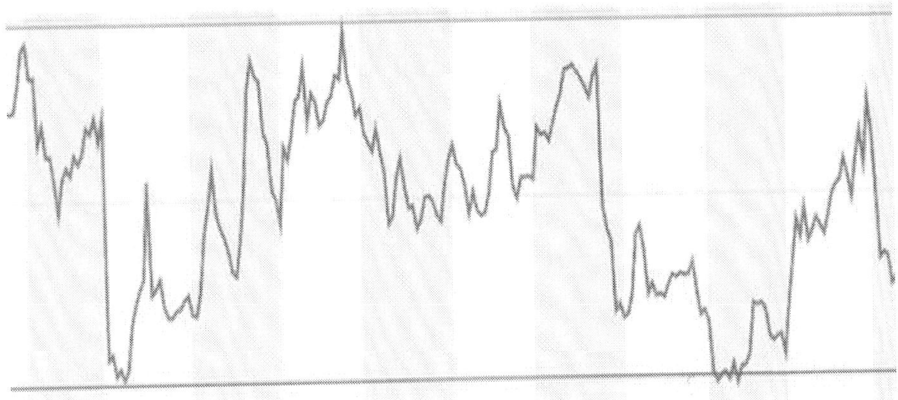

In the above chart, the price level of resistance is indicated by the upper red line. The price level for support is indicated by the lower, purple line. Ranges can last for any length of time, and can even go on for months. The key to finding a trading range is that it lasts over a time frame that is of interest in your particular case. Remember that trade ranges don't last forever, at some point there will be a breakout to the upside or the downside, and the stock will settle in with a new level of support and/or resistance. These are guidelines only.

## Trading Strategy for Ranges

However, notice that the price fluctuations within the range offer opportunities for profit. Once you have established a level of support, you can use that as your price level to enter the position. You also have an idea of the price the stock will reach before trending back down. So you use the resistance pricing level as a guideline to set a price point to sell your shares.

It's possible that you will miss out on the upside, but a smart trader takes a methodical approach. Rather than being greedy or waiting around to see if the price might continue increasing, the smart trader sets up rules for their trade beforehand, and they stick to their rules. It's better to ensure a limited profit and duplicate the process, than it is to wait too long hoping for higher highs and find yourself losing money. Unfortunately that happens all too often.

# Chapter 4
# Chart Patterns

Traders also look for more complicated chart patterns than the ones we've looked at so far. Certain chart patterns can be used as guidelines that indicate a future uptrend of the stock or a coming downtrend. They can also be used to determine when a stock has stalled at the top of an uptrend or if it's bottomed out.

The main reason that we use chart patterns in our analysis is to spot trend reversals. Trying reversals are important for two reasons. The first reason is that it provides a clue when you should enter a trade. If you're looking to go long on a stock, the first thing you're going to do as a trader is look for the price to hit bottom. That is obviously when you want to answer your trade. Of course more analysis is required. It's possible that you can get in that kind of situation, and the stock only pauses, before continuing a downward trend. Later on in the book we are going to look at some other tools which will help us distinguish that situation from a trend reversal. Nonetheless, chart patterns can also help with that as well. These are more intuitive, and to certain extent based on the long-term experience and knowledge of traders. Most of the time or maybe it's better to say more often than not, the chart patterns are correct in indicating when a trend reversal has arrived. Or should I say is about to arrive. We begin by considering Head and shoulders.

## Head and Shoulders

Head and shoulders is considered a reliable chart pattern which forecasts a trend reversal. It's a chart pattern that can occur at the top of an upward trend, or at the bottom of a downward trend. The main feature of this chart pattern is that it indicates sellers or buyers have run out of momentum driving the price up or down.

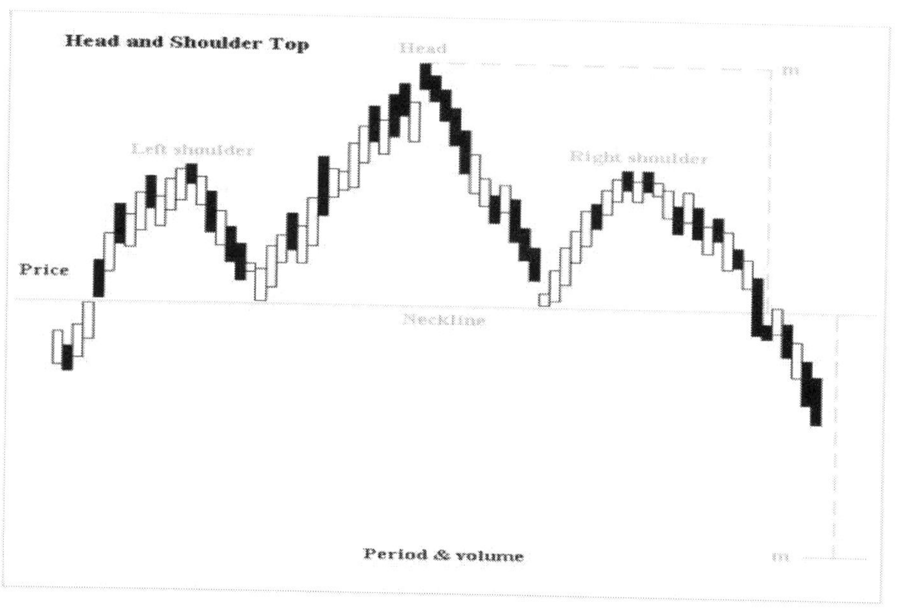


Image created by By Altafqadir (talkhttps://en.wikipedia.org/w/index.php?curid=28356046

It's pretty easy to spot a head and shoulders chart pattern. Let's take the condition of an upward trend first. At many points on an upward trend, there appears to be a pause in the rise of price. Many times that's an illusion, or a short-term phenomena, and the price continues its rise which seems inevitable. But then you see a pattern that indicates multiple attempts to breakout higher, but and up failing. With a head and shoulders, you see a large or high central price peak in the center of the pattern. It is flanked buy two smaller peaks which are called the shoulders. Obviously the central higher peak is the head. Typically, the volume of the right side shoulder is lower than the volume on the left side shoulder. So to confirm the pattern, you also want to take a look at the volume of trading.

In between the formation of the first shoulder on the left side and the head, there is a low point in price which sets a level called the neckline. You can draw a straight line to estimate where the low point following the head will be. After this point, the price will rise again and form the right shoulder which is going to be about the height of the left shoulder. In other words it's going to reach about the same pricing level. Then the price will start dropping off as the decline begins. There may be some temporary reversals or retracements, where the price goes back maybe about to the neckline.  After that it's more than likely the reversal and downward trend will continue.

There are two ways to look at this situation. If you are long out of stock and you see this pattern, which means it's time to sell your position. If you want to short the stock, or are you are interested in buying puts on the stock, when you see a head and shoulders pattern it's as good a time as any to answer your position.

You can also see a head and shoulders pattern at the bottom of the downtrend. In this case it's going to be upside down. That means it takes a little bit of practice in order to recognize it, because the fact is people are conditioned to think in terms of rising prices. And in the case of a head and shoulders at the bottom of a trend, it's flipped over.

So what happens is you're going to see the downward trend hit a certain point and then reverse and rise a small amount. It's then going to decline to a deeper point or should I say lower price, before reversing and rising again. When it rises, it's going to rise till point that matches the previous rise in price level. Once again he can draw a line from point-to-point, and that will form the neckline. After reaches the second peak the price is going to decline again. That decline is short-lived, and prices will reverse and start rising and that will be the start of an uptrend.

So we've describes what to look for, but what does this all mean. Let's stay focused on the top patter which occurs at the top of an uptrend. Basically what this means is that the trend has run out of steam. The stock has been bit up high enough in price that it's getting harder to keep attracting buyers at higher prices. Put in more simple terms, the bullshit run out of momentum. So there simply aren't traders willing to pay higher prices for the stock at this point. The three humps that form indicate that buyers keep coming in but just not enough to keep to the rise going. Soon enough, there simply aren't enough buyers around at that price to keep driving the stock higher.

## Double Tops

The next chart pattern to consider is called double tops. Quite simply this means that the stock rises to a peak, and then there's a small peak followed by a small decline, and then another small peak. Then the stock price clients back down again matching the low point that came previously. So you get the appearance of a peek with two hills next to each other at the top.

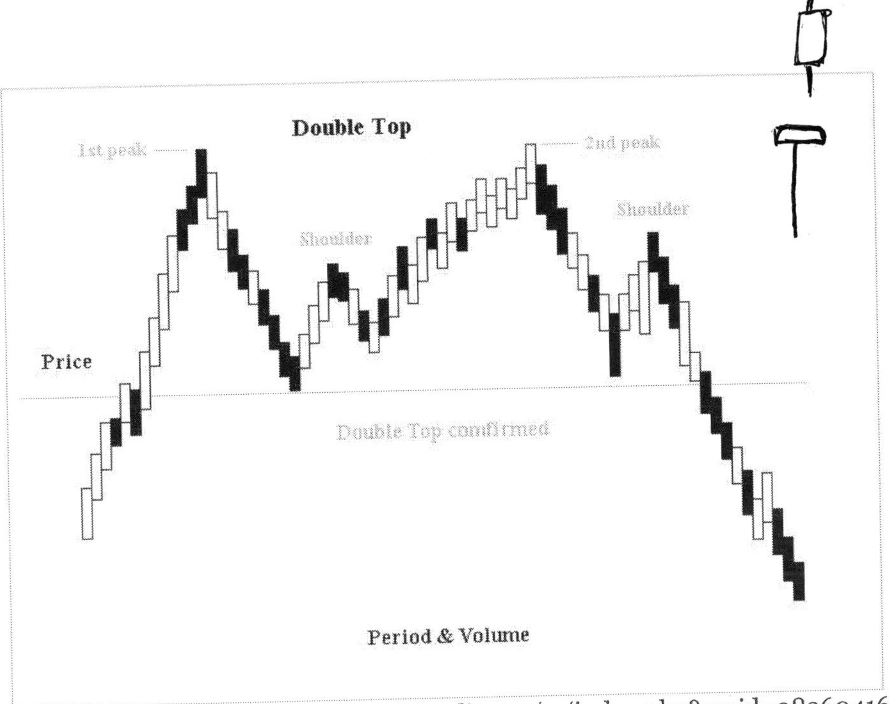


By Altafqadir (talk) - https://en.wikipedia.org/w/index.php?curid=28360416

The double top can also occur in a downtrend, that's the price will decline to a certain level and then it's going to decrease in price again for short period, coming to a stop and reversing. Then it will decrease in price again, and it will match up with the same low price that the first hump generated. It will once again reverse, and at this point the price will start rising.

The principles behind double tops are basically the same as those we saw with the head and shoulders. With a double top, at a peak, you essentially see a price point reached where there are not enough buyers to keep it going. The fact that the pattern forms is something that indicates we aren't in for a sideways move. So the price tries to rise again, which means that some buyers are coming in willing to pay a small amount above the current market price, but there aren't enough buyers to keep driving the price up. At so it quickly runs out of momentum and after another try it starts reversing, and then heads down.

## Triangles

The next chart pattern will consider is known as a triangle. A triangle forms as a contraction or slight reversal in price as part of a major trend. So you will see a price go up and then immediately reverse, and it will stop at that point which meets where the price began rising previously. If you'd your tramlines on the chart, they would converge at the peak or apex of the triangle. Triangles are not trend reversal patterns. Rather, they are small stops along the way of the larger trend. There're three types called the symmetrical triangle, the ascending triangle, and the descending triangle. The type of triangle that you have will depend on the overall trend in which the triangles found. Since it's a continuation pattern, an ascending triangle which means the peak of the triangle is at a higher price to where the base of the triangle would be, is found within an uptrend. Often times you are going to see multiple triangles in a row. The base of each triangle is going to be higher then the base of the previous triangle. This is why they are known as ascending triangles. So in this case the price level of the base of the triangle is what's higher than the price level of the previous triangle. That demonstrates the triangles are continuation patterns within a trend rather than indicating a reversal.

Of course we can see the opposite pattern, where are you having triangles on a downward sloped portion of the chart. Those are descending triangles, and in this case the base of each triangle is lower then the base of the previous triangle. That means that the price is continuing on his downward trend.

## Cup and Handle

A cup and handle it as a chart pattern that forms during a rising stock prices. So the stock price will rise to a peak, and then it will gradually decline forming around the chart. It will then start reversing and rising again slowly and gradually. And so this produces a soft landing or cup shaped pattern in the middle of the chart. It then rises to a peak sharply, with a high price level that matches the price level of the previous peak. It Ben stays at that peak price for a very short time. It starts declining. The handle portion of the pattern which includes the peaks last a few weeks. This is not typically a pattern that forms over the short-term. The middle of the pattern which is the cup part, can last for long time. Up to a month or more. Of course you would have to zoom out the chart, or examine the chart on long enough timeframe to actually see the pattern. Otherwise you're just going to see some sideways movement. A cup and handle pattern is taken to be a bullish signal. Therefore, it could indicate future price increases for the stock in question.

## Wedge

A wedge forms on a stock chart after a long trend in one direction or the other. Let's consider a rising trend first. When a wedge forms, prices will be rising steeply. Then a peek is reached, and then the trend starts reversing. At each step for training session on the chart, you will see declining prices. Each price will decline to a lower level than the previous price. As these prices go out in time, it forms the shape of a wedge, or you might think of it like a door jam.  At the end of the pattern, the upward trend resumes. It often resumes quite steeply. As a result, this pattern is considered to be a continuation pattern, and not a reversal.

You can also have a wedge forming in a downtrend. In this case the price will drop steeply. Then it reaches a low point, and then begins rising. The price will start rising in the same way that it dropped in the other case. That is each trading session will show a higher price than the previous one. This will go on for a significant time period forming a wedge. In a previous case in the middle of an uptrend, the wedge formed a downward slope moving left to right. That is because as you go further out in time, each successive price is lower than the previous one. In this case, it's going to work the opposite way. Some moving left to right, it's actually going to slope upward, since each price for the training session is higher than the price for the previous trading session. Then is finally going to come to an end and the overall trend will resume.

Typically speaking, a wedge pattern will last up to a few weeks in time.

## Summary

Chart patterns can be an important thing to recognize for the trader. I can't tell you that the chart patterns described here are going to be important for all traders. You may have noted that some of the chart patterns discussed have longer time frames those others. Therefore, they aren't necessarily of much interest to day traders. However, these types of patterns will be of interest to swing traders, and position traders. In any case, no matter what your trading style is you should learn what patterns mean and how to recognize them.

# Chapter 5
# Candlesticks

You may have noticed that a lot of stock charts have bars on them of different colors. These bars are called candlesticks. The purpose of candlesticks isn't for decoration. Candlesticks provide a wealth of information that traders use to get a handle on sentiment of other traders in the market as a whole. More importantly, candlesticks provide a method whereby traders can estimate fairly accurately when a trend reversal is coming.

It is the trend reversal which is the bread-and-butter of trading. Trend reversals provide an opportunity. If you're looking for a point to enter a trade, for example you might want to bet on a stock rising in price, when you see a low point where there is evidence of a trend reversal, this is a good point to enter your trade. Or if you are already in a position, and prices are rising to a peak, you need to have an idea when to sell.

Candlesticks are an old invention, used long-ago by Japanese traders. They are still useful today and the old traders would be amazed to see that they are used worldwide in virtually every financial market. This humble invention is very well-suited to determining when there is a trend reversal.

## Introduction to candlesticks

The candlestick has three parts. The first thing to notice, which is immediately obvious, is that thick body in the middle. The top of the body and the bottom of the body indicate beginning and ending prices of a trading session. Candlesticks can represent trading sessions of various lengths, you select the right time frame for your situation. For example, you can use candlesticks to represent "trading sessions" of 5 minutes, 4 hours, or 1 day, among others. There are two types of candlesticks. These are bullish candlesticks, and bearish candlesticks.

Let's take a look at bullish candlesticks first. If you see these candlesticks on a black and white chart, they are going to be hollow, that is the body is just indicated with an outline. On color charts they are usually green. Sometimes people use black backgrounds on their charts, in which case a bullish candlestick will have the outline form but it will be green in color. But typically these are green in color.

The top of a green or bullish candlestick is the closing price for the trading session. The bottom of a green or bullish candlestick is the opening price for the trading session. Therefore we see a simple relationship described by the candlestick. Since top is higher than bottom, the price associated at the top is higher than the bottom price. And remember the top in the case the closing price. So this kind of candle stick tells you that during the trading session the price increased.

Now consider a red or bearish candlestick. This type of candlestick will be solid black on a black-and-white chart. When traders use a black background, sometimes they color bearish candlesticks as solid white. But most of the time they are red in color. The positions on the candlestick represent the opposite that they do on a bullish candlestick. That is, the top of the bearish candlestick represents the opening price for the trading session. The bottom of a red candle stick is the closing price. So what this means is during the training session prices dropped.

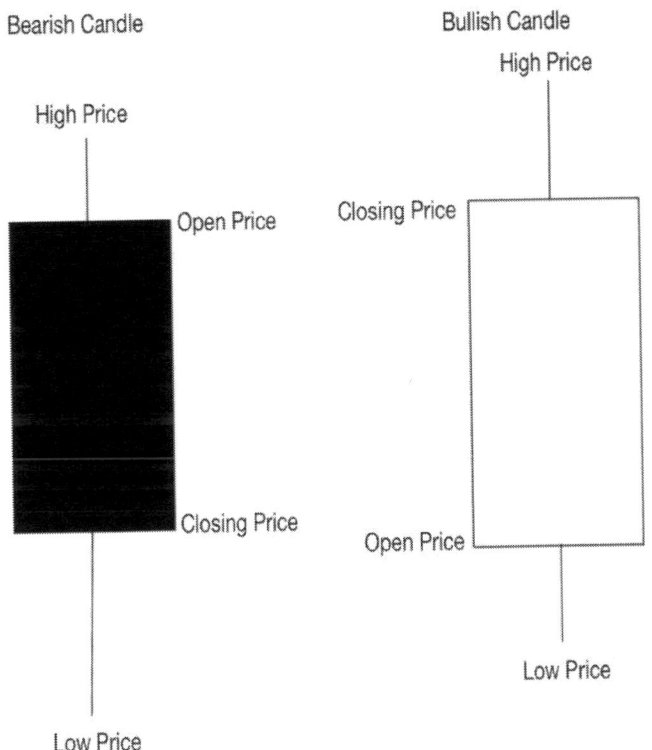


The next thing we need to learn about candlesticks is they have single lines coming out of the top and bottom. These are typically called wicks, but some people referred to them as shadows. The wick coming out of the top represents the high price of the trading session. The wick coming out of the bottom represents the low price of the training session.

So we also need to know a couple of general characteristics that can't be observed by the shape of the candle and the wicks. Perhaps shape was a bad choice of words. What I mean by that is a candlestick can be long or short. If I candlestick is long, there is a large difference between opening and closing prices of the training session.

## Using Candles to Spot an Uptrend

Candles give you a measure of trader sentiment, and they can help you forecast coming trend reversals. In this section we will begin to examine how you can look to candles on your stock charts to estimate whether or not a downtrend is about to reverse and become an uptrend. This can be done for any reasonable time frame, ranging from minutes to days, and out to weeks. A day trader will only be concerned with time frames lasting minutes. A swing trader may look at a wide variety of time frames.

First let's think about what candles represent. They represent the price spread for a trading session. If the candle body is long, that means that the session closing price went well above the opening price for a green or bullish candle. In other words, during the trading session the price was bid up by a traders looking to buy the stock. If the candle is red, which means it's a bearish candle, that means the trading session was dominated by a selloff of shares. In that case, the opening price would be higher than the closing price.

Candles that have a narrow body are going to represent a situation where there is not much change between the opening and closing prices for the trading session. That can be taken as a signal of indecision. These differences are illustrated in the next image.

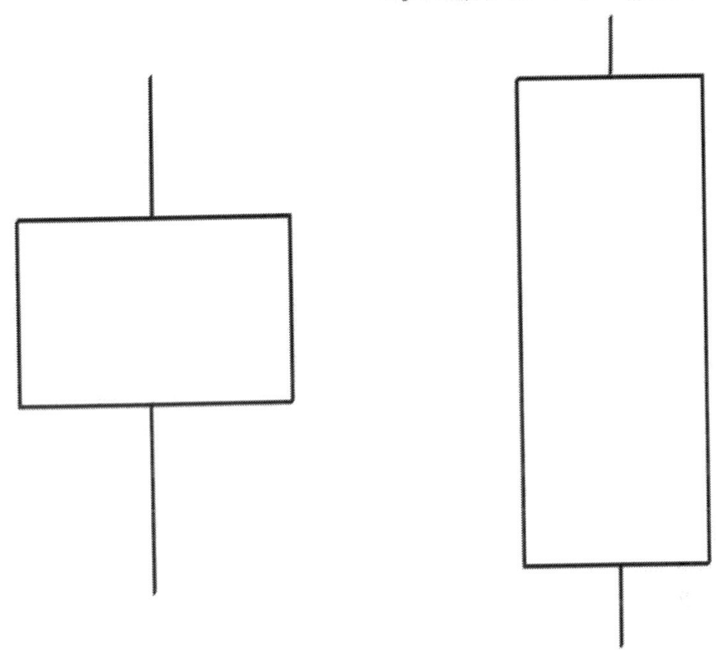


Now imagine that we are in a downward trend in prices. One of the signals you'll want to look for is a reversal in sentiment indicated by a switch from a bearish candle for one trading session, followed by a bullish candle in the following trading session. This should always get your attention, but one of the most important patterns to look for is called the *engulfing candle*. In this case, the size of the green or bullish candle that comes for the next trading session is much longer than the last bearish/red candle. In other words, in the subsequent trading session the price was driven up by a large amount from the opening price, and the price change was a lot stronger than in the previous session. This is a stronger signal when the opening price of the last trading session is below the closing price of the previous session. The pattern will look like the following:

Here we see a perfect example from Apple. After a downward trend, there is an engulfing withe candle (bullish), which signals the start of a coming upward trend in pricing.

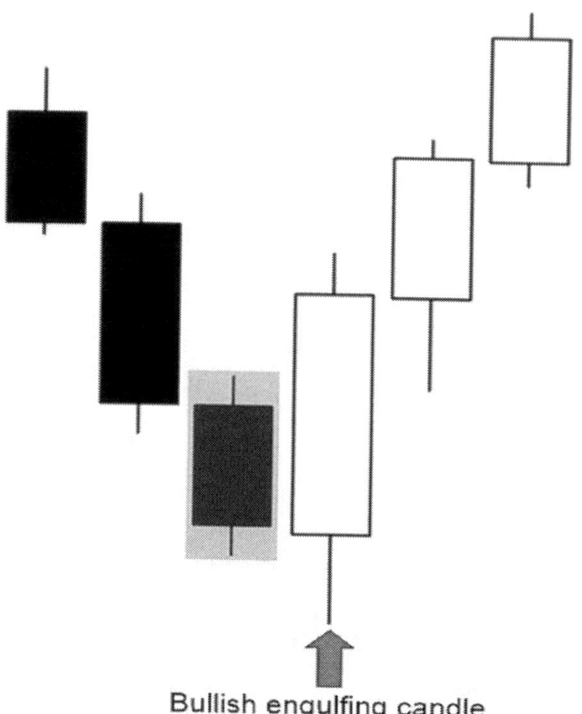


You'll also want to look for other confirming signals, but this is a solid signal that usually indicates a coming trend reversal. You will also want to check trading volume. If the volume of trading for the session is high, this is a strong indication that traders and investors are moving to buy the stock, and bid up prices.

Generally speaking, an engulfing bullish candle is a strong buy signal if you are hoping for price appreciation.

Another important signal of a trend reversal from a downturn is known as three white soldiers. This might seem strange since bullish candlesticks are green, but the term is a reference to the days when charts were published in black and white, and bullish candlesticks were shown with a boxed outline. In that case they had a white color in the center.

What you are looking for here are three green candlesticks in a row after a downturn. In fact, the signal shown above for Apple was very strong, indeed. The first green candle was engulfing and followed by two more green candlesticks. However, you don't need an engulfing candle. Here is the general appearance of three white soldiers:

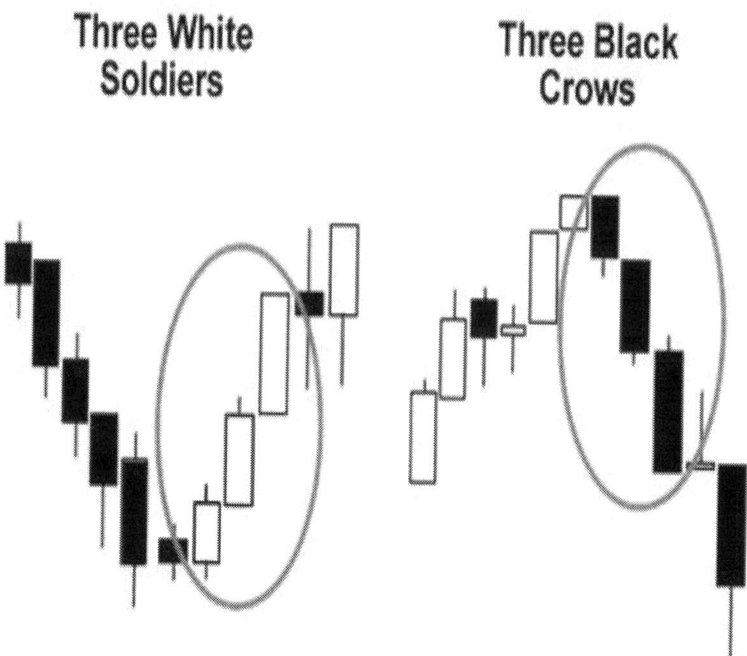


The relative sizes of the candlesticks aren't that important, you simply want to see three bullish candles in a row. However, caution might be exercised when you see a very strong movement to the upside, as this can indicate that the security is *overbought*. That means there is a frenzy of buying driving prices higher than the market will really tolerate and so a downward trend in price could follow.

There is a quantifiable way to check for this condition rather than guessing from the sizes of the candlesticks. It's called the Relative Strength Indicator or RSI. If it's above 70, that tells you that it's overbought. So if the RSI is below 70, this is a good signal to buy the stock. We will discuss the RSI in more detail in our chapter on indicators.

The next signal that you want to look for in a downtrend is the *hammer*. This tells us that the stock is nearing the bottom out point for the downtrend. It will have a narrow gap in opening and closing prices, but the closing price will be higher than the opening price indicating that the price is moving up again. There will be a long wick on the bottom of the candle, indicating that during the trading session the price was pushed far downward during the session, but there was a very strong bullish push into the stock that pushed prices higher and above the opening price. It looks like this:

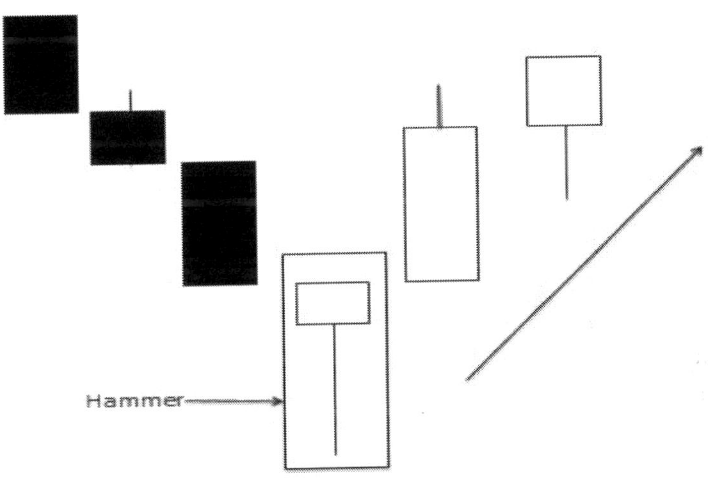


The next trend reversal to look at is the piercing line. This happens when the opening price of the next trading session following a bearish candle is lower than the previous day closing price, but the price rebounds to the midpoint of the previous day price or higher. So the midpoint price between the previous days open and closing price is breached, with a new higher closing price.

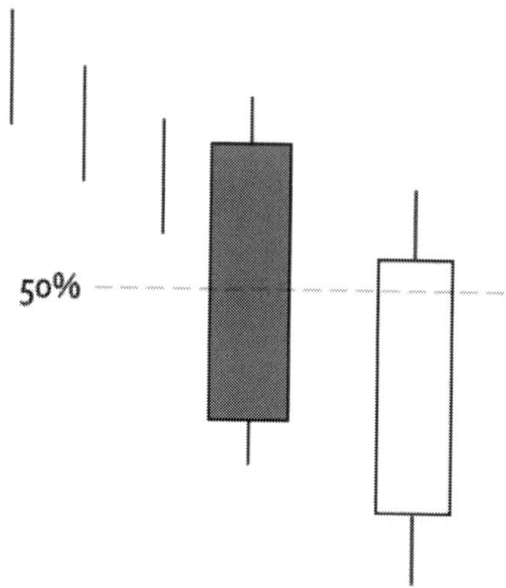


Next we have the morning star pattern. This is a three candle pattern that indicates a reversal from a downtrend. The left candle (earliest in time) is red or bullish. The middle candle has a narrow body and is known as a doji "indecision" candle. It can be either bullish or bearish. On the right, we get a larger bullish candle. For this signal, be sure to check trading volume. You are looking for trading volume to increase in the final trading session on the right side.

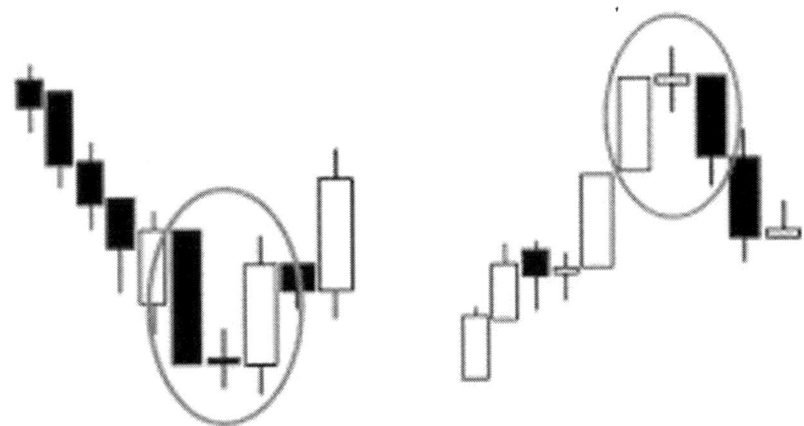

The inverted hammer is the last signal in a downtrend you need to be aware of. Like a hammer, an inverted hammer has a narrow body. While the hammer has a low price that is well below the opening and closing prices, the inverted hammer has a high price that rises well above the opening and closing prices. However it's still taken as a signal of a trend reversal because the market rallied to a higher closing price.

**Inverted Hammer** **Shooting Star**

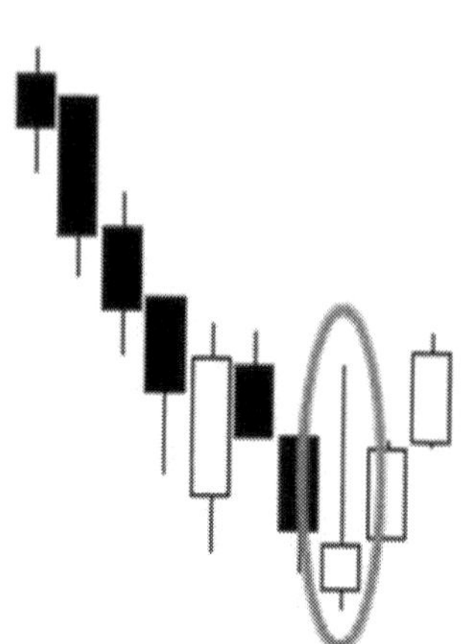

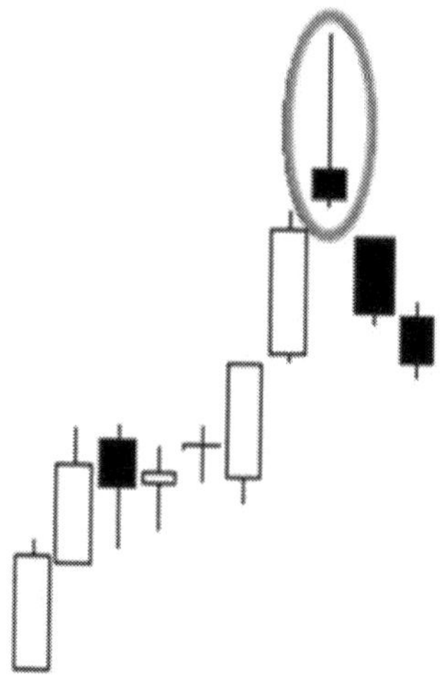

## Forecasting a coming downtrend using candles

This brings us to looking at chart patterns that indicate a coming downturn in stock price after there has been an uptrend, or even when the market is moving sideways. The signals are the same but with bullish and bearish candles reversed, and an uptrend or sideways move proceeding from the left.

When you see an inverted hammer at the top of an uptrend and it's a bearish candle, this is called a morning star. It is taken as a strong signal that the uptrend is coming to an end, and will soon be followed by a downward push in prices.

In an uptrend, you also want to be wary of engulfing candles, when the candle to the left is bullish and the engulfing candle is red/bearish. That indicates that there was a lot of activity pushing prices downward, and people are feeling like they need to exit the stock. Check for signals that the stock is overbought.

The analogue to "three white soldiers" is "three black crows". Most people don't use black and white charts anymore, but the terminology is a reference to the use of black candles to represent declining prices in a trading session. So in this case, you are looking for three red/bearish candles in a row, with successively lower closing prices in each trading session.

One important pattern to take note of is the *two black gapping* pattern. This will occur after stock prices have reached a peak. After the last significant bullish candle, you'll see a bearish candle. Then it's followed by another bearish candle that shows a significant shift to a low closing price.

## Confirming Candlestick Patterns

A trader should not rely on candlestick patterns alone. First, you can utilize what you've learned about trend lines and chart patterns to look at any candlestick patterns in the context of the larger picture. Second, you are going to want to confirm your forecast from the candlestick pattern using indicators. We will discuss these in the next chapter so that you can know what you need to look for, and what tools are best to use.

## The danger of overreliance on candlesticks

The market is an extremely competitive environment. Candlesticks have always been used in trading, but in recent years it's become somewhat of a fad. This has not been a uniformly positive development. Large institutional traders and hedge funds have become aware of the fact that the retail investment community (that is small independent traders) are relying on candlestick patterns. As such, they've been using them too, but to make trends go in the opposite direction as compared to what the candlesticks indicate. It's possible for them to do this because large institutional traders can rely on software tools and other methods that give them a speed advantage. They also have a volume advantage, and are able to buy and sell extremely large numbers of shares in an instant. That can literally shift market direction.

That doesn't mean candlestick patterns have lost their usefulness. If you start studying the stock charts and examine them, you're going to see that they largely conform to what we've described here, most of the time. But it's important to be aware of the impact that large traders can have on the markets.

The way to get around this problem is to take the signals you see with a grain of salt, and always verify them before taking action. Discipline is one characteristic that every trader needs to have. Making impulsive moves because of panic or because you see some candlestick pattern is a path to failure, not success. By the time you finish the book you'll understand how to trade effectively by taking all signals into account.

You also have to realize that trading is not a guarantee of profits. Rather it's a game of probability. So you are attempting to set up a trade that has probability in its favor. Always keep in mind how probability works. If you have a trade that is going to have a 75% probability of being a winning trade, then you're going to lose at least one time for every four times you enter that trade.

## How to use trend reversals

A trend reversal signal, if confirmed using other tools, is a signal to enter or exit a position. The possibilities are:

- You are not in a position currently, but you intend to go long (that is buy shares in hopes of price appreciation) in a position. In that case, any signal of a trend reversal after a downturn is a buy signal.
- If you hold a long position, and see signals of a trend reversal after an uptrend in price, it's time to exit the position (sell your shares and take profits) before the position deteriorates by entering a major downturn, or at least dropping back to the price level where you purchased the shares.
- You are interested in shorting the stock. It's at the top of an uptrend, and you see a trend reversal signal. At that point, if you are going to short the stock and have margin, you can borrow shares from your broker and sell them now on the open market when you can get a high price for the shares. If you are doing options trading, you can invest by purchasing put options or selling a call credit spread.
- Stock price drops to a low and will reverse, but you're shorting the stock. In this case, you sell your put options or buy back the call credit spread. If you are shorting stock, you buy the shares at the low price and return them to your broker.

# Chapter 6
# Indicators

Candlesticks and eyeballing charts to spot trend lines, support, and resistance are all very useful. These are subjects that you should study very carefully if you intend to become a trader. However, you'll need to add 2-3 indicators to your tool bag if you expect to become a successful trader. Indicators help take the noise out from stock market data and help you do things like get a dynamic representation of the standard deviation in price ranges for the stock. This can help confirm signals that you are seeing from the candles or in your trend analysis and these tools can also help you identify the best entry and exit points for your trades. We begin with a discussion of moving average.

## Moving Average

Stock market data is noisy. You can instantly make out the noise on any line chart of stock prices. It's very jagged, and seems random. If you want to analyze the data and get an accurate view of where it's headed and what kind of price ranges the stock is going to have in the near future, it would be helpful to smooth out the curve. To pick out trends, it would also be helpful to look at curves that rely on more recent data and compare them to curves containing long-term data.

This is what the moving average does. You know what an average is. A simple average means you simply add up some data points and then divide by the number of points. So for example, we can average the test scores in a class with six students:

55, 67, 71, 78, 86, 94

The average is just:

Average = (55 + 67 + 71 +78 +86 +94)/6 = 75.2

A moving average is an average of data in a time series that moves along with the data, by a fixed number of periods. Suppose that for the first 10 days of July the high temperature was:

87, 88, 85, 90, 92, 87, 93, 95, 97, 94

The average is:

Average = (87 + 88 + 85 + 90 + 92 + 87 + 93 + 95 + 97 + 94 )/10 = 90.8

A *moving average* calculates the average at each given point. It's defined in part by the number of time periods or periods used for the average. So we could have a 3 period average, which means at each point it would calculate the average of the three most recent data points. We could start a moving average calculation for our temperature data on day 3:

Moving average at day 3 = (85 + 88 +87)/3 = 86.7

Then you re-calculated it at each point, moving over one step. The moving average on day 4 is:

Moving average at day 4 = (90 + 85 + 88)/3 = 87.7

Then on day 5 it would be:

Moving average at day 5 = (92 + 90 + 85)/3 = 89

This type of moving average is called a *simple moving average.* It calculates the simple average at each data point. This is a common type of moving average used to analyze stock market trends. You can compute moving averages using different numbers of periods. Some commonly used moving averages are 9-period, 20-period, 50-period, and 200-period. The period can be any period used in your analysis, swing traders often use days.

It produces a smoothed out curve of the pricing data in the stock market. In the chart below, we see how a 10-day moving average produces a nice, smooth curve that flows along the general trend of the stock market pricing data.

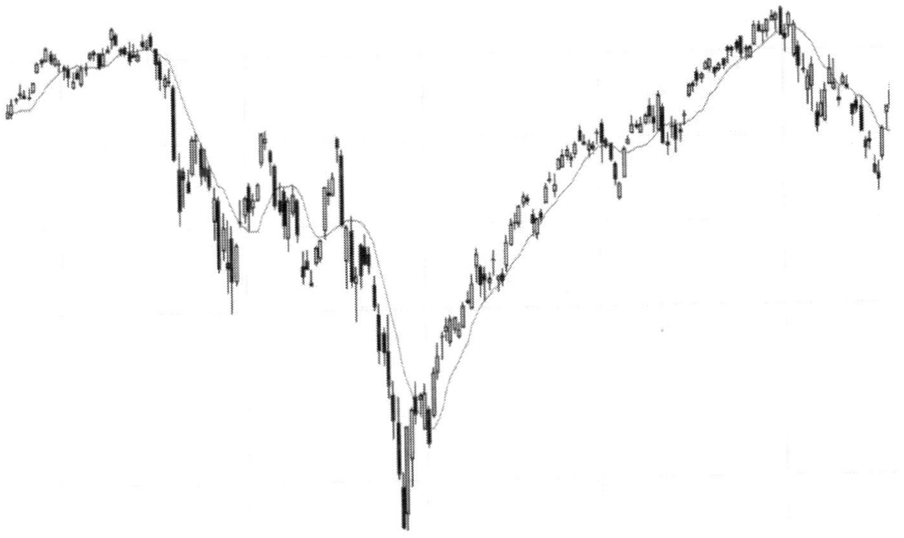

One thing you'll notice about the simple moving average is that it's got some accuracy problems, despite the overall fairly good fit of the curve. At some points, it can lag the data.

## Weighted Moving Averages

A major criticism of the simple moving average is that it gives equal weight to distant prices and recent prices. In fact any data in the moving average calculation has the same weight as any other. I am sure that you will agree that it's more likely that recent prices are going to be more influential on the trend. Market sentiment 10 days ago isn't as influential as market sentiment today, yesterday, or the past three days.

For this reason many *weighted* moving averages have been developed. The most frequently used weighted moving average is the *exponential moving average*. It was developed using a complicated formula that helps make the data more relevant. You don't need to bother with knowing the formula behind the exponential moving average. The only thing you need to know about it is that it gives the prices from more recent trading sessions more weight than it gives prices from 5, 10, or more trading sessions ago. This helps make the curve more accurate.

There are other more advanced moving averages that can be used for indicators, although it's debatable whether or not they are very useful or not. Many traders even stick to using simple moving averages, and exponential moving averages tend to be the most popular among traders operating over shorter time frames. Exponential moving averages have a lot of popularity on the Forex markets.

You can calculate the moving average using different data. The most commonly used metric is the closing price of each trading session. However, you can use the opening price as well. Other options include the high price, the low price, or fractions of each.

It's also possible to calculate moving averages based on volume of trading. That can be very useful information, since volume of trading can correspond to real price movements on the markets.

In the chart section displayed below, we've shown two moving averages, one in thick black and one in thin black. The moving average in thin black is an exponential moving average, while the thick black curve is a simple moving average. I'd like to call your attention to the fact that the simple moving average curve lags the change, as seen by the dip in share prices toward the right hand side. It's more accurately tracked by the exponential moving average.

## Crossings to forecast trend reversals

The most important information that an indicator can give you is forecasting a trend reversal. In order to forecast trend reversals, you'll use two moving average curves of the same type but with different periods on your stock chart. The focus is on what short term pricing is doing with respect to the average pricing for the given stock you are looking at.

A trend reversal is indicated when the short period moving average crosses the long period moving average. If the short period moving average crosses above the long period moving average, this indicates a coming upward trend in price. On the other hand if the short period moving average crosses below the long period moving average, this indicates a coming downward trend in price.

The following chart shows this effect, comparing a 9 period moving average (in thin black) to a 50 period moving average, thick black. The moving averages in this case are simple moving averages. One thing to notice is that while the crossings do indicate trend reversals, simple moving averages tend to lag the actual pricing data.

Starting from the left hand side, while the short period moving average follows the data fairly well, notice that the downtrend in prices takes place before the short period moving average crosses below the long period moving average. Note that the candlesticks gave strong indication of a downward pressure in prices before the crossing of the moving averages took place.

A similar phenomenon is visible moving from left to right across the chart. Notice that in the center there is a mild uptrend in prices, but there is no crossing of the moving averages that is evident. By the time the short period moving average crosses above the long period moving average, the upward trend that starts a bit past the end of the final major downturn in prices was already well underway.

However, we observe a similar situation using the 50-period exponential moving average together with a 9-period exponential moving average. Again, the prominent upward trend in the right section of the chart is well underway long before the crossing of the curves occurs. If you were relying on the moving average indicators, you would have missed quite a bit of significant price movement – so you would have erred in deciding when the best time to enter the trade was.

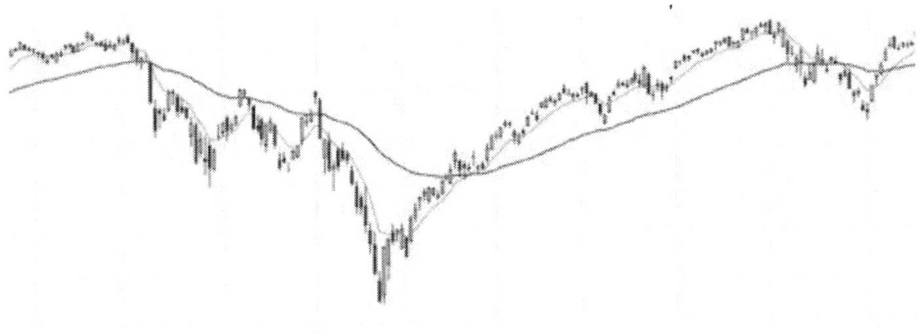

## Comparing shorter period moving averages for more accuracy

We can get a much better handle on the trends by using a shorter period moving average. Instead of using a 50-period moving average, we can compare a 20-period moving average against a 9-period moving average. Now you'll see that the cross overs indicate a trend reversal far earlier.

That may not be surprising. You have to ask how relevant a 50 period moving average is when looking for trend reversals in the present day. Even the example shown here – which is far better and so would help you capture a lot more of the pricing gain – the price moved from $274 a share to $283 a share before the crossover on the right side occurred. On the other hand, the large bullish candle that starts the uptrend is a pretty clear indicator.

This example clearly demonstrates how tricky this type of analysis can be. It also illustrates why you can't rely on one indicator alone. The candles also prove their worth yet again, and despite problems with the candles, especially recently, they remain one of the most accurate forecasting tools available to the trader.

It turns out going to shorter period moving averages won't help much. You'd still be at $283 a share up from $274 a share if you waited for the crossover of the moving averages in order to enter a position, losing out on $9 in price appreciation. A trader using candles however wouldn't have missed out.

## Heightened accuracy using Hull moving averages

When you use Hull moving averages instead, you're going to find that the cross overs are far more accurate. In fact, in the case of the Hull moving averages, you will often see crossovers before they are indicated by the candles. In the chart below, we use a 9-period Hull moving average together with a 20-period Hull moving average. Notice that this time, we don't miss out on any of the price gains, if we used the crossover as our guideline to enter the trade.

Let's zoom in, so that you can clearly see the crossover of the Hull moving averages happens *before* the candlesticks indicate an upward trend.

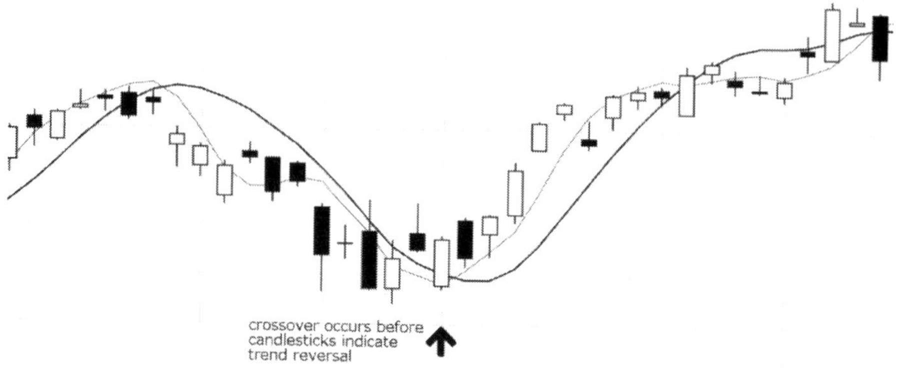


## Golden Cross

A golden cross occurs when the short-term moving average crosses above the long-term moving average. To look for a golden cross, most traders compare the 50-period moving average to a longer-term 200-period moving average. If these moving averages indicate a trend reversal, it is a strong signal that the stock may be heading into a rally.

A golden cross is considered to be a breakout pattern. That is, the stock may have been fluctuating within a certain range of prices for some time. During that period it would reach high prices, but they would not break above a resistance price level or go very far above it. And in each case, the price would drop back down. Price may then drop down to a lower support price level. A breakout is when the stock finally breaks above resistance and begins a longer term upward trend. The upward trend signals a rally and it can last for long time periods.

When applied to major stock indexes like the S & P 500 (or using an exchange traded fund like SPY that tracks it as a proxy), a golden cross can be taken as an indicator of a bull market. If you are looking for trends during a recession or bear market, you may be interested in the ability to forecast when the market has hit bottom. After that point, the market will begin a new rally and we can consider that the bear market has come to an end. While it's certainly not a guarantee, a golden cross is a strong indicator of a coming bull market. It can be helpful to compare the major indexes or their proxies in exchange traded funds, such as the Dow Jones Industrial Average, NASDAQ and other market segments such as the RUT (Russell 2000).

For an individual stock, a golden cross is a strong buy signal if you are looking to go long on the stock and take advantage of a major price swing.

## Death Cross

The death cross is the opposite condition when compared to a golden cross. In this case, you look for a short-term moving average to cross below a long-term moving average. When looking for a death cross, the 50-period moving average and the 200-period moving average are the best time periods to use for this purpose. Therefore, with a death cross you are looking for the 50-period moving average to cross below the 200-period moving average.

While a golden cross can signal a long-term (in relative, or absolute terms) price increase, a death cross signals a coming long-term drop in prices. If you are long on the position now is a good time to sell your stock. If you are looking to short the stock, a death cross is a good entry point.

We can also look for a death cross when studying the major indexes of the markets. A death cross for the Dow Jones

Industrial Average or the S & P 500 can be a strong signal of a coming bear market.

## Relative Strength Index (RSI)

Every trader should include the relative strength index in their analysis. This helps you determine the momentum of a trend. The range of the RSI is 0 to 100, and it's shown as a graph below your stock chart. The RSI is known as a *momentum oscillator*.

The relative strength index helps you determine if a stock is overbought or oversold. If a stock is overbought, the price has reached an unjustifiably high level. That means the price has gone above the intrinsic value of the stock. You can check fundamentals like the price to earnings ratio to help determine this as well.

With traders and investors now paying too much for the stock, they are going to start pulling back. This can lead to a downward trend in prices. An RSI that is signaling overbought conditions often correlates with continued uptrends that quickly pull back. There is no longer enough buyer interest in the stock to keep pushing prices higher.

The condition used to determine if a stock is overbought is an RSI that goes over 70. If you have bought shares hoping to profit from an upward trend in price, this is a good indicator that it's a good time to sell your shares, or that you should sell your shares in the near future. When a stock is in overbought conditions, it's not typically going to stay at the high price level for very long.

During a strong uptrend in price, the RSI can range between 40-90. You can look at the RSI chart and use the same chart analysis you do for stock charts. That is you should look for patterns like head and shoulders and double tops that indicate a coming price reversal. These often show up on an RSI chart while failing to appear on the stock chart itself.

An important pattern to look for when doing your momentum analysis is a so-called *failure swing*. When there is a failure swing the price of the stock moves up to a higher price, and then drops down to a previous, temporary line of support. This might happen more than once. The key characteristic of a failure swing is that there is not enough upward momentum in the stock to push the price past a certain point.

The RSI can be used to confirm a general trend in stock prices as well, if it's above 40 but less than 70, this indicates enough momentum to keep an upward trend going. When your other indicators and candles are all signaling uptrend, you can confirm the strength and momentum of the uptrend by using the RSI. You can ride the uptrend until the RSI reaches a value in the range 70-90.

RSI doesn't also tell you the momentum for trends or signal price reversals, you can also use it to help establish a price level of support. If you are seeing what appears to be support in the charts, confirm with the RSI. Levels of 40-45 indicate pricing support for the relative strength index. A level of resistance can be found if the RSI is anywhere in the range of 65-75 and it goes along in this range for sometime without increasing. Confirm with what you're seeing on the stock chart itself.

Look for downward trends in the peaks reached by the RSI in the same manner that you would when looking at charts. If the RSI reaches some peak value and drops only to rise again, but fails to reach the first peak without entering a new decline, this is a strong signal of a coming price reversal. Again, these patterns may appear on the RSI without showing up on the stock chart. Do not dismiss them even though they are not showing up on the stock charts, this is a strong indicator of changing momentum.

When it comes to downward trends in pricing, if the relative strength index falls below 30 this can indicate oversold conditions. Now the stock is becoming undervalued and a price reversal can be imminent. This is a strong signal that indicates it's a good time to enter a position, if you are going long on the stock. Resistance can be indicated when the RSI won't drop below 20 during a downtrend.

If there is a very strong uptrend, seeing an indication of overbought conditions should not be taken as an automatic sell signal. Prices can often continue with an upward trend in overbought conditions for some time. Remember that people do not always act in rational ways. On the stock market, greed can set in and people will be overcome by excitement and exuberance, hoping to see ever-higher prices. There are also latecomers to any uptrend. These two factors can sometimes lead to a continuing uptrend even though the RSI is telling you there are overbought conditions. In this situation, you should seek confirmation from other signals before using the overbought conditions as a reason to exit your position.

The same logic applies to downtrends. There may be an indication of oversold conditions, but emotion can take hold and rule the day here as well. As investors start panicking, and they see other investors exiting their positions to avoid what they mistakenly believe to be a catastrophic crash in stock prices, more will join the selloff and cause prices to continue going lower for some period of time. Therefore, as you should be doing in the case of uptrends, confirm what you are seeing with the RSI by looking at other tools. This can include looking for crossovers in your moving averages, examining chart patterns, and keeping a close eye on candles.

Swing failures occur at price peaks when the stock reaches high prices and then breaks down to a new low before increasing again for a short time period. This is taken as a strong signal of changing momentum, and it's a good time to exit a long position – you've probably gotten as much profit out of the trend as you can get at this point. This is called a *Top Swing Failure.* So you will look for the price to rise to a peak, then drop down to a low value we will call *A*. Then the stock will rise again, this time probably reaching a peak price that is a little bit lower than the previous peak, only to drop to a new low price *B*, before rising again. The key piece of data to confirm a Top Swing Failure is if *B* < *A*.

Swing failures occur at the bottom of downtrends as well, indicating that a selloff is running out of momentum. This is called a *Bottom Swing* Failure. Here we simply look for the opposite pattern to that described in the last paragraph. In this situation, the price declines to a new low price *A*, and then pushes against the trend over a short time period to reach a high point *C*. The price then reverses and falls to a low price *B*. If *B* > *A* and the price starts rising again to *C*, this is considered a Bottom Swing Failure and indicates a price reversal into an uptrend.

## Bollinger Bands

One of the most useful indicators in technical analysis are the *Bollinger Bands*. Bollinger bands combine three useful pieces of data into a single indicator. Bollinger bands include the moving average, a lower boundary curve determined by the moving one or more standard deviations below the average, and an upper boundary curve determined by going one or more standard deviations above the average.

Typically, Bollinger bands are used with a 20-period simple moving average. This will be the central line seen on the charts. For the standard deviation, it's common to use two standard deviations to set the upper and lower boundary curves. An example is shown below.

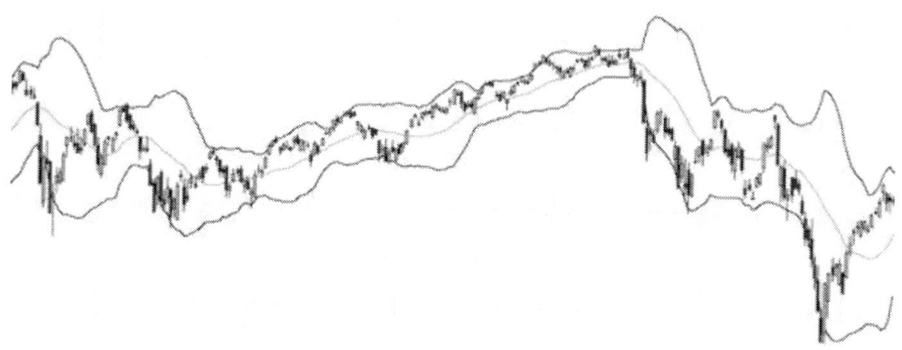

Bollinger bands, like the RSI, can be used to determine whether or not a stock is entering overbought or oversold conditions. When prices fall outside of the two standard deviation range, this is taken to be a strong signal of a price reversal. That doesn't mean, by itself, that a breakout is coming. It may only mean that the price will revert back to the mean. In the above image, we see both conditions. You can note in the image several points where the price reverted back to the mean, but there is a strong uptrend slightly to the right of the center of the figure.

Notice that the strength of the trend can usually – but not always be confirmed with candles. In the figure the point where there was a shift from the lower Bollinger band to the upper Bollinger band with a strong uptrend, there is a gap between the candles and the second candle after reading the bottom of the downtrend is a strong bullish candle.

The Bollinger bands can be taken to be dynamic representations of support and resistance price levels for the stock. This is seen clearly in the figure. Although it's not particularly useful in this case, since the particular security used (SPY) went though a significant downtrend followed by a significant up trend, using the Bollinger bands as a guideline in a ranging market is particularly useful. A ranging market is one where prices are staying within relatively fixed levels of support and resistance for a prolonged time period.

When using Bollinger bands, traders look for "tagging". This happens when the wicks of the candles touch or go outside one of the bands. It's considered that you should use a candle as a signal of a price change when it goes with the trend but there is a tagging indicator. As an example, you would look for a bearish candle at the peak of an uptrend that tags or even goes outside the Bollinger band all together.

It's important to use other signals and not rely on Bollinger bands in isolation. For example, during a long uptrend you will often see prices rise a small amount and then drop a little, forming a hump shape, before rising to a higher level. These small price humps can occur as part of a larger uptrend. Mistaking a hump for a peak because it touches or goes outside a Bollinger band can be a major mistake, causing you to miss out on further price increases for the stock.

It's common to put two sets of Bollinger bands on the same stock chart. In this case, a one-standard deviation set of Bollinger bands is included with the two-standard deviation set. The trader can then look for pricing trends where prices stay in between the one and two standard deviation zone. If this takes place during what appears to be an uptrend, the zone in between the two standard deviations is taken to be a "buying zone" where traders looking to enter long positions can do so (that is buy the stock in hopes of price appreciation). Likewise, when prices are staying in the lower range that is they are largely confined between one standard deviation below the mean and two standard deviations below the mean, this would be a "selling zone". This is a signal indicating a downward trend in prices. Alternatively, a short seller would use a buying zones as an indication to exit a position, or if they are not already in a position to wait for the price to show signs of peaking. Likewise, a selling zone is a buying zone for those shorting the stock.

The example below illustrates a selling zone, and you can see the downward trend. The grey zone indicates one-standard deviation, while the white zone indicates two-standard deviations, and you can see that for a significant amount of time the share prices are falling in between the two, forming a good example of a selling zone.

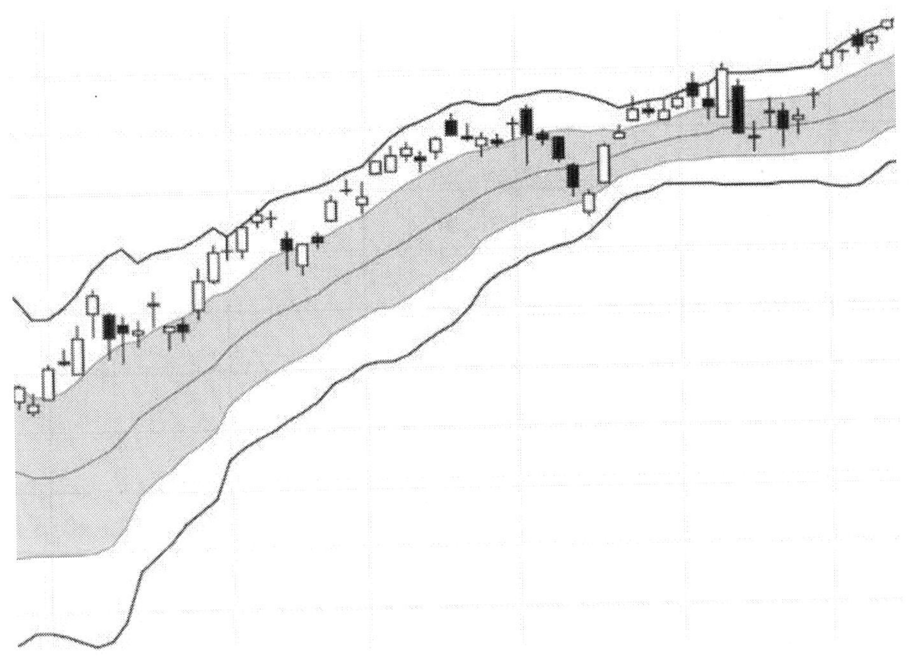

This example shows a buying zone. Prices for the most part are within the 1-2 standard deviation range.

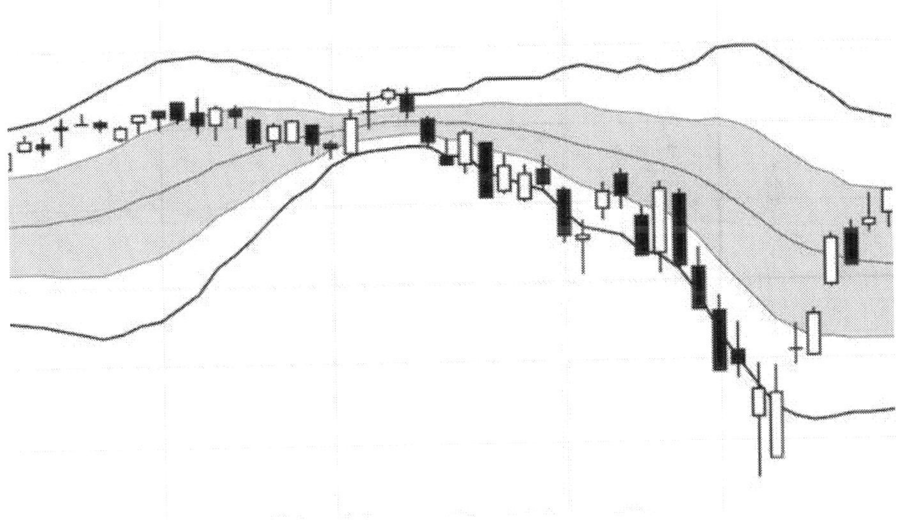

## Volatility and Bollinger Bands

The volatility of a stock is closely tied to the size of the standard deviation at any given time. Taking this into account, we recognize that Bollinger bands can be used to measure or estimate the volatility of a stock at any given moment or observe how it's changing with time. Remember that volatility is a measure of the magnitude of price swings for the stock. That is, if stock A ranges between $50 and $55 with a mean of $53 over the course of a week, but stock B ranges between $40 and $60 with a mean of $50 over the course of a week, we'd consider stock B to be more volatile. High volatility implies larger and more frequent price swings over a given period of time. More volatility is going to result in a larger standard deviation.

In the case of Bollinger bands this is represented visually by the width of the Bollinger bands. When volatility is getting larger, the Bollinger bands are going to be wider. When volatility is decreasing or smaller, the Bollinger bands are going to be narrow.

Small adjustments in the standard deviation used are suggested for longer and shorter periods used with the moving average. A two standard deviation width is the default value used with a 20-period moving average. If the moving average is longer, then it's recommended that the standard deviation be slightly increased. For a 50-period moving average, it is advised that you use a 2.1 standard deviation width. On the other hand, for a shorter period moving average, you should slightly decrease the standard deviation. In the case of a 10-period moving average, it's advised that you use 1.9 standard deviations.

Below, we see a chart for Apple, using a 10-period moving average and 1.9 standard deviations for the Bollinger bands.

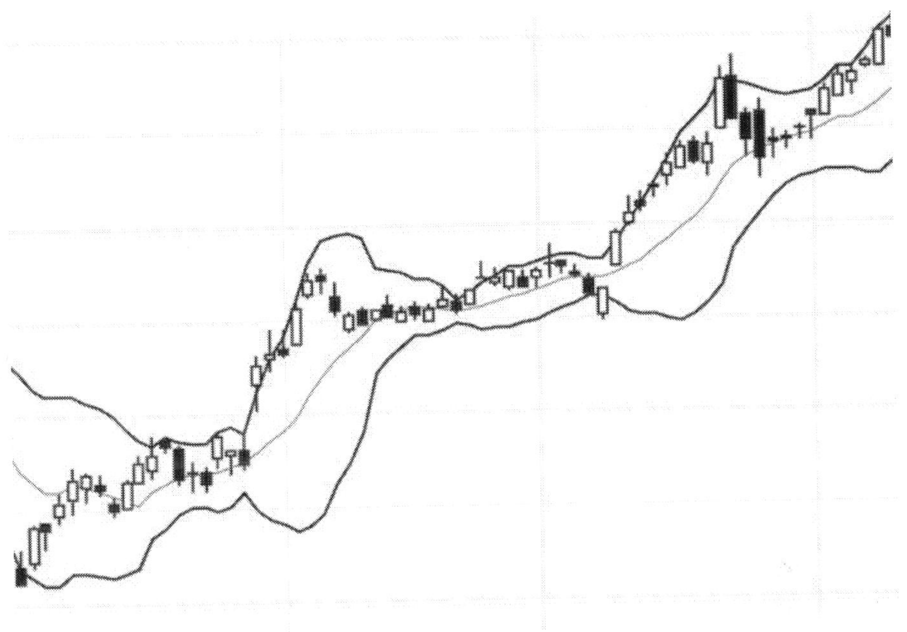

## The W bottom and M top pattern in Bollinger Bands

One key thing to look for with Bollinger bands are patterns that show a reversal back to the mean, either at the bottom of a downtrend or at the top of an uptrend. These can indicate a coming trend reversal. At the bottom of a downtrend, a *W bottom* is indicated by a price drop that hits the lower Bollinger band, then prices reverse back to the mean. Then it drops a second time, again reaching the lower Bollinger band. Once again price reverses and starts increasing again. If it reaches the mean a second time, this is a W bottom. That is a strong indicator that the price will continue rising forming an uptrend above the mean.

An M top works in the reverse. This time prices rise from the mean and peak when hitting the upper Bollinger band, only to revert back to the mean. Then they rise again, but can't break through the top pricing level, so prices stop rising at the upper Bollinger band and then reverse, going back down to the mean. This is usually followed by a downtrend in prices below the mean and perhaps beyond.

## Band Walking

It's important to recognize that when prices touch or even go slightly outside the Bollinger bands, that in itself isn't a buy or sell signal. It needs to be confirmed by looking at other metrics and signals, including crosses of moving averages and looking at the candles themselves. Price trends also do what traders refer to as "walk the band". This means that a long string of prices will touch the band without a trend reversal. This can happen when the price is following an upward trend or when the price is declining.

## Moving Average Convergence – Divergence

This indicator is another "momentum oscillator". It utilizes two exponential moving averages. But rather than just plotting them on a chart, it calculates their difference. The standard is to subtract a longer period moving average from a short period moving average, and this is normally done with a 12-period EMA (exponential moving average) and a 26-period EMA. The difference between the two curves is called the MACD line.

But that isn't all that is included with this indicator. It also includes a curve which is called the signal line. The signal line is calculated by computing the 9-day exponential moving average of the MACD line. The results are then used to look for buy and sell signals.

Traders seek points where the MACD line crosses above and below the signal line. If it crosses above the signal line, using a standard bullish perspective, that is taken to be a buy signal. Therefore, if you are hoping to profit from a price swing that leads to appreciation of the stock price, you are looking for the MACD line to cross above the signal line.

Conversely, if the MACD line crosses below the signal line, this is taken to be a sell signal for those who are bullish on the stock. On the other hand, if you are shorting the stock or buying put options, this is your point to enter the trade.

Since the MACD line is calculated by subtracting one moving average from another, it can have positive and negative values. It's going to be positive when the 12 period exponential moving average is above the 26 period exponential moving average. In addition to giving buy and sell signals, the MACD gives you a measure of the momentum of a pricing trend. The MACD is usually displayed below stock charts with a histogram which gives a bar chart representation of the difference between the two moving averages.

The MACD has been criticized for not always being accurate, so it is not something a trader should come to rely on 100% of the time. It will often miss trend reversals and can give signals of a price uptrend or downtrend that will fail to materialize. Many traders study market momentum looking at the MACD and the RSI together. In any case, if you use the MACD to do technical analysis, it is recommended that you utilize other tools with it, and don't take the MACD alone for a buy or sell signal. Always confirm with other indicators.

## Parabolic Stop and Reverse (SAR)

The parabolic stop and reverse or SAR indicator is a simple trend indicator. It appears on stock charts as a series of dots or dashes, that fall below or above the actual prices. When the parabolic stop and reverse curve is above prices, that indicates the market is in a downtrend. When it's below prices that indicates that the market is in an uptrend.

Therefore, traders look for the parabolic stop and reverse to change its appearance above or below prices. If you purchased shares of stock at the bottom of an uptrend, then you would watch for the parabolic stop and reverse curve data points to start showing up above prices as a sell indicator. Alternatively, someone looking to short the stock at that point would use that as a signal to enter their trade.

The parabolic stop and reverse indicator isn't useful in a ranging market. It's useful when the stock breaks out into a trend, and it can be helpful when other indicators are giving confusing signals.

## ADX

ADX stands for average directional index. This is another oscillator that can give you a measure of the strength of a trend in market prices. Despite its name, it actually doesn't give the direction of any trend, it only tells you if it's a strong or a weak trend. This is an important distinction, because many indicators simply give buy and sell or trend reversal signals. The range of the ADX is from 0 to 100. To look for a strong trend (regardless of direction), you are looking for the ADX to be above 50.

If the ADX is 20 or below, this is considered a weak trend. That means it lacks momentum and not many traders and investors are behind the trend.

You will remember that the MACD can give some false positives. You can utilize the ADX with the MACD and other indicators to help weed out false positives. There is no question this has applications when using the MACD, but you can also use the ADX with any indicators you are relying on to forecast trends. It can act as a double check to indicate whether or not entering or exiting a position is really a good move.

The ADX is good to check when you have been riding a trend to the upside. It will help you see when the trend is weakening, even though prices may be continuing to increase. This may be a reasonable point to exit the trade.

## The Stochastic Indicator

In mathematics, the word *stochastic refers to a random process.* The stock market is certainly infused with a great deal of randomness. So it's natural that getting a handle on it is the basis for an important indicator. The *stochastic indicator* is considered to be a highly accurate indicator by the trading community. The stochastic indicator seeks to determine the relationship between the current price and the price range of the stock over a period of time. Like some other indicators, it can be used to determine if a stock is overbought or oversold. The stochastic indicator uses 14 time periods, but it's flexible. It can use days, weeks, or months, so is useful to all styles of trading. That means you can zoom in and out, viewing 14 days, or 14 months. The stochastic indicator uses a fundamental observation, which you can see from candlesticks. That is the closing price of a stock tends to be in the upper range of prices for the trading session, when the stock is in an uptrend. Conversely, when the stock is in a downtrend, the closing price tends to be in the low range of stock prices for the trading session.

The stochastic indicator determines the stock's high and low price over a given period of time. It can then compare the current price to the range defined by the high and low, and express that as a percentage.

The stochastic indicator ranges over 0 to 100. If it's below 30, this is taken to indicate oversold conditions, and so it's a buy signal. Over 70 represents overbought conditions, and so would be a value indicating a sell signal. Anything in between 30 and 70 should be ignored.

## Stochastic Momentum

The stochastic momentum index is a more sophisticated version of the stochastic indicator that is used to seek out oversold and overbought conditions. The indicator is supposed to provide an accurate forecast of coming shifts in momentum. This indicator focuses on the high and low prices of each trading session, and uses them to calculate the median price value. It then calculates the difference between the closing price of each trading session and the median price. The purpose of developing this indicator was to avoid false buy and sell signals that resulted from false price swings. It ranges from -100 to +100.

When you set up the stochastic momentum index on a stock chart, you'll be asked to specify overbought and oversold ranges. The standard values are +40 for overbought conditions and -40 for oversold conditions. Therefore an indicator value of +42 would be overbought and an indicator value of -42 would be oversold.

Like the ordinary stochastic indicator, the stochastic momentum index does not tell you the coming trend, it only tells you there is going to be a shift in momentum. The trader has to get the trend direction using other tools. The main use of the stochastic momentum index is to help traders decide when to make their trades.

The indicator line is denoted by the obscure symbol %K, so when you set it up and it asks you for the number of periods for %K, it's asking you for the number of periods to use for the indicator. The standard value that is used is 10 periods, so if you are using days for your trading sessions, %K will be 10 days. The signal line is given by %D, with a standard period of 10. The signal line is an exponential moving average (it's a simple moving average for the regular stochastic indicator). The trader looks for line crossings. A downward crossing of the indicator line below the signal line is a bearish signal, while an upward crossing is taken to be a bullish signal.

## Indicators – A Summary

A trader should never rely on any single indicator or chart pattern to enter or exit a trade. Instead, you should develop a practice of using a few specific tools. There are many more tools available, this description is only introductory and gives you an overview of the most common tools that are used. The key is to avoid jumping off and sinking a large amount of capital into a trade just because one indicator gave you a "go" signal. Likewise, you should avoid a premature exit from your positions by again only relying on a single indicator.

Many indicators are redundant. So, a Hull moving average and an exponential moving average with their crossover signals are going to provide the same information. In that case, you should experiment with the different moving averages and find on moving average that works for you. Checking across multiple moving averages is simply beating a dead horse.

As a trader, you should definitely be a master of the candlesticks. That means being able to eyeball the candlesticks to spot probable trend reversals. They can also help you get an idea of momentum in a trend or toward a reversal. Candlestick chart analysis should be used in conjunction with moving averages.

Beyond this, you should utilize one or more of the other indicators described in this chapter. For example, using the relative strength index to determine when a trend you're looking at is getting into overbought or oversold territory. Second, you would use the ADX in order to determine whether or not a trend is a strong or weak trend.

It's not necessary to use all the indicators, and when you start researching this you will find that there are a large number of indicators. It's far better to pick out about 3 or at the most 4 and get to know those indicators well. Take the time to study examples of those indicators and read articles about them. Add them to past stock charts and then look at what happened when the indicator behaved in the ways that you're being taught to look for.

You should also spend some time practicing with indicators in real time, before you start making real trades. This will help you develop an ability to read the stock charts along with the indicators to more accurately forecast coming price swings.

Keep in mind that despite all the effort you are going to put into this, you cannot ever attain 100% accuracy. The indicators are not prophets, they are guides. If you view them correctly then you won't be disappointed. It's inevitable that at time all the indicators are pointing in one direction but you still end up with a losing trade. Most of the time they work, but not all the time.

When you are learning your way around stock charts, which you should do before making trades, follow along in real time during the trading day using different indicators. This will help you find the ones that you like best and feel the most comfortable with, and that appear to you to be the best indicators as far as predictability. Practicing will also help you recognize the signals they give in real time. It's one thing to see the data in past history, it's another to recognize it as it's happening. Something that can be helpful is to buy a small number of shares to practice swing trading in real time. Just buy 3-5 shares at a time of different stocks, and then follow along with your chart patterns and indicators to make buying and selling decisions with some real psychological pressure. A side note – don't make day trades while doing this. You might find yourself in a panic and making day trades by exiting positions early, the same day that you bought them. This often happens to new traders who tend to panic far more than is really justified. Don't worry if it happens to you, we've all been there.

# Chapter 7: ABCD and Swing Patterns

In practice, various ABCD patterns remain an important part of the traders toolkit. In this chapter we will basically review the most common ABCD patterns and how they play a role in trading decisions. ABCD chart patterns were characterized in the 1930s by a stock trader named Charles Gartley.

As the name implies, an ABCD chart pattern involves four price points. There are three general types of ABCD patterns; Classic, Price and Time, and ABCD extension. We explore each of these below.

## Classic ABCD Pattern

A bullish ABCD pattern is used to estimate the best pricing point that should be used to buy stocks. Price points A and B form the swing points of the pattern. This is a downward trend in price, with A first making a large drop to point B. There is then a retracement to a higher price point C, but C is lower than A. The distance to C is between 61% and 79% of the distance from A to B. The price then drops to a new low point D, with the distance from C to D being 127.2% or 161% of AB. The trader will enter a long position on the stock at point D.

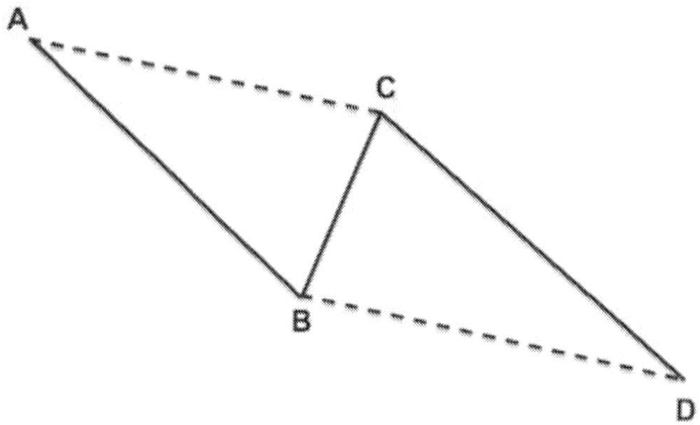


## AB = CD Pattern

The shape of this pattern is the same, but in this case the time between the different points plays a significant role. The time span between the high price A and the low price B should be equal to the time span between price point C and price point D. In this case, reaching point D is again a point where stock should be purchased.

## ABCD Extension

In this case, the ABCD pattern is again repeated, but this time the line between the price points CD is 127.2% or 161.8% longer than the line AB. Once again, there is a general downtrend in price with each successive high price lower than the previous price, with D being a low price. It represents a buying opportunity.

## Bearish Classic ABCD Patterns

These are the same as the patterns discussed above, but with rising prices. The point D is taken to be a selling point.

## Bullish Gartley 222

A bullish Gartley 222 is a pattern like the one shown below.

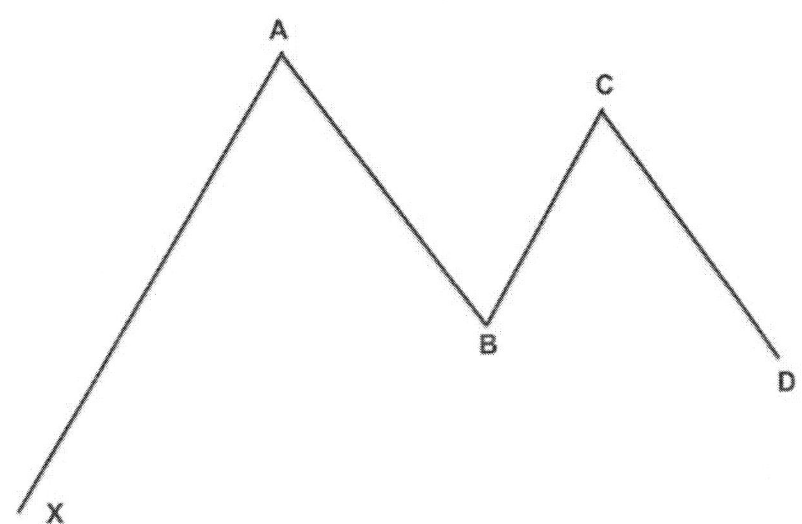


The price drops a distance AB that is approximately 61% of the distance XA. It then rises along BC, a distance that is taken to be approximately 85% of the distance AB. Finally, it drops about 75% of the distance of XA to point D. The trader takes point D as the entry point into a trade anticipating a gain in a large uptrend. Note that the bullish Gartley begins with an upswing from point X to A.

## Bearish Gartley 222

A bearish Gartley is an indication that the trader should exit their position. Unlike the bullish Gartley, the bearish Gartley 22 begins with a large swing down in price. Then it's basically the inverse pattern. AB will be a rising price trend, with the line AB about 65% of the XA leg that was the entry into the pattern. Then, BC will be about 69% of the length of AB. Finally, CD rises in price, about 77% of the distance of XA. At point D, the trader would exit a long position. However this can be an entry point for a short.

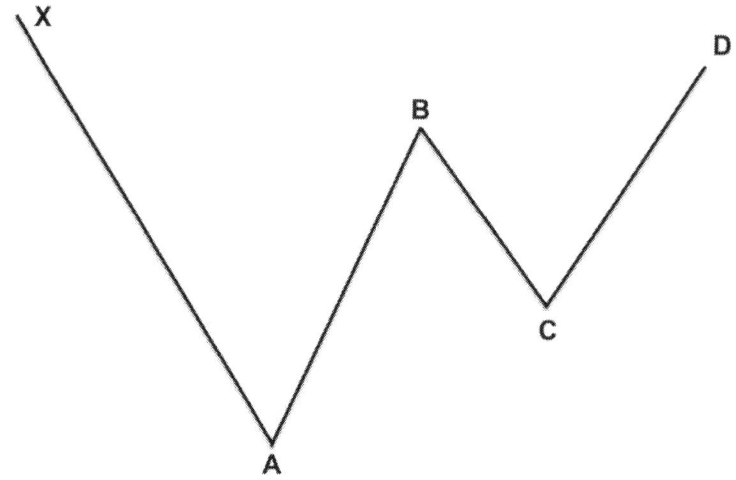


The important thing to note is that while there is an increase in price at the end, this is a bearish pattern. The same can be said about the previous examples. A bullish pattern might for a time take the shape of a downward trend in price. Consistently identifying classic ABCD and Gartley patterns on real stock charts is a craft that must be learned. It is more art than science, even though it's basically quantitative.

## The Importance of Charting

We have barely touched the surface here. You should buy as many books as you can and learn about all the known chart patterns. As a trader it's going to be important to be able to see them in real stock charts, and know when to get in and get out of positions based on what the charts are telling you. My position is that a trader should not rely on any single method in isolation. That message applies to these patterns as well. The thing to remember about any tool used by a trader is that these tools are not fool proof. There are going to be times when you definitely see these chart patterns but they don't produce the expected result. In part, this is due to the unpredictable nature of the human mind, so you can't always know what people are going to do next, even in herd behavior like trading. It's also going to be due in part to the actions of large traders, who may be sitting on the sidelines and then come in with an unexpectedly large move that shifts things in a new direction. So don't put your faith in any one chart pattern, use the other tools at your disposal to confirm or deny any signal given by any other tool. In the case of these chart patterns, you can look to candles and your technical analysis to confirm or deny.

# Chapter 8: Supply, Demand, and Buyer Traps

Supply and demand zones are an extension of the idea of support and resistance. However rather than thinking in terms of an exact price, we think instead of a range of prices that fills out a "zone". In this chapter we'll also discuss traps, which are chart patterns that incorrectly signal pricing trends. A bear trap will incorrectly signal a rising price trend, while a bull trap will incorrectly signal a declining price trend.

## Supply and Demand Zones

The goal of using supply and demand zones is to get a handle on the buying and selling done by large institutional traders. This can help you identify trend reversals and breakouts earlier. A demand zone forms around a level of price support. So this is a range of low prices below which the stock won't fall for a given period. This is known as a demand zone because demand for the stock will rise, driving prices up to the resistance level. That means the low price of the stock will lead to increasing demand for the shares by traders and investors. A demand zone can be estimated by taking the support level as the top of the zone, and the low prices of candles on each side of the area where the support has been established to indicate the low prices of the demand zone. In a supply or demand zone, you are seeking out price ranges that have a large imbalance between buyers and sellers. You're going to be looking for a chart pattern that looks something like this, with a large drop off in price.

Notice there is a clustering of price before it sees the large drop off. This is a supply zone. In this price area, supply is overwhelming demand. This presages a coming drop in share price, which is can be followed by an uptrend as shown in the figure. A supply zone may indicate a selloff by sophisticated and institutional investors. When you see price bouncing downward from a supply zone, this is typically a sell signal.

A demand zone occurs at the bottom of a downtrend. When price shows a bounce upward, this can be a buy signal.

## Bear Traps

A bear trap occurs when the market is really trending upward. However, it gives all the signals that the market is entering bear territory. A bear trap can actually be created by large institutional investors and hedge funds, the so-called "smart money". Thcy intentionally push the price down by selling shares. This is done in order to capitalize on the fear of losing money among small and novice traders. After there has been a significant selloff, prices will start rising again as institutions get back in their positions. Since there was an illusion of a downward trend in prices, small and novice investors were trapped into selling their positions.

The rising prices will entice small and novice traders back into the market. This helps increase demand as the price approaches previous highs. This is the goal of the bear trap from the perspective of the institutional investor, to increase demand in the market so that prices will be pushed higher.

Although a solid opportunity exists to buy at the bottom of a bear trap, small traders, especially novice traders, tend to wait too long to get back in the market. They end up buying as prices are rising past previous highs.

It's not possible to predict a bear trap with total accuracy. However, there are signals you can look for that may indicate a bear trap is around the corner. The first thing to look for is a breakout in price, which is the price breaches a previous level of resistance. Then you're going to want to see increased trading volume at that moment. This can be a signal that a bear trap will occur in the near future.

The point of a bear trap is even though you see a price decline, you don't necessarily want to exit your position. You can either hold if you had entered the position at a higher price, or if you do exit your position, then you're going to want to quickly get back in when prices drop, so that you can take advantage of the bear trap. The key to success with buyer traps is to be aware of how the institutional investors trade to manipulate price, and take advantage of it.

## Bull Traps

A bull trap is essentially the opposite situation. When there is a bull trap, prices have been declining. Then they show signs of a breakout, which entices investors to enter positions. But after a small rise in price, the shares turn sharply toward decline, resuming the main downward trend. Buyers who entered positions during the apparent breakout are trapped by their purchase of shares.

When there is pressure from the smart money, in this case, prices are trending downward, and institutional investors move in to buy shares to give an artificial bump in price. That gives the illusion that an upward trend is commencing, and the hope is that enough small and novice investors will take it as a buy signal. Then institutional investors will do a large sell off, shorting the stock. This will cause a major price drop, which traps those investors who took the bait, and entered long positions. Fearing losses from a major decline, they will exit their positions causing an increased selloff and drop in prices, strengthening the positions of the smart money investors who were seeking a downward trend in price in the first place.

## Avoiding Traps

It is not possible to avoid bull and bear traps all the time. However, you can tip the odds in your favor by carefully analyzing your trades. In other words, always check with multiple indicators before entering or exiting a trade. This cannot completely eliminate the risk of a bull or bear trap, but it can significantly reduce it. Look for volume and momentum to confirm a true breakout in price.

# Chapter 9
# The Best Indicator

As a new trader, you're probably wondering what the best indicator is. We hope to address that question in this chapter as best we can, but you should be aware that there isn't a right or wrong answer to this question. The real answer is you should use the indicators that you are comfortable with. You should also make sure that you have got everything that can be covered matched with an appropriate indicator. We address this problem toward the end of the chapter, so if you aren't sure that that means right now sit tight.

## Why there is no "best" indicator

New traders are hoping there is a "holy grail" or a fortune teller they can use to forecast the best trades. Unfortunately no such thing exists. As we stated earlier, indicators are only guides. Many indicators actually provide the same information. That said it's important for all traders to use indicators to follow price action. However, oftentimes it's really just a matter of taste.

## What not to do

A new trader may be tempted to load up on a large amount of indicators. They may feel that the more information they have, the better. When it comes to stock trading this actually isn't true.

Information overload can actually hamper your ability to make good trading decisions. As we've said, many indicators actually provide similar or the same information. Some might contradict each other, leaving a novice trader in a confused state.

## The recommended approach

The best thing for any trader to do is try and cover different types of data with one indicator, rather than piling on a large number of indicators. But before you even get to that point, you should put yourself in a position where you are not letting the indicators tell you what to do, but rather you're using them to support or refute your own trading positions. That means coming to your own trading positions before looking toward indicators to give you the answer.

This begins by learning chart patterns inside and out. You're going to need to be able to spot support and resistance, and you'll have to be able to draw trend lines. Then you'll need to be able to recognize important patterns like double tops, so that you can make an estimate of when a trend reversal is coming.

The second approach is to learn candlesticks inside and out. Then you'll want to be studying candlestick charts so that you can estimate on sight where the trend is heading. You are going to learn that while it works more often than not, candlesticks are not a surefire way to predict coming prices or trends with complete accuracy.

Trading is part craft and part science. Candlesticks and chart patterns are the craft side of a trader's toolkit, but they form the foundation. Your analysis should begin here, and then you come to a tentative conclusion on when to enter or exit a trade. At this point you use technical analysis to confirm or reject your decision.

## Cover all bases

As we've said, you can gather together a large number of indicators that all do the same thing, but there are many types of indicators. The key to success is to make sure that you use the smallest number of indicators possible, yet make sure you cover every important piece of data that can be forecast by the indicators.

There are five major areas that you want to cover with your indicators. These are:

- Trend: Estimate the trend direction of the market, and look for trend reversals. Using two moving averages will satisfy this requirement. Moreover, crosses with moving averages can be used together with candles to get a firm picture on the coming direction of the market. Remember that trend indicators and candles are lagging indicators – that is they tell you what's happened in the past. However, we also know that behavior in the recent past is a good predictor of what's coming next.
- Relative Strength Indicator: The strength of a trend is the second most important thing to note. If a trend isn't strong or it's waning, it's not likely to continue in the future.
- Momentum: A momentum oscillator helps you determine how rapidly prices are changing.
- Volume: the volume of trading is important. If you see prices rise on low volume, it might not be a very important signal, since during that trading session most traders and investors were sitting on the sidelines.
- Mean Reversion: A mean reversion indicator can help you estimate how far away from the mean a price breakout will head.

Here are our suggestions for the indicators you can use as you start your trading career to cover all five areas. As you gain experience, you may come up with your own preferences. But these are good to get started, and many traders will find them to be satisfactory.

- Trend: Exponential moving averages are better than simple moving averages, because they take into account how long ago a price occurred, and they give more weight to recent prices. You will need two moving averages on your stock charts. One will be a short period moving average, and one will be a long period moving average. The exact periods used may depend on your style of trading (day, swing, position). Traders generally prefer a 50-period and 200-period EMA. You can also get good information using a 9-period and 20-period moving average.
- Relative strength indicator: You can utilize the RSI as a part of your analysis. A stochastic indicator can also be used.
- Momentum: The MACD is a good indicator to use to estimate trend momentum.
- Mean Reversion: Use Bollinger bands for this purpose.
- Volume: Stock charts give you the option to display volume bars at the bottom of the chart, so that you can quickly determine the level of trading volume for any given trading session. This should be used in conjunction with the On-balance volume indicator.

The wide range of indicators that are available often leave new traders feeling confused. We hope that our suggestions have helped make the concept of using indicators in your trading more manageable and understandable.

# Chapter 10
# Market Cycles and Other Topics

## Market Cycles

A free market economy (or a regulated one that is close to being a free market economy) is going to go through business cycles. These are periods of expansion and growth that are followed by recession and contraction at some point. Market cycles occur on all levels of economic behavior, for the same basic reasons. In fact market cycles form the basis for stock trading. A security will go through a repeated cycle where it's undervalued, and demand begins increasing for the stock, pushing prices up. Prices will continue being pushed up as more traders and investors get into the stock, and exuberance can take over. People who have been sitting on the sidelines and waiting too long will jump in, continuing to push prices higher as demand keeps increasing. This will push the stock into overbought conditions. It's simply human nature for this behavior to go on.

When the stock reaches overbought conditions, people will begin worrying about getting out of it as soon as possible, when they start worrying about being stuck with an overpriced stock. As a result, a mad dash to the exits begins and there is a large selloff. This will continue until the stock enters territory where it's oversold. The price then becomes undervalued again, and the cycle starts all over again.

These types of cycles are simply a result of the rules of supply and demand. What happens for an individual stock will be happening for the market as a whole and for the economy at large. For the market and the economy, a boom and bust cycle is followed with unusual regularity. Of course at the present time we are in a period of what seems to be continual expansion, but history shows that the bust part of the cycle always comes. Luckily it's temporary and the economy regains its footing as resources are slowly reallocated to better uses.

During a period of expansion, there are increases in priced and economic production. Eventually because the economy itself ends up in "overbought" conditions, a crisis ensues and investment comes to a halt, leading to sharp declines in investment and economic output. Eventually – just like with an individual stock going through the cycle – prices will drop far enough that demand resumes, and the entire cycle begins again.

There have been some unusual manias that have occurred throughout history. For example in the 18th century, there was tulip bulb mania in the Netherlands. People began "investing" in tulip bulbs and prices for tulip bulbs skyrocketed, creating massive amounts of wealth on paper. Some people probably had real wealth as well, if they were smart enough to exit and sell their tulip bulbs to someone else who was willing to pay the price to get them. Eventually people came to their senses and demand for tulip bulbs collapsed, leaving a disaster in its wake. It's hard to know from where we stand now, but one has to wonder if cryptocurrency might become a similar phenomenon.

The dot com crash of 2000-2001 was a similar phenomenon. When the internet was made available to the general public and online companies began growing and becoming prominent, a bit of hysteria took over. People believed that the market could only go one way –up. They also invested in virtually any internet company regardless of profits or price to earnings ratios – which went sky high. People were even paying millions of dollars just for domain names. Eventually, even though there were some definite gems among the mess like Amazon (although buying domain names hoping to make money was no better than buying tulips), the hysteria came to a stop and demand ceased. The markets collapsed and a recession hit.

Even after all this, the U.S. economy went right into the housing boom, following the exact same process. This time houses were the new thing that could "never lose value". Low interest rates and lose credit policies began pushing housing prices to unheard of heights that went far beyond what would be considered fair market value. Banks got leveraged to the hilt and everyone caught tulip fever, thinking that it couldn't end. But of course it did, and we had the crash in 2008.

Human nature being what it is, despite the obvious lesson of the dot com crash, people went headlong into the next mania and the inevitable crash that followed. Interestingly, people also acted like this was a surprise. This led a pair of Harvard economists to write a famous book called "This time is different".

The market is on an interesting trajectory now, because we've had several years of modest, and one might say sustainable growth. Even 3% GDP growth is modest in historical terms. It's hard to say when the next end of the business cycle is coming, it used to be a routine phenomenon but the market has been on an amazing long-term run.

There doesn't seem to be any regularity or predictability to market cycles. Let's look at the post civil war era in the United

States. Major recessions occurred in 1873, 1887, 1890, 1893, 1896, 1899, 1902, 1907, 1910, 1913, and 1920. The frequency of these downturns was alarming, but if you study them it's interesting that they were quite short lived. In those days, there was no government intervention, and the economy reallocated itself quickly and began booming again in some other direction. The high frequency of the recessions (which were called panics at the time) may have been due in part to the extremely rapid growth the United States was having at the time. Also, there was no centralized money management until 1913.

From 1929 onward we have, starting with the great depression – 1929, 1937, 1945, 1949, 1953, 1958, 1960, 1969, 1973, 1981, 1990, 2001, and 2008.

Although the frequency is still quite high, it's important to note that the "panics" of the earlier era, with the exception of the great depression and the 2008 financial crisis, were much larger downturns. Of the recessions here, the only crises were the 1929 great depression and the 2008 financial crisis. In comparison, the other downturns were fairly mild and short lived. There is argument among economists about how much government intervention there should be during a crisis. Surprisingly, in all of the previous recessions before the 1929 crash, the government did little or nothing. At the time the attitude was to let the free market sort it out. It always did, but the high frequency of crashes in the business cycle led many to believe that the government should "do something" to soften the blow. Probably the biggest innovation was the creation of the Federal Reserve to help manage the money supply. Unfortunately, during the great depression the Federal Reserve made the absolute wrong move, and contracted the money supply. This helped deepen what was at the time just a recession. Restrictive trade policy which was put in place by the Smoot-Hawley tariff act combined with an excessively tight money supply turned the recession into what we now call the great depression. This lesson has been learned by many prominent economists, and that is why Ben Bernanke greatly expanded the money supply and the banks were bailed out in the 2008 financial crisis. These moves helped prevent a contraction of the money supply like what happened to help trigger the great depression.

For sometime, it appeared that there were cycles of about 5-10 years. It's been 12 years since the last recession began forming, so it's pretty amazing that the economy and stock market seem to be continuing upward without losing any steam. Trying to predict when a downturn might occur seems to be a foolish exercise. The bottom line for you as an individual trader is that you should be ready for one no matter when it occurs.

## Traders and Market Cycles

As a trader, you have to keep your head on and avoid letting market cycles cause panic. In fact, a smart trader knows that they can profit when there are market declines. You should prepare yourself ahead of time so that you can act if you find yourself in the midst of a major market decline. This means you'll want to be able to short stock. You can also buy put options and take advantage of declining share prices. Nobody knows when the next market decline is coming, but it will definitely come at some point. The key is being prepared ahead of time.

You should also be investing in funds that short the market now. Most people only think ahead with a – short – time horizon. But if you are thinking long term, you know what a recession will hit at some point. Funds that short the market are cheap to buy in good times. When the economy starts crashing, their value skyrockets. By planning ahead now, you can be ready to jump on such an opportunity and make good money when everyone else is scrambling for the exits. That is what planning ahead is all about, being ready to deal with any situation that comes your way.

## Using Leverage

It is possible to obtain leverage from your broker. Leverage is increased buying power in your brokerage account. This will allow you to buy more stocks that you would be able to buy with the cash you have on hand alone. The amount of leverage that a broker gives you is expressed as a ratio of (buying power): cash.

Buying power is the sum of margin plus the amount you can borrow. For most stocks, it's a 2:1 ratio. So to get the buying power, you take the amount of cash that you haven't used and multiply by 2.

When you open an account with your broker, leverage is not automatically accessible. To get leverage you need to have a margin account. What this means is that you deposit an amount of cash which serves as your margin, and the amount of leverage you can use is reached by borrowing from the broker. By law, you must deposit a minimum of $2,000 in a margin account. Typically brokers will give you 2:1 leverage. That means if you put $1,000 toward the purchase of stocks you can buy $2,000 worth of shares, borrowing the difference from the broker.

Each stock will have a margin requirement listed with its details. If the margin requirement is 50%, to buy $2,000 worth of stock you have to deposit $1,000 in your account. In order to buy $5,000 worth of stock, you'd have to deposit $2,500 in cash.

If you haven't used any margin, and you have $2,000 in your account, your buying power is $4,000. But if you use some of your margin, say $500 to buy $1,000 worth of stock, then your buying power gets reduced by $1,000. You should be able to look up your buying power on your account at any time.

To calculate leverage for a given stock, divide 1 by the margin requirement expressed as a decimal for the stock. For example, if the margin requirement is listed as 25%, then use 0.25. The leverage in this case would be:

Leverage = 1/0.25 = 4

That is, the broker is giving you 4:1 leverage on that stock. Keep in mind that the standard margin requirement for stocks is 50%.

The actual amount of cash that must be put up to enter a trade is known as required margin. Let's say that you have $3,000 in your account, and you want to buy 20 shares of IBM that is trading at $140 a share. IBM has a 50% margin requirement, and the total cost of the shares is $2,800. That means you'll have to put up $1,400 in required margin, which is cash directly out of your account, with the broker lending you the balance.

Another way that a margin account can be used is to borrow stocks from the broker, to use when shorting a stock. We have alluded to his in a few examples earlier in the book. The amount of shares you borrow must be covered by the buying power you have in your account. When you get the shares, you sell them on the market immediately. This is a risky move, because if the stock doesn't go down in price like you think it will, you might end up owing the broker money. But if it works out and the stock drops as expected, you can buy them dirt cheap on the market and return them to the broker, pocking the difference. If the price of the shares rises, then you will end up owing money, because you'll have to buy them back at a higher price and return them to the broker.

If you make bad trades and end up using your entire margin, you will get a margin call. The broker will close all of your trades and possibly shut down your account.

When you use margin and leverage, you are borrowing money. That means that you're going to have to pay interest. This type of stock trading has to be used with extreme care, and many traders have gotten into serious financial trouble using it. If you are careful, it can help you get into larger positions. The advantage of margin for a swing trader is that you're not holding your position very long, and if you can exit the position and make a profit, then you can pay back the money you borrowed without paying a lot of interest.

As an example, suppose that a stock is trading at $100 a share. You have $5,000 in your account, so you could buy 50 shares. But you use your leverage and buy 100 shares. This completely wipes out your buying power. You have borrowed $5,000 from the broker. Let's say that the stock rises to $102 per share and you exit your position. So you make $10,200. You return the $5,000 to the broker, and your account also has the original $5,000 that you received in payment for the stock. Your profit from the deal is $200. In short, you've turned a deal that would have given you 2% into a deal that gave you 4% instead, since you were able to enter into the trade using far less of your own money than would have been required to buy 100 shares of stock. Traders use this technique all of the time, and it's fairly common in swing trading. But you have to remind yourself that not all trades are winners. Let's say that the stock drops to $98 a share instead, and you have a stop-loss order at $98.50. So the shares sell for $9,850 and you still have to return $5,000 to the broker.

That leaves you with $4,850 in your account, since you have to take the loss. Now your total buying power has been reduced from $10,000 to $9,700. It's not the end of the world, but it shows the importance of using stop-loss orders.

## Conservative Trading vs. Aggressive Trading

In financial markets there is a direct relationship between level of risk and possibility of reward. There is also the possibility of being a reasonable trader and being a reckless trader. It's possible to do trading and be conservative. In that case, you will be very careful about entering your trades, and do a large amount of analysis before taking a position. You will also have conservative stop-loss and take-profit orders in place. A conservative trader is going to go with the standard recommendation of a 1% risk. That means he or she will only risk 1% of their account on any given trade. This can result in very conservative downsides on any trade. That is, depending on the size of the trade, the conservative trader will only let the stock drop 25 cents or 50 cents a share, and then the stop-loss order will be executed. This will save the trader from significant losses, but as you know stock will often drop by a fairly significant amount only to rebound to new highs. Not every decline in share price is long-lasting, even beyond a 5 minute trading session. As a result, a conservative trader is going to end up missing out on a large number of profitable moves. So if they have purchased shares of Apple at $187.25, and they have a stop-loss order at $187 a share, consider what happens if Apple drops to $186.50, but then climbs to $193 a share. The conservative trader will have missed a very significant upside in their pursuit of safety.

Being a conservative trader often means opting for safety at the expense of large rewards. Conservative traders are also likely to have take profit orders in place that ensure that they can exit a trade profitably, but again, it will be another missed opportunity on the upside.

Aggressive trading makes the same trade-offs, but in the opposite direction. An aggressive trader is going to be more willing to take risks. Hopefully the aggressive trader is also a disciplined trader, so that they will use tools like stop-loss orders to prevent catastrophic loss. But by being more liberal in their application of such tools, they are often going to end up reaping rewards that the conservative trader misses. In that same trade for Apple we described above, the aggressive trader would stay with the trade and take the profits. But this cuts both ways. If there was a catastrophic loss, the aggressive trader will end up taking much larger losses than the conservative trader.

So which trader are you? Answering this question is something you will have to wrestle with, and often you really won't know until you're actually trading. There is nothing like the emotions you experience when real money is on the line. No matter what you think now, you'll find out in a real situation which type of trader you are. It may be important to adjust, if you find that you are not getting the results you are seeking. For example, are you too willing to take risks? If you keep finding yourself on the end of losing trades when you held on too long or bought too many shares (more than you can afford), then maybe you need to step back and work on becoming more conservative.

There are downsides to being too conservative as well. If you find that you're doing well as far as estimating the right positions to be in, but making very little profits even though you are winning the trades, then you might be too conservative. A clue of this is going to be when you find that you're taking profits but you keep missing out on large upsides.

The worst type of trader is the emotional trader. It's difficult to do, but you need to work at keeping your emotions out of trading. This is really important for beginners. When it seems that you might lose a large amount of money on a trade, you will panic and exit your positions early if you are an emotional trader. If you hold onto your positions so long that you end up losing after the stock has made a major shift upward in price, then you're being too greedy and this is another symptom of being an emotional trader. Getting over being an emotional trader is something that takes experience. One therapeutic way to do it is to make small trades until you get comfortable with trading in general. But the best thing to do is plan out everything ahead of time. Know what your limits are, use stop-loss orders to prevent catastrophe, and use take profit orders (that is limit orders to sell at a profitable price) to exit your trades. Under those conditions, you don't even have to follow the trade, you can just let it go through to completion and work out the way it's going to work out. That of course, is something that is hard for many traders to do, especially if you are just getting started.

# Chapter 11
# Trading Exchange Traded Fund

Exchange traded funds represent an opportunity for the trader. This happens in two ways. The first is that exchange traded funds enable the trader to follow leading stock market indices. In case you haven't noticed, the daily fluctuations of the Dow Jones Industrial average and the S & P 500 take up a regular spot on the news. These fluctuations in price, along with the overall trends of these indexes and others, represent an exciting opportunity for swing traders and position traders. There are many other indices that can be incorporated into this strategy, including tracking small cap stocks, the entire market, and many others.

Exchange traded funds offer a second opportunity for the trader, the ability to trade swings on a diversified set of financial assets including U.S. Treasuries, municipal bonds, real estate, and precious metals, among other things. Simply put, exchange traded funds provide a mechanism by which the trader can gain exposure to every kind of financial asset there is (except cryptocurrency, at the time of writing) via the stock market.

## What is an exchange traded fund?

Exchange traded funds grew out of the concept of mutual funds in the early 1990s. Basically, mutual funds created a way for investors to get diversified exposure to the market without being a big player. However, mutual funds suffer from many drawbacks, the least of which is high costs due to the professional management the funds require. While there are no-load mutual funds today, they are still far more expensive and cumbersome than exchange traded funds. Mutual funds are only traded once per day, after stock market close.

The invention of exchange traded funds sought to keep the benefits of mutual funds (massively diversified exposure), but get rid of the downsides. Exchange traded funds are passively managed and have far lower expenses than mutual funds. As the name implies, they are traded as stocks on exchanges. Therefore you can buy and sell them at any time the markets are open, and so take advantage of price swings.

## SPY: The Granddaddy of them all

SPY is one of the most popular exchange traded funds, and with good reason. This fund tracks the S & P 500 and is one of the most widely traded funds on the market. By following this stock, you can literally swing trade the S & P 500 index, and take advantage of price swings that impact the market as a whole.

Another option closely related to SPY is DIA, which tracks the Dow Jones Industrial average. Which fund you trade is a matter of taste, but it's possible to trade both funds. In either case, these funds give you an opportunity to profit from the price swings that frequently occur following major news events, whether it's political news or simply the release of economic reports.

## Sector trading

It's possible to find exchange traded funds that track virtually everything, which is part of what makes them so fun. And one very useful characteristic of exchange traded funds is the ability they give the trader to get involved in trading different sectors. This can help you keep your trades diversified. You can trade sectors like healthcare, real estate, or energy/utilities. The possibilities are literally endless. Many financial advisors recommend sector rotating, so that you can take advantage of the price movements that occur in different sectors but not in others. Think about the 2008 financial crisis, for example. The banking, auto, and real estate sectors suffered mighty blows. And you can look at those from another perspective, that they provided opportunities to short stock.

## What makes an ETF a good candidate?

The first factor that makes an ETF a good candidate to swing trade is high volume. You want to make sure there is a lot of action surrounding the ETF, and that you are going to be able to enter and exit your trades in a timely fashion. Liquidity is always vitally important for a swing trader (position traders may be able to get by with less liquidity, since they are not as time pressured with their trades). In any case, you don't want to be stuck in a position that you need to get out of quickly.

For example, you might be interested in trading a precious metal like gold. The SPDR Long Dollar Gold Trust has a decent share price at $141.76. But it's got low volatility and low volume. The average volume is only 1,625.47. That is quite low. Let's compare that to GLD, another gold related exchange traded fund. The average volume for this one is 7.8 million – an orders of magnitude difference. As you might imagine, it's going to be a lot easier to get out of a position while trading GLD than it is trading the Long Dollar Gold Trust.

For comparison, the volume for Facebook is 22.74 M.

Volatility is another consideration when trading exchange traded funds. It's not necessary to trade a highly volatile stock. There are certain conditions when the volatility isn't all that important, for example if it's a steadily uptrending stock, that can make is a suitable candidate for a bullish investor. All other things being equal, however, a more volatile stock is preferable. That will ensure that you actually get the kind of price movements that lead to profits while trading.

To measure volatility, you really can't get an absolute answer. What you can do is compare the volatility of one stock to another. In fact stocks are given a volatility score called beta that compares the volatility of each stock to the volatility of the market as a whole. If beta = 1.0, this indicates that the stock has average volatility. If beta is less than 1.0, it's a low volatility stock. The relationship is quite straightforward. So if beta is 0.75, that means it's 25% less volatile than the stock market. If beta is 0.6, it's 40% less volatile than the stock market, and so on.
If beta is larger than 1.0, this is a stock that is more volatile than average. In general, these are the stocks or funds that you want to seek out to trade. If beta is 1.25, that means its 25% more volatile than the market, on average.

Of course a stock may not be that volatile and still have some mighty price swings. SPY is a good example of this. SPY has large price swings and has generally followed the upward trend of the overall market since the last recession. The volume is an astounding 85 million shares, but beta is just 1.05. Even so, remember that is average behavior. Every jobs report that comes out, every GDP growth report, and any major news item, can send SPY to new heights or cause it to crash down. Looking at a recent chart of SPY, you can see that you have plenty of swings and trend to work with. The high volume means it will be easy to enter and exit trades. Another good ETF to consider is QQQ, which tracks the NASDAQ 100.

For any given index or sector, there are a wide variety of ETFs. You should carefully study each ETF to determine which one meets your trading needs. The primary difference between them is the weighting given to different companies on the index. For example, we could create two funds to track fast food stocks. One fund could buy 100 shares of McDonalds, 50 shares of Burger King, 25 Shares of Wendys, 25 shares of Taco Bell, and 25 shares of KFC. Another fund could track the same companies, but with completely different weights. Instead it would buy 100 shares of Taco Bell, 25 shares of McDonalds, 25 shares of Burger King, 100 shares of KFC, and 100 shares of Chik-FilA. The different weighting used can mean different levels of performance and different levels of volatility for each fund. They may also have different share prices, even though they are tracking the same index.

Small bid-ask spreads can be important for a trader, and you are going to find that lots of exchange traded funds fit the bill as far as this is concerned. High volume ETFs like SPY are definitely in this category. A small bid-ask spread is an advantage for a trader, because it means you can sell your positions quickly or buy at a price that you want relatively quickly.

## Other Financial Assets

ETFs offer an opportunity for swing traders to gain exposure to other financial assets without having to do anything other than stock trading. The possibilities include commodities, real estate, bonds, and Forex. There are multiple ETFs for each one of these categories as well as several others. You can simply study each fund and use the same tools we've been teaching you in this book in order to determine which trades you want to make. So you can utilize stock analysis to trade funds that track currencies, without having to learn the ins and outs of the Forex market and all the specialty knowledge required to actually trade Forex. The same approach can be used for bonds of different types.

## Seasonal Trends

Exchange traded funds make it easy to swing trade with seasonal trends by sector or for specific assets. Many sectors or assets are more active during specific seasons or time of year as compared to others. By using exchange traded funds, you can trade them as stocks and have diverse exposure. Examples of this are farm products like soy, corn, and wheat. There are exchange traded funds that invest in futures markets. You can trade these funds on the stock market. Two examples of this include JJG and GRU, which track grains futures. As you can see from the chart, these types of exchange traded funds offer opportunities for trend trading.

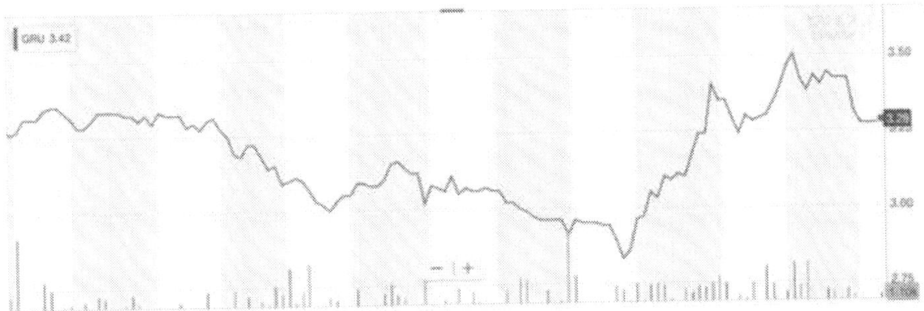

## Find something you like

Exchange traded funds have something for everyone. So you can select funds that you are interested in and excited about to trade. Trading them is exactly like trading stocks.

# Chapter 12
# What kind of Trader are you?

Trading is a field that is exciting and also diverse. Deciding what kind of trader you'd like to be is an important question. You should largely settle on it before you start trading, because mastering your "trade" is going to be something that will have a large influence on your profits. You are less likely to be successful if you are indecisive and playing around with different things without becoming a master of any of them. Focus is much better. Remember that when trading your hard earned money is on the line. So even if you keep your day job, this is not a game or a hobby, it's a real business. And I am sure you wouldn't try starting and running a business on an ad hoc basis, or trying launching a restaurant, hardware store, and home cleaning business at the same time. In the same way, you should decide whether you want to be a day trader, a swing trader, a position trader, or an options trader. Then go from there, and master whatever you choose. Trying to focus on too many alternatives means spreading yourself thin; and it's likely to lead to losses, or at best sketchy and minimal profits.

Let's review some basic considerations, with the idea in mind of matching your own personality with each trading style/type.

## Day Trading

Day trading is definitely a trading style for action-oriented individuals who can focus 100% of their attention. You are also going to need to be at your computer 2-4 hours per day during day time trading hours, so it's a full-time commitment and not something you're likely going to be pursuing as a hobby. Day trading uses the tools of technical analysis extensively. You will spend hours each day doing research on stocks to trade. You'll also spend a great deal of time researching and observing, in order to decide the best point where you should enter your positions. Once you've entered a position, you're going to have to stay glued to your computer. Because of the way day traders stick to highly volatile stocks because they need to earn profits within a single trading day, you're going to have to keep a close eye on what's going on. Your exit point is going to have to be precise. It's a high stress style of trading that is high risk, with the possibility of losing thousands of dollars in a couple of hours. If you are risk averse when it comes to money, being a day trader is probably not your cup of tea.

To be a day trader, you also need to have a lot of capital on hand as we mentioned in the firs chapter. That means $25,000 in your account in the United States. Don't risk the $25,000 if you can't afford to lose it.

## Swing Trading

If you are not quite cut out for day trading but like the idea of profiting off price movements and doing some technical analysis, swing trading is probably more your style. Swing traders still use all the tools described in the book. But as we mentioned in the introduction, a swing trader holds positions for days or weeks. That makes it lower pressure, although pressure can get high if you can't wind down a position profitably. While you'll be using technical analysis, it's not going to be to the same level of "live or die" in the moment. Swing trading is a much more relaxed lifestyle. You can do it on a part-time basis, and you can trade large caps and index funds which are generally avoided by day traders. Swing trading represents a good middle ground, and it's a good alternative for those who don't want the high pressure, or who would like to trade on a part-time basis. As we mentioned in the introduction, swing trading doesn't have capital requirements.

## Position Trading

Position trading is really just swing trading on a longer time frame. Position traders don't trade very frequently, and they are looking for long term price swings or even price appreciation. The time frames are from months to even 1-2 years. Unlike long-term investors, position traders aren't looking to hold positions for the long haul. Position trading can fit naturally into a swing trading business. Alternatively, it's something that can be used in conjunction with traditional buy and hold investing for the long-term. More fundamental analysis is needed when doing position trading, but otherwise there is no specialized knowledge used, and therefore it would be similar to swing trading, just over a longer time scale.

## Options Trading

The beauty of options trading is that a trader can get started for a few hundred dollars. If you are disciplined, that is you can avoid trading on a large scale until you know what you are doing from some experience, you can build up profits slowly over time. And when you have losses, they are going to be limited to a couple of hundred dollars or less. Keep in mind that options trading do require lots of specialized knowledge. So while you could in theory do it in conjunction with other types of trading, it's not recommended. Instead, if options trading appeals to you, then you should devote all of your attention to it. That is, other than any long-term investing in stocks that you have on the side. We don't advise trying to swing trade and options trade at the same time. Become a master of the one that appeals to you more and ride it to maximum profits.

## Minimizing Risk

No matter what trading style or method you decide to adopt, mitigating risk is an important part of any trading business. Mitigating risk means that you never risk more than you can afford to lose. It also means that you have defined points where you take profits and exit trades. Let's look at each of these in turn.

The standard recommendation is that you can risk 1-2% of your account on a trade. That means if you can afford to lose $500 on a single trade, then if you are willing to lose $1 a share, you can buy 100 shares of stock. In order to get the amount you can afford to lose from a single trade, you simply calculate 1-2% of the total value of the cash in your account. Certainly you should not put your life savings on the line trading stocks. It's quite possible that over time you'll find them evaporating into nothing. You can decide as a percentage what you are able to risk. You can stick to 1-2% or if you are comfortable going higher, that is your business. However, you should probably not go above 3% as a beginning trader. Whatever rule you choose, you should stick by. It's important to stick by rules and not "adjust" them when you find yourself in a desperate situation.

Begin by taking the amount in your account and multiplying it by the percentage you can afford to lose. Let's say we have an $8,000 account, and we are willing to risk 2%. That means the gross amount we can risk on a single trade is $240.

When we enter a trade, we use this figure to determine how many share we are going to buy. The next step is to determine how much we are willing to lose on a single trade. If the stock is highly volatile, you may not want to exit the position at the drop of a pin. The stock might drop down and rally, so we wouldn't want to miss that. So the amount you are willing to lose per share on a given trade is something that is going to be situational. On one trade, you might only risk $0.50, while on another you might be willing to risk $2 per share. Some traders will decide to standardize and risk the same amount on all trades. The amount you can risk (that is the percentage of your account) is divided by the amount you are willing to risk per share. So if we can risk $240, and we are willing to risk $0.50 per share, we can buy $240/$0.50 = 480 shares.

The amount you are willing to risk per share is not something to keep in mind. It's something you are going to immediately enforce after buying the stock. This will be done by submitting a good until cancel limit order after you buy the stock – in order to sell it. If a stock is trading at $50 a share when you purchase it, then if you've determined your loss per share that you are comfortable with is $1 per share, then you'll enter a limit order to sell with a $49 per share limit price. So it won't be executed unless the stock price drops to $49 or lower per share.

With a limit order in place (called a stop loss order in this context), you don't have to sit in front of your computer all hours of the day hoping to prevent a catastrophic loss. You've defined how much you are willing to lose. So you should be able to relax knowing how things are setup, and take it as fate if the situation arises where the shares are sold at a loss. In that case you can take note of what happened and hopefully learn from your mistakes to do better next time.

We can also enforce discipline by using the same method with take profit orders. In this case, you enter a good until canceled buy order, and set the price to the one you are willing to accept. So this is another limit order submitted with your broker soon after you've purchased the stock.

If you do nothing but implement these rules, you are well on your way to becoming a successful trader.

## Trader Mindset

The trader mindset that is one that will correlate with success has many characteristics. However, rather than trying to list them all, let's list the flaws that you need to get rid of to have the mindset of a successful trader.

First off, always keep in mind that trading is not a get rich quick scheme. Yes, it's possible to get rich quick trading. However, it's not likely to happen to very many people. And most people don't become rich, quick or otherwise. Treat trading like a real business and work on building up small profits over time.

Being ruled by emotion is a negative characteristic that traders can have. Unfortunately you may not realize you're ruled by emotion until you become a trader. You might not have had the kind of financial pressure put on you that trading capable of doing. It's only when you're under pressure that you can see how you react. For example, we mentioned in the last chapter that if you are selling options, you could be assigned if the share price moves the right way. Are you going to panic if that happens? Or can you keep a cool head and think it through? For example, you could recall that while an option could be exercised before the expiration date, they usually aren't exercised unless the options expire in the money. A trader that will give into panic might immediately buy back the position to close. And then they will miss out on profits when the price rises.

Panic isn't the only emotion you have to worry about. Someone with the right trader mindset is not going to be someone who gives into greed, even though that may be the stereotype. Greedy traders can make it big, but most of the time when people let themselves get taken over by greed, they are going to make ill-advised decisions while trading, which is going to lead to losses, not profits. For most people, greed should be left out of their trading business. What happens is you'll get greedy hoping to ride a trend of rising prices as far as the eye can see. But being greedy and overwhelmed by your emotions, you start making bad decisions like staying in positions too long. When that happens, you'll probably end up seeing profits you could have taken disappear in a flash as the stock begins its inevitable rapid downfall.

This brings us to the next trader mindset, which is a trader needs to be disciplined. Don't ever cut corners. Always do your technical analysis, rather than just guessing which stock is going to rise in price. Make sure that you never enter a position without putting in a stop loss order and a limit order to take profits.

Finally, the trader mindset should be one that favors continual learning. Be willing to read books, watch videos, and take courses. Use your common sense, that doesn't mean blowing thousands of dollars paying some guru for tips. But you should be willing to educate yourself to help improve your game.

We also have a bonus – the mindset of the successful trader means you are willing to accept wins and losses with your trades. The goal is profit over time, not profit on every trade. Losses are inevitable, that is a fact of life and even experienced traders are going to lose a lot of the time. Don't lose on a trade or a couple of trades and let yourself get so emotional and frustrated that you quit early.

That does it for our list of the key characteristics that make up the successful trader mindset.

# Conclusion

Thank you for reading my book about trading strategies!

For those who want to take an active role in their investment activities, trading is one option to consider. It's not the same as traditional investing. Trading is aimed at earning profits over the short term. Therefore it's more like a business than investing. Depending on the level of commitment you can give to trading, the amount of money you can risk, and your own personal tolerance for risk, you can chose a trading style that is the best fit for your situation.

Remember that trading is risky. You should never risk more capital in trading than you can afford to lose. By taking some reasonable steps, however, you can protect yourself and your capital from catastrophic losses.

Don't get fooled by early losses. Beginning traders can expect to have some losses and make mistakes along the way. That's inevitable when taking up any new occupation. As long as you are not risking huge amounts of money on one single trade, you should be able to dust yourself off and get up and try again. Some people will find it to be too much to deal with but my hope is that you will learn from your failures and do better next time, and build yourself into a successful trader with time.

I hope that you have found the book interesting and informative. I also hope that you have found it exciting. Remember that trading is a fun and exciting world to be in. You can directly participate in the world of free market capitalism by becoming a stock trader. It's also flexible, you can start a full-time business doing it, or have a part-time operation you do from home. No matter what, if you approach trading as a business and take it seriously, you'll be able to substantially grow your income.

My hope is this book has communicated the exciting world of trading to you and that we've given you a solid foundation upon which you can build in your trading education.

# Options Trading

## *A Simplified Guide for Beginners with Secrets Strategies to Make Profit Fast! Basics and Tips on How to Trade Options for a Quick Start to your Financial Freedom.*

*William L. Anderson*

# Table of Contents

# Introduction

Congratulations on downloading *Options Trading 1* and thank you for doing so.

Books about the subject flood the market; we thank you for personally picking this one! Efforts were made to make sure all information here is useful. Please enjoy!

Are you eager to jump into the world of investments? Perhaps, you've heard of the benefits and million dollars stories in this seemingly magical world of investments. Slow down, as you risk losing your life's investment in an unfamiliar market. For so many new investors, the world of stocks might look like legalized gambling. They think of scenarios like this: if your stock goes up - you win! If it goes down - you lose! How? You don't know since it has become a game of luck. With this type of mentality, the stock market more or less becomes a game of roulette. However, the more you understand the true nature of stocks, the better you will manage your money.

Therefore, in this chapter, you will learn the basic and common terminologies used in the stock market, the reason why companies sell shares, an in-depth analysis of the mechanics of the stock market, and how to recognize a bearish or bullish market. So, let's start with the basic terminologies you will come across while trading in the stock market.

# Basic Terminologies Used In the Stock Market

## *Shares*

In the financial market, shares are a unit of capital that depicts the ownership relationship between the shareholder and the company. In such transactions, investors buy or sell shares through a stockbroker who acts as the middleman. The market value of the shares you buy is determined by the performance of the company and other economic factors such as wars, elections, and new economic policies. In addition to this, dividends are the income you earn from shares.

## *Bonds*

Bonds are an interesting alternative to dividend investments. Bonds are defined as fixed income structures that represent a loan made by an individual investor to a borrower. Most times, the borrower is the government or a corporation. Fixed or variable interests rates are attached to these loans, and the end date is fixed for the payment of the principal to the bond owners. Some investors prefer bonds since they are seen as safe, and can be easily traded with other investors or brokers. Companies or other entities issue bonds to investors when they need to raise money for a new project or re-finance existing debt. They issue bonds that contain the terms and conditions, the time at which the loan (principal) must be paid back, and the interest rates that will be paid. The interest rate is a fixed income that bond owners earn for buying bonds. You should know that the face value or value of bonds differs. In addition to this, you don't have to wait for the bond to expire before you can sell it off.

## *Equity*

In the financial market, the term equity has various definitions. Generally, these definitions revolve around the concept that equity is the difference between the value of assets and liabilities. You can think of equity as the degree of ownership in any asset, once we subtract the cost of the debt associated with it. Here's an example to simplify this term. Imagine you had a car that was worth $15,000, but you owed $5,000 worth of debt against the car. In this case, your equity for the car (asset) was $10,000. Furthermore, equity becomes negative when the cost of liabilities exceeds assets. In terms of shareholder equity or capital, this represents the total number of assets subtracted from liabilities, as divided between shareholders.

## *Shareholder*

You become a shareholder when you own shares of stock in a corporation. Shareholders are the owners of a company since each share of stock they possess entitles them to have a say in the way a corporation operates. However, just because you are a shareholder doesn't mean you can barge in and start firing workers. There are laws in place that protect the company from such actions. Shareholders have the power to elect a board of directors to make major decisions in the company, such as the number of shares to be sold to the public. Besides this, some long-standing corporations pay out dividends to their shareholders.

## *Initial Public Offering (IPO)*

This is a term used to describe the process of a company selling its share of stocks on the stock market for the first time. This is when you hear terms like: "the company is going public". In IPOs, the company's shares are sold to institutional or retail investors, who later sell the investors to others via brokers

[WU1]. Investment banks who act as underwriters calculate and establish the value of the company's share, and a detailed overview of the public offering is given to initial investors in the form of a lengthy document known as a prospectus.

## *Earnings per Share*

This is the total profit of the company divided by the number of shares. This is an important factor you must consider before investing in a company. Each part of a company's shares can be likened to pieces of a pie. The larger your share in the corporation, the bigger your pie slices. To know the earnings per share, the investors calculate how much income after-tax each share will receive. Therefore, if a company generates more and more profits annually, but only a little profit makes its way to the shareholders on a per-share basis, then it is considered a terrible investment.

## *Ticker Symbol*

Ticker symbols are used to represent corporations listed on the stock market. They are usually a short group of letters. For instance, Johnson & Johnson has a ticker symbol of JNJ and Coca-Cola has a ticker symbol of KO.

## *Book Value*

This is the total asset of a company that's useful to shareholders. It determines what a shareholder will get in case of liquidation. The book value of a company is calculated as the total asset of a company, excluding the liabilities and intangible assets like patents. Investors can use a corporation's book value to gauge if their stocks are overpriced or undervalued.

### *Corporations*

Here's a term that you will come across countless times in this book - corporations are different from businesses. How? Well, any business that sells shares of stocks to investors needs to first become a corporation. A business must undergo a legal process known as incorporation before it becomes a corporation. It's important to understand that a corporation is different from a sole proprietorship or partnership. In fact, it is a virtual person in the eyes of the law. It is registered with the government and has a federal tax number. More so, a corporation can sue, make contracts, and own properties. There are certain laws put in place to ensure uniformity in the way a corporation operates, and how the public and shareholders are protected. For instance, it is compulsory for every corporation to have a board of directors. The shareholders hold yearly meetings to decide who gets to sit on the board. Shareholders also use corporations as shields against liquidity in case the corporation goes bankrupt.

## What Are Stocks?

Also referred to as equities, stocks are issued by companies in a bid to raise capital in order to expand their business operations or take on new projects. To shareholders, stocks represent a claim of ownership on the company's assets or earnings. Your ownership stake becomes higher as you acquire more stocks. You should know, however, that owning stocks does not give you control over the properties of the corporation, as it is protected under laws of ownership. Now that we've got that out of the way, let's take an in-depth look at the different types of stocks companies issue to investors.

## Types of Stocks

Companies issue two main types of stocks that get listed on the stock market to their investors. It is important to know the type of stock that you are dealing with since each type of stock comes with its own benefits and setbacks. So, let's get right to it!

## Common Stocks

When you hear people talking about stocks, it's very likely that they are referring to common stocks. In fact, common stocks make up a large percentage of the total number of stocks traded on the stock market. A common stock confers voting rights on investors and gives them a client on profits or dividends [WU2]. With common stocks, investors often get one vote per share to elect a board of directors to oversee operations. What's more, these types of stocks come with higher returns than corporate bonds. However, this high return comes with many risks. If a company goes out of business, you stand to lose your entire life's investment (one of the reasons why you need to diversify). If a company goes out of business (bankrupt) and liquidates, common shareholders will not receive their money until bondholders, preferred stockholders, and creditors have been paid.

## Preferred Stocks

Preferred stocks have a similar bill function to bonds, and don't usually come with voting rights. Sometimes, some companies offer voting rights with their preferred stocks. With preferred stocks, investors will get a fixed income in the form of dividends. The dividends are guaranteed, unlike common stocks which have variable dividends that are never guaranteed. In fact, many companies don't pay out dividends to common stockholders. Also, in the case of liquidation, preferred shareholders are paid first, before common shareholders. The company settles creditors and bondholders before getting to preferred stockholders.

What's more? Companies can buy back preferred stocks from shareholders at any time. Therefore, you can consider preferred stocks as a blend of the features of bonds and common stocks. Aside from common stocks and preferred stocks, companies can also create classes of shares in a bid to fit the needs of investors. Companies create classes of stocks when they want to keep power concentrated in a certain group of shareholders.

## Why Do Companies Sell Shares?

After examining the core terminologies used in the stock market, it is time to take a look at why companies sell their shares, how stocks are issued, and the role of investors in creating a relationship that will benefit both parties. I'm not going to bore you with a vague or uninteresting description. Instead, we will paint a scenario that you can relate to. So, let's use a pizzeria as our case study.

Will has a pizza business with annual earnings of $350,000. His total after-tax profit is $100,000 per year, which is quite a fair amount. However, Will wants more. He wants to expand his business to a neighboring town, which has more potential and a higher population. So, how does he go about this? First, he calculates the cost of building a new pizzeria. The land and equipment required for the new pizzeria will cost up to $500, 000 upfront. Then, he has to consider the cost of staff, ingredients for the products, and a delivery vehicle to ensure smooth operation. Right now, Will is looking at a sum of $750,000 to cover all his expenses. He is faced with two options; either getting a loan or going public to get funds from investors like you. On the one hand, he has to consider the interest that comes with loans, and how he could lose everything if he defaults. In addition to this, banks don't always lend money to companies, especially small businesses. Therefore, he makes the decision to give up a percentage of his own control in order to raise cash for his dream. Will invites an underwriter from an investment bank such as JP Morgan or Goldman Sachs to evaluate his total asset, and to set the price for his stocks. As mentioned before, Will's Pizza shop earns $100,000 after-tax profit each year. The company also has a book value of $4 million. Then, the underwriter carries out research and finds out that the average pizza company on the stock market trades for 25 times its company's earnings. Therefore, the underwriter will multiply the company's earnings of $100,000 by 25 and add the book value to the result. This means Will's pizza shop is worth $6.5 million.

Will can decide to sell a certain percentage of his stocks to investors in order to meet his financial target. If he sells 40 percent of his company to the public as stock, this means he gets to keep $3.9 million worth of the business. The underwriters search for investors that will buy the stock, and will ultimately offer Will a check of $2.6 million. With a huge income from sold shares, Will can build not just one but two pizzerias anywhere he wants. On the other hand, investors should expect a minimum profit of at least 10 percent of their investment - it's a win-win for both parties!

This is a scenario that depicts the mutual relationship between shareholders and corporations. Now that we have got that out of the way, let's delve into the basics of the stock market and how to understand its technicalities.

## What Is The Stock Market?

The stock market is not like your neighborhood grocery store: you can only buy and sell through licensed brokers who make trades on major indexes like NASDAQ and S&P 100. This is where investors meet up to buy and sell stocks or other financial investments like bonds. The stock market is made up of so many exchanges, like the NASDAQ or the New York Exchange. These exchanges are not open all through the day. Most exchanges like the NASDAQ and NYSE are open from 9:30 am to 4 pm. EST. Although premarket and trading after closing time now exist, not all brokers do this.

Companies list their stocks on an exchange in a bid to raise money for their business, and investors buy those shares. In addition to this, investors can trade shares among themselves, and the exchange keeps track of the rate of supply and demand of each listed stock. The rate of supply and demand for stocks determines the price. If there's a high demand for a particular stock, its price tends to rise. On the other hand, the price of a stock goes down when there's less demand for it. The stock market computer algorithm handles these varying fluctuations in prices.

# Chapter 1
# Options Trading and the Individual Investor

This chapter looks at the setups for profitable trades - to get a rough overview and to see where the market is in general development. Then we turn to the technical tools to find an entry point, stop-fall protection, if you're wrong, and the likely candidates for the price moves. As in the real estate business, trading is the most important factor: the location, the location, the location. Then there is the timing, the timing, the timing. The setup gives you a rough overview of the market's current state of development - key information when looking for short-term reversal or confirmation patterns. Ideally, you open your position in the area where the likelihood of success is greatest.

## How Does The Stock Market Work?

A Stock market analysis definitely looks like gibberish to beginners and average investors. However, you should know that the way this market works is actually quite simple. Just imagine a typical auction house or an online auction website. This market works in the same way - it allows buyers and sellers to negotiate prices and carry out successful trades. The first stock market took place in a physical marketplace, however, these days, trades happen electronically via the internet and online stockbrokers. From the comfort of your homes, you can easily bid and negotiate for the prices of stocks with online stockbrokers.

Furthermore, you might come across news headlines that say the stock market has crashed or gone up. Once again, don't fret or get all excited when you come across such news. Most often than not, this means a stock market index has gone up or down. In other words, the stocks in a market index have gone down. Before we proceed, let's explore the meaning of market indexes.

## Stock Market Indexes

As mentioned earlier, when people refer to the rise and fall of the stock market, they are generally referring to one of the major stock market's market indexes. Market indexes track the performance of a group of stocks in a particular sector like manufacturing or technology. The value of the stocks featured in an index is representative of all the stocks in that sector. It is very important to take note of what stocks each market index represents. As mentioned in the first chapter, you should invest in a niche you are comfortable with. In addition to this, giant market indexes like the Dow Jones Industrial Average, the NASDAQ composite, and the Standard & Poor's 500, are often used as proxies for the performance of the stock market as a whole. You can choose to invest in an entire index through the exchange-traded funds and index funds, as it can track a specific sector or index of the stock market.

Bullish and Bearish Markets

Talking about the bullish outlook of the stock market is guaranteed to get beginners looking astonished. Yes, it sounds ridiculous at first, but with time, you get to appreciate the ingenuity of these descriptions. Let's start with the bearish market. A bear is an animal you would never want to meet on a hike; it strikes fear into your heart, and that's the effect you will get from a bearish market. A bear market depicts when stock prices are falling across several of the indexes mentioned earlier. The threshold for a bearish market varies within a 20 percent loss or more.

Most young investors unfamiliar with a bear market as we've been in a bull market since the first quarter of 2019. In fact, this makes it the second-longest bull market in history. Just as you have probably guessed by now, a bull market indicates that stock prices are rising. You should know that the market is continually changing from bull to bear and vice versa. From the Great Recession to the global market crash, these changing market prices indicate the start of larger economic patterns. For instance, a bull market shows that investors are investing heavily and that the economy is doing extremely well. On the other hand, a bear market shows investors are scared and pulling back, with the economy on the brink of collapsing. If this made you paranoid about the next bear market, don't fret. Business analysts have shown that the average bull market generally outlasts the average bear market by a large margin. This is why you can grow your money in stocks over an extended period of time.

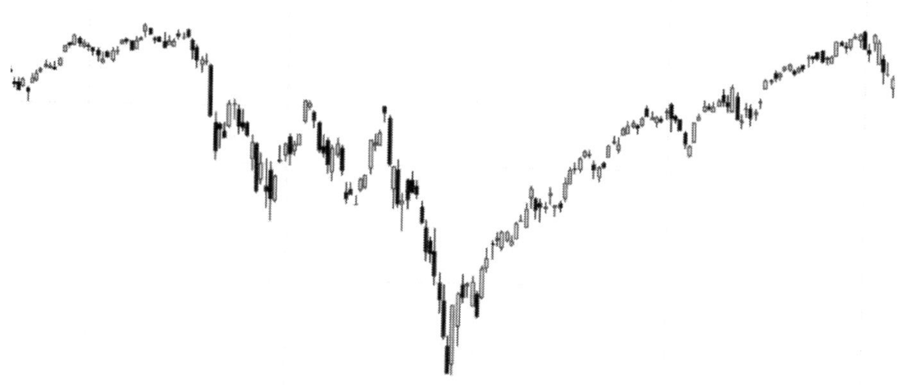

## Stock Market Corrections and Crash

A stock market crash is every investor's nightmare. It is usually extremely difficult to watch stocks that you've spent so many years accumulating diminish before your very eyes. Yes, this is how volatile the stock market is. Stock market crashes usually include a very sudden and sharp drop in stock prices, and it might herald the beginning of a bear market. On the other hand, stock market corrections occur when the market drops by 10 percent - this is just the market's way of balancing itself. The current bull market has gone through 5 market corrections.

## Analyzing the Stock Market

You are not psychic. It is nearly impossible to accurately predict the outcome of your stock to the last detail. However, you can become near perfect at reading the stock market by learning how to properly analyze the components of this market. There are two basic types of analyses: technical analysis and fundamental analysis.

## Fundamental Market Analysis

Fundamental analysis involves getting data about a company's stocks or a particular sector in the stock market, via financial records, company assets, economic reports, and market share. Analysts and investors can conduct fundamental analysis via the metrics on a corporation's financial statement. These metrics include cash flow statements, balance sheet statements, footnotes, and income statements. Most times, you can get a company's financial statement through a 10-k report in the database. In addition to this, the SEC's EDGAR is a good place to get the financial statement of the company you are interested in. With the financial statement, you can deduce the revenues, expenses, and profits a company has made.

What's more? By looking at the financial statement, you will have a measure of a company's growth trajectory, leverage, liquidity, and solvency. Analysts utilize different ratios to make an accurate prediction about stocks. For example, the quick ratio and current ratio are useful in determining if a company will be able to pay its short-term liabilities with the current asset. If the current ratio is less than 1, the company is in poor financial health and may not be able to recover from its short-term debt. Here's another example: a stock analyst can use the debt ratio to measure the current level of debt taken on by the company. If the debt ratio is above 1, it means the company has more debt than assets and it's only a matter of time before it goes under.

## Technical Market Analysis

This is the second part of stock market analysis and it revolves around studying past market actions to predict the stock price direction. Technical analysts put more focus on the price and volume of shares. Additionally, they analyze the market as a whole and study the supply and demand factors that dictate market movement. In technical analyses, charts are of inestimable value. Charts are a vital tool as they show the graphical representation of a stock's trend within a set time frame. What's more? Technical investors are able to identify and mark certain areas as resistance or support levels on a chart. The resistance level is a previous high stock price before the current price. On the other hand, support levels are represented by a previous low before the current stock price. Therefore, a break below the support levels marks the beginning of a bearish trend. Alternatively, a break above the resistance level marks the beginning of a bullish market trend. Technical analysis is only effective when the rise and fall of stock prices are influenced by supply and demand forces. However, technical analysis is mostly rendered ineffective in the face of outside forces that affect stock prices such as stock splits, dividend announcements, scandals, changes in management, mergers, and so on. Investors can make use of both types of analyses to get an accurate prediction of their stock values.

## Why You Need To Diversify

According to research by Ned Davis, a bear market occurs every 3.5 years and has an average lifespan of 15 months. One thing is clear, though: you can't avoid bear markets. You can, however, avoid the risks that come with investing in a single investment portfolio. Let's look at a common mistake that new investors typically make. Research points to the fact that individual stocks dwindle to a loss of 100 percent. By throwing in your lot with one company, you are exposing yourself to many setbacks. For example, you can lose your money if a corporation is embroiled in a scandal, poor leadership, and regulatory issues. So, how can you balance out your losses? By investing in the aforementioned index fund or ETF fund, as these indexes hold many different stocks, as by doing this, you've automatically diversified your investment. Here's a nugget to cherish: put 90 percent of your investment funds in an index fund, and put the remaining 10 percent in an individual stock that you trust.

## When to Sell Your Stocks

One thing is sure - you are not going to hold your stocks forever. All our investment advice and energies are directed towards buying. Yes, it is the buying of stocks that kick-start the whole investment when chasing your dream concept. However, just as every beginning has an end, you will eventually sell every stock you buy. It is the natural order. Even so, selling off stock is not an easy decision. Heck! It's even harder to determine the right time to sell. This is the point where greed and human emotions start to battle with pragmatism. Many investors try to make sensible selling decisions solely based on price movements. However, this is not a sure strategy, as it is still sensible to hold onto a stock that has fallen in value. Conversely, selling a stock when it has reached your target is seen as prudent. So, how can you navigate around this dilemma? Before touching on other parts in this section, let's first tackle the reason why selling is so hard.

## Why Selling Is So Hard

Do you know why it's so hard to let go of your stocks even when you have a fixed strategy to follow? The answer lies in human greed. When making decisions, it's an innate human tendency to be greedy. Here's an example: An investor purchases shares at $30, and tells herself that when the stocks hit $40, she will sell. Here comes an all-too-familiar trend - when the stocks finally hit $40, the investor will hold out and see if her stock prices will rise beyond $40. You can see that human nature is already creeping in. Surely, the stocks hit $45, and greed takes over logical thinking. She decides to wait to see if it rises beyond $45. Suddenly, the stock prices plummet down to $36. At this point, she tells herself that once the stocks rise again to $40, she will sell. Unfortunately, this never happens. This stock continues to plummet down to $25. Finally, she succumbs to her frustrations and sells at $25.

From the above example, you can see how greed and irrationality took over her sound investment plan. In this scenario, sound investment plans were replaced with gambling tendencies. Although the investment was a loss at $5 per share, her true loss stands at $20 per share. This is because she had the opportunity to sell at $45 but she held out, hoping for even higher prices. Knowing when to sell is truly a paramount factor. Sometimes, a good selling decision that brings some profits to your table might look like a poor selling decision. However, in this scenario, it's advised to say prudent. To remove human emotions from your decisions, you can consider adding a limit order which automatically locks in your selling decision. The limit order will sell once it reaches your target price.

Wait! Ask Yourself These Questions before Selling Your Shares
You have held out long enough, and you feel it's time to take the big leap. Perhaps, you have seen the haphazard rise and fall of stock prices, and you don't want to be at the short end of the stick. Hold on! Ask yourself these questions before you sell.

## Is The Company Suffering From Any Setback?

These days we have access to a lot more information than we ever had. As you have nonstop access to the internet, it can be extremely difficult not to constantly check market data. However, beware that doing this can make you succumb to emotional triggers, and this might ultimately lead to poor selling decisions. The best thing you can do in this situation is to get some perspective. Compare the company's total revenues to its benchmark and to others in the same sector. This can help you to discern if the slow performance is an indication of falling stock prices or just a random market movement.

## Is Your Portfolio Out Of Balance?

As an ideal investor, you have diversified your investment across various sectors. Over time, some stocks begin to perform better than others in that portfolio, making your investments shift towards the out-performers. Therefore, it is necessary to bring your investments back in line to conform to your fixed asset plan. In this situation, you are faced with two options to even the scales: you either buy more of the stocks that have fallen behind or sell the outperforming stocks.

## Will You Get A Tax Break?

Yes, your investments have reached your target price and you can wait to sell. Before you do, remember that selling a stock that has increased in a tax-prone brokerage account can trigger a tax bill. The rate of the tax depends on whether you have held the investment for more than a year. If you have, you are eligible for a reduced long-term capital tax rate. If not, you will attract higher short-term tax rates.

## Is There A Better Investment For Your Money?

According to billionaire investor and guru, Warren Buffet, the best holding time is forever. However, that's pretty unrealistic for an investor with a finite income. Sometimes, we sell off investments in order to meet up with certain needs such as retirement, college funds, vacations, and anything else that requires capital. Admittedly, it's a wise choice to sell off stocks to meet up with current cash needs and to avoid the volatility of the market. However, I advise not to use your long-term funds for your immediate needs.

## How Will You Make Your Exit?

Once again, you are not psychic. It is nearly impossible to time a perfect sale - you don't know when a stock is at its lowest point or when it's at its highest point. Running to sell off your stocks can save you from losing more, and it also denies you the opportunity to gain additional income if the stock rises. Those are the uncertainties that you have to deal with as an investor. However, there's a trick to selling your shares. You can sell shares at different time periods. If you sell them all at once, you might lose out on additional opportunities. If the stock has good potential, then you should sell part of it and hold on to the rest.

## Becoming a Super Investor

Every day, you come across internet ads and brokers promising to make you a "super" investor. You must come across a few of these adverts every week. It's a pity that many jumps on this bandwagon of investment without learning how to properly navigate the world of stocks. The word, "investor" has been bandied around so many times that it has lost its value. It is therefore not surprising to see some lose their life fortune all in the name of investment. Investing your money allows you to build wealth. More so, it involves putting your money in areas that have the potential to create huge returns. You really deserve to accomplish your dreams. However, if you are still undecided about investing or not, here are a few reasons to get you on board.

## Why You Need To Invest

Here's another question for you: How would you feel on retirement day if your friend or work buddy was sitting on a million-dollar investment, and you weren't? Regret? Pain? Disappointment? Depression? These negative emotions will definitely crop up in the future unless you take the necessary steps against this.

## Save For Retirement

The government retirement funds just aren't enough to meet your future needs. There is plenty of uncertainty surrounding the future, and it is wise to safeguard it. You can invest your retirement savings into investment portfolios, such as bonds, real estate, stocks, and precious metals. So, you can comfortably live off funds earned from investments when it's time to retire. Here's another angle to this: you can earn a continuous income every month or annually by investing your retirement savings in dividend stocks. You can also re-invest income from dividends into more stocks. Wait! Don't let me spill the beans just yet. I will explain all the principles of dividend investments in the next chapter.

## Earn Higher Income

Well, this part is obvious. What's the essence of investing if you can't achieve your financial goals? However, this part is quite tricky as not all stocks are worth investing in. The stock market appreciation can remain stagnant for years. A typical example is the Dow Jones, which remained stagnant for 17 years. The Dow Jones is one of the oldest running US market index. This market index reached 995 in January 1966 and it did not surpass the 995 price level until December 1982. Now, imagine if you had invested in this index. This means your investment portfolio was stagnant for 17 years, with no appreciation at all. Therefore, always invest in stocks that will guarantee a continuous income despite the upheavals of the stock market.

## Reduce Taxable Income

This is a win-win situation. First, you get to invest and at the same time, you reduce your taxable income. By putting part of your pre-tax income into an investment plan, you will save more money. In addition to this, if you incur a loss from an investment, you may apply that loss against any profit from other investments, and this lowers the amount of your taxable income.

## Help Businesses to Grow

No matter how small you invest, your money can make a huge impact on an ailing business. Investing is about more than just gaining profit, it involves backing new ventures with the potential of creating cutting-edge products. Ultimately, you are building a future for yourself and the businesses you invest in.

# How Much Money Should You Invest?

How much should I save and put into my investment portfolio? This question has always been on the lips of new investors. Although it's a straightforward question, its answer has always eluded many. Since there's no clear-cut rule on how much you need to invest, most investors often save or invest lower and this can affect their long-term financial goals. Before we proceed, it is important to know the difference between savings and investments.

## Difference between Savings and Investments

Fact is, many investors don't know that savings and investments are two completely different entities that play different roles, and have different functions. So, before you set out on the journey to building wealth through passive income, you need to understand these concepts.

Savings is the process of storing cold hard cash in an extremely safe yet liquid account. Liquid, in this context, means that it's stored in a place that allows you to easily access your cash within a short time frame. These include savings accounts supported by the FDIC, checking accounts, and treasury bills. Some savings accounts come with interest rates, but these are usually too small to create a passive income. Many investors including those who lived through the Great Depression recommend keeping a store of cold hard cash in case of a meltdown or market crash.

Investments, on the other hand, is the process of using your capital to procure an asset that you think has a good chance of generating an acceptable income during the course of your investment. You are reading this book to learn how to invest due to the promise of a continuous source of income. You should know that there are many factors that threaten your investment, and a single mistake can wipe out part of your investment portfolio, or even worse, wipe it out in its entirety.

Before you embark on a journey of becoming a super investor, it is necessary to save. Think of savings as a foundation upon which you build your financial structures. You should know that your savings are what provide you with the capital for your investments. Those who don't save are likely to sell off their investments in hard times, and this is not a recipe for getting rich. Therefore, as a general rule, you ought to save an amount that's sufficient to cover all your personal expenses, including your mortgage and utility bills for a span of six months.

## Questions to Help You Determine How Much You Want To Invest

First, start by asking yourself these questions, which will help you to arrive at your answer.

How much passive income do I want to earn from my investments? Perhaps you want enough passive income to buy a new house or pay off your mortgage. While trying to arrive at your desired figure, take into account the price of the things you want and the cost of upkeep.

## How Much Tolerance Do I Have?

In other words, how high is your risk tolerance? Can you tolerate watching your investment value move wildly up and down? The quicker you want to reach your target financial goals, the bigger the fluctuation in your investment value. Sometimes, you may have to watch your accounts go up by 50 percent or go down by 70 percent.

## When Do I Need To Access The Money?

This question is vital, especially when you are using tax-deferred accounts like 401[k] or Roth IRA. You can invite heavy penalties and taxes if you withdraw your money from these accounts before the age of 59. Furthermore, you need to calculate the number of years you want to build up your portfolio for in order to increase the compound interest rates.

## Are You Willing To Sacrifice Your Current Standard of Living For Your Dreams?

The Answer

Now, let's look at how we can provide an answer to the main question: how much should you invest? I would say that you already have a fair idea of how you want to live in the future. Perhaps, you have picked your dream house, car, or holiday on an exotic island. Or, you have calculated the sufficient amount for your kids' college fees? Now that you have those images in mind, ask yourself this: how much money do I need to achieve this and live the way I want? Would it take $10,000 per year? Perhaps it would take $150,000. Calculate your total income per year and divide it by 0.4 to discover the assets it would require to back that level of annual income. The next thing you need to figure out is how soon you need the money. Let's say you are 30 and you plan to retire by the age of 60. That gives you 30 years of continuous savings. By increasing the amount you save every month, you effectively reduce the number of years needed to reach your financial target. Mind you, do not take this to the extreme. Money solely exists for you to create opportunities for your loved ones and lead a better lifestyle. Don't overdo it!

## Adopting the Traits of Super Investors

Successful investors have certain traits in common, irrespective of their investment portfolios. Whether you earn a tidy sum every month from invest incomes and dividends, or you are a financial genius with a laudable portfolio of high investment returns, these traits will ensure that you stay afloat the uncertainties of the financial market. So, before you jump on to the notion of becoming an investor, you need to adopt certain traits to survive the financial market.

## Acquire the Right Temperament

Yes, having the right temperament can make a lot of difference in the financial world. Mind you, this has nothing to do with discernment, intelligence or wisdom. It simply means developing the right attitude. For instance, patience is a strong trait you need to develop, as you should understand that some things take time. As I mentioned earlier, investing is not a get-rich-quick scheme. Your investment will not magically turn into a huge sum overnight. Heck, you will hardly see the result of your investment in the first few years.

In addition to exercising patience, learn to stay away from the crowd. Yes, you must be willing to stick to a plan while ignoring the will of the crowd. This brings to mind the 1990's dot.com bubble when some of the world's best investors refused to be swayed by public opinion. These super investors recognized that bubbles don't last. So, you should know that not every stock or asset is worth investing in. Some investors stick to earning dividends, rents, and interest incomes in order to avoid the uncertainties of the stock market.

Lastly, don't get too emotional. In fact, you will hardly reach your financial goal if you are clouded by emotions. Learn to separate market fluctuations from the inherent value of your assets. For example, let's say you bought an apartment building that nets you $100,000 per year in passive income, and someone comes around and offers to buy the building for $200,000 – you would probably laugh in their face since you know the inherent value of the building.

Learn the ropes! There's no shortcut or cheat for this method. It is vital for you to know how to calculate the intrinsic value of your assets, and this includes getting familiar with the terms, regulations, and laws of investment. It doesn't matter if it's a government bond, a share of stock or a car wash business; you will be at a disadvantage if you don't know to pull out a calculator and punch in the figures yourself. Yes, the calculations involved looking daunting or impossible. However, don't lose heart. All you have to do is to continually ask yourself this question - "how much do I have to pay for a dollar of net present earnings?". Your net present earning is the difference between the current value of your cash inflow and the current value of your outflows. By asking yourself this question over and over again, you will notice your thoughts becoming clearer. In fact, it will help you to sieve genuine and high returns from shady investments. Remember, it only takes a few good financial decisions to reach your desired target.

## Understand the Risks Involved

You need to understand that the market won't be rosy all the time. The market isn't fallible. Heck! Stock prices went down when the New York Stock Exchange was shut down for 136 days during World War I. During this long hiatus, investors counting on capital appreciation from their stocks were disappointed. However, those with dividend stocks kept on receiving their paychecks. So, it is important to place your eggs in the right basket.

You should also keep track of trends and the financial history of the stock you are investing in. In fact, you need to have a firm grip on your financial history in order to build your net worth and manage your money. If you take a look at the Dutch Tulip Bubble, the dot.com bubble, and the real estate bubble, you can see that there isn't much difference between them. Therefore, by arming yourself with these turning points in history, you get to delve into the psychology that influences the selling and buying decisions of individuals. This will help you to avoid financial mistakes that will haunt you and your loved ones. Additionally, mental models are an important tool that you can use to avoid mistakes. In the following chapters, I will show you the strategies you can employ to succeed in investments.

## Understand Your Investments

Do you know that stock funds are different from bond funds, and a stock index fund is not the same as stock? Most people are generally unaware of the different terms and regulations of investing in the stock market. It is probably not a surprise that Warren Buffet, billionaire and investment guru, made it a rule to never invest in what he does not understand. In other words, it is risky to invest in a niche that's difficult to explain. It's no surprise, then, that Buffet has steered clear of investing heavily in the tech industry. Books are also an excellent way to get information on the stocks you are interested in. Yes, I love the internet and its array of free information; however, nothing beats a good book when you want in-depth knowledge on a particular subject.

## The Ultimate Timing for All Markets

Short-term trades that did not perform well or that I did not get out in time became my long-term investments. Maybe you have heard this before: "We all know that things have to go up again." I would like to assure you that the market has nothing to do. But if I had to say exactly when and at which price the market will turn around again, then certainly just when I close my position and not a minute earlier. Get to know this principle well, because it will save you a lot of money. It has already brought me a lot of money. Investors often called me in the hope that I would support them on the assumption that the market in which they were invested would soon recover. My answer is always the same:

"Get me to know when you get off, then I will buy." If a position does not perform well, get off. Do not cling to positions. Then you still have enough capital for the next trade. Learn to love the small losses.

## The Technology Revolution

The average security holder can now easily check these formulas using cost-effective software package. Nevertheless, the promise of fast wealth is always tempting even for the best. But the philosopher's stone just does not exist. If it existed, then surely someone would have won everything for a long time, and we would have no more markets. But you can work out a technical advantage by studying charts, and you also have to control your psyche. Some people could not even make money by giving them a copy of the Wall Street Journal. And this, you should realize yourself.

A successful trader needs to have knowledge. But possessing knowledge does not necessarily make you a successful trader. The knowledge and the successful trader are separated by a gigantic divide. Few of us can jump over this gap, and those who make it must be very careful not to rush back into the abyss. Once you have reached a certain level of wealth, accumulating more things will increase neither your satisfaction nor your freedom. Trading has the potential of being truly enjoyable, but like overdoing anything else, it can become an addiction.

## The Stages of the Price Movement

All speculative markets go through the following stages of price movement:

1. Accumulation (Congestion) - The low of the market
2. Rise or breakout
3. Distribution (Congestion) - The high of the market

4. Waste or burglary

The fundamental understanding of these different stages of the market movement is essential for successful traders. Approximately 85% of the time the market is in a phase of congestion during which you should settle for modest gains. We will look at different market phases to see the different stages and know when to make a quick profit in a congestion phase or benefit from a breakout or break-in. First, look at the market situation in a rough overview and look for favorable opportunities. You usually use a chart set for a longer timeframe. Then your analysis is finely tuned with the observation of a shorter-term chart. So, you'll find out when to board, when to take profits, and perhaps most importantly, when to leave the sinking ship because you're on the wrong side of the trade. When looking closely at bar charts, it often becomes clear which direction will be most likely for the course. A chart contains a lot of information: if the demand exceeds the bid, then the price rises until a balance is established. The chart is also a reflection of fear and greed.

- Greed: "If only I had bought more, I could have made millions."
- Fear: "Man, if the course continues to break, then I lose everything I have!"

Fear is the stronger of the two emotions, so markets fall faster than they rise. After a breakout or collapse, the market may enter a phase of re-accumulation or re-distribution. This is where Newton's theory comes in: a moving body tends to move on. This means that once a trend has begun, it tends to continue with periodically recurring periods of interruption or rest. The basic wave theory with the five main waves up or down deals with this type of course movement. As a result, price action usually continues after a period of consolidation in the original direction. If the evidence is not reversed by important chart information, then you should trade in the same direction the course was before the congestion. Be wary of reversals after the second or third rest period during a break or break.

Although these patterns may differ in detail, they still repeat themselves in all securities markets. Some stocks were trapped for years in congestion phases. These were mostly the bad fundamentals that mostly stay there.

## Setup for Accumulation

### *Phase 1 - The Peak Of Sales*

Accumulation setup usually begins with a peak of sales. This is the first sign of the fatigue of the decline and the beginning of accumulation. The last bar shows the largest span with strongly increasing volumes.

The sales peak is followed by a sharp rise in prices. This price rally exceeds every step down in the previous move down both in terms of time and price. This is a prerequisite for the transition of the market into the accumulation phase. Without this sharp rally, you cannot say whether the downtrend is over or not.

This rapid increase in price is followed by a test of the previous lowest price. This movement either turns up early or leads to a new, slightly deeper low.

### *Phase 2 - Support and Resistance*

Now the market is entering a phase in which supply and demand are more or less balanced. Here are the areas of support and resistance. The range of support is the range of the lowest bar of a sell peak or a succeeding low. The area of resistance is the exact opposite: accumulation lows on positive days increase slightly and become weaker on negative days. Towards the end of this phase, the tops and bottoms will be higher than previous rallies and reactions.

After a sharp rise in prices, there will be several price declines followed by significant rallies. After two or three unsuccessful attempts to reach a new low, you should pay more attention to positive bars with a large span. These indicate that each approach to these lows will buy heavily. The third time points to a very high probability that the market will break out. A tendency towards a rally towards the end of accumulation is likely. A potential entry point for purchase is the second or third brief collapse in accumulation.

The term "clear" means that the rise exceeds the earlier tops by at least an average length of the curve. The extent of exceeding one or more earlier tops indicates the completion of the accumulation phase. If earlier tops are broken only timidly, and the price falls back quickly, then we go from sufficient supply and a possible relapse into the deeper areas of support.

Conversely, a significant breakthrough with further subsequent increases implies continued demand. Additional confirmation is given by a course that lasts several bars long over these previous tops. From this, we conclude that the accumulation is complete and that there is likely to be an increase.

After the signs of strength, the price generally corrects to about 50% of the previous price movement. This marks the beginning of the rising phase. Resist the urge to buy when the price reaches new heights. Often, these are impulsive buyers who are afraid of not being present at the big breakout. But there are countless other stocks that are just at the end of the accumulation phase just before the outbreak is up. Open your positions on your terms and do not chase after the course. If you chase the course and buy on the top, you are often stopped out by normal course corrections.

Brief summary:
1. The first rise after a peak in sales rarely lasts.
2. If you buy in the early stages of accumulation, then small gains are likely until the end of accumulation.
3. The best odds are when you buy towards the end of the accumulation phase.
4. The biggest gains are made during the rise and break-up phases.
If the congestion phase of the course becomes obvious, then the good points for profit taking are in the area of resistance. Sell orders should be placed early enough, as these areas are often only reached very briefly before the price falls again. The profit opportunity can be over quickly when the target price is reached, and the order is not. It's a wrong thing to wait and check what the course does when it enters the resistance zone. Watching a shorter timeframe can be helpful.

## Last Market Adjustment

At the end of accumulation, a final market adjustment may occur. This shows up as a sudden slump in the course below the total accumulation area with increased volume. This is followed by an equally rapid increase, which makes up for the whole loss. Then often comes a short drop in price, which reverses quickly and increases again with high volume and strong thrust. The latest market adjustment is trapping the traders who sell at a new low. These trades can quickly lead to large losses. This price movement is also called V-bottom.

## Setup for the Distribution

### *Phase 1 - The Peak of the Purchases*

The setup for distribution usually begins with a purport. This is the first sign of the fatigue of the price rise and the beginning of the distribution.

On the heels of the sale follows a sharp price slump. This price decline exceeds every step up in the previous uptrend, both in terms of time and price. This is a prerequisite for the transition of the market into the distribution phase. Without this sharp decline, one cannot say whether the uptrend is over or not. This rapid rate of decline is followed by a test of the previous highest price. This movement can either turn back down early or lead to a new, slightly higher high.

### *Phase 2 - Support and Resistance*

Now the market is entering a phase in which supply and demand are more or less balanced. During distribution, the volume will increase a bit on negative days and on positive days will be weaker.

After a sharp price collapse, there will be several price increases followed by significant reactions. After two or three unsuccessful attempts to reach a new high, you should pay more attention to negative bars with large margins. These indicate that each time you approach these high points, you are selling heavily. The third time points to a very high probability that the market will break down. A tendency towards a rally towards the end of accumulation is likely.

The term "significant" means that the waste falls below the previous bottoms by at least an average bar length. The extent of under-run of one or more previous bottoms indicates the completion of the distribution phase. If earlier bottoms are broken only tentatively and the price rises quickly again, then we assume sufficient demand and a possible relapse into the higher areas of resistance. Additional confirmation is given by a course that stays several bars below these earlier bottoms. From this, we conclude that the distribution is complete and that price collapse is likely.

After the sign of weakness, the price usually corrects to about 50% of the previous price movement. This marks the beginning of the break-in phase. Resist the urge to sell when the price drops to new depths. Often, these are impulsive buyers who are afraid of not being there when the price plummets. However, there are countless other stocks that are just at the end of the distribution phase just before the outbreak down. Open your positions on your terms and do not chase the course. If you chase the course and sell on the bottom, you are often stopped out by normal course corrections.

If the distribution phase of the course becomes obvious, then the good points for profit taking are in the area of support. This area is located in the area around the former bottoms of the Congestion. Sales orders need to be placed in advance, as the profitable ranges are often reached only very briefly before the price rises again. The profit opportunity can be over quickly when the target price is reached, and the order is not. When the course enters the support zone, waiting is dangerous. Watching a shorter timeframe can be helpful.

## Re-Accumulation

Trading securities would be easy if one could always assume that a peak of buying follows a phase of distribution followed by a downward movement. In reality, of course, that looks different. The course is entering a congestion phase, but it can also be a re-accumulation. Everything can point to an imminent price decline after a buying trip. But that does not mean that the course is sure to break. It can also be a period of rest during which the powers of supply and demand decide which direction to continue. The course can often go through several rallies and reactions. After the second or third rally in this congestion phase, the span and the position of the bars in the course area often indicate the direction of the next move. As a rule, after a congestion phase, the courses maintain the direction they had been following before the congestion. If a stock that moves into a congestion phase after a buying spike and if you trade at all in this congestion phase, then you should sell up to the gradual slope flattening and buy at bottoms. Note that the lows are higher and the price for some bars is in the upper range of the price range. This indicates a re-accumulation with a probable further price increase. In the case of re-distribution, the opposite is true in the opposite case.

## The Phases of the Rise and Burglary

The stages of increase and burglary are the most promising. However, these price movements account for only about 15% between the successive congestions. The theory of parallel motion excels at fast markets. Basically, this theory states that rallies and reactions correspond to previous rallies and reactions. Buy at the same levels of reaction and take your winnings in equal rallies or spurts. The break-in phase is the approximate mirror image of the rising phase. The course usually falls faster and deeper than it rises. After all, fear is a stronger feeling than greed.

## The Exhaustion of the Course

After a long climb or even three consecutive bars in one direction, prices are often in the most critical situation, which can lead to correction and the beginning of a new trend. A strong reversal bar in such situations is a good indication that one should worry about a short position. Close the position again if the price does not really break in the next few days. A lower opening price is one of the first signs of fatigue and perhaps the end of the movement.

Five indications that a rising price is going into a congestion phase:

1. The course forms two negative bars with a large spread.
2. The price does not reach a new high over a period of ten bars.
3. The course has non-overlapping days that are opposite to the trend. A non-intersecting bar is a bar whose upper end is below the lower peak of the previous bar. This can occur three or four bars after the highest bar.
4. The course shows a sharp kink or a jump after a steady rise. The drawback is that the price drops to a new low, does not find an offer and then rises aggressively. The jump occurs when the price suddenly rises to a new high, finds no demand, and quickly falls back.
5. The course goes back 75% or more of the last move.

## The End of the Movement

The end of the price movement is displayed if the existing high of the movement cannot be broken up with three attempts and no new high forms. Here profits are taken, or the stops are set closer.

# Chapter 2
# Understanding Options

The big question is: how do you apply your skills to make money on the stock market? Before you finish reading this book, you will get some answers. You need to see the patterns and setups as they appear, not just after that - anyone can see them afterward. This is followed by a possible application method. Rules are created. Charts show patterns and the locations where the rules for determining entry and exit points should be applied.

Determine whether the congestion is a re-accumulation or re-distribution based on the last increase or break. Assume this until the congestion pattern tells you otherwise.

## The Stop

We propose two steps: an average spread below the last reaction low or the span of the entry bar below the entry bar. Once we have some freedom of movement, the stop will be tightened. Close the position if the price does not behave within three bars. Then do not wait until the stop is triggered.

## Trade or Not?

You do not risk your capital if you are not invested in the market. This trading style limits exposure to approximately 10% to 15% of the total observation period. Between 85% and 90% of the time, you are not in the market. During an accumulation or distribution phase, a position can be held. Although there is nothing wrong with this approach, it involves the risk of losing significant portions of the profits. The pattern may be distribution rather than accumulation. You need to study many charts until you find that this approach is workable and fits your trading style. This approach requires a lot of judgment. They should try to automate as many rules as possible to minimize uncertainty.

## Trade High-Value Assets

Active trading is best suited for the stocks and/or futures that are moving or in trend phases, and not the boring ones like the securities that are constantly going sideways. The definition of a value that moves is quite subjective. Many sources cite lists of securities that outperform and outperform others, and one of the best is Investor's Business Daily.

Moving securities may have the following characteristics:

- Increased volatility
- Reaching a new four-week high
- Securities in the rising phase
- Significantly upwards or downwards inclined sliding average of the last 20 days
- The leading values in a specific market segment

Brief Summary

Remember, the goal of this game is to win, not that you're in 90% of all price moves. Open your positions when certain patterns occur and realize your profits when the target price is reached or at the first sign that the offer exceeds demand.

These basic principles apply to every time horizon, including day trading. If you are long-term oriented, use weekly charts. This will lead to many false signals, but there are indeed the stops.

You will only earn money by studying countless charts and drawing your entry points, exit points, and stop loss. Thereby you internalize these approaches and make them suitable. After that, you could succeed in trading. One of the hardest things in trading is closing a position towards the end of an outbreak or during a buying spike. Just tell yourself that you are a nice person: everyone wants to have the stock, and you give yours.
The General Motors study might be one example of how you can create a supply-demand based trade system. Create two charts: one shows what you should have done and the other what you really did. Learn by comparison. Recognize the forces that act at important turning points.

## Practical Application of the Elliott Wave Theory

The Elliott Wave Theory confuses many traders. In this chapter, we do not want to discuss the ambiguity of this theory, but we apply it to a trading plan that should develop into a successful approach. This theory is one of the best theories of the Cycle because it allows non-harmonic movements.

There are many different approaches to securities trading. These are roughly divided into fundamental and technical approaches. Some technicians like to mix both methods for an optimal market approach. The fundamental access includes bushels, hectares, consumption units, revenues, book values and so on. Technical Analysis examines past price movements and predicts future ones. In 1939, Elliott published a series of articles describing the principle of Elliott waves. The Elliott Wave Theory is one of the best technical methods for market analysis, and the serious-interested should certainly include it in his studies.

Is it possible to predict price trends using the Elliott Wave Theory and use this information profitably? The answer to that is a cautious yes if you do not make the theory an exact science. The Elliott Wave Theory allows harmonic and non-harmonic course movements. Most cycle theories use principles based on harmonic movements. As soon as nonharmonic movements occur, it becomes difficult.

The following summary of the Elliott Wave Theory reduces the ideas to a useful size:

1. Ascending moves consist of five waves, two of which are corrections. Falling movements are counterproductive. The odd waves run in the direction of the main motion. Straight waves run against the main direction. Shaft 2 corrects shaft 1. Shaft 5 corrects shaft 4. Sometimes there are nine or more waves. Elliott solves this problem by calling these movement extensions.

2. The endpoint of shaft 4 is higher than the height of shaft 1. Elliott specifies lengths proportions exactly, such as that the shaft 4 should be shorter than the waves 3 and 5. However, it has been found that this is not necessarily true.

The movements are divided into waves that are one degree smaller. What does "one degree smaller" mean? This question is difficult to answer, and that is one of the reasons why applying the theory is so difficult. One suggestion is to look for it in the next shorter timeframe. If you have a daily chart, look for the smaller grade on a 30-minute chart. The next smaller degree also needs five waves to complete the higher-order wave 1 and is therefore identical to the daily chart.

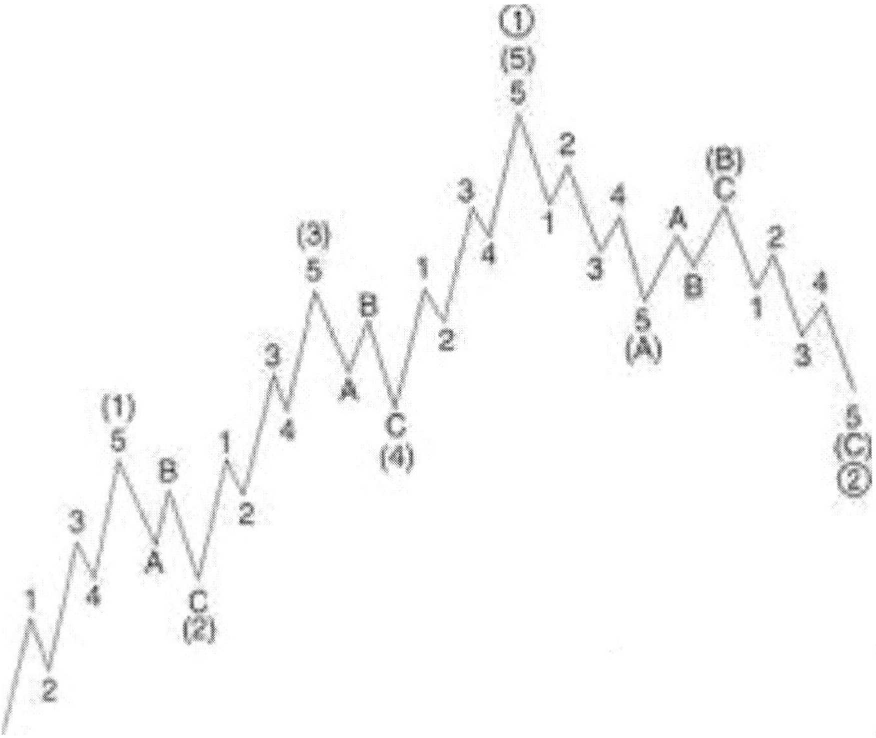

## *Triangular Corrections*

Triangular corrections consist of a five-point pattern (ABCDE) after a thrust. The type and position of such a pattern often allow conclusions to be drawn as to whether a turnaround is pending or not.

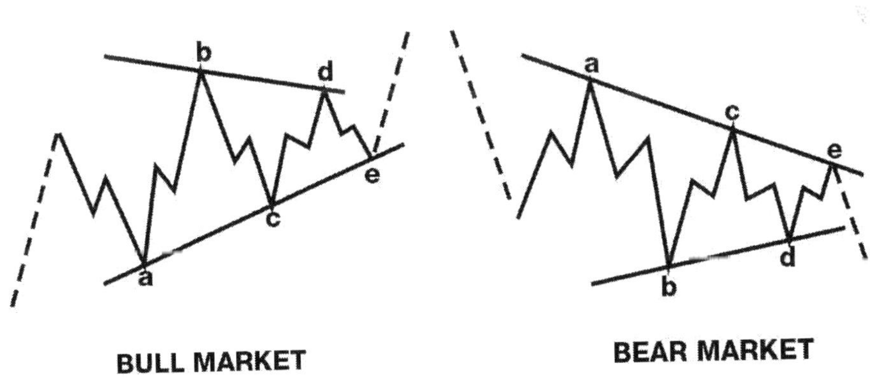

### *A-Shaped Corrections*

The length and duration of the first correction wave or A-shaped correction of the thrust are of utmost importance for determining the further course of the total correction and the probability of a turnaround.

Look for the application of the A-wave (the first correction wave to increase) to determine the type of correction and the probable direction of the price after the correction has been completed. Then, you can see four possible price movements. If the extent of the A correction wave is the same, the following should be deduced:

- 25% - 35%: Indicates a single correction wave.
- 35% - 50%: Indicates a three-wave correction.
- 50% - 75%: Indicates a five-wave correction.
- Over 75%: mostly a possible trend reversal.

### *Prediction of the Corrections*

This type of price development can lead to a turnaround. Here are the forces of supply and demand at work. A reaction at a distance of 75% from the starting point makes a clearer statement than a low-25% reaction.

## Understanding Options Terminology

For logical reasons, the option's duration is a factor. If you'll like an asset to be controlled for five years rather than one year, normally, having it controlled for a longer period of time would cost more. Alternately, it would not cost as much, in the event that you needed the asset controlled for just one day,

This is because the more the asset is being controlled, the more likely it is that something can happen (there's that word again) to affect its price. If for example, the property was controlled for just one day, it isn't too likely that a major real estate bargain involving your property will be reported that day.

# Chapter 3
# Options Risk and Reward

Money management is only included in the trading plan by about one-tenth of all private traders. Just because a trader does not have a lot of capital does not mean that he cannot apply the principles of money management. Many traders are of the opinion that these ideas can only be used by large asset managers and institutions.

Money management also implies that the potential risk, taking into account the preferences of the trader, is set in relation to the expected profit. The goal is to set a desirable yield rate and then minimize the associated risk. Trading generally requires four decisions:

1. Buy/sell (system or strategy)?
2. Which security is traded?
3. How many contracts or shares of value are traded?
4. What is the share of capital risked on a trade?

The first decision is about the trading process itself without taking into account money management. The other three decisions involve maximizing profit and minimizing risk directly. The foundations of risk and reward should be considered from the start in the development of a trading system and must become an integral part of the system.

If a trader works profitably right from the start and has thus increased his trading capital, then he cannot be ruined by four losses (as long as his bet remains the same). Although the number of consecutive losses that would lead to ruin increases with time, so does the likelihood of multiple losses following one another. The following formula calculates the probability of ultimate ruin (WR) over time:

WR = (1-VT / 1 + VT) AH

VT stands for the trader's advantage (percentage winners - percent losers), and AH is the initial trading units. If the initial capital of a trader is $ 20,000 and his bet per trade is $ 5,000 then AH = 4. The following example calculates the probability of ultimate ruin:

| | | | |
|---|---|---|---|
| Total Capital | § 20,000 | Total Capital | $ 20,000 |
| Deployment | $ 5,000 | Deployment | § 2,500 |
| Advantage of the Trade | 10% | Trades' Advantage | 10% |
| Chance of Ruin | 44.8% | Chance of Ruin | 20.1% |
| Total Capital | $ 20,000 | Total Capital | $ 20,000 |
| Bet | $ 2,000 | Bet | $ 1,000 |
| Advantage of the Trade | 10% | Advantage of the Trade | 10% |
| Chance of Ruin | 13.4% | Chance of Ruin | 1.8% |

These numbers apply only when you trade one contract at a time. With changing contract numbers, the risk of ruin changes dramatically. Moreover, these calculations assume that, in the case of a profit, the amount is always the same and corresponds to the loss in the negative case. As mentioned above, the risk of ruin is determined by the percentage of winners, the ratio between winners and losers, and the size of the bet. So far, we have disregarded the relationship between winners and losers. In real life, most successful trading systems score less than 50% winners and win-loss ratios above 1.2.

The risk of ruin is an interesting indicator, but it does not give much insight into how to use or manage capital efficiently. For self-preservation, it is best not to put everything on one card. If you choose your bets well and follow a system with a positive bias, the risk of ruin is very low.

## The Capital Allocation Model

Now you know the tools you need to understand our capital allocation model. First, we'll show how capital is allocated to a one-market portfolio using a small selection of data. Later, we will apply the same approach to a two-market portfolio. At the end of the chapter, we will show the efficiency of the capital allocation model using a true system of small and medium accounts.

As you know, our goal is to maximize profit while minimizing risk. This goal must be achieved without exceeding the limits of justifiable risk. To reach the goal, we need to know how much capital is to be allocated to each market and what number of contracts should be traded. In this model, capital is calculated from the market value of the account, the average monthly returns, and the market risk. The market value is simply the starting capital with which we begin our trading. In these examples, the returns do not add up; we use the initial capital for all calculations. The average monthly income is the capital that we can expect to gain from our system. Market risk is the amount we can lose per day on a trade. Asset managers use a variety of metrics to assess market risk:

- Mean Range: The average of the ranges of the last three to 50 Days, which is converted into a monetary amount in US $. For example, if the average spread is 40 points for the Swiss franc over the past 10 days and the Swiss franc is $ 12.50, the market risk is $ 500. The likely amount of market movement is the average spread of the last x days. This does not always have to be right, but the capital allocation model needs to be built on certain probabilities.

- The average change in closing prices: The average change in closing prices over the last three to 50 days says more about the risk, as this value indicates the expected risk if the position is held.

- Mean change in positive closing prices versus negative closing prices: the average change in the negative closing prices over a period suggests the risk of holding a long position.

- The standard deviation of closing prices: The standard deviation of the closing prices gives a more accurate picture of the risk, as the daily deviation is displayed with a probability of 68%. This calculation is a bit more complex, but it does not cause any problems with the computers available today.

In whatever way we measure the risk, it is the most important variable to watch and the most important component of the capital allocation model.

## A Market Portfolio

Whether the system trades futures or stocks makes no difference. Before we can allocate capital, the average monthly income and market risk must be determined on the basis of a contract. We also need to determine how much of our capital we are willing to risk per trade. But we cannot know that yet, because that's exactly what we want to find out.

## Cumulating Of Results

Cumulating means here the process of capital allocation based on the current portfolio or deposit value. The current portfolio value results from the start-up capital as well as the already completed positive and negative trades. When it comes to large sums of money, accumulation is very good: the capital invested increases or decreases depending on the current value of the deposit. If a trading plan is successful, then each trade will be given more capital; but if it is bad, then there is less capital available for each trade. Note that we have found that cumulating is very good when it comes to large sums. This limitation stems from the belief that the allocation should not be extended until the seed capital of smaller accounts has not been at least doubled or tripled. Even good systems can crash after a series of wins, and if a smaller account does not cumulate, there is still some capital left for bad times. If accumulation is of interest to you (and it should, if you have significant sums of money), then you can build it into the capital allocation model with a small change. In the formula, do not use seed capital as total capital (GK), but use the current value of the deposit.

# Chapter 4
# Analyzing Mood Swing in the Market

## The Main Configurations of the Market

The high volatility of the markets shows how important it is for a trader to know how to rank the various market configurations. We can distinguish three main configurations (uptrend, downtrend, trading range). Before developing these configurations, we will explain the interest of the trader to master them.

There Are Three Main Types Of Markets:

- The uptrend market;
- The market in a downtrend;
- The market without trend (trading range).

Each type of market presents opportunities on which the trader can capitalize only by adopting an appropriate strategy:

In a bullish market, he will have to favor a mainly buying strategy; in a downtrend, it will have to adopt a sell strategy in a market without trend, the trader will have to favor the quick return and therefore a strategy of options trading or day trading by positioning itself to the purchase around the important supports and the sale around major resistances. Modern markets are so volatile that a simple buy-and-hold strategy no longer has a place even for the long term.

## The Market Is Uptrend

A bullish market is characterized by a succession of lower and higher points, and higher and higher points. In a clear uptrend, the corrective phases (drop legs) are less important in amplitude than the impulsive phases (legs of rising). This property is very important because it provides a valuable indication of the possibility of a trend reversal. When a corrective leg has a greater amplitude than the impulsive leg (bullish in a bull market), then the uptrend is likely to be challenged. The trader will have to reconsider the current trend and avoid positioning himself for the purchase under these conditions.

A downtrend market is characterized by lower and higher points, but also by lower and lower points. In this type of market, rebounds often have less amplitude than bearish legs, the main characteristic of a bear market. In a trending market, the movements that go in the direction of the dominant trend are still the most powerful. As for the uptrend, the turnaround can be anticipated. This requires the recovery to be larger than the last bearish wave.

## The Market without Trend

In a trendless market, there is no clear trend, and low points and high points are often confused. Buyers and sellers are testing themselves and no clear consensus is at work.
According to Wilder, markets evolve in trend one-third of the time and do not draw any clear trend during the remaining two-thirds. This property is important because investors are often victims of momentum bias. They tend to mechanically prolong the recent course evolution. If the course progresses during the

last sessions, they are convinced of the continuation of its rise and many traders are trapped by positioning themselves around resistance or slightly above2. Conversely, in the case of a decline in stock prices, investors say that this decline will continue and are trapped by opening a position around major support.

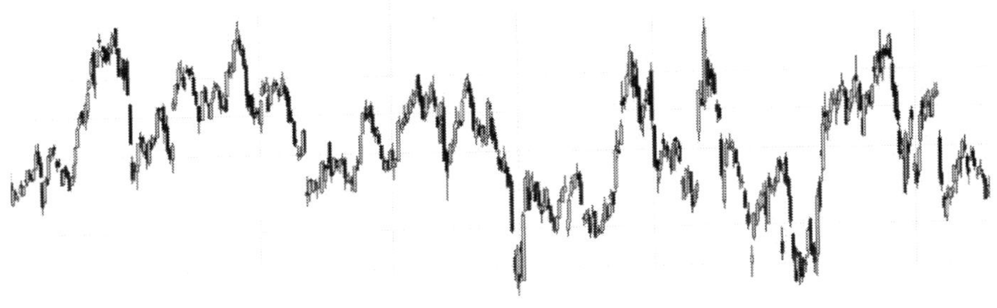

The good trader can wait patiently for the right moment before opening a position. Professional traders seek to position themselves at the beginning of an impulsive movement and avoid exposure by taking unnecessary risks when the market is not predictable. Good traders are people who can adapt to changing market conditions. As we will see later, markets fluctuate differently depending on whether we are in an uptrend, bearish trend or a trending market. In a bullish (bearish) market, the trader will be able to afford to buy (sell) up (down) and sell (buy) even higher (low), even if that is not ideal.

This is not the case in a market without a tendency where the trader will have to buy low and sell high, that is to say, sell the resistors and buy the supports and do not hesitate to go in and out quickly if the conditions require it. In a market without trend, many investors lose patience and position themselves impulsively, thus losing their capital and therefore the opportunity to participate in the real movement. They will often buy resistors and sell media. In trend markets, on the contrary, they will have the annoying habit of taking their profits hastily. These errors, consequences of psychological bias present in traders, must imperatively be corrected.

## Trend Lines

Trend lines are often used by traders to identify bullish points in an uptrend and highs in a downtrend. In a bull market, the trend line goes through at least two low points. Conversely, in a downtrend market, the trend line will join at least two high points. It is possible to adjust trends over time based on new information: sharper, more marked trends may indeed appear as the trend initially traced becomes obsolete.

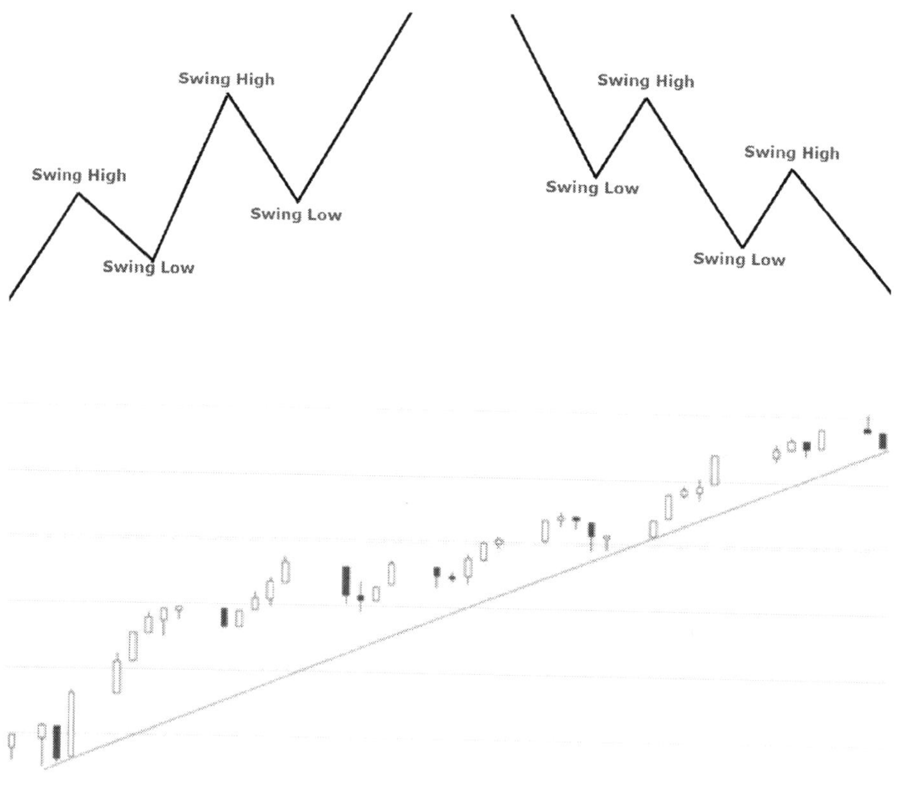

## Conditions of Effectiveness of a Trend Line

The success of trend lines is justified by their effectiveness in identifying good levels of support and resistance. In other words, they sometimes make it possible to give with surprising precision these minor levels of reversal when a trend has already started. They also offer the possibility of identifying the state of the trend and anticipating reversals or simply corrective movements. In what follows, we try to give some elements to explain their effectiveness.

A first approach advances the argument of a stock market evolution respecting a "natural" phenomenon. There would exist on the market, and on all time horizons, trends that would respect a speed of progression and therefore a certain angle. The famous trader and analyst WD Gann explains that to last, a trend line must have a 45-degree angle. Not to mention natural phenomenon, we can say that a course of courses with a low slope indicates a slow movement that will probably abort. Conversely, when the slope is steep, the movement is too impulsive and will quickly run out of steam. The ideal is, therefore, to have an average slope (45 degrees), a sign of a healthy impulsive movement.

Another militant element in favor of trend lines is the fact that they are known to most operators. As we have seen, their validity will be strengthened because of the phenomenon of self-fulfilling prophecies. In concrete terms, a bullish trader will draw a trend line to identify the probable drop-off point for the stock, which will be a good buy with low risk. In the opposite case, it will draw a downtrend line to identify sales levels.

The importance of a trend line depends on the number of points it connects. The higher the number of rebounds on the right, the greater the importance. This is explained in particular by the mimicry of operators, which reinforces the strength of this line. In addition, the trend lines can be plotted over several time horizons (long, medium and short term), but the long-term trend lines or just to take them are those whose reliability is the most important. The trader will enjoy a return to the right of support (resistance) to strengthen its position buying (seller) and especially as the quality of the trend is proven.

Finally, a trend line, to be effective, should not be too steep. A parallel can be drawn with running: a sprinter will run out of steam quickly and will not be able to travel a long distance, while a runner will have the resources to travel the same distance. Similarly, if prices accelerate strongly, a consolidation is likely because it will allow the market to catch its breath before continuing its impetus.

We see on the PPR stock that the break in the trend line did not stop the market from continuing its upward movement. The stock just consolidated before heading back up. It is not uncommon for a rise to continue for a long time without being exhausted. Many traders will be trapped because they will seek to anticipate the turnaround. This is why the trader should always wait for the convergence of several signals before playing the corrective movement, and not be content with recent progress to justify his sell decision.

Finally, Elder recommends when drawing a trend line to avoid extremes because they are not representative. He prefers to use the support areas as levels to connect.

## Finding a Trend Reversal Using a Trend Line

Rupture of a trend line is an important reversal signal. This signal is all the stronger as the trend line is significant (it has been used on many occasions to support the current trend). The break of a bullish or bearish straight line materializes the end of a market dynamic: the operators who should have strengthened their positions near the trend line proved to be weaker than the opposing side (the bearers), thus allowing the rupture of the right and all the dynamics of the market. The change in trend thus seems clear.

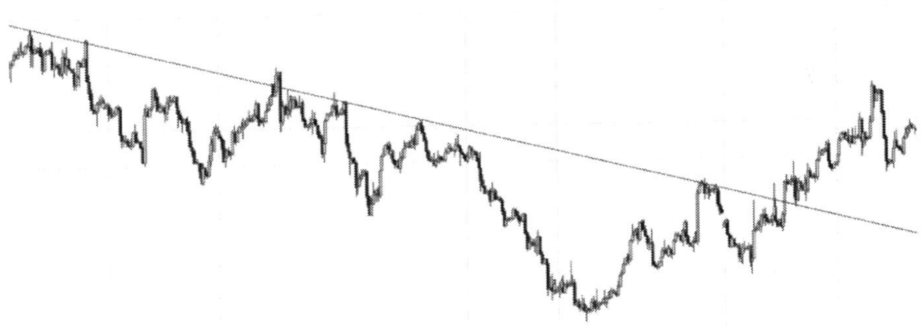

A broken bullish straight line immediately becomes a line of resistance against which the market will crash; this is very often shown by a pullback (return to the right of a trend that has just been broken). The market thus tests the strength of the support that has become resistance (or vice versa). Beware; the break of a trend line cannot alone constitute a signal of a reversal of the market, as shown by the example of the title PPR. It only alerts the trader about the possibility of consolidation.

## Canals or Channels

A channel (Canal) is a figure directly related to the analysis of trend lines studied previously. The tracking is simple: once a bullish trend has been determined, it is a question of finding a parallel to the tendency to cover all the evolution of prices. Over the period when the trend is observed (straight line connecting the extreme points), we thus obtain a channel in which the courses evolve harmoniously.

The channel will tuck into a trend by allowing impulse turning points to be determined through trend lines, but also corrective turning points through the upper channel of the uptrend channel - or the bottom line for a downtrend channel.

The courses thus vary between these two lines: the first constitutes the support line of the canal, where the courts come to rest; the second represents the resistance line of the channel (or top of the channel) against which the market stumbles.

As for trends, it is possible to distinguish short, medium and long-term channels. The importance of a channel depends on its duration of evolution, but also on the number of times each line of the channel has been affected. To be considered a canal, you need at least two impacts on each side. The higher the number of impacts, the more important the channel is.

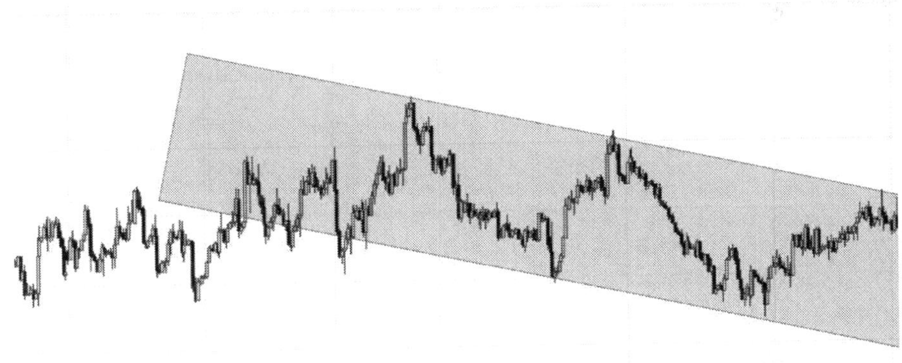

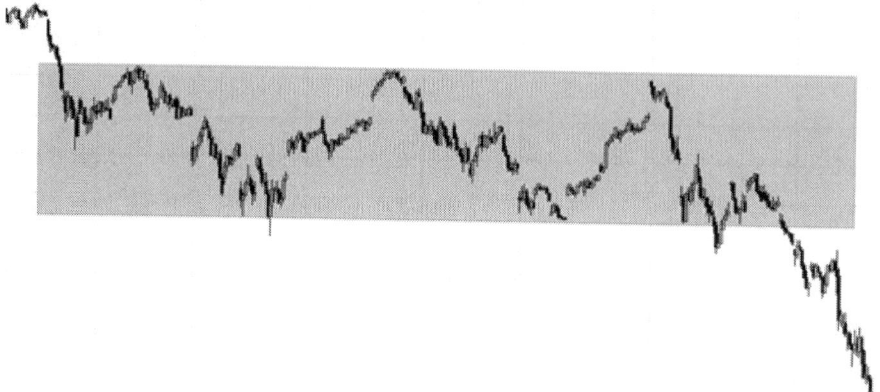

## Intermediate Lines

In practice, prices do not move stubbornly between the lower bound and the upper bound. They sometimes have trouble passing intermediate areas within the canal. It is possible to draw parallel straight lines to the channel which constitute as many lines of support or minor resistance for the courses. However, the number of real intermediate rights is limited; one generally finds only one, even two. They are very often halfway through the channel and are real tests to know if the courses will reach the top or bottom. In the case of a bullish channel, the break in the intermediate resistance line often indicates that the market will reach the top of the channel.

It is also possible to distinguish within a channel small intermediate channels that allow, for example, the market to move from one terminal to another. Sometimes, too, a new channel emerges inside the canal, which appears more and more relevant, and which will eventually replace the old one that has become obsolete.

For the operator, the use of a channel is very simple: if it is a bullish channel, it will buy at the bottom of the channel to sell at the top, and eventually, become a seller. This rule will apply depending on the quality of the channel; for example, if the channel's resistance line seems fragile, it will not sell itself, it will simply take profits. We will also use the information given by the behavior of the courts facing the intermediate line. We will also use the information given by the small intermediate channels, or small lines of minor tendency.

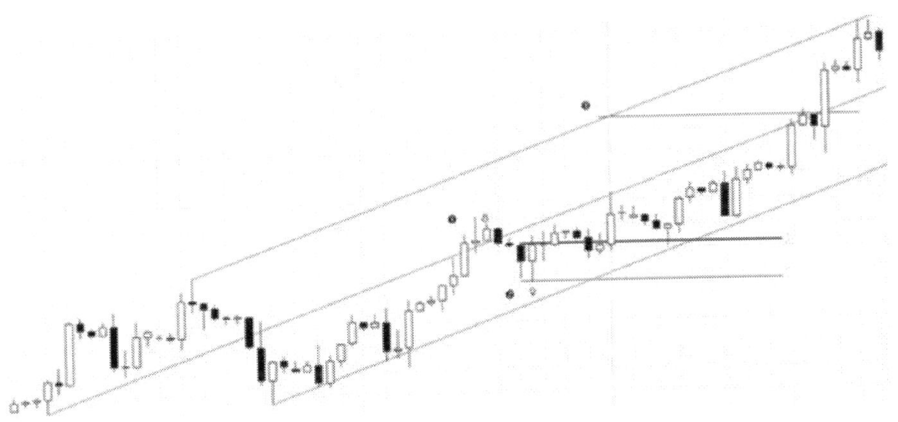

## Rupture of the Canal

Two kinds of breaks can be envisaged: either the trend is confirmed and reinforced (it is an upward outflow of the uptrend channel or the decline of a downtrend channel), or it is reversed, and it is then a possible change of trend (downward release of a bullish channel and exit up a downtrend channel). The break is all the stronger as it is done in a large volume.

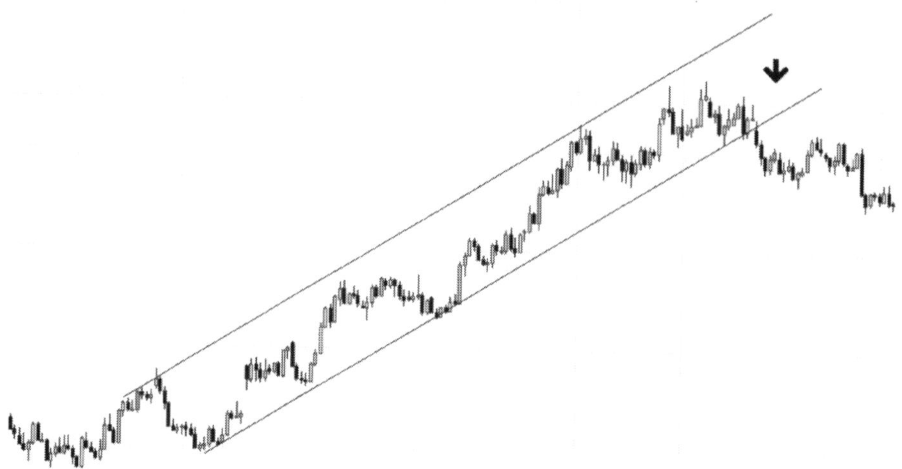

The operator has several elements to identify a possible rupture of the channel: in the case of a downward exit of a bullish channel, we usually notice that the courses have no strength, they do not arrive for example more to pass the intermediate right but stumble against it regularly. These elements are usually the first alarm signals.

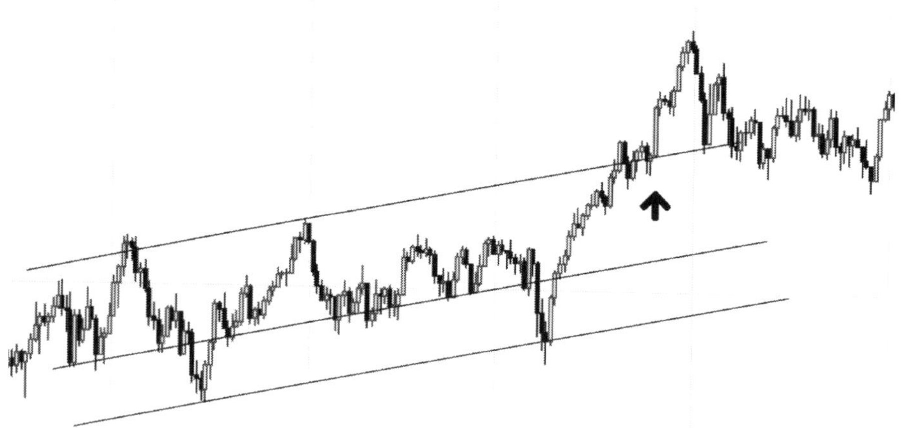

## Precautions When Detecting a Signal

The breaking of a bullish channel does not necessarily mean a sell signal, just as the break of a bearish channel does not always correspond to a buy signal. This is a simple indication that will need to be supported by other elements to become a relevant signal.

The trader must convince himself that there is no absolute truth about the financial markets and that he must position himself only when the probabilities are favorable to him.

## How to Detect the End of a Trend?

Can trend reversals be identified using chart analysis? We will see that it is possible to plot a reversal graphically, but for this, the trader will have to make sure that several criteria are respected: it is necessary to have a clear trend (for example, a trend line whose impulsive movements have a greater amplitude than corrective movements); the breaking of a major trend line or a major support is often a precursor signal of reversal; and finally, the various researches show that a figure of large turnaround (thus which took some time to be formed) will often be at the origin of an important corrective movement.

## The Trend Reversal

After a downward movement (bullish), the title draws a bullish leg (bearish) whose amplitude is greater than the previous bearish (bullish) leg. This configuration signals a probable reversal of the trend and indicates the imminence of a bullish (bearish) departure or simply the cessation of the current trend and the entry of the market in a phase without a trend.

This presentation of trends has been deliberately simplified because, in fact, the range of movements is much richer. Nevertheless, it is important to have a clear idea of the main trends in the markets before refining the analysis. The AGF stock is the typical case of a stock that draws a strong uptrend with very few corrections. It was difficult for a buyer to find a low point allowing him to position himself in the direction of the trend.

## How Are Trends Formed?

Trends are a common phenomenon in the markets, but their training is often misunderstood by operators. Dow has developed a theory to provide relevant explanations for this phenomenon and can usefully be applied to current markets, regardless of the period used.

# Chapter 5
# Sector Analysis: Technical and Fundamental

## The Basic Principles of Technical Analysis

To better understand the technical analysis, we will summarize its fundamental principles; we will show the importance of the psychological dimension of technical analysis.

### *Fundamental Principles*

Based on the work of renowned technical analyst John Murphy, we will present the main properties of technical analysis:

Technical analysis focuses on what is, rather than what should be. It is interested in the market itself and not the external factors that it reflects or that may have influenced it. It describes market movements, not the reasons behind them.

This method focuses on the psychology of the operators and not on the fundamentals. Indeed, what matters is not the news but the way operators react to it. This is a strategic approach to the stock market and not a fundamental approach, whose main purpose is the search for the intrinsic value of the asset. The technical analysis does not question the concept of fundamental value but argues that there may be lasting divergences between the stock price and the latter.

The market value is entirely and solely determined by the game of supply and demand. Supply and demand depend on many factors, some of which are rational and some not. The market results from the permanent interaction of all these behaviors and the differences of interpretation of the speakers. Fundamentals are just one price determinant among many others.

The courses evolve according to trends that can last a certain time. The trend changes are due to a change in the dominant consensus that will change the balance of power between suppliers and applicants. The graphs consider all the information available at a given moment. History repeats itself and markets are governed by the psychology of crowds. The phenomena of euphoria and panic are very often found on the markets and this cyclically. The following sentence, attributed to the famous speculator Jesse Livermore, sums up perfectly these words:

"I learned early on that there was nothing new on Wall Street. Indeed, speculation is as old as the hills. What is happening today in the markets has happened in the past and will happen again in the future."
These basic principles are favored by many leading operators (analysts, traders ...)

## Consideration of the Psychological Dimension

Fundamental analysis focuses on the real value of a financial asset but neglected psychological component, determining for the proponents of the behavioral approach. This approach has shown that psychological biases explain price shifts in relation to the fundamental value. Technical analysis, therefore, takes into account this psychological dimension and focuses on the emotions of operators.

The fundamentals are supposed to be known to all, and the technical analyst's main task is to determine how the operators react to economic news. Basic information (growth rate, inflation rate, unemployment rate, contracts signed by a company, etc.) has a significant impact on stock prices, but most professional traders attach importance even greater at the behavioral reaction of traders.

Finally, as we have seen above, history repeats itself, and in financial markets governed by crowd psychology, it is common to note that the phenomena of euphoria are followed by panic movements.

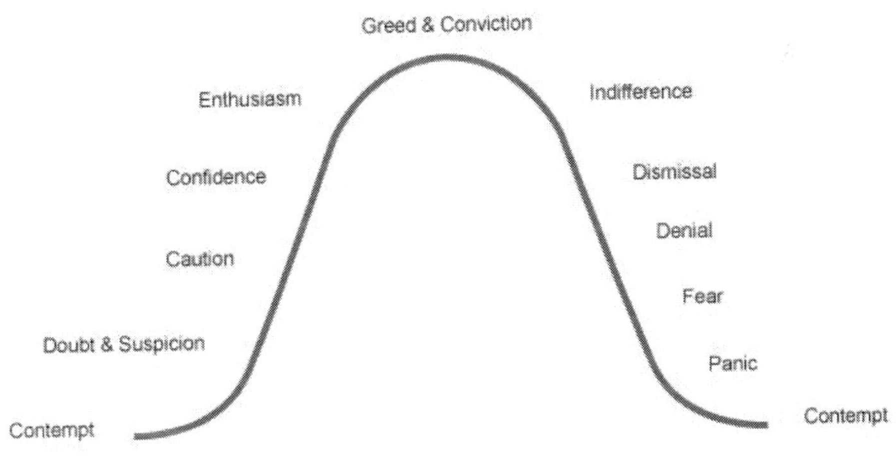


In a reference book, Gerald Loeb explains that a stock market price is only partly determined by a balance sheet and an income statement:

"It is much more by the hopes and fears of humanity, by greed, ambition, events beyond the reach of humanity such as natural disasters, inventions, stress and tensions in the financial world.

Time, discoveries, fashion, and innumerable causes that it is impossible to enumerate."

The famous American financier Bernard Baruch going in the same direction as he explains:

"Fluctuations in the stock market do not correspond to the recording of events as such, but to human reactions to these events or how millions of men and women feel the potential impact of these events on the future. In other words, the stock market is a reflection of individuals."

Technical analysis also helps to take a strategic approach capitalizing on the emotions of other traders. The great economist Keynes was also a great speculator. In his financial operations, he relied heavily on crowd psychology and put aside basic analysis, which may seem surprising to a person who has had such a strong impact on economic theory. In fact, we owe him the following sentence: "There is nothing more irrational than investing rationally in the markets. This sentence does not mean that the investor must be irrational, but rather that the use of analytical tools considered rational must be used vigilantly. In his General Theory of Employment, Interest, and Money, published in 1936, John Maynard Keynes describes the markets as follows:

"Most professional investors and speculators are less concerned with making accurate forecasts in the long run than with predicting the future changes to the conventional valuation base shortly before the general public. In fact, the unacknowledged object of enlightened investment is to steal the departure, as Americans say so well, to be smarter than the public and to pass the wrong or belittled piece to the neighbor."

# The Law of Supply And Demand

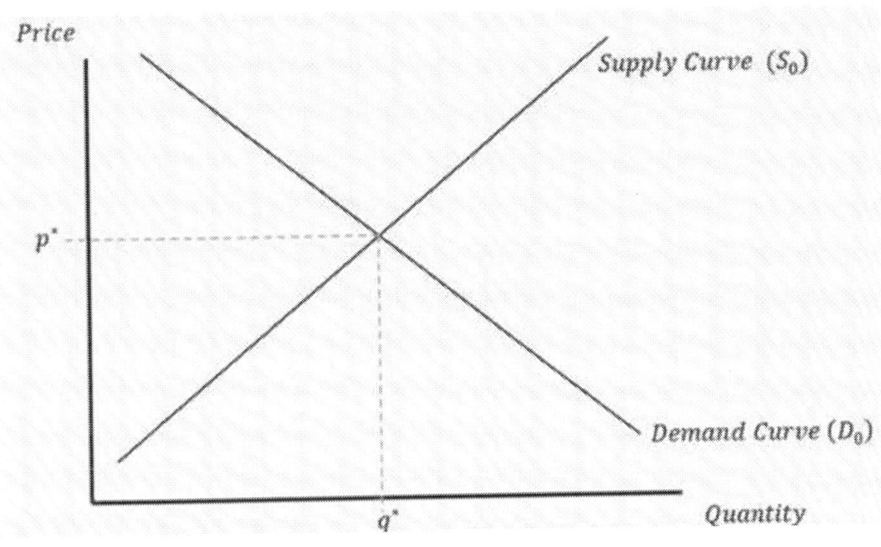


Technical analysis assumes that all the necessary information to the decision is contained in stock prices. The graphs represent a good barometer of investor psychology. Indeed, the technical analysis considers that it is the operators who are at the origin of the stock market fluctuations and not the economic and financial news. If a stock goes up it is that there are simply more buyers only sellers; conversely, if a stock is down, it means that the sellers are in surplus and plummet the stock prices. If this view of market fluctuations is also shared by fundamental analysis, the two methods diverge on the determinants of stock prices:

For the fundamental analysis, the officers and the plaintiffs focus essentially on the real value of the security. Security will be asked if it is undervalued (price below its fundamental value) and conversely it will be offered when the stock price is higher than its intrinsic value. Investors are rational and position themselves solely on the basis of the fundamental value of the security.

For technical analysis, the concept of fundamental value is not necessarily called into question. However, the security can fluctuate quite a bit before returning to its fundamental value. In addition, technical analysts consider it difficult to gather all the information needed to perform a fundamental analysis worthy of the name. It is for this reason that technical analysts seek, first of all, to identify the forces involved in order to determine the probable evolution of prices. The technical analysis simply seeks to answer the following question: "Which bull or bear will win the fight?”

The reality is that behind every offer or each application, there are many explanatory factors of fundamental and psychological. The theory of conventions explains that it may be rational to include in its analysis factors that have no connection with fundamentals, such as fashion phenomena for example. The stock price results from the permanent interaction of all these behaviors and the fundamentals11 are only one price determinant among all the others. The prices evolve according to "tendencies", which can last a certain time, because of the existence of a dominant convention. A change of trend can be explained in different ways: the fragility of the convention is updated by the financial community which turns away quickly from the financial asset (example of the technological values); the players have positioned themselves massively for the purchase and cannot, therefore, more support the market. Any bad news will have a massive effect and will cause massive sales related to the panic of operators.

Some technical analysts consider that there is no contradiction with the assumption of market efficiency since the graphs take into account all the information available at a given moment. Nevertheless, they forget that fundamental analysis considers operators to be rational, which is not the case for technical analysis. Market movements are predictable because the stakeholders regularly make the same mistakes and systematically deviate from this state of rationality.

## Technical Analysis Is Not a Crystal Ball

Technical analysis is a method that can predict the evolution of prices with some reliability, even if it is not an exact science. This pragmatic method focuses primarily on the psychology of operators. It was developed by people operating on the financial markets (Charles Dow, GANN, Homma, Schabacker, and others). The technical analysis serves mainly as a market barometer and can detect excessive movements of crowds. Some of its detractors equate it with a crystal ball, whereas it is simply an effective tool for analyzing market movements.

There is no such thing as a martingale on the financial markets, that is, an infallible system that makes it possible to win every time. First of all, the only "martingale" is the result of hard work, iron discipline and the courage to stand up even when events are unfavorable.

Operators generally have imperfect knowledge of technical analysis. In addition, it should be noted that the mastery of this approach is insufficient to succeed in the markets. Indeed, it is not enough to correctly predict the evolution of stock prices to beat the markets. The trader must also develop certain qualities that have nothing to do with his analytical know-how (independence of mind, absence of ego, self-control, acceptance of uncertainty and risk).

## The Reasons for the Current Success of Technical Analysis

Technical analysis is now more and more popular. We will list some explanatory elements of this current success.

### *The Limits of Fundamental Analysis*

First of all, part of the success of technical analysis can be explained by the somewhat dull assessment of the fundamental analysis. This approach has been strongly criticized in recent years due not only to the bad - or even "misleading" - recommendations of financial analysts but also because of the numerous financial scandals.

Laura Unger (president of the SEC13 in 2000), in a report, showed that 99% of the recommendations of the 28,000 US financial analysts were to "buy" or "keep" securities in March 2000. In addition, some stars of financial analysis did not stop their buying recommendations despite the market downturn. This has been very misinterpreted by individual investors and has given rise to numerous lawsuits.
Henry Blodget, an analyst at Merrill Lynch, waited until August of 2000 to lower his rating on e-Toys Inc. and Pets.com Inc. (which he recommended for buying when they had already lost more than 75% of their value.)

Mary Meeker, a senior analyst at Morgan Stanley, gained tremendous notoriety by issuing a very positive report on Internet values in 1995. After March 2000, she remained on the purchase and the titles she advised, including Priceline.com and Drugstore.com, literally collapsed.

Even after assuming that fundamental analysis has a predictive quality, the many financial scandals have shown that it is very difficult for an investor, whether individual or professional, to obtain complete and reliable information on the fundamental value of a security. Operated by insider operators taking advantage of their privileged position.

# Chapter 6
# Designing a Trading Plan

## Flexibility: Adapting Your Strategy to Market Conditions

The trader must never be obstinate, he must agree to adopt. This situation is obviously delicate. A good trader must rigorously apply his trading plan, while not considering the rules of the plan as immutable. Traders often apply the same strategy regardless of market configuration. The good trader considers the different market conditions and develops the most effective strategies for each situation. Thus, some day-traders have a strategy for opening, another for mid-day and finally one for closing. Others have adopted specific strategies for bull markets, bear markets and for trend-free markets. A good trader is able to adapt to changing markets and new conditions.

In addition, market conditions change over time (the market of the 2000s is different from that of the 1990s). Some effective strategies have not been effective today.

Nevertheless, the adaptation of the strategy must be based on in-depth research work and a critique of the methods used. The trader should never question his system when operating in real-time because it can be harmful. This phase of reflection should always be conducted calmly: the trader must prioritize strategic thinking before the fight and apply his strategy calmly in the heat of the moment.

Finally, for the great trader Mark Weinstein, "no approach in technical analysis works all the time. You have to know when to use each method. I do not believe in mathematical systems that approach markets in the same way. I use my person as the system and I constantly change the input to achieve the same output: profit."

The professional trader is constantly adapting its strategies to market conditions. He questions his system and tries to improve it with the aim of performance. Some principles are immutable, but it is still possible to improve certain rules or techniques of opening and closing positions, and this is what the big trader should be trying to do by being flexible and adapting himself to the evolution of the market

## Look For the Line of Least Resistance

The strategy must always stick to market circumstances. The trader must know the direction of the flows because it is by marrying that he dominates them. In trading, you should never oppose the course of things and respect the famous saying "trout is your ally". We must leave the market to dictate the procedure to follow and not pretend to want to impose our certainty.

Thus, when a market is without trend, it is dangerous to apply a trend tracking strategy. In this case, the trader will only have to buy support and sell resistance. The trader must pierce the intentions of his opponents, the object of the analysis. He must decipher the intentions of professional traders, including detecting the right signals and eliminating false signals.

## Lessons Learned

A successful trader lets his profits run and quickly cuts his losses. As a result, it maximizes profits and minimizes losses and achieves gains on average greater than losses.

In low-performing traders, the average loss is usually greater than the average gain: they quickly exit their winning positions and return to hope mode when the market invalidates their point of view instead of facing reality. Everything seems linked: the successful trader has a high payoff ratio and an honorable probability of success, which allows him to take more risks and thus to record a superior performance.

### *Example of a Trading System*

Suppose that the trader relies on the following criteria to open a position:
- To position himself only in the presence of a double-bottomed graphic figure;
- Bullish divergence on the validated RSI, - MACD higher than its signal line.

The trader has tested his system over quite a long history and he finds that it has a probability of success of 60% and a payoff ratio of 2. It is a profitable system that can be used in the markets. Nevertheless, the probability of success, as well as the payoff ratio, is based on past data, which the trader will never know for sure if they will happen again. The only thing he can handle is a risk, which proves the importance of money management.

## Vary The Size Of Its Positions?

Some traders use the same size regardless of the market configuration. They consider equiprobable events and believe that each configuration must, therefore, be assigned the same risk capital. This approach does not seem optimal for us and we think that it is necessary to vary the size of the position according to the opportunity that presents itself: to increase the size of its position when the opportunity seems excellent and its potential still important; reduce the size of the opportunity does not really give satisfaction, or even completely out of it.

It should be noted that novice traders do the opposite: at the outset, they allocate the same risk to all opportunities (good or bad); after a series of gains or losses, they increase the size of the position, whatever the opportunity, and take significant risks. They are suffering new losses that push them to engage more and more transactions, but also to increase the size of their positions, which can sometimes lead to ruin.

The performance relies heavily on the trader's ability to vary the size of his exposure based on opportunities. Likewise, it involves taking bigger risks and accepting higher drawdowns. Despite this, we remain convinced that good traders take much less risk than others and remain cautious in their decisions, even if they are not afraid to take positions. They consider that without risk-taking there are no possible gains.

This point of view was also defended by Thorp in his famous book Beat the dealer, which discusses the importance of increasing one's risk when probabilities are in our favor. Nevertheless, he also insists that conditions only favor 10% of the time and that it is during this period that we must maximize our chances of success. The payoff ratio must be favored over the probability of success.

Many traders place a lot of importance on the probability of success because it means that they are often more right than wrong. In fact, the payoff ratio has much more weight than the probability of success.

The payoff ratio is often low for traders because of the psychological bias highlighted by Kahneman and Tversky. In fact, individuals have a much greater aversion for losses than the satisfaction gained from the gains made: a loss is twice as painful as the satisfaction gained from a gain of the same amount. It is for this reason that people tend to take profits very quickly and not take their losses (so not to execute their stops) or even to ignore any information about them because they seem too painful.

# Chapter 7
# Different Options Styles

## Options Trading

Options' trading is an extremely well-known trading style for a wide range of investors. It tends to be utilized when investing in a range of financial instruments as well as options, for example, futures, foreign currencies, and stocks. It's basically a style that is somewhere close to the specific short-term style of day trading and the longer-term approach of utilizing a buy and hold strategy.

It's typically a style utilized by those generally new to options trading, but at the same time, it's frequently supported by those who have higher experience also. There are various advantages to options trading and specifically, utilizing this style for trading options. Similarly, as with investment, there's a great deal of information, you ought to learn before really beginning.

## What Does Options Trading Involve?

Options' trading is tied with searching for short-term price momentum and attempting to profit from that price force by buying and selling suitably. As the value of options contracts is to a great extent dependent on the value of basic securities, you are basically hoping to recognize the price energy of any financial instrument, for example, stocks, and afterward trade the significant options contracts as indicated by how you anticipate that the hidden security will move.

By and large, you will enter a position and after that exiting it a short period of time later. That period of time can be anyplace between several days or half a month, contingent upon to what extent you are anticipating that the price momentum should last.

With this style, you aren't as worried about the basic value of the securities involved and how they will perform in the long term as you would utilize a buy and hold investment strategy. While some basic analysis of the securities can surely be valuable, you are basically hoping to distinguish circumstances where a specific security is probably going to move sensibly altogether in price over a generally short period of time. This depends on trends and patterns. When you have recognized that circumstance, then you would then be able to buy or sell in like manner with a view to profiting from the price movements.
Options' trading is achievable utilizing most sorts of options, and you can utilize diverse orders to take short positions or long positions on distinctive contracts. You can even utilize a mix of various contracts and orders to make spreads which can significantly expand the number of chances for profiting. Spreads can likewise be utilized to limit risk presentation on a specific position by limiting potential losses.

There are really two distinct types of options trading options: discretionary and mechanical. Discretionary options trading depends on using your own analysis and judgment to make a decision. Mechanical options trading entails following a fixed regulation to determine fixed entry and exit spots, and you can even utilize software to determine what transactions you ought to make and when.

## Why Use an Options trading Style?

Of the two most broadly known and acknowledged trading styles, options trading and utilizing a buy to hold investment strategy, options trading is the best style for options. The buy to hold strategy isn't generally appropriate by any means since options are basically short-term trading instruments. Most contracts end following a couple of months or shorter, and even the longer-term LEAPS become invalid at the end of a year. Thusly, options are the ideal instrument for options trading.

Options' trading is much less serious than day trading and furthermore significantly less time-devouring. With day trading, you must be ready to spend the entire day checking the markets while trusting that the opportune time will enter and exit positions. The levels of attention required can be exceptionally depleting, and it requires an unmistakable range of abilities to fruitfully utilize this style. Options trading, then again, is an ideal center ground for those that need to see a sensibly fast return on their money yet don't have room schedule-wise to devote to buying and selling throughout the day, consistently.

It's an incredible style for those that are relative amateurs and those that have full-time occupations or have other time responsibilities amid the working day. It's feasible to emphasize potential swings, enter the important position, and after that simply check how your position is faring toward the finish of every day, or even every couple of days, before choosing whether or not to exit that position.

You can end losses or utilize spreads, so you are never in peril of losing more money than you are okay with. You can really utilize spreads by different strategies, some of which are especially valuable for options trading when you aren't for all time checking price changes in the market.

The fundamentals of this style are moderately simple to understand, which another valid justification for giving it a go is. You don't need to have an immense measure of knowledge to begin; you simply need to know how options function and be ready to devote a sensible measure of time to search for the correct chances. Some risks are definitely involved. However, this style to a great extent, allows you to take absolutely any level of risk that you are alright with and allows you to make some fair profits.

## Guidance for Options Trading

Investigating and planning is essential for anybody hoping to utilize this style. You should be very ready and have a smart thought of precisely what sorts of examples and patterns you are searching for and what kind of transactions you will make in some random circumstance. You definitely want a level of flexibility in the manner in which you trade, though it can have an unmistakable arrangement of targets and a characterized plan for how you will accomplish those objectives. The market is unstable, and it will require you to make changes in like manner. A strong plan, however, gives you a platform to work from.

Great investigative abilities are exceptionally helpful. You don't need to settle on choices as fast as though you were day trading, so you have time to break down circumstances and work out the best entry and exit spots purposes of a specific trend or pattern that you recognize. It's likewise critical to be quiet. If it happens that you can't find a decent entry point to exploit a price swing, at that point you need the discipline and persistence to hold up until the point that an open door presents itself. It's not necessary to make trades each day if there are no appropriate ones to be made, and the way to progress is actually about picking the correct chances and carrying out your transactions at the perfect time.

It's a smart thought to set the greatest losses on any position that you enter. It's improbable that you will get your expectations and conjectures right every time you enter a position, and sometimes the prices will move against you. You should, at all times be prepared to cut your losses and escape an awful position; it can and will occur, and you simply need to ensure that your great trades exceed your terrible trades.

So also, you ought to dependably have an objective profit for a position, and close your position when you have achieved that profit. Endeavoring to press additional profit out of an open position can simply bring about losing your profits. Your parameters for limiting losses can simply be set and locking in profits by options spreads, stop orders or a blend of both.

## Options Brokers for Trading Options

A standout amongst the most imperative choices you have to decide on before beginning with this, or some other style, is which stockbroker would it be advisable for you to utilize? Utilizing an online broker isn't as important for options' trading as it is considered for day trading, yet you could utilize a conventional broker in the event that you needed. Notwithstanding, there are as yet numerous advantages to utilizing an online broker; for instance, they usually sell less expensive fees and commissions which will enable you to submit your requests.

- Position: Trading

- Trading Intensity: Low
- Holding Period: 1 to a half-year
- Time Commitment: Low
- Risk Level: Low

Not like other options trading styles, position trading isn't usually utilized for most financial instruments. Actually, it is practically one of a kind to trading subsidiaries, for example, futures and options. It is a generally safe style that is utilized to make a profit by exploiting a portion of the sure window that options can present. It isn't a style that ought to be embraced by novices, as it requires a complete comprehension of options and all the related elements.

Position trading is a style that is only utilized by professional and institutional traders. Market makers, for instance, would utilize this style to satisfy their job. However, it is truly not a style of that any easy-going or home trader ought to consider. Options trading is typically the best decision for many, or day trading for those that can make a full-time responsibility. It is still necessary to see how this style operates, however.

## What Is Position Trading?

Position trading is a technique that is generally utilized by professionals that stand for banks and other big financial institutions. It's principally utilized for transacting derivatives and, specifically, options contracts. If this style is to be used, a trader has to know significantly something beyond how options function; really deep information of all the important qualities and elements that influence options and their prices is required.

Furthermore, it is necessary to have an entire comprehension of all the diverse strategies that can be utilized, how they operate, their advantages and disadvantages, and how they can be used relying upon winning market conditions.

The basic aim of this style is that as much as possible, the risk should be reduced, regardless of whether it implies making a low percentage of profits. Position traders often want to profit from directional moves in the market like the majority of the investors. However, their exercises are generally founded on supporting existing portfolios against those directional moves and endeavoring to make a profit from the time decay of options contracts.

Holding positions for really long periods of time is usually required, with the end goal to amplify the potential profit, and options are regularly held straight up until lapse. In spite of the fact that position traders may just hold positions for short periods sometimes, contingent upon the strategies being utilized and the market conditions, the fundamental meaning of a position trader is somebody who holds a position as long as possible.

## Profiting From Position Trading

We have just clarified how this style is not generally appropriate for the occasional investor on account of the extraordinarily deep knowledge that is required. It ought not totally to be disregarded even if you truly feel you have understood all about options, however generally you will constantly be in an ideal situation utilizing an alternate style. Another explicit purpose behind this is the manner in which that position traders make their profit.

The general purpose of this style is to dependably reduce risk to the barest minimum. The level of risk is indicated by the profit levels to be made like most types of investing. While the facts confirm that the professionals can make a huge amount of money, this is on the grounds that they are managing large measures of capital.

The vast majority of the strategies utilized are based on endeavoring to ensure a specific sum of profit, anyway little that profit is. Maintaining reduced risk is considerably more essential than attempting to make the most profits. When trading with a big measure of capital, achieving returns of minuscule percentages can be particularly beneficial. Notwithstanding, for those that have a littler beginning capital, making any sort of huge money utilizing this style is extremely hard in fact.

Positions trading options aren't probably going to be the best style for many of options traders. It's basically the space of professional and institutional traders for two basic reasons. To start with, it requires a deep knowledge of everything identified with options trading, every one of the elements included, and all the achievable strategies that can be utilized. Second, it's just actually feasible to make any sort of huge profits with substantial beginning capital.

## Market Makers

Market makers assume a critical job in options trading, and in certainty, they exist in the markets for a wide range of various financial instruments. They are basically there to keep the financial markets running productively by guaranteeing a specific level of liquidity. They are not your normal trader; they are professionals that have legally binding associations with the significant exchanges and complete a substantial volume of transactions.

It isn't important, that you comprehend what market makers do, except if you have goals to join a financial institution and secure occupation as one. Be that as it may, having an idea of why they exist, and the impact they have is in any case valuable.

## The Role of Market Makers

The fundamental job of market makers in the options exchanges is to make sure that the markets run easily by empowering traders to buy and sell options regardless of whether there are no open orders to suit the required trade. They do this by keeping up the substantial and various arrangement of an extensive variety of various options contracts.

For instance, if a trader needed to buy certain options contracts yet there was nobody else at that time selling those contracts, at that point a market creator would sell the options from their very own portfolio or hold, to encourage the transaction. Moreover, if a trader needed to sell certain contracts yet there was no open buyer, after that, a market creator could execute the transaction by buying those contracts and adding them to their portfolio.

Market makers ordinarily ensure that there is both profundity and liquidity in the options exchanges. In the absence of the two, there would be altogether fewer transactions done, and it would be a lot harder to buy and sell options. There would likewise be fewer options in the method for various contracts accessible in the market.

Allowing traders to execute transactions immediately, regardless of whether there is no ready buyer or seller, thusly, guarantees that the exchanges work effectively and traders can generally buy and sell the options they desire to.

## How Do Market Makers Operate?

As said earlier, market makers keep their very own portfolios that comprise countless options contracts. They trade in substantial volumes and can buy options from traders who want to sell and sell them to traders willing to buy. Without the producers, the market could easily cease, and options trading would turn out to be greatly hard.

In return for the imperative job they play in options trading, they have significant right inside the marketplace that allows them to basically make some type of profit on every single transaction they make because of the manner in which options are priced.

There are two primary perspectives to the price of options that any options trader ought to get. To begin with, the real price comprises two major segments: extrinsic value and intrinsic value. Besides, and this is applicable to how market makers work, they are priced on the exchanges with an asking price and a bid price. Anybody hoping to buy options contracts would pay the asking price from those contracts, while anybody composing or selling contracts would get the bid price.

The bid price is lower than the asking price; this means that any person buying contracts would pay a higher price than the person selling them would get. The difference between these two prices is referred to as the spread, and it's from this spread the market makers gain from. They are essentially allowed to sell at the asking price and buy at the bid price, consequently profiting from the spread.

Let's assume a case of specific options contracts that are trading with an asking price of $2.20 and a bid price of $2. Should a person place a request to buy these contracts, in the meantime as another person submits a request to sell these contracts, the market creator essentially goes about as an intermediary. They buy from the dealer, paying the bid price of $2.00, and afterward sold to the buyer at the asking price of $2.20, consequently making a $.20 profit for each contract traded.

Obviously, it won't generally be workable for a market creator to buy and sell contracts at the same time – generally, there would be little requirement for them in any case. This means that they are still strongly presented to the risk of price movements and time decay of the options they claim. The essential point of a market producer is to trade whatever a number of contracts as could be expected under the circumstances to profit by the spread, however, should likewise utilize viable positioning strategies to guarantee that they are not presented to a lot of risks.

In spite of the natural advantage of being a market producer proffered by the spread, it's still very feasible for them to lose money.

## Who Then Are The Market Makers?

Market makers are typically people that work for banks, brokerage firms, and other financial institutions that are specifically contracted with an exchange or exchanges, to satisfy the job. As they are not permitted to trade in the interest of open investors and traders, they will utilize their very own capital to fund every one of their transactions.

They must show great prowess at what they do, with great expository capacities and a considerable measure of mental quality. At the point when the significant firms enroll market makers, they would more often than not be searching for a great deal of appropriate involvement and an unmistakable sign of the required range of abilities.

# Chapter 8
# ETF's, Options and Other Tricks

## Best Brokers for Options Trading

E-Trade's OptionsHouse platform and mobile application are the highest quality levels of option trading platforms. OptionsHouse at present gives traders premium-quality tools without the top-notch price tag. Best options trading platform.

Fidelity platform shows traders the correct way and gives them every resource they require as the trading goes. Options trading can be scary and confounding for new traders. Fidelity offers a monstrous measure of free research and information introduced in a way that is not overpowering for inexperienced traders. Best research and training.

Tastyworks has become famous in options trading. The brokerage, driven by its parent financial media organization, Tastytrade, offers probably the best rates in options trading matched with incredible tools and options for traders. The brokerage flaunts a low commission structure, finish with zero closing trade fees, depending on the kind of opening contract: options on futures, futures, options on stocks, and stocks. Best lost cost broker.

EOption gives a proficient, nitty-gritty platform for active investors who prefer low expenses to an extravagant platform.

The investment funds can be critical for cutting-edge stock and options traders who have different sources for the research and information they require.

Honorable mentions: Lightspeed, Merrill Edge, Options House, and Trade King

## Do Not Believe Everything You Hear

One last admonition about picking a broker: Just because a sales representative or promotional material says a brokerage firm offers some new feature on their software or an exceptional service doesn't imply that it's quite true. As we know, some marketers are emissaries of frivolity, preferring to promote the positive and disregard the negative. In this manner, the cases you read in writing delivered by the firms themselves might be painfully exaggerated.

In all truth, managers and programmers frequently tell advertisement marketing specialists that some new service or product highlight will be available when the promotion turns out, and then fail to meet their own schedule. What's more, sales representatives are every now and then told things that are non-existent work better than they do—and, not being experts and ready to decide for themselves, just pass the misrepresentations along.

Our point is: Try to do more other than converse with the brokerage agent. Look at some reviews; online and in popular financial magazines here and there. Then speak with people who have to be in the industry long before you.

## Secure Yourself with a Backup Plan

Be absolutely mindful, nonetheless, that regardless of how good a brokerage firm is painted as being, you'll more likely have an issue or two preceding all said and done. These could be the consequence of disturbances at the exchanges, with your broker's database, or with your own computer, Internet connection, or telephone line.

Or, you could even commit an exorbitant error as the consequence of stupid calculation errors. Approximately fourteen years back, we signed onto our internet browser to check the news and opening market indices —and nearly hopped into frenzy mode when the EarthLink™ start page showed the Dow down 397.85 for just 10 minutes after the opening. Obviously, it was simply a terrible calculation; the Dow was extremely down simply 7.85—however, the browser's numbers weren't right throughout the day. Had we followed up on those numbers, it could have been a catastrophe. Be that as it may, that is only the manner in which it is in today's powered-up world, kept running by PCs, encouraged by telephone lines and absolutely subject to the ideal execution of electrical transmission lines.

To shield yourself from the impacts of these mechanical caprices, build up a reinforcement plan that goes past simply hoping to get the telephone and call your broker when the framework goes down. This plan ought to include:

- Be certain you generally have limits and stops set up on your weak positions—both profitable and unprofitable.
- Be certain you completely comprehend the risks before attempting new strategies or starting new plays.
- Printing out day by day printed copies of your open positions in the event that the broker's server fails.

- Closely observing your account status, particularly your equity balance, and printing hard copies of key account outlines at any rate week by week.

With those protections set up, technical issues may cost you a little loss. However, you'll never confront overwhelming financial difficulty. What's more, should the broker encounter a total framework disappointment, your paper duplicates will kill any plausibility of debate in regards to your positions and value of accounts.

Concerns such as those highlighted earlier are legitimate. However, they're not really motivations to shy away from options trading—particularly given the technological and innovative advancements.

# Chapter 9
# Options Strategies

## How to Trade In Stocks

### *The Advantages of the Options Trading System*

By opening a part of the position (half for example), we avoid losing a lot of money if we make a mistake on the meaning of the market. In a way, the trader tests the market. We only strengthen our position when the market gives us the reason. In this case, we expect confirmation or a new low point (in a bull market) or high point (in a bear market) in the current trend. For example, if we are buyers it is possible to strengthen one's position when the RSI lands on the neutrality zone. The placement of the stop will be slightly below the base which has been broken to strengthen the position.

This technique allows the trader to avoid the classic mistake of getting out of a winning position too early and hesitating to cut a losing position. If the position results in a loss, it will not be too big and therefore the trader will not hesitate to cut it. Indeed, when the loss is heavy, it is often painful and traders prefer to go into hope mode rather than face it. In addition, this approach allows the trader to play the movement in all its amplitude since it will strengthen its position which will prevent it from going out quickly.

In addition, the trader who strictly applies his plan will avoid downward averaging. This serious fault is often fatal. From now on, with this method, the trader will strengthen his position only when the market evolves in his direction and will not cut it too fast or with a small gain. Finally, the last advantage of this method is that it allows testing the market. If the stock does not react as expected, the loss will be only 50% of the loss that would have been incurred if the entire position had been opened at the very beginning. Thus, this method allows the trader to strictly adhere to the stock market adage: "Cut your losses and ride your winners."

## The Limits of the Options Trading System

This method presents the risk of strengthening a position while a market reversal is emerging. It is not effective in a market without trend because the trader will strengthen its position on an extreme level (high point or low point). He must, therefore, be convinced that there is a tendency to apply this approach. This method adapts badly to a market without trend but even in this case, it presents limited risks.

## The Classic System: Open Its Position in One Time

The classic method is to fully open its position and then take profits during the upward movement (for a purchase) or downward movement (for a sale).

## The Limits of the Classical System

This system is mainly adapted to a market without a trend. It should be noted that the losses are much greater than for the options trading system and that the performance is not necessarily greater. Nevertheless, when the market is volatile this system is the most efficient. The trader will have to focus on carefully selecting his positions (thus increasing his probability of success) and taking profits faster.

## A Pragmatic Method to Maximize Trading

One of the main attractions of technical analysis is that it does not present huge barriers to entry. It is less demanding than the fundamental analysis in terms of knowledge to acquire. Fundamental analysis generally requires long and solid academic training in economic and financial analysis. This training is usually difficult to acquire, which can discourage more than one.

The researcher Olivier Godechot conducted a sociological study on traders operating in a Paris trading room. This research found that traders and other financial operators had little control over economic reasoning. The author even goes ahead to say that the market economist was merely popularizing the economy and did not push his analyzes very far.

Moreover, even with this method of analysis, investors are not necessarily well equipped to understand the significant and persistent discrepancies in the price of a financial asset compared to its fundamental value. The tests conducted by Meese and Rogoff (1983) have shown that it is impossible for fundamental analysis to predict the evolution of exchange rates. They even go so far as to argue that a naïve model was often more efficient than a model based on fundamental analysis.

The frequent and large discrepancies between the price of a financial asset and its fundamental value (assessed by financial analysts) are hardly explained by the fundamentals or they are posterior. Finally, the technical analysis is not reduced in the short term as many experts say. This method offers reliability in the forecasts made, and this as well in the short term as on the medium and long term, as we will see it thereafter.

## Equal Treatment for All Stakeholders

For the Orthodox school, an efficient market is characterized by the transparency of information. But many insiders (employees of a company, business bankers, family, friends, financial analysts, etc.) have some privileged information, which they can take advantage of. Everyone is not equal in the phase of information.

For the proponents of technical analysis, all the information available at a given moment is integrated into the courses. If a company intends to report poor results, it is likely that this information is visible on the price, and the technical analysis offers the opportunity to anticipate this negative news. Very often, insiders will seek to get rid of their securities, which cause a decline in stock prices (no apparent news) and are a sure sign for seasoned operators.

The role of the technical analyst is to detect the moments when a title will shift without valid reason and therefore to be alert all the time. The graph contains all the information investors' need, which puts them on an equal footing. Some economists even go so far as to say that technical analysis does not necessarily contradict the assumption of market efficiency since it is based on the same assumptions. This approach is attractive and reassures private investors, who have the same information as professionals.

With technical analysis, performance will be primarily a function of personal discipline and experience. Indeed, having the same information does not mean that its use will be the same for everyone. Some people will know how to exploit it better than others and will react appropriately. Implicitly, this means that using the same analysis tool does not necessarily imply consistency in decision making. The psychological dimension that explains the effectiveness of technical analysis also makes it possible to understand why individuals do not make the same decisions while basing themselves on the same information.

## Technical Analysis Is Better Accepted By the Academic World

Considered originally as a naive model by the academic world, technical analysis is increasingly accepted today. Indeed, the assumption of the efficiency of the markets, dominant yesterday, is more and more questioned. The work done by behaviorists and conventionalists supports the idea that prices can strongly and durably shift their fundamental value for no good reason.

A. Orlean defends the idea of self-referential rationality, at the origin of rational speculative bubbles that can be formed even in the presence of perfectly rational individuals. Stakeholders will rationally use the dominant convention to make their decisions because they believe that it is better to follow the market than to refer to fundamental value.

Better yet, the work of the behaviorists gives an almost scientific character to the technical analysis. H. Krow likened technical analysis to behavioral analysis. In the preface of his book, he highlights three main schools of thought: fundamental analysis, random walk and finally the behavioral approach. According to Krow, technical analysis is the counterpart of behavioral analysis.

Closer to home, an article in The Economist in 1993 establishes a link between behavioral finance and technical analysis. This is only fair because technical analysis has focused on the behavior of individuals well before the emergence of the behaviorist approach. This pragmatic approach had, moreover, highlighted the existence of recurrent errors, the peculiarity of human nature. Thus, the famous: "Let your profits run and cut your losses quickly" is symptomatic of market reality. Indeed, stakeholders would tend to cut their winning positions too quickly and hesitated for a long time before closing their losing positions. This stock market adage, which cannot be dated precisely, has been demonstrated by the experiments of Kahneman and Tversky.

## An Approach Acclaimed By Major Traders

A method is judged by its success. In a pragmatic way, the success of technical analysis can be explained simply by the spectacular performance of some of its users.

The problem of technical analysis is that it can be of formidable efficiency in the hands of a great trader, and represent an extreme danger for a novice trader. O. Godechot quotes in his work a trader who explains the reason for the success of the technical analysis in his trading room:

"The chief economist of the trading room makes many mistakes or justifies an economic event posterior while the chartist of the room is right in nearly 70% of cases."

On many traders surveyed by high-flying J. Schwager, over 80% said they only use technical analysis or in addition to fundamental analysis. Ed Seykota is a perfect example: a graduate engineer from MIT, this trader has achieved a performance of 25,000% over a period of sixteen years. He does not hesitate to say that he does not touch fundamentals - which he even calls "funnymentals" - and only uses models that use technical analysis.

According to him, "a good surfer does not have to master fluid physics and resonance to get a good wave. The goal is to feel when the wave will take shape and have the courage to seize it at the right time". The famous trader Bruce Kovner goes in this direction when he explains the effectiveness of this method:

"I use a lot of technical analysis and it's a fabulous method. It helps to clarify the fundamental analysis. Technical analysis is like a barometer. Fundamentalists who say that graphs are useless are like the doctor who feels it's pointless to take the temperature of his patient. That does not make sense. If you are a serious trader, you need to know where the market is, whether euphoria is dominant or whether pessimism prevails. The trader must know everything about the markets if he wants to have an advantage."

The approach of Kovner is rich in information. Indeed, according to this manager, technical analysis should not be considered as an exact science, but rather as a market barometer. It allows to know the forces involved and to guess the dominant feeling of the market. It is, as for the doctor, to take the temperature of the market, to make a diagnosis before recommending a remedy. However, Kovner being an exceptional trader, it is difficult to generalize his approach. It is true that operators often use technical analysis without real control and rarely operate as strategists.

These non-standard traders are an excellent ad for technical analysis. This method, which may seem esoteric and unscientific, draws its credibility and quasi-scientific character from the success of "some" of its users. What better argument for market efficiency than a person who has regular earnings over a long period of time and consistently uses the same method of analysis?

Nevertheless, these remarks must be nuanced. The success of these traders is not only explained by the method of analysis. Strong market experience, iron discipline, and personal talent have probably played a significant role in their success. It is important to note that many traders have been ruined several times before accumulating considerable fortunes, and that experience plays a fundamental role in the success of a trader.

Finally, the signals used in technical analysis evolve over time. If the phenomena of euphoria and greed are recurrent, the way in which they emerge can evolve. A good trader must, therefore, have the ability to adapt to changing markets.

# Chapter 10
# To Do and Not to Do

## The Strategist Trader

According to the strategic approach, price is the product of individual beliefs. For a strategist, only the beliefs of others count, even if they are unfounded. Yamina Tadjeddine took into account two scenarios: the other entire actors act as strategists and they will try to anticipate what others will do. André Orléan speaks of self-preferentiality to characterize this phenomenon: the trader will be determined by the beliefs of other stakeholders because the absence of a referent collectively admitted to base the price forces him to do so. It seeks to reduce uncertainty, and to do so it will mimic others ... only one operator is a strategist and all the others are naive stakeholders or rely on an untrained model to make their decisions.

This situation gives rise to two possibilities:
- The strategist cannot influence the prices and, in this case, the price corresponds to the fundamental value;
- The strategist has substantial financial means and enjoys a significant credit with the financial community. It has enough capacity to influence prices and will use it to maximize profit.

De Long, Shleifer, and Waldmann have shown by their model, in 1990, the rational investor will be determined based on ignorant or irrational investors. It will be prompted to handle the work of ignorant investor's passive investors in a destabilizing direction in order to increase their profits. If the myopic investors are trend followers, they buy when the prices go up and sell when the price drops. The interest of the rational investor will be to raise prices, to provoke a purchase by ignorant investors, and then sell on top to take advantage of the market downturn.

The best attitude is that of the strategist because the short-term movements are hardly explained by the fundamentals. Depending on the situation, the strategist will have to adapt his answer. In some cases, it may influence stock prices and use this capacity for its own benefit. In others, it will not have the financial power to do so, but may still adopt a strategic attitude without really influencing the markets. The fundamental value is not fixed and evolves according to different parameters. Take the case of a company with a potential deemed satisfactory by most financial analysts. It goes without saying that a simple political decision or a major technological innovation is enough to upset the game and therefore the fundamental value. What is good at one time is therefore no longer necessarily good at another, and we understand the interest of the investor to adopt a strategic attitude that is not limited to the fundamental value and takes into account the behavior other operators.

The optimal strategy for a trader is, therefore, to make the most profit on an action. The professional trader will prefer to sell undervalued security if he considers that the downside potential is not exhausted then will position himself to buy on a low point to play the movement of recovery: this investor will not be satisfied with part of the movement but will prefer to play the movement in all its amplitude.

To summarize, the trader whether institutional or particular must integrate that:

- Institutional traders master the art of strategy and have more resources than a trader. The risk of shifting the markets and suffer many constraints (legal, liquidity, etc.). On the other hand, they have reliable sources of information, advantageous brokerage fees, which gives them an undeniable advantage on the markets- the private trader is often in a weak position compared to the institutional ones: he can easily be manipulated but can hardly handle the big traders. On the other hand, there are niches from which it will be able to profit because its main advantage (compared to the institutional ones) remains the flexibility: a particular trader fixes his pro-rules and evolves freely on the markets. It does not really have constraints in terms of rules, markets worked, size of positions, liquidity, etc.

## The Importance of Strategy

There is no perfect and ideal technique in trading that applies to all traders and all situations. We can even say that there are as many trading styles as there are traders. The market operator must be wary of the one-size-fits-all solution or miracle system simply because the markets are changing, and what works today will be less effective tomorrow. He must not try to be right, but to maximize his chances of success.

After defining the strategy, we will highlight the main strategies adopted in the business world and we will see to what extent they can be applied to trading.

## Strategy Definition

A trading strategy can be defined as the art of detecting the best opportunities offered by the market and allocating the necessary resources to profit from it. It will consist of understanding the psychology of the speakers and developing a method to capitalize on this knowledge. The goal of the strategy is to be original, powerful and offer a real advantage over the competition.

The development of the strategy and its implementation imply for a trader to have a strong trading system and control his emotions. In fact, we realize that the trader is often the victim of his own bias, that he does not have a real system and that even if it is the case, it will systematically deviate.

The strategy is materialized by the strict and rigorous application of a trading plan including tested and tested rules that will allow the trader to capitalize on recurring figures without neglecting the risk. This strategy will make it possible to define:

How it will determine the entry points by taking into account the money management aspect as well as the technical aspect; the different techniques to make profits; the manner in which the stops will be fixed; the contingency plan which specifies the different approaches of the trader in the face of the disaster scenarios.

Strategy and tactics are often confused: the strategy aims at absolute performance, in other words, victory, whereas tactics are a means to achieve it. Strategy plays an important role as it allows the trader to get out of the chaos that reigns in the fight by keeping in mind firmly rooted principles.

Tactics are at the service of strategy and must never take too much liberty with respect to strategy. This principle is the key to victory, but it is often forgotten by traders and explains for a large part the failure of many of them.

The trading plan will, therefore, include different tactics but must also specify the global strategy of the trader that can be called vision. That is to say that the trader must in his trading plan specify how he sees himself in a few years (the vision) and indicate the strategy that will be put in place to achieve it

## The Different Strategies

Several types of strategies make it possible to succeed. The strategy of global dominance by the costs mainly benefits institutional traders who have extremely low transaction costs and can benefit from small market movements. Generally, they work for large institutions and have a real advantage over individuals. Their fixed costs (hardware, software, offices, etc.) are reduced because of their size and the large sums they brew. In addition, they have an important information network that gives them a real advantage over others.

## The Differentiation Strategy

For a company, differentiation is about creating a product that offers qualities that justify a higher price and a real advantage over the competition. This is the case of innovative products, quality of service, a more efficient organization of work, etc.

Similarly, the trader has every interest in differentiating himself from his competitors by developing a concrete advantage. He can, for example, find a niche and develop an advantage in it. He can also develop an original method and apply it on a regular basis. It is important to note that in the most important trading is not to find a revolutionary method to predict the evolution of stock prices, but simply to find a method with an interesting probability of success9 and to apply them on a regular basis. But often, traders will not respect their system and will be victims of their emotions. Differentiation consists in having an irreproachable preparation and developing a solid and efficient system.

## The Emerging Strategy

This strategy does not question the two previous strategies. A trader can opt for global domination by cost or for differentiation and from time to time adopt an emerging strategy.

An emerging strategy can be defined as a strategy that arises from action. A trader can, for example, be bearish on the market and sell short several securities, then realize that the market holds, that it is not really bearish and that some elements point even in the direction of a bull market. The trader realizes that his idea of origin no longer works and his action [short sale] makes him realize that the markets are bullish. It will be able to be based on this observation and to place itself in the purchase.

To illustrate the concept of emerging strategy we are mentioning the experience of a financial author, from March 2000.

On March 26, 2000, I gave a lecture on the technical indicators at the Technical Analysis show in front of a sold-out room. My diagnosis on the NASDAQ was still bullish and I explained, showing the index graph, that there was currently no danger in this market which remained well oriented with an RSI above 50%. Nevertheless, the main risk was the presence of a bearish divergence not yet validated. If it were to be, we could see a bearish stall.

A few days later, Abby Joseph Cohen, chairman of the investment committee of Goldman Sachs explains "that it reduced from 70% to 65% the share of the shares in its standard portfolio, because of the recent rise of the courses". It was not necessarily bearish as it held 65% equities in its typical portfolio, but the sharp drop in markets validated the bearish divergence.

Then, I understood the issue and I realized that the market is really drawing a major reversal. Indeed, the bearish divergence on the NASDAQ was confirmed by other downward divergences validated on the main European stock market indices (CAC 40, Dax 30, etc.). I, therefore, went bearish on March 29, 2000, on the main indices IS & P 500, CAC 40, DAX 30, MIB ...] and I recommended my clients to sell their securities. This was certainly an emerging strategy since I relied on new elements that I did not have."

This example shows how important it is for a trader to be flexible and never stubborn. It's a good trader's job not to have a fixed opinion and to let the market behavior dictate what to do.

## The Primary Goal of the Trader Must Be His Survival

According to Sun Tzu, one of the most important characteristics of the art of warfare is to make oneself invincible and never to take undue risks. Thus, the trader must aim above all for survival and closely monitor his exposure.

## Manage Your Resources Well

The trader must win by saving himself. He must reserve himself for the best moments and avoid positioning himself simply to kill time. Sun Tzu expressed the same idea 2,500 years ago: "By calculation, consider whether the enemy can be attacked, and only then should the population be mobilized, and the troops lifted; learn how to distribute munitions of war and mouth always, never to give in the excesses of too much or too little."

According to Paul Tudor Jones "always thinking about what we will lose not that we will win, I never risk large amounts of money when figures are going to be released because it is a bet and more than trading."

By positioning the trader is comforted as it feels to be part of the game, but he does not realize he is about to sign financial death. This is the point of view of the great trader Larry Hite who claims not to be in the markets for excitement but to win. The trader should not afford to lose money on positions with a low probability of success. Indeed, it will not be in optimal conditions when the real opportunity will appear: he will be too afraid to position himself and will not open a position; he can take his courage with both hands and try. But in this case, his position will not be consistent because of previously recorded losses that have reduced his capital and therefore decreased his capacity for action.

Often, in trend-free markets, traders will lose lots of ammo and energy instead of booking for the most profitable times (trend markets for example). So when the real movement starts, it's already too late. Much of their capital has been decimated and they no longer have the psychological strength to participate in the movement.

## Never Measure Yourself against Yourself

For Sun Tzu, we must avoid attacking the fortresses and prefer to put the enemy strategies at risk because they are much more malleable. Always wait for the best time to position yourself, never before. The markets are always right and the trader must avoid any ego or seek to impose his point of view on them.

## Stay Discreet About Your Intentions

"The great art of a general is to make sure that the enemy is always ignorant of the place where he will have to fight and to carefully remove from him the knowledge of the posts he keeps. If he comes to the end and can conceal even the least of his steps, he is not only a skillful general; he is an extraordinary man, a prodigy. Without being seen, he sees; he hears without being heard; he acts noiselessly and disposes of as he pleases the fate of his enemies." – Sun Tzu.

The trader has every interest in being discreet about his intentions. This idea applies perfectly to institutional traders. Indeed, if a particular trader is not likely to move the markets due to limited capital, an institutional trader because of its significant positions can quickly be spotted by other operators. Therefore, it is in his best interest to remain discreet about his intentions and never open his position in a single time. Often, important traders split their positions so as not to let their intentions show through.

If for example, a trader wants to get rid of a million titles, this operation will cause a sharp decline in the title if it is performed at once, which will result in an unfavorable average selling price. It is therefore in the interest of the trader not to declare his plans and remain discreet in the way he operates.

Some big traders claim to mentally place their stops so that they are not known by their competitors since some traders can quite easily get this information from brokers and take advantage of it.

## The Interest of Never Revealing Its Strategy

"Let the enemy never know how you intend to fight him, nor how you will attack him, or defend yourself. For if he prepares for the front, his rear will be weak; if he gets ready in the back, his forehead will be fragile; if he prepares on his left, his right will be vulnerable; if he prepares on his right, his left will be weakened; and if he prepares himself everywhere, he will be everywhere in default. If he absolutely ignores it, he will make great preparations, he will try to make himself strong on all sides, he will divide his forces, and that is precisely what will make his loss." – Sun Tzu.

The trader should not make the task easy for his competitors by revealing strategic information. It is better to leave a doubt about one's intentions and wait for the error to come from others. Like chess or poker, you have to have nerves of steel to succeed in trading.

## A Preparation without Flaws

Attack and defense techniques must be mastered by traders. Nevertheless, they must be supplemented by solid preparation. The best traders spend a lot of time preparing for them. They know the markets in which they operate their competitors and have powerful tools.

## Know Your Environment

Sun Tzu insists enormously on the importance of preparation:
"Consider that with many calculations one can win the victory, fear their inadequacy. It is thanks to this method that I examine the situation, and the outcome will be clear. Before coming to a final battle, you must have foreseen it, and have been prepared for a long time; never rely on chance in everything you do in this way. Anticipate everything, dispose of everything, and rely on the enemy when he still believes you a hundred leagues away."

The trader must be familiar with the markets in which it will work (rhythmic, historical development, key support and resistance levels, indicators work best, etc.). He will also have to identify the false signals generated on this market.

## The Importance of Preparation

The trader must take care to establish a solid strategy and to set himself the entry levels, the main pivots, the levels on which profit-taking can be made, the levels around which he can increase his position, cut his position, etc. Before opening a position, the trader is able to determine when he is going to strengthen it, as well as the circumstances that will lead him to take his profits or simply get out of his position. He has already visualized multiple scenarios and mentally prepared for their occurrence. Jean Brilman declines the four-step strategy that we will apply to trade.

## Analyzing the Situation

First of all, the strategist must know his business and the initial situation. The OM / FF model (also known as SWOT) of the Harvard School (strengths/weaknesses, opportunities/threats) recommends that the strategist perform an analysis to assess his strengths and weaknesses, and also, to identify in its environment the main opportunities and threats. The objective of the strategy is above all to develop a sustainable and sustainable competitive advantage.

The trader will have to proceed in the same way by controlling his environment, that is to say by having a perfect knowledge of his main competitors. He will also have to determine his strengths and weaknesses, i.e. the financial means he says, his analytical skills, his trading skills as well as the skills he will have to acquire and develop in the future.

## Specialize

After the preliminary analysis of the situation, the trader will have to determine the market on which he intends to operate (equities, currencies, futures, options, etc.), which method will be used (technical analysis, fundamental analysis, analysis order book, etc.) and finally the time horizon (short term, medium term, long term). This decision will depend heavily on the analysis of the situation, his skills and the means at its disposal.

## Develop a Competitive Advantage

The trader will seek to develop a competitive advantage based on the means at his disposal and his skills. A particular trader will avoid difficult markets and sophisticated techniques and will specialize in medium-term investment. A well-capitalized institutional trader with the most up-to-date technology and very favorable terms from his brokers will be able to specialize in short-term trading.

Beyond this specialization, each trader will have to identify a niche, that is to say, adopt a technique tested on a long enough history and generating positive profitability. It must also be certain that the implementation of this strategy gives it an undeniable advantage over its competitors.

## Deploy Strategy

This step represents the implementation of the strategy. The trader can only start it if the three steps mentioned above have been carefully carried out. Deploying the strategy requires the trader to have a flawless discipline and a good knowledge of his psychological traits.

The strategy is not an exact science. The trader must essentially aim to develop an advantage over the competition and strive to implement it optimally on the markets. For this, it can use methods such as technical analysis or fundamental analysis and look for low-risk and profitable configurations. Its strategy will have to be tested on a long enough history and prove its veracity to be retained.

## Who Are Our Competitors?

Every trader has to list his enemies or potential competitors. Who are they? What can be their impact? How to minimize their impact?

In each market, the competitors are different and arise where we least expect it. Moreover, the competitors are not necessarily located on the markets and can be for example time-consuming elements (meetings with repetition, information sparse and not enough centered on the essential, etc.). The trader will have to identify his competitors but also learn to better control his emotions to operate effectively in the markets.

The goal of the trader is to shelter while waiting for others to make mistakes. He must in no case succumb to the error of exposing himself. For a trader, the enemies are the portfolio managers, investors, brokers, and himself ... By controlling his main enemies, he puts on his side every chance to succeed.

## Be Ready To Fight

"May your principal forces be all on the same side; if you want to attack head-on, make a choice of a sector, and put at the head of your troops all that you have of the best. One rarely resists a first effort, as, on the contrary, it is difficult to recover when one first from below. The example of the brave is enough to encourage your cowards. They follow without difficulty the path shown to them, but they cannot themselves spawn it. If you want to give the left-wing, turn all your preparations on that side, and put on the right-wing what you have weaker; but if you want to conquer by the right-wing, let it be on the right-wing as well as your best troops and all your attention." – Sun Tzu.

Gary Bielfeldt does not believe in diversification. His philosophy is to say that you have to specialize in one area and become an expert. The most important thing for a trader is to have a method to keep his winning positions and get rid of his losing positions quickly.

Specialization is of paramount importance in trading, especially the early days. Novice traders tend to want to do too much at the beginning and disperse. The losses they suffered forced them to give up while a specialization at the beginning would have allowed them to limit the damage.
Too much information kills information: do not scatter. Some traders want to know everything about everything. They think that by having the most sophisticated instruments, the best software, they will be able to conquer the markets. Nothing is further from reality. In fact, the best traders have simple systems that they master perfectly. They know that by wanting too sophisticated things they risk losing their discipline and taking unfavorable positions.

## Visualization

Great traders are used to visualizing their different tactics before markets open. They imagine themselves operating and mentally repeating the most appropriate movements. When markets open, they are already ready.

Mental training trader allows him to be ready and condition when the markets open. He has in mind what he is supposed to do in this or that situation. His strategies must be fully assimilated and mastered so that he can react almost instinctively to situations. Like the general, he must be prepared for the most catastrophic scenarios. The trader must be prepared to act in situations where everything turns against him and be ready for the unexpected.

He knows his weaknesses well and does everything to limit their negative impact. A day trader who loves action should be vigilant during quiet market phases because he may be bored, which will incite him to initiate positions impulsively.

## Cunning

Many traders will forget about any trading plan and let their decisions be dictated by the markets. For Sun Tzu, it's important not to let the game take you and take the lead.

"There will be occasions when you will lower, and others where you will affect to be afraid. You will sometimes pretend to be weak, so that your enemies, opening the door to presumption and pride, will come to attack you improperly or allow themselves to be surprised and cut to pieces shamefully. You will make it so that those who are inferior to you can never penetrate your designs. You will keep your troops always alert, always in motion and in occupation, to prevent them from being softened by a shameful rest. "

## Cunning: The Art of Manipulating Opponents to One's Advantage

In the financial markets, there is no need for manipulation since traders fall into the trap of their psychological biases. They often have a poor understanding of the financial markets and rush when to wait and wait to take action. Sometimes, some traders will seek to provoke these reactions by for example breaking support or resistance so as to trigger an emotional reaction in their competitors.
The best traders know how to use the psychological bias of other traders for their benefit. They have studied their attitudes and are able to guess how they will behave in certain situations. Thus, they will voluntarily provoke these psychological biases to obtain desired effects among novice traders that they can use for their benefit. They are inspired by that of Sun Tzu.

"The great science is to make him want anything you want him to do, and to provide him, without his noticing it, all the means to assist you."

This is for the trader to decide when the transition to action should begin. Nothing must be imposed on him. Thus, a trader can artificially raise prices to create a certain euphoria among traders and encourage them to position themselves for the purchase. Conversely, in a bear market, professional traders will have an interest in exacerbating the fears of novices.

In trading, this means that the trader must use the psychological bias of others to his advantage instead of being a victim. The trader should never rush and make sure his competitors work for him. He waits for the best moment before positioning himself, that is to say, the one where the other traders make mistakes, victims of their impatience. In a market without trend, it is not uncommon to note many false breaks support or resistance.

## Fulcrums and Turns

An upper pivot point is the highest point of a price movement before the low of the highest bar is broken down. A lower pivot point is the lowest point of a price movement before the high of the lowest bar is breached upwards. An upper fulcrum becomes a resistance, a lower fulcrum becomes support. The movement from one fulcrum to the next is called momentum.

## The Direction of the Trend

The trend rises as long as new highs and higher lows are reached. The shift to the downtrend occurs when the last low before the highest high is breached.

## Closing Prices

A number of close-out prices within a relatively small range indicate a market that is in a state of equilibrium. Moving away from this close range of close prices suggests an imbalance where demand exceeds supply or vice versa. On the basis of this assumption, patterns can be developed with which one obtains a technical advantage when dealing with the trend. Be very careful if you want to use such patterns as an entry point against the prevailing trend. You can minimize the risk by making a correction after the closing price points the way.

A two-bar closing price reversal with increased spread is likely to signal a significant reversal when it occurs in the direction of the trend. The odds increase when the closing price is below the end of the previous bar.

If several closing prices occur within a narrow range, then the last closing price often indicates the direction in which the breakout will occur from this equilibrium. If the first thrust comes from a close formation of several closeouts with a long bar, then it usually points in the direction the course will take in the short term.

## Closing Prices with Non-Overlapping Bars

An even weaker pattern is a three-bar pattern with a non-overlapping bar - a bar whose height is below the bottom of the last bar with the top pivot point.

## The Direction of the Trend

A bar running against the direction of the four previous final curves may indicate a trend reversal. If the four closing prices are close to each other and not all rising, then the trend changes to the bottom. If all four closing prices are rising, then the reverse bar is likely to correct only the overbought situation and the shift is neutral.

Once the course has reached its goal, the profits can be protected as follows:

1. Close the position upon reaching the target course
2. Tracing a stop at least three ticks below the lows of each bar
3. Set a stop a tick below a correction that corresponds to the extent of the previous correction
4. Hold the position until a four-bar reversal occurs
5. Closing the position if higher closing prices occur over three or four bars
6. Closing the position when reverse patterns occur in the next shorter time frame

This is often an indication of the validity of the breakthrough. It is generally statistically significant and gives a small advantage to the trader if the previous bar shows signs of demand closing above the opening price (point 3 above). However, this advantage is not enough to make up for the slippage and day trading fees. You could do more research by keeping a profitable position longer and securing it with a tight stop. This is how successful trading systems are developed.

## Reversal Day

A reversal day signals a one-day change from the bulls to the bears or vice versa. From a statistical point of view, this pattern alone cannot be used profitably, but in combination with other technical indicators, it can be very useful.

A reversal day is a day on which a value trades below (above) the pre-tort rate and then closes above (below) the low (high) and opening price of the previous day. This type of price movement may mean a temporary or permanent end to a smaller prevailing trend.

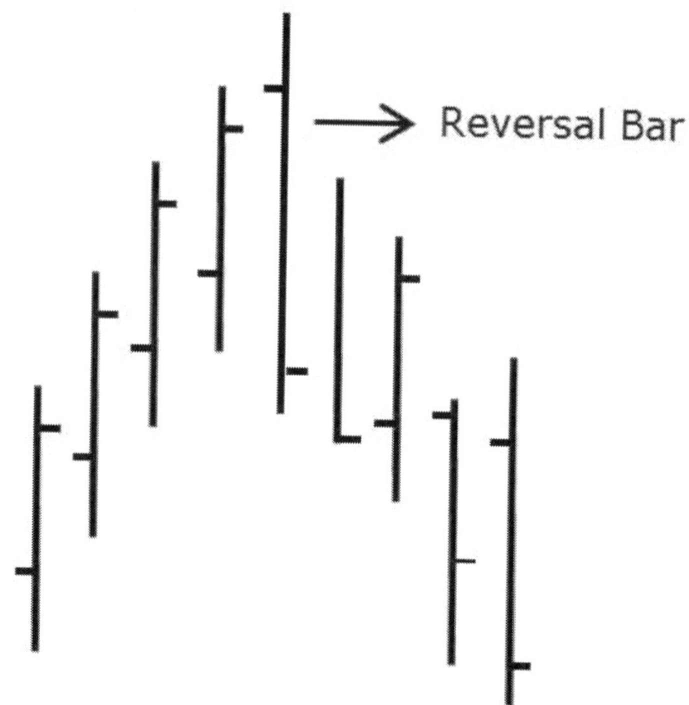


## Type and Occurrence of the Reversal Days

The following factors influence the meaning of a reversal day:
1. The span of the beam
2. The number of closing prices that are reversed
3. The number of pivot points that are above and below

Using computers, the reverse tag pattern was tested for its suitability as a market entry. The following filters have been added:
1. Buy / Sell at the end of the day on which the simple round-trip day is trained.
2. Exit: After the opening of the position, the exit takes place on the first day on which the price opens higher or lower by 50% of the previous day's spread.

3. Trend filter: A purchase will only be made if the previous day closes above 50 days ago (and vice versa).

The use of the reverse-day pattern has a significant technical advantage. Nevertheless, the profit is insufficient to cover the fees and slippage. However, further attempts could lead to a successful trading system.

## Three-Day Balance and Reversal

The price movements of the last three days often point in the direction of the next small step.

The strongest three-day equilibrium (3DE) reversal occurs when the high and close of the current day are above the high of the previous two days and the closing price is higher than the opening price. Negative reversal is the opposite. This pattern occurs approximately 35 to 40 times a year in equities and futures. One way to successfully use this pattern is to wait one day and buy it at the closing price of the following day.

# Conclusion

Thank you for making it through to the end of *Options Trading 1*, let's hope it was informative and able to provide you with all of the tools you need to achieve your goals whatever they may be.

Concluding a book is not easy because a book is never a culmination but first and foremost a beginning. This first step traveled together is nevertheless the most important in our training (or your development) because it aims at access to knowledge. Trading, like any other activity, can be learned, and this is what we have tried to show by bringing many theoretical arguments, but also drawn from the practice to support our remarks.

I hope that our goal has been achieved and that the apprentice trader now has a reference book to better understand the financial markets, to anticipate movements in stock prices but also to develop successful strategies to capitalize on inefficiencies steps. I hope I have convinced you that trading was above all an art and not a science and that success in this area was possible if the trader agrees to make the necessary efforts. As in any activity, the trader will have to successfully complete several stages before being able to claim the title of master in trading.

My second objective was to prove the effectiveness of the technical analysis, so often decried in the academic world, and to improve its image by providing solid arguments. Over the course of my professional career, I have made many successful forecasts thanks to this approach and I found it unjust that it is not yet considered worthy. I hope that other people in France, and elsewhere, will take up the torch and will try to enrich the results in this book in terms of stock market analysis and strategy. I would also like to acknowledge the remarkable work done by the French Association of Technical Analysts and its senior leaders in promoting this approach.

Today, market access is easy. Anyone can have quick, real-time access to major exchanges around the world, 24 hours a day. In addition, you do not have to be a full-time employee. To stay in front of your computers continuously (except for day traders). Modern technologies allow us to place electronic orders that will perform for us various tasks (profit-taking, exit a title when a certain threshold has been depressed). However, if the physical presence in front of the screen is not necessary, the trader will not be able to save a lot of preparatory work. Indeed, this ease of access is a double-edged sword. Having analytical tools no longer means a decisive advantage in the markets. During my seminars, I met people who performed spectacularly and who lost everything as a result of an opposing movement. Trading is not an easy activity and I have tried in this book to provide many "strings" that I consider important to survive at first, then to succeed for the most enduring. These remarks are not intended to discourage you, but rather to prepare you mentally for the hard task ahead. Success in trading is possible but it is not easy. Trading is an activity that requires many psychological qualities, which most people do not have: only those who are able to control their emotions can capitalize on the emotions of others and therefore their mistakes, which explains the existence of opportunities recurring on the markets. A good trader must have foolproof patience, a real will and a good dose of humility. Finally, it is a solitary job where one is alone to savor one's victories and one cannot blame others for his mistakes. This loneliness is also posed as one of the conditions for success by many high-flying traders. This aspect of trading activity may seem tricky in a society where one only exists through one's status and where socialization goes through work. Nevertheless, the situation seems to be changing in the 21st century. We are immersed in an economy of knowledge and knowledge where remote work is becoming more and more widespread. Trading is undeniably a profession of the future for perfectly prepared people.

In this book, I strived to show that trading is not a natural process and requires specific qualities. I am talking here about private traders operating for their personal account from home, and non-professional swing traders who are in a stimulating environment. Sometimes, some traders organize themselves into a group to work together in the same trading room. This is sometimes a good thing when there is coherence in the group and real support. And I hope this book finds you in the best of spirits, and by this time, you would be raring to go, learn, practice and win.

Finally, if you found this book useful in any way, a review on Amazon is always appreciated!

# Options Trading

*Pricing and Volatility Strategies and Techniques. A Crash Course for Beginners to Make Big Profits Fast with Options Trading. How to Trade to Get Your Financial Freedom*

*William L. Anderson*

# Table of Contents

# Introduction

Congratulations on downloading *Options Trading: Pricing* and Volatility Strategies and Techniques and thank you for doing so.

There are plenty of books on this subject on the market, thanks again for choosing this one! Every effort was made to ensure it is full of as much useful information as possible, please enjoy!

For someone who invests or speculates in the market, for what reason would it be advisable to know how to use options? The straightforward answer is that options can greatly improve your profit from stocks and/or offer the means to protect your portfolio. Familiarizing the amateur with call and put options as well as demonstrating some of the basic ways that options are used is the goal of this chapter.

Assume you buy a stock at $30 per share, and it rises to $33. The stock price has increased by 10%, and in like manner, you have a 10 percent profit. That is good! You may make a 100 percent profit or significantly more, for a similar 10% raise, if you buy the right option that as opposed to buying the stock. That is more than good. That is great!

## The History of the Stock Market

To understand the history of the stock market, we should have a grasp of the inner workings of a stock exchange first—specifically the bid-ask spread that also influences prices of shares. The bid-ask spread is a sort of register that consolidates the demand and supply of stock in a central position. On the one hand, it allows people who need to buy stocks to place an order of the number and price of shares they intend to buy. On the other, it gives the sellers an opportunity to list the number of shares they intend to sell, as well as the target price for them. The final price of the stock depends on whether the buyer is willing to settle for the price of the buyer or whether the buyer is able to buy the stocks at their listed price. The laws of demand and supply also come into play, with buyers being forced to increase their purchase price when the competition is higher and sellers accepting a lower price for their stocks if there are not enough buyers to drive demand and price up.

Now, the stock exchange facilitates this conversion of ownership from the seller to the buyer by bringing them together in one platform. It is essentially a platform comprising of stockbrokers where they congregate to perform the business of exchanging (buying and selling) stocks. But who exactly runs the stock exchange? The stock exchanges as they currently exist were founded so long ago that the issue of who owns them seems immaterial. For the most part, the stock exchange is just the building or platform on which brokers buy and sell. The most important aspect of the stock exchange is the stocks that are listed in it. And because companies only list where they can be sure of attracting investors (stockholders), this is a very important aspect of their operations. It is no surprise, therefore, that the oldest bourses were started as corporations by stockbrokers to facilitate the exchange of securities among themselves.

The stock market has had a long and eventful history, one that is almost as long as the banking industry, by far the oldest financial institution still surviving today.

## 1100s–1400s

The earliest versions of the stock market were rather different from the bourse as we know it today. In France, the country of origin for these early stock exchanges, courretiers de change agents oversaw the agricultural debts issued by banks to farmers all over the state. They could swap and renegotiate these debts, an equity exchange that formed the foundation for the current stock market. Over time, the business of exchanging debts grew, and these men expanded to new markets, including government securities. As the first stockbrokers, the Venetian courretiers de change established stocks as a legitimate way for "common" people to make money in the financial markets.

Interestingly, these men carried on a system of cross-transactions with each other, buying debt and equity of each other based on risk and various other factors. Because they represented different banks in the debt issuance and collection sector, this interlinkage would later evolve to become the present-day interbank lending system, whereby banks issue each other with cheaper short-term loans. The people involved in this trade were mostly commodity traders, with the value of commodities changing hands but not the commodities themselves. This was a virtualization of the business functions that was way ahead of its time at the time.

The merchants of Venice started trading in government securities in the early thirteenth century. They were soon followed by banks in Verona, Genoa, Florence, and Pisa as it became evident that government securities presented a wonderful investment opportunity. Trading between the merchants was done by word of mouth and handwritten agreements. The extent of organized trading was limited to the houses of prominent traders where many of these courretiers de change could congregate and negotiate terms and conduct their transactions.

From France, the development of the securities market moved to Belgium and Netherlands, where traders started stock markets in Antwerp, Bruges, Ghent, and Rotterdam between the 1400s and the 1500s. In Antwerp, a clan of traders named the Van der Beurze family established a hub for stock traders to exchange equities, forming the first formalized stock market, except it still traded in agricultural debts, commodities, and government bonds. The concept of private companies using the stock markets to raise money had not yet been born.

## 1500s–1700s

In the meantime, before the first publicly-traded company made it into the bourse, England joined in the "stock" trading enterprise. As usual, government securities were the main commodities traded, but debts and commodities also changed hands. By this time, as European civilizations continued to expand, there was a stock market in pretty much every country that had a banking industry. Business ownership also started to change, with partnerships and corporations becoming increasingly popular as businessmen recognized the profit of combining their financial muscle. New philosophies of a business organization birthed the limited liability system of business organization and paved the way for the modern conglomerate.

The first publicly traded company would emerge from an unexpected area: risk. At a time when the Western world was discovering the rest of the world and venturing out to explore it, merchant ships were making many traders extremely rich. Explorers had discovered the West Indies as a land filled with business opportunities and tremendous riches, but the sea routes they took exposed them to piracy, with numerous voyages turning up zero returns because a ship was ransacked at sea. In fact, losing a ship meant that the trader, who had put up the money for the voyage, including the commodities to be bartered for gold and other treasure, wound up losing a ton of money.

To reduce the risk of losing a merchant ship at sea, a group of traders formed the East India Company, with each owning a portion of the assets but shielded from personal liability for any losses suffered beyond their investment in that particular expedition. This format of overseas trading quickly caught on. By keeping one's eggs in separate baskets, so to say, traders could have one out of three or four of their invested ships lost at sea and still end up making some money from the transaction.

A shareholding in a company became more and more liberalized; the Dutch East India Company became, in 1602, the first publicly-traded company. The shares of the company were listed on the Amsterdam Stock Exchange. Every share was entitled to an equal percentage of the proceeds of the company's profits. However, the trading of shares was not done in dedicated exchange houses. For example, the business of the New York Stock Exchange was conducted in coffee shops. Brokers would meet in coffee shops and conduct their business there, but this soon proved to be too ineffective, and the business of trading shares was moved into the stock exchanges.

The systems that even today moderate stock trading were put in place back then, enabling the traders to physically identify the person with the shares they wanted, approach them, and negotiate to buy them off. The counter was soon discovered to be a better alternative to tracking down traders with a particular stock. People intending to sell would just list their shares at the counter, and people wanting to buy would place their orders at the counter. An easy and effective system of centralized control was established, but having a centralized buy/sell counter meant that the market forces of demand and supply were also let loose. Someone with stock could wait until so many orders had been placed that they could name their price, however exorbitant, and get a buyer.

# Chapter 1
# Financial Contracts

## The Basic Concept of Options

### Choosing a Brokerage Account

When selecting an online broker for your options trading, there's one essential principle: There is a replacement for options experience. Obviously, make your own decisions. Because somebody loves a broker doesn't mean you will—or that you need to utilize them. What you do need to do, in any case, is build up a plan for assessing the brokers you consider, so you'll guarantee that the one you eventually pick offers the features you need—and certainly require.

Luckily, assembling such a "shopping list of services" isn't very hard. I won't say it is "as simple as 1-2-3," however, it surely is "as easy as 1 to 10"— the following ten things being the least number of capabilities you should request in any online options broker you pick.

## Factors to Review When Choosing a Broker

1. **The standard of the trading software.** For online traders, this is the most basic issue, and it takes various

inquiries to decide exactly what number of features is incorporated—and how great they are. These include:

- Is the software user-friendly; easy to comprehend and simple to utilize?
- Can I get it on a disk or would I be able to download it from the internet?
- Is it hard to install on my PC? Will I require help?
- Does it require any unique equipment or communications highlights, for example, high-speed modems, specialty internet browsers or DSL lines—with the end goal to make it work proficiently?
- Does it incorporate adequate pricing and logical, analytical tools for my requirements?
- If not, is it built to be effortlessly incorporated into independent quotation frameworks and analytical services? Let's assume this is the case, are there any exceptional pricing plans?
- Is satisfactory customer documentation given—both printed and online—to enable both to understand the framework and manage any technical issues?
- Is it attractive to look at—and, in the event that I don't like it, would I be able to change such things as size or color or display? (This may appear to be unimportant, yet in case you will be an active trader, you might take a look at it on and off for six or seven hours every day. In this manner, you don't need something you hate on a stylish premise.)

2. **The simplicity of order entry and the speed of transmission to the trade.** This is additionally critical for active traders, who might put in heaps of requests and need the procedure to be as programmed as possible. Some key things to ask:

- What number of fields on the order-entry screen do I need to fill in to put in a request?
- Do I really need to type in all the data, or will the software import it from the logical or pricing screens in the event that I need?
- Do I need to manually go back to the firm's order screen, or would I be able to get to it by tapping on the screens given by incorporated trading partners?
- Does the program send the order to the trade when I submit it, or does it need to be prepared elsewhere inside the firm first?
- Do I need to indicate the trade where the order is sent, or does the program shop around at the best cost and course the order as needs are?
- Do I put orders specifically through your software, or must I have a browser to get to your framework?
- Can orders be entered at night-time, for execution the next day—or just while the market is open?
- Do you additionally have a site—and, provided that this is true, would I be able to put orders from the site and also through the software?

3. **Quality of service to options traders.** Still another area where you have to make a few important inquiries, including:

- Are there independent order screens for stocks and options?
- If not, can the order screen be personalized to take into account options traders?
- Are the options quotes given in the order screen constantly or deferred?

- In the event that you call up an option chain; is it a real-time preview, or a delayed collation of last prices? Furthermore, is it spread out in an orderly way, or do you need to search for the option you need?
- Does the option-pricing framework give you access to current bids and offers, or simply last trading prices? What about volume numbers? Open interest?
- Does the framework include multi-option strategies, for example, spreads, and give you a chance to order them as a unit?
- If so, does it charge one commission for such orders—or survey fees for every option in the combination?
- Will the framework settle for stop and stop-limit orders on options? What about stops and buy orders that are dependent upon the price of the basic asset?
- Do any of the incorporated quote services spend specialize in options?
- If yes, will their program give me a chance to punch in trade parameters and screen for good trading chances?
- Does the brokerage firm's program have any comparable services to assist me with options analysis?

4. **Timely executions and confirmations.** The broker's order entry program ought to give guide access to the electronic trading frameworks of the suitable trades and, once your trades qualify for programmed execution, report back a confirmation in few seconds—ideally to an area of the order-entry screen where you can quickly observe that you got your fill. In the event that the trade doesn't qualify the bill for programmed execution, it ought to show up in a corner on your screen intended to give you a chance to monitor your working orders.

5. **Ability of the framework to deal with high-volume circumstances.** The broker's database ought to have the adequate reserve processing capacity to deal with additional overwhelming order stream—and the firm ought to have a framework set up to manage quick economic situations as successfully as possible. (No firm is flawless when such circumstances occur, yet they ought to make an attempt to at the very least—not simply hurl their hands and say, "Sorry" or "Too bad!")

6. **Commission costs.** Numerous traders would put commissions much higher on the list than No. 6; however, our reasoning is unique. To mind: What great are low commissions in the event that you get lousy prices, moderate executions and terrible (or no) benefit? Ensure the broker gives you all that you need—and require—and don't stress on the chance that it cost a couple of additional dollars. You'll likely influence it up on your trades, at any rate. Do, in any case, demand that the broker's fees, at any rate, be competitive; you need to pay for what you get—not pay to get gouged. Additionally, make sure to get some information about possibly precarious things covered up underneath a guarantee of low commissions—e.g., a commission rate of $1 per option won't help you a whole lot if the firm forces a $50 least on each order.

7. **Customer support.** Very important! It's a must-have—ideally by telephone, not only online, by email or through a self-improvement menu on the site (in spite of the fact that it's pleasant to have those choices too). Likewise, see if support is accessible simply amid business hours — or terribly, just when the market's open. Your goal is to

guarantee that the help services will be accessible on the occasions you really require help.

8. **Backups for order execution in case of technical issues.** As we'll talk about in one moment, there will be times when things turn out badly—even with the best broker and the most superb programming. In the event that it occurs within trading hours, your broker must have a backup framework to manage it. That implies having enough telephone lines and in-house individuals to deal with client calls and the sudden flood of disconnected order stream. All things considered, no trader who frantically needs to escape a position 30 minutes before the end wants to call his broker and hear a tinny, computer voice: "All agents are at presently occupied; however, your call is vital to us. Please stay on the line; a delegate will be with you in roughly 45 minutes"— soon after you've lost your shirt!

9. **Simple access to account data.** Trading capability isn't the sole key to accomplishment in options trading—money management is similarly vital. But it's difficult to deal with your money in the event that you can't easily access the status of your account. With a decent broker software program, you ought to have the capacity to get to all key data—including open positions and their values, balances, total equity, available equity, result of recent trades, and profit/loss statements (ideally, the ones you can ask for by period or on a year-to-date premise). The perfect framework will likewise play out the majority of the math and the greater part of the accounting capacities for you.

10. **Security of individual and financial data.** Numerous individuals fear to do anything online in light of the fact that they fear a hacker or another person will discover excessively about them, take their personalities—or, surprisingly more terrible, take their money. Insubstantial part, these fears are unreasonable—particularly inside the frameworks of America's financial services systems, which were planned in view of security and had unique assurances, set up. Therefore, most brokerage frameworks are as secure as it's presently conceivable to make them. All things considered, it never hurts to make an inquiry.

## Strive For the Perfect Choice

I said the broker shopping procedure would be "as basic as 1 through 10"— yet, with all the sub-questions listed, it, in fact, got more complex. All things considered, it's just for your advantage.

Clearly, not very many firms will have the capacity to give the affirmations you need regarding all of the worries just made reference to—yet, you ought to make progress toward perfection. The more things you need to consider with respect to the "mechanics" of online trading, the more opportunities will be made available for you to end up diverted and falter as you move along the way to options achievement.

Keeping that in mind, survey the 10-shopping process listed above over once again, and choose what highlights you completely should have—and which you might have the capacity to live without. At that point, when the forthcoming brokerage firm says something isn't accessible, you'll know in a split second if it's enough to make you leave.

In case you're a genuinely new trader, you may likewise need to check whether the broker offers any close to home, one-on-one investment counsel, or proposes trading chances to customers. Relatively few online firms do, yet in the event that such things are important to you, it doesn't hurt to inquire. You may, at any rate, get a referral to a partnered warning service or data site that can help give some trading thoughts.

This enables a client to manage a prepared options broker to deal with orders and questions. The commission charges are not quite the same as the online rates—yet the value included by having a live broker will most likely be worth the expense in case you're simply taking in the trading ropes.

Obviously, the essence of online trading is accomplishing direct access to the trades so you can perform your transactions precisely like the experts. In this way, you should attempt to wean yourself from the requirement for broker help before going online—or as fast as possible from thereon.

# Chapter 2
# Forward Pricing

Low margins can be very useful when trading. To use them successfully, they must be integrated into the overall pattern. The basic idea is to enter the market as soon as it breaks out of the state of equilibrium that exists. If the price rises sharply from this point on and then falls back down there, an increase in demand is expected. This is a classic double bottom. In combination with the Accumulation / Distribution, this becomes the basis for an interesting trading approach. Choose only the trades in the direction of the thrust. Place stops at the opposite end of the short bar.

## Trading Beams with Large Margins

A wide-span bar can be either bullish or bearish, depending on where it appears in the formation. If it appears at the end of a buy peak, then it is to be classified as bearish, at the break from a formation, however positive. Most beams with a large span are followed directly by a correction beam. The buy zone is in the lower half of the bar, and the profit-taking area is located at around 50% to 100% of the span above the high of the bar. Of course, this only applies to short-term traders. The course tends to be varicd, with a short track following a long bar. Of course, this is not always the case, and the definition of a wide-span bar is subjective. This is where the art of chart reading comes into play. This ability can only be learned by analyzing many charts over the years.

## Purchase Zones

The buy zone describes the lower half of a push. While the relapses are causing the price to rise, the buying zone also moves upwards. In these areas, you should look for opportunities to get started. Before you open your position, you should know where to set the stop and set a price target. Mark the buy zone, the stop loss and the area of the price target in the chart. Do not chase after a quick course! Among the countless stocks, there is always a good candidate for a better start. Opt for a boarding area. The following steps could help:

1. Buy only in the purchase zones.
2. Place your stop loss immediately after opening your position.
3. Be sure to close the position when you reach the winning zone. Is this done by means of a stop, or are you simply selling? Any possibility is a compromise: if you sell, the price could rise even higher. Waiting for the stop to be triggered will often result in significant portions of the potential win.

The following options are available:

- Make the stop tighter.
- Close only half the position. So, your decision is only half wrong or half correct.
- Close your position at the first sign that the supply outweighs the demand.

- Use a shorter time frame to set the stop. For example, if you trade on a daily chart, choose a 30-minute chart to place your stop more accurately.

## The Stop

If you do not know what you are risking, you risk everything. There is no stop-loss option that is equally satisfactory for everyone. Everyone has to find out for himself which ratio of risk to the potential profit he feels comfortable with. Here are some suggestions for placing stop orders:

1. Three ticks below the low of the last or penultimate fulcrum
2. An average range below the closing price or the low of the day on which the purchase was made
3. 50% of the breakout or break-in after opening the day after entering the position. This stop works especially well when combined with the other possible stops. For example, a value sometimes opens below a stop at a level, which then turns out to be the low of the day. We like to see it move about eight ticks or half the span of the previous bar after opening.
4. Three ticks below the lower low or lower end of the last two bars
5. Close the position after three bars, if it is not yet in the profit zone.
6. Release the trade and try to exit without loss if the trade runs too far against you after the opening and your stop is not triggered. Do not think about a possible profit anymore. Their only interest is the stopping and preservation of your capital.

It is of utmost importance to always have a good plan ready for your investment. When opening a position, ask yourself if this is a long-term investment for five or ten years or not. Then you should not panic in the face of short-term price fluctuations. Are you a trader? Unfortunately, many people set their exit point or stop loss according to the following criteria:

1. The stop-loss is at a point where the losses are already huge.
2. The stop is based on the general market situation. If the whole market collapses, my positions will be closed.
3. As soon as everyone is frantically trying to close their positions in my stock quickly, then I sell too.
4. Any analyst or broker says you should get out now. That reminds me of a story.

A few years ago, I had the honor to come on the Mark Haynes show. I was invited by CNBC. Mark introduced me as an expert on the futures market. He asked me how the gold would develop. I replied that I knew exactly how the gold price would continue to behave. But before I answer that question, I'd have to make the audience aware that until now, I've only been 23% right, and I'm on the rise, so the main danger is that sometimes I could be right. And if that were known, I added, and then I could barely pay for the bus ride to my house. Of course, after this interview, CNBC tried to select the invited guests in a better manner.

The moral of the story is that you should beware of people who have all the answers to all questions. If you want to be a trader, then you must realize that success must be hard-won and that you will pursue a monster all your life that you will never master. But maybe you learn to live with it, and you get more than you give.

## Profit Taking

If you have a long position and the price goes into profit, then you can protect your profit by:

- Best selling
- Sell when a closing price is below an opening.
- Sell when the price falls after the opening by half the average range.
- Set the stop below the previous day's low.
- Sell when the price closes below the two previous closing prices and below the opening.
- Sell at the third strong positive bar of the next smaller time frame. For example, if the price breaks into the profit zone on the weekly chart, then you sell after the third consecutive day in a row.

## Anticipation

The following factors are important in anticipating the completion of a pattern or reversal. You can build parts of a position at an early stage before all criteria are met. Remember: The stated goal is to make profitable trading and not to be in the market at 90% of all price moves. Learn to settle for small pieces of the market. Either you secure your profits by means of a best-order, or you sell at the first sign that the supply exceeds the demand.

1. The seven possible times to anticipate a pattern are:
2. The closing price of the bar, if a short spread indicates a low supply or low demand.
3. An opening course in the direction of completing the pattern.

4. An outbreak after opening in the direction of completing the pattern.
5. An outbreak after 30 minutes towards the completion of the pattern.
6. The course is midway through the opening and in the direction of completing the pattern.
7. At the closing price if the pattern is fully developed.
8. For a correction movement after completing the pattern.

For many patterns, it can be seen that the price will fall back into the buy zone, but the pattern will be completed above the buy zone. Then it has to be decided on a case-by-case basis which measure is the right one.

## The Time-Break-Out Rule

A common approach is to trade the breakout from the first 30-minute bar, with the stop loss at the other end of this bar. This approach has been tested using S & P's market data over 14 years. Trading according to this rule leads to huge losses. It should be noted that this method has been profitable in recent years. But one must always keep in mind the fact that how dangerous it can be, if too short a test period is chosen to check a method. When entering a position, the 30-minute rule may be useful, but as with most tools, isolated use will not work.

## Price Gaps

Normally, a positive price gap is considered a sign of strength and a buy signal. In verifying this assumption, it turned out that the exact opposite is true. The review was based on two methods:

1. Sale with a positive price gap.
2. Sale on a positive price gap, but only if the price falls back to the previous day high.

For purchases, the opposite applies. Both approaches were tested by computer without stops and as day trades. The second approach turned out to be almost twice as successful as the first. It is used approximately 60 times a year per future. The course must go in your direction before doing anything. This signal provides a clear market advantage, but in most cases does not make up for the fees and slippage. But when combined with other filters and more meaningful stop management, this is a valuable addition to your trading arsenal. Coincidentally, the review found that this could be a profitable trading system for bonds.

This pattern is very similar to a pattern developed by Larry Williams called Oops. The starting point is the same, but we do not know which entry and exit criteria were used by him. The information can be reused as follows:

1. The signal is likely to be more reliable if the price has already gone one way and the expected end of that price movement is within range. Then this could be a good way to realize profits and perhaps build up counter positions.
2. Other ideas are:

    - Watch out for introductory signals on reverse movements of the last closing price, several previous closing prices, and several previous highs and lows.
    - Consider setting a half-span stop after boarding.
    - Watch price gaps above or below a cluster of close closing prices.
    - Look for a reversal after half the gap in the price gap before opening a position.

These simple computer tests will tell you quickly whether such an opening with a price gap will give you a technical advantage in view of past price developments or not. Larry Williams and Toby Crabel have made a name for themselves in this field. Whole volumes could be filled solely with the study of price movements in relation to the opening and the movement away from the opening price.

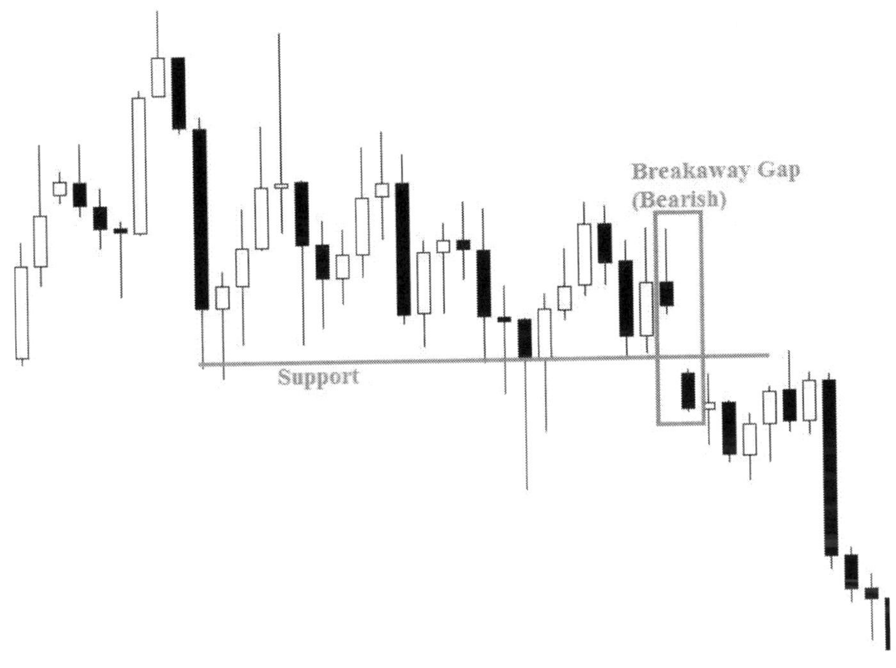
Breakaway Gap
(Bearish)
Support

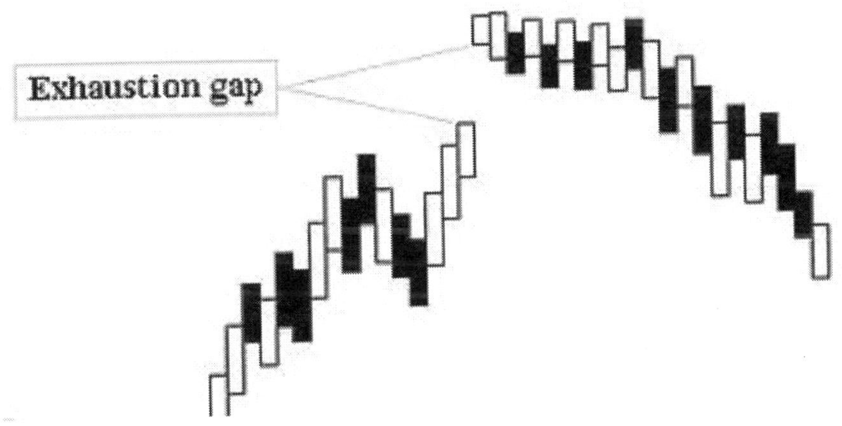
Exhaustion gap

## Channels and Trend Lines

The information in this chapter will help you identify the most advantageous opportunities for trades, as it is about identifying smaller and larger channels. This is especially important when it comes to trading decisions on reversal or continuation patterns. The use of simple trend lines, combined with some basics of wave theory as a starting technique, is also covered. Some of the methods in this section are not the same as transferring them to a computer system, but the ideas that are discussed will certainly be very clear if you look at a chart with the registered lines and channels. From this, a systematic approach can be developed.

One of the most valuable tools for the trader is trend lines. Many use indicators that are calculated by a sophisticated computer program. Roughly speaking, all these indicators try to answer the same question: how much is the market overbought or oversold? Simple trendlines with a few extra rules can be used most effectively in timing your trades. Learn to read the charts, not just the indicators. So far, we have not found an indicator that tells us that there has just been a kink or a jump and that we should do better when we are in the market. The drawback is that the price drops to a new low below a pivot or support finds no-bid, and then rises aggressively. The jumping occurs when the course suddenly rises to a new high above a turning point, finds no demand and quickly falls back. These procedures are discussed in more detail further in the book.

## Trend Line and Parallel Movements

A major high on a pivot is followed by at least two deeper pivot points before it hits a new high (and vice versa at lows). The main trend line connects two main highs or main lows that are at pivot points. The parallel motion is a parallel line that passes through the main pivot point. The goal of the movement is where the price hits the parallel line again, that is, the boundary of the trend channel. Smaller trend channels are constructed by connecting lesser pivot points. The target range is the parallel trend line, the other side of the trend channel.

## Trading With the 0-2 Line

The following setup: The market is experiencing a surge of strong demand but is currently in the correction phase. If wave C remains above the level of the lower pivot point A, then the purchase takes place when the 0-2-line breaks through. If the pivot point C is below half of A, then you should wait with a possible entrance to wave 4.

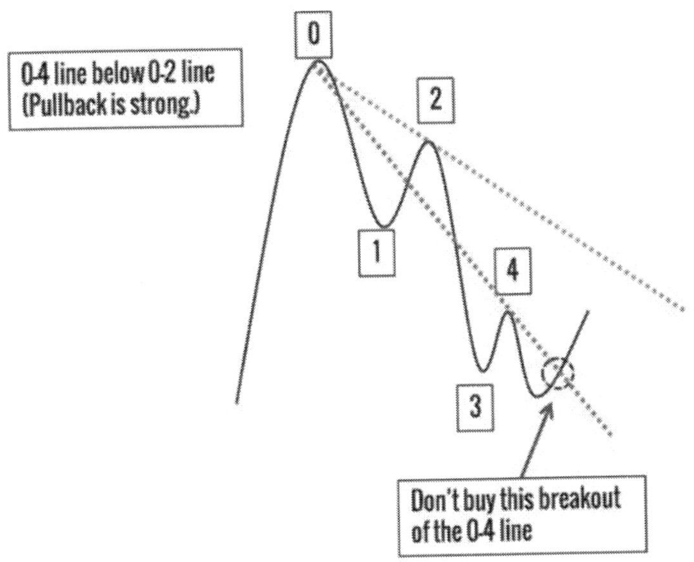


The trade-in parallel moves, the 0-2 and 0-4 lines requires some subjective decisions. The logical sequences that would be necessary for programming in a computer system are enormously complex and difficult. Still, the rules are pretty simple, and entry and exit points are easy to determine. You do not need a computer for that.

## Trend Lines and the Four-End System (TL4S)

This is a simple system that can be followed without a computer. You just have to be able to assess the trend correctly and decide whether the profit potential is worth the risk taken. The setup for the purchase (the opposite applies in the case of sale):

1. Always act in the direction of the trend.
2. Drag a trend line that joins the last two top pivot points.
3. In the last 20 days, two or more rising or equal high lower pivot points formed.

Buy on a price move, though

- The closing price is above the four previous closing prices.
- The span is above average.

The stop is below the last lower pivot point. Sell immediately if there are signs of a false signal or outbreak. Push the stop further upwards to the breakeven point, as soon as you have some leeway, so that the risk of a loss is banned, and the fees are covered. The evaluation of the margin is at your discretion, but the following suggestion may help: Place the stop just below the low of the entry day as soon as the high of the entry day is exceeded by half the span.

## Realize Your Profits

1. When reaching the target area.
2. In a breakthrough of the four-closing trend line against the trend direction.
3. In the event of an outbreak halfway through the opening after the price enters the sales area.

These are all suggestions. The basic idea is to break the position as soon as the first signs become apparent, that the supply exceeds demand or that a buying peak is emerging (in the case of shorts, of course).

The trend channel system

If the price falls on the lower channel line, buy/sell at the first positive indication of a trend change:

- Purchase at a higher opening
- Buy after the 11:30 am Rule (mid-day course above the opening)
- Buy on a reversal day
- Buy with smaller reversal patterns
- Buy at the correction
- Shorter-term time frame. Observe the 30-minute chart and buy near the parallel line (on the daily chart) at the first sign of strength in the shorter time frame.

## Types of Options Traders and Trading Styles

Most would agree that, in spite of the fact that the fundamental options trading are not extraordinarily hard to understand, there is a great deal of information that should be understood before you probably feel okay to start. The basics are generally clear; you need to know what it entails, the advantages, what the risks are and how options truly function.

One of the few different things to know is the diverse trading styles that can be utilized along with the distinctive sorts of an options trader.

As a rule, traders can be grouped into two. To start with, you have the professionals, those that typically work for big financial institutions, trading specifically in the interest of those institutions or for the benefit of customers. These professionals can likewise fill the job of market makers.

Also, you have private people that trade entirely for themselves utilizing their own capital and for the most part, they trade from home. A few people trade full-time, depending on their profits as their essential source of pay, while others trade temporarily while additionally having a principal work.

Day trading is a style that can be utilized for practically any type of financial trading, including forex, futures, and stocks, and in addition, options. Customarily, it was a style utilized just by financial institutions and professionals. However, it has turned out to be known among locally established traders as well. There are various purposes for this. However, it's to a great extent because of the impact of online technology which has made it less difficult to make financial transactions rapidly and furthermore expanded the measure of information and data that can be gained access to.

Day trading usually includes exploiting little price movements, the way you utilize leverage when buying and selling option makes them an especially reasonable financial instrument for this style.

## What Does Day Trading Options Entail?

The fundamental idea of day trading options is straightforward; the idea is that you make various transactions during the day with the intention of making fast profits. The general standard is that you close the entirety of your open positions by the close of business, so you know precisely where you remain toward the day's end. With this style, you can buy and sell a wide range of options and can utilize various diverse strategies.

A few trades can include taking a position early in the day and closing it close at day end while others may include buying and selling options contracts in a few minutes. This depends to an extent on what openings you find and what kind of strategies you are utilizing.

The interesting thing about this style is that it is, in fact, at least, feasible to make fast profits many times during the day. Those that utilize this style successfully know about discovering openings that have a good chance of selling positive returns. Obviously, there will never be an assurance that every single open door will be profitable.

This style is sometimes referred to as active trading, and you do need to be active to utilize it successfully. You should have the capacity to spot open doors for-profit and respond rapidly. The fundamental rule is to exploit little price movements in the hidden security of options, so timing is imperative. A couple of minute's postponement can possibly mean a botched chance or no less than a decrease in the potential profits.

## Who Uses This Style?

As said earlier, day trading any sort of financial instrument used to be done just by the master professional that worked for banks and other financial institutions, and possibly the periodic private investor. Nowadays, in any case, it's a style that is supported by a lot of private investors, and it's proceeding to be known by people. The apparent advantages of having the capacity to make fast profits, rather than clutching investments with a view to making a return later have brought about it winding up essentially more standard.

Day trading options, specifically, makes it achievable to make great returns from generally little sums using leverage. The objective is to profit by little movements in the prices of stocks, and other hidden securities and options can increase the potential gains from such losses.

Options are amazing means whenever utilized effectively, and there are numerous traders that profit simply through making fast trades over the span of every single day. It should be noted that utilizing leverage can likewise increase potential losses, and there are risks involved.

The fundamental point, essentially, is that basically anybody can be involved with day trading; you don't have to work for a big financial association, and you don't require a large amount of money to begin. Anybody that is ready to dedicate the needed time to fully realize what they have to know and after that, examine the markets every day to highlight openings, will eventually be successful. All things considered, it is not encouraged for a total amateur.

## Guidance for Day Trading Options

There are some recommendations that anybody keen on day trading options ought to know about. As a matter of importance, it's serious and time-devouring, and you should be ready for what it entails. It's unrealistic to execute this style very well except if you have time and a dedicated personality to devote yourself to watching the markets for the duration of the day.

You should be cautious every time and be prepared to act when it's a perfect time. In that regard, you additionally require the capacity to investigate circumstances rapidly and carry out your trades as need be. In the event that you believe you cannot adapt to the requests, you ought to think about different styles.

You should have a deep insight and understanding of the different strategies that can be used, know how to use them, and when to utilize them. You should be exceptionally disciplined and have the capacity to keep feelings out of the situation. You also need to be ready to accept the risks that come with it (if it happens).

You can, to a certain level, reduce the risk that you are presented to by utilizing spreads and stop-loss orders to limit losses. However, there will be risk included. Risks are especially high when the market is unpredictable, even though unstable market conditions give the most profitable situations.

Even though you don't really require a large amount of capital to begin, you ought to have sufficient money to cover yourself if a few traders don't go right or if there are long unprofitable days depending on the amount you are hoping to make. You additionally need to make transactions at the suitable level for the spending you have; numerous beginner day traders become bankrupt basically in light of the fact that they come up short on capital due to not dealing with their money accurately.

It is true that money can be made from day trading options. It is in no way simple, however, and you truly need the correct aptitudes, devotion and a sense of responsibility. Should you feel you are prepared to give it a go, it is a smart thought to paper trade for a short time before really utilizing genuine money. This will get you used to what it entails and give you some signs concerning whether you have the correct character and ability to make it work.

## Options Brokers for Day Trading Options

Picking the correct broker is an imperative choice for an options day trader. Specifically, there are two things that you truly require: the capacity to put orders immediately when you recognize a chance and low commissions. Since the plain idea of this style is tied with responding rapidly, any postponement in directing your broker can have great consequence. You will likewise be making a lot of trades, so low commissions are considerably more essential than for different styles.

The sole intelligent decision is to utilize an online broker. Online brokers will, in general, be the least expensive in terms of commissions, and you can submit your requests substantially more rapidly than if you needed to make a telephone call to your broker.

# Chapter 3

# Options Trading Simulators

You've most likely heard everything before: If it's too good to be true, then it probably is, and trading options without risking your money definitely falls into that class. Conventional investors and specialists alike would reveal to you that there's no such thing as risk-free trading – which is valid, obviously (can't contend with the specialists!).

However, note that you can learn and practice options trading without putting any money hanging in the balance. Market novices and prepared investors alike can utilize virtual options trading to increase significant experience and test trading strategies without risking any hard-earned money.

I will prescribe the best platforms accessible online to open your options trading account with.

## Free Options Trading?

Virtual options trading — or paper trading—includes investing virtual money in business sectors defined by different online platforms. With a paper trading simulator, you have the chance to work on trading hands-on with zero risks.

You've most likely inquired about options trading and may definitely know fundamentals, yet the buck doesn't stop there. A few people would state that you can hop into the universe of options trading promptly. However, I exceptionally advise against that. The complexity can be scary for any dimension investor.

For entry-level traders, free trading simulators are the ideal place to begin: you'll have the chance to practice and handle the fundamentals in a risk-free condition, and most will likewise incorporate accommodating assets in the event that you lose all sense of direction in the dialect of options trading. It's likewise incredible for experienced traders alike, as you can be permutated and masters your strategies and approach before taking your risk in genuine trading.

A considerable number of these trading platforms are free. Not only do you not risk losing your well-deserved money, but you also don't need to spend a penny to practice virtual options trading. What else would you want?

## The Best Free Paper and Virtual Options Trading

Trading simulators have been utilized in the financial markets to prepare younger traders. Indeed, even before the business sectors turned out to be overwhelmingly electronic, the utilization of basic, offline trading amusements, for example, Liar's Poker to instruct the basic aptitudes of trading was at the center of many preparing programs. Financial market simulators are risk-free and a charming method to learn!

Be that as it may, most present-day simulators are a long way from flawless. Some simply offer 'phantom' market information whereupon 'phantom' trades can be executed. This is limiting on the grounds that the simulator is just accessible when the basic market is open. What's more, a couple of simulators give the client much feedback on their execution or about how to make strides. Truth be told, most simulators are simply simulators; they make no endeavor to really show the client the financial markets.

Here's a survey of my most loved platforms to rehearse options trading online. All are appropriate for both learning and expert traders, so pick the platform that best suits every one of your needs, and registers to get a practice trading account.

- **Investopedia.** Obviously – you've known about Investopedia; While Investopedia is more popular as a result of its huge measure of instructive assets utilized in fund and trading, the site likewise brags of its simple-to-use stock simulator. You begin with $100,000 worth of virtual money to invest, and you can even view different options chains through this platform. While the simulator as of now has some valuable aides accessible in it, the Investopedia site is as of now an extraordinary asset for every one of your inquiries when you feel overpowered with the trading dialect you may not be comfortable with.
- **Options Industry Council.** The Options Industry Council trading simulator furnishes clients with real-time analyses of markets – considering their current economic situations. This is ideal for the individuals who are anxious to get the hang of trading options in the current financial condition today. The simulator is totally free, and you can decide to use the accessible information from the simulator, or you could enter your very own information to work with. The OIC simulator isn't as complete

contrasted with next couple of simulators I will specify. Be that as it may, once more, in case you're a learner, this simulator may be the opportune place to begin.

- **Market Watch.** Market Watch is prominent among experienced clients and even specialists of the market – likely in light of the fact that Market Watch frequently opens challenges where the best trader gets featured on an article on their site. In case you're an amateur, MarketWatch can likewise work for you, as you can still trade alone – without the stress of rivalry – utilizing virtual cash and real-time data access. Their primary site additionally contains the most recent updates in financial and investment-related news, which can be valuable for your upgrade execution in the game.
- **Thinkorswim PaperMoney.** Thinkorswim is apparently the best options paper trading simulator online and in light of current circumstances. In the game, you would be given $100,000 worth of virtual money, which you can invest in forex, options, and stocks among others. Thinkorswim additionally gives a cover of instructive webcasts. Thinkorswim PaperMoney is accessible for download. In case you're an accomplished client searching for an all the more energizing platform and are searching for more its advanced highlights, you will discover the value of utilizing Thinkorswim. Thinkorswim additionally has a dream stock market game.

Any trading simulator needs to combine realism with satisfaction. The simulators above are practical; in addition, a great deal of amusement to play on. However, to be an incredible piece of training innovation, a simulator needs to go past these fundamentals. I trust the rundown are compelling training tools in light of the fact that they were developed starting from the earliest stage with this as the main priority.

Now that you know it's possible to trade options without risking money, what are you sitting tight for? Register on these platforms and improve your options trading strategy today! Go on, trade without risking any money!

## Technical Analysis of Options

It's inescapable that the more you trade, the more you will feel a wide range of emotions. You'll experience all the full range of emotions, from the sadness of taking a loss to the bliss of closing a winning trade. You will question your life choices, and sometimes wonder why you ever decided to go into trading, and in other cases thinking you are in charge are destined to be a trader.

Greed and fear will be the two main feelings driving the choices you make. It doesn't make a difference whether you're making your hundredth trade or you're first. Greed and fear are inescapable.

Technical analysis works because everybody has to manage greed and fear, and it is something that can be found in the charts. Human habits don't change. You can trade technical analysis once you learn what they are.

To be successful as an options trader, you have to create and rely on strategies. Remember the time a move takes because options lose value over time. Comprehend the stats identified with options.

You want to make sure you can still see the chart whatever set of indicators you utilize. An excessive number of traders fill up their charts with so many lines and indicators that you can no longer see the price and volume. So you can concentrate on the data that genuinely matters, keep your charts clean. Add indicators that improve your insight, not cover it up. Just include the ones that will matter to your trading and keep all the others off your chart. Maintain your attention on price and volume.

# Chapter 4

# Specific Strategies for Trading Options

Stocks represent a unit of ownership that is issued by companies to the general public, allowing them to take possession of its assets and earnings. It is this claim to earnings that justifies earnings distribution to shareholders in the form of dividends. By simple calculation, an investor's claim to the assets of a company in which they hold shares increases as the percentage of their share ownership increases.

However, there are a few points about the finer details of stockholding that most people do not appreciate. First off, a stake in a company does not really equate to a stake in its assets. Your shares do not really make you a partial owner of the corporation you hold shares in because shares are issued by companies as more of a stake in their financial performance than the conventional kind of ownership. Corporations, being legally recognized persons, own their assets, file their own taxes, are sued and sue other legal entities and have the ability to take loans for their own expedient use.

So does owning the stocks of a company equate with the right to their assets? Not by a long shot. The principle of separation of rights and control governs the way shareholders interact with the assets of holding companies. With this principle, your share ownership is restricted to the amount of equity a company has offered to the public, not their assets, or even a portion of the company equivalent to the percentage of shares you own. This separation of shareholders' equity and the corporation itself is very important because it restricts liability for both. Even in the event of a bankruptcy, only the company's held assets may be sold. Your stake will remain as a nominal value of whatever value the stock market places on the company. In those adverse events, only the value of your shares will drop, but your ownership of them is not enforceable by any state body, which is to say that not even the courts can compel you to sell—you decide. For the corporation, its assets are protected from appropriation even by the shareholders who purportedly own a share of the business.

Even though shares do not constitute ownership rights in a business, they do equate to voting rights during shareholder meetings. The shareholder is also entitled to a share of the company's profits in dividends for those companies that reward its shareholders with them. The process of buying and selling shares is also simplified by the fact that there is no transference of asset ownership. Higher up in the share ownership hierarchy, shareholders also have enough voting power to be involved in seating the board of directors. In large corporations, the board of directors runs the company on behalf of the shareholders by appointing the senior managers, crafting the long-term strategy of the business and authorizing massive expenditures like acquisitions.

If stocks are not really a portion of the company a shareholder buys, and then what exactly are they? In many instances, companies issue stocks to the public to raise large amounts of money, distributing the capital risk to thousands (or millions) of people. Money raised in the initial public offering is then used to fund new business projects and propel it to greater heights. But raising capital is not the only reason why companies go public. Some companies, like software giant Microsoft, went public because of government regulations that require companies with a certain number of shareholders (over 500) to release their financial reports publicly. Rather than release financial reports like publicly traded companies but not enjoy the surplus of capital that comes with a public issue, companies like these opt to issue a portion of the business to the public. Another motivation for issuing the shares of a company to the public is to make it possible for employees to trade out their stakes in the company (usually offered as an incentive during employment) for real cash.

The stock market is the institution through which brokers and traders exchange their shares with other traders and brokers. A large number of them are involved in the stock trade whose liquidity of shares is quite high—there is always a willing buyer and a willing seller. Stock markets also facilitate the transfer of bonds and other securities. Only in the stock market can a shareholder hope to turn their stocks into liquid cash, especially because, as mentioned above, the assets of the company whose shares they hold are out of bounds.

There are two types of stocks issued by corporations—common and preferred.

## Comparison

What we have discussed above is essentially the common stock type of share ownership. Common stocks enable a person to hold a portion of a business but not take possession of it even though it gives them a limited right to influence the business operations of a company. On the other hand, preferred stocks, a hybrid share that is issued by a company for a very specific capital requirement, gives the holder zero say on a business's running—no voting rights, no right to influence the board of directors placement, and no consultation in the making of huge business decisions. For that reason, preferred stocks are little more like bonds than shares.

Investors with common stocks are entitled to a share of the company's profits in the form of dividends. These dividends are determined by the board of directors on a per-share basis. As for preferred stockholders, their claim to dividends is usually greater, taking precedence over common shareholders in terms of yield per share and priority. In the event of a company missing a dividend payout, preferred shareholders receive their arrears first. Preferred stockholder also takes precedence over common stockholders in the event of a company liquidating its operations. In fact, because of the greater claim of common stockholders to the business as owners (making decisions, voting, etc.), they are paid absolutely last behind holders of bonds, credit, and preferred shares.

The common stock is the most popular type of share for people to transact in. It performs much better than preferred shares in the stock market, but it is also more volatile. With a flexible interest rate, the return on capital invested in stock is determined solely by the perception of the stock market on the company's financial strength. The fixed interest rate of the preferred stock makes it less susceptible to market volatility in the stock market. Instead, their value is affected by interest rates of the general economy in an inverse manner. When the interest rates rise, the value of a preferred stock drops, and when it declines, their value climbs.

Another important distinction between common shares and preferred ones is the rights of the issuer to call them back. While common stocks may only be bought back in the event of a company going bankrupt or folding, preferred stocks may be repurchased at a prefixed time or any time the company decides to call them back. The company then pays shareholders a redemption rate to investors, often a higher rate of return than expected. One of the factors that affect the price of preferred stocks is actually the anticipation of a callback. The sooner a company is likely to call back preferred shares issued to the public, the more in demand those shares become as investors seek to capitalize on the premium redemption rate.

## Stock Issuance: The IPO Process

The initial public offering (IPO) is the process through which a company issues shares to the public. An IPO represents the blowing wide open of the shareholder register, previously dominated by founders, early and angel investors and employees (in those companies where the stock option is an incentive for attracting and retaining employees) to include as many of the public as the number of shares a company offers. The price of a company's stock, especially shortly after the IPO, is determined in part by its book value and the number of people who are willing to buy its shares at a certain price. The higher the demand, the higher the stock price climbs. As a prospective investor in the stock market, it is only natural that you are fascinated by the whole IPO process. After all, the understanding of what goes on behind the scenes of an IPO often determines whether an investor considers the freshly issued shares worth buying or not.

There are several ways for a company to go public, but the Securities and Exchange Commission (SEC), a government department mandated with overseeing the stock market and enforcing fair play rules, follows each and every one of them very closely. The most popular format of public issuance is one where an investment bank spearheads the process. In fact, this format is so popular that it is referred to in most literature as the legitimate definition of an IPO.

However, there are other alternative procedures for a company to follow in issuing their shares to the public. They are direct listing and Dutch action.

## Investment Bank

A bank-issued initial public offering is a five-step journey from private holding to public trading that is overseen by an investment bank from start to finish. First, the business leaders in a company decide to go public, with the intention of raising money or simply in compliance with government regulations. However, because the offering process is a complicated and tightly regulated process, having a firm that specializes in the stock market can be a very good idea.

### Selecting the Bank

The first thing to do in the IPO process is to select a bank to underwrite the whole process. By underwriting, we mean that the bank buys or commits to buying in principle all the shares a company intends to issue to the public and then re-issue them in the secondary stock market.

This is an important role for a bank to play in such a key process of a company's financial maturity, so some due diligence is very much in order. Usually, what a business looks for in an underwriter is reputation. Investment banks, like Goldman Sachs, have taken many iconic companies public because their ranking, as some of the best investment firms on Wall Street, gives them a certain appeal to wary executives. An investment bank with a specialty in a business's line of operation gives it an edge because it is perceived as having a better grasp of the institutional investors who might be brought on board during the IPO.

Talking of institutional investors, they are very critical to the success of an initial public offering for a few reasons. But to understand that better, let us first jump slightly ahead and consider the landscape immediately after a company goes public. A spike in the price is usually expected soon after the IPO. This is the most effective way to create a stable foundation for a company's shares to take off and increase in value over time. To do this, some companies offer their shares to the public at a point where confidence in their future financial performance is high. The SEC enforces a period of lockdown, where transactions are restricted. This quiet period ensures that market hype does not drive the share price too far above its real value and exacerbate the volatility of the whole stock market. When employees and initial investors start selling to take advantage of the short-term rise in price, the share price often drops drastically because of oversupply. Institutional investors, on the other hand, invest for the long haul. They are unlikely to engage in this kind of maneuverings, which makes the stock more stable. This makes it more important for a business to select an investment bank that can rope in the big fish to increase hype and subscription rates.

## Due Diligence

The next process in the investment bank format of IPOs is the performance of due diligence checks and conducting the regulatory filings. As mentioned above, the investment bank assumes the responsibility of getting all the shares a company intends to sell to the public and resells it, acting as the middleman between it and the investors. There are various arrangements that the company can enter with the investment bank on the process.

A firm commitment entails a bank undertaking to buy all the shares and re-issue them to the general public. For an investment bank to agree to this arrangement, it has to be very confident that it will be able to make money on the IPO from the underwriting fees and mark-up of selling at a higher price than what they buy the shares for.

Another strategy is called the best effort agreement, whereby the underwriter speculates the amount of money they anticipate to raise from the IPO. Because there is no assurance that the target will be hit, the bank does not undertake to buy all the shares. Its job is simply to issue the stocks to the public for the company. Nonetheless, the bank is expected to promote the shares to the public and institutional investors.

For IPOs that are too big for one underwriter to handle alone, a syndicate is created, with each member contributing to the pool of money required to purchase the whole issue in full from the issuing company. The bank that raises the largest share takes the lead on the offering, keeping the books and overseeing the more crucial aspects of the IPO for a greater share of the underwriting fees. This way, an investment bank distributes the risk of the IPO to a large group of competing banks.
In fact, this is the most intricate process of the offering. Important documents are crafted, SEC requirements have to be followed, and some very delicate accounting mathematics has to be done, often with a contracted accounting firm for impartiality. A reimbursement clause protects the investment bank from losses in the event of the issuing company withdrawing the offer midway through the process by stipulating that the expenses are to be reimbursed either way. In a letter of intent, the underwriter

commits to the offering process by promising to dedicate every effort to ensure that the shares will perform well in the stock market, including promoting to investment bankers among other promotional efforts. On its part, the issuing company commits to provide all information needed by the underwriter and to cooperate in the whole issuance process.

Other important documents in the due diligence process include the registration statement, which is submitted to the SEC showing the financials, management background, ticker symbol suggested for use in the stock markets, holdings by company insiders, and the legal history of a company. The registration statement filed with the SEC identifies the issued company as a component of the stock market and allows the SEC to keep tabs on their financial, legal, and accounting practices.

A prospectus is drafted for all investors, showing the strengths and weaknesses of a company, as a way of giving every prospective investor sufficient and reliable information about the impending share issue. From the prospectus, investors can speculate on the future of the company and make a better decision of whether to participate in the IPO. Another item created for the investors is the red herring document, which is used during the promotional roadshows where the underwriters and issuers promote the impending share issue to the public. The roadshows allow both the bank and the issuing company to gauge interest and demand for the impending share issue, which is important for the next part of the process—pricing.

## Stock Pricing

After evaluating the prospectus and verifying that all records are in order, the SEC gives approval for the IPO. The issue date is decided between the SEC, the issuing company, and the investment bank underwriting the process. And on the eve of the effective offering, the issuer and the investment bank sit to decide on the best price for the shares. Haggling on share price often comes down to a few cents per share. With millions of shares and billions in net worth often being the stake, every cent counts.

The price set for the stock during this seating depends on a few factors. The most important of these is the subscription rate for the share. During the roadshows, pre-orders are recorded in the order books. Shares that have been oversubscribed are preferred because this indicates greater confidence in the company's future by the stock market. Another consideration is the price at which the issuing company intended to sell its shares in the first place. In order to decide this, the share price for companies in the same industry is assessed. The issuer may want to have their shares sell at a higher or a lower price.

The stock price is calculated against the amount of money expected to be raised to determine the price of each share. The money a company expects to raise and the share of the company to be issued dictate the number of shares and value of each share on the negotiating table. But in the market, after trading opens up, all that matters is market hype, because this determines the enthusiasm of the market and, subsequently, the prices to which the share rises immediately after the IPO.

## Trading

The first day a company trades in the stock market is usually very exciting. Depending on the levels of excitement exhibited by buyers, the price either falls higher or lower to the one that the issuer agreed to with their investment bank. The trend established on the first day in terms of volumes traded and price trend may continue for a while, but restrictions placed by the SEC on trading soon after the IPO somewhat limit the volumes of transactions. As such, it is not until a few months after the initial offering that a stock stabilizes.

## The Stabilization Process

The undertaker does not disengage from the sharing process immediately after the stocks start trading publicly. They stick around to provide the market with analysis and expert commentary to boost demand. Other mitigating actions to maintain the stock price at the desired price include batch buying or selling to influence the direction of the price shifts that take place soon after the IPO. During this time, the SEC restrictions on price manipulation are usually suspended to allow the stock to pick up at a price that is more realistic.

Incidentally, it is for this exact reason that it is ill-advised to buy into a company soon after its IPO. The price, immediately after the initial offering, is usually artificially modified, which makes it unpredictable afterward when the laws of demand and supply finally take over.

While complicated, the process of issuing shares through an investment bank presents the issuer with greater control over investor interest and stock price after the IPO. The expert guidance of the investment with the SEC regulations that come with initial public offerings also goes a long way in smoothing the process out. The main disadvantage of using an investment bank is that they charge quite an exorbitant underwriting fee and also make a ton of money on the mark-up between the price agreed with the issuer and what the public ends up paying for the shares. Perhaps it is for these reasons that some companies decide to go directly to the public.

## Direct Listing

By listing the company's shares on the stock exchange at the same time that they are offered for purchase by the public, a company skips the process of hunting and negotiating with a bank to take the company public. The company also saves on underwriting fees and enjoys all the sweetness of an oversubscribed stock with a price higher than the book value. However, a company that opts for a direct listing forfeits the advantages of having an experienced Wall Street firm promoting the IPO. The stock price from a stock that has been listed directly starts off rather sluggishly.

The companies that are well suited for direct listings are those that are considerably well known already, offering a product that the public is already well aware of. Even if the institutional investors may not join the fray earlier on, the market buzz for its products more than makes up for the lack of an investment banker. Moreover, when investors show more genuine interest in the stock, the price grows organically, driven by real demand rather than blatant price manipulation. One of the most recent direct listings was the 2018 Spotify Technology SA.

## Dutch Auction

A Dutch auction allows the buyers to set their own price for a share. A company approaches investors and requests for the number of shares they would like to buy of their company and their price of those shares, relying on the market perception of the business's financial well-being to set a reasonable price. The highest bid price almost always wins the auction and sets the price of a company's shares. Dutch auctions rely on connections to spread the word and give investors the chance to buy shares.

One of the most iconic Dutch auctions of the twenty-first century is that of Alphabet Inc., Google's parent company. Some other companies like Morningstar Inc. and the Boston Beer Company, Inc. have also helped Dutch auctions, issuing their shares to a selected group of people.

## Why Invest in the Stock Market?

There are many reasons why investors, both professional and beginners, choose the stock market as their preferred vehicle for investment. The main reason why people do so, however, are those stocks having a better interest rate than most other investments? Unlike a savings account, money devoted to the stock market makes returns way above the inflation rate—as long as the investing has been done with a bit of skill.

## Investment Value

Over the long term, stocks have the highest rate of returns when compared to other asset classes. For example, the Standard & Poor 500 Index (S&P 500) had an average annual interest rate of about 11% from 1928 to 2016. To put this in perspective, the Rule of 72 is used to determine how long it would take for an investment to double in value at a certain rate of return (RoR) by dividing the RoR with the number 72. With 11%, the time frame falls somewhere between six and a half years and seven years. For other investments like treasury bills that have an estimated annual rate of return of 3.46%, the time it takes to double the investment comes in at slightly over 20 years! That is a long time difference between two asset classes that are both traded in the same stock market.

## Return on Investment for Stocks versus Short-Term Bonds

Investments are evaluated by the value for money that they generate for the investor above and beyond the inflation rate. Whatever the rate of inflation in a given year, it should be factored into the calculations when considering true returns. The higher the rate of return, the better the gain on capital will be even with inflation being high. The stock market, therefore, presents all investors with value for their money in the form of greater rewards, a variety of investments that one can put their money into, like mutual funds, index funds, ETFs, international indexes, etc. Finally, the fees are considerably lower if you decide to go for discount brokers. More pricey stockbrokers also offer some investing advice, which is a surefire way to increase potential returns.

## Dividends

A dividend is the share of a company's annual earnings that is shared out with the investors, with every share allocated a fixed payout depending on how much the company made that year. Dividends are viewed by most investors as free money because they add to your already appreciating initial investment whose value is dictated by the market forces in the stock market. For example, if you buy the stocks of company X for $50 and one year later they have risen to $56, then that is an average rate of return of about 12%. However, if the company also issued a dividend payout of 3% on every share, then that is an extra 3% in returns that your investment just produced for you in that year. It is so great because a dividend is money you get on top of the nominal rate of return for your stock investment—free money, so to say.

The dividend is paid out in various forms, but the most prominent buyback and cash reward are the most common. In the cash reward option, the company credits every investor's account with a sum of money equivalent to the number of shares they hold with the company multiplied by the dividend payout rate. If the investor wants to reinvest this extra money back into the company, they can do so at their discretion. The buyback option is where a company offers investors with a dividend reinvestment plan to use their dividends to buy more shares at better terms.

The announcement date is the date on which a company discloses to the public that they intend to pay a certain amount of money to every shareholder. This payout is approved by the shareholders, so announcement dates usually come after the annual general meeting. The record date is the latest time an investor has to have bought the share for them to be eligible for the dividend. After a certain time, the ex-dividend date, shareholders are ineligible for dividends because they bought after the company had already settled on a certain rate based on the existing shareholder register. And of course, the payment date is the time at which the dividend payout is actually injected into the accounts of the shareholders.

## Bonds

Bonds have been in existence since time immemorial. They were used by ancient governments to raise money for various capital-intensive causes, which is the same used to which they are put even today. So what exactly are bonds? In the stock trading sense of the word, a bond is like a unit of a bigger loan that a company or government takes from a large pool of investors for a specific purpose. The whole loan, thus taken, also falls under the definition of a bond. What individual investors hold in their hands as the bond is usually the certificate given to signify the borrower/lender relationship they enter into with the borrower. In the bond certificate, the terms of payment and details of the loan are indicated, including the interest rate and maturity date. Trading in bonds can either be over the counter in the bourse or between lender and borrower.

## How Bonds Work

The system of bond borrowing can be traced way back to the ancient Mesopotamian financial systems, where corporations borrowed grain with the promise to pay back the principal plus interest at a certain date. Instead of placing the company assets as surety, a bond was used instead, symbolizing the borrower's deepest commitment to repay the loan. This obligation to repay the debt became to represent the bond the current world knows as financial systems evolved. Bonds are necessitated by a number of realities that only the insider might know about the capital markets.

The capital requirements of large corporations are quite extensive. To start a new project, finance ongoing operations (especially in R & D), and repay old debts that have not been repaid yet, companies need to raise massive amounts of money. From large infrastructural projects to war efforts, governments have an appetite for capital that is tax remissions from citizens and businesses do not meet.

In some cases, the banks cannot meet the demand for these needs simply because the amount of money these entities require is so great. The risk of a bank going under in the event of these massive borrowers defaulting is too great, which means that corporations and governments have to become creative about how they raise the money for whatever their super-important need might be.

The way to do this is by distributing the risk to so many people that the effect of a possible default is blunted by the very fact that it is spread over many people. Having 10,000 people risk $1,000 each is preferable to one entity risking the $10,000,000 because the impact would be less serious on each person. With a single lender, such a huge default would definitely take the lender under.

Bonds are considered to be quite conservative as investment options, mostly because the possibility of losing one's money is way low. Short of going out of business, bond issuers repay their debt obligations in full, and even in the event of going bankrupt, bonds are treated as creditors and paid first from the liquefied assets of a company. Governments absolutely pay their bonds, sometimes issuing a new bond just to repay the old.

## Characteristics of Bonds

While there are quite a number of types of bonds, some of their characteristics are uniform to them all. Understanding the characteristics and terminologies used to describe them is crucial to learning how to invest in them.

The face value is the principal amount that the issuer is expected to pay the holder of a bond when the period that has been agreed upon passes. The face value remains fixed over time even when the supply and demand drive the price up in the stock market. These external influences of the stock market determine whether the bond sells at a premium (higher than the face value) or a discount (lower than the price indicated on the bond certificate).

The maturity, of course, is the due date for the bond's principal. The issuer decides the maturity period for the bond, and the market responds by buying into the idea with their money. A lengthy maturity time increases the risk of nonpayment, so the issuer has to promise a higher yield to entice investors.

At the time of issuing the bond, the borrower promises to pay a certain amount over the face value, which is otherwise known as the interest rate or the yield/coupon. The coupon is the equivalent of servicing a loan, with the borrower expected to pay a certain amount every year or semi-annually. This coupon could be fixed (which means that it never changes despite the state of the economy), or it could be adjustable, allowing the borrower to vary their coupon payment depending on certain market conditions.

Because their interest rates are either fixed or more rigid than the rest of the stock market, bonds are considered to be a safe haven for conservative investors during an economic crisis. Lower interest rates in the general economy drive the interest of a bond higher due to increased demand. The increased demand comes about because investors suddenly view bonds as being more profitable even if their price remains the same. Bond yield thus moves in an inverse direction with interest rates in the rest of the market—down when the former is high and high when it is low. Another factor that affects yield is the rate of inflation. With their low-interest rates, bonds become attractive when the inflation rate is lower because the net yield increases. Short-term bonds that are expected to be exposed to a shorter period of inflation tend to have a lower interest rate while those with a longer maturity period (and thus risk) require a greater interest in recompense.

Based on the yield, we have several types of bonds. The common one is the coupon bond where the issuer pays a certain amount of money above the face value of a bond. Another type of bond is the zero-coupon type, which is issued at a discounted rate compared to the face value. When the bond matures, the bond is paid in full, and the investor makes their money that way. The United States treasury bills are traded as zero-coupon bonds, so a $100 note sells at, say, $98. At maturity, the inflation-adjusted interest rate will be around 2.5%.

Another type of bond is the convertible type. This one allows bondholders to take the decision to convert their bond principal and use it to buy stocks. The option to convert debt into equity when the share price reaches a certain level allows private bond issuers to reduce the coupon. The lowered interest rate at the point of issuance serves the company better as the project takes off, and the fact that the debt is converted into equity dilutes the stakes of other shareholders at no cost to the company. As for the investors, the convertible bond presents double insurance for their investment. If the share does not reach levels attractive for purchasing, the bond yield is still high enough to give a considerably good return. But the fact that they can convert the bond into stock at any time, at any stock price, means that the investor gets their pick of the best moments to buy shares, which could be very profitable.

A similar but somewhat different type of bond is the callable type that may be redeemed by the issuer at any point before the maturity. The callable bond allows the issuer to buy back the debt at lower interest rates and re-issue at a cheaper cost. Because issuers buy the bonds back when interest rates are in decline, it means that the bondholders are relieved of their bonds at just the point when the price is in an upward trajectory. For that reason, investors do not overly like callable bonds and opt for noncallable types when the coupon rate, maturity, and credit rating of the company is the same.

## Bonds Issuers

The three main types of entities issue bonds are corporate, municipals, and governments. The government is the main bond issuer, responsible for more than 50% of all bonds floating around in the stock market. The treasury issues bonds on behalf of the government, with the word assigned to them varying by their maturity rate. Bonds that are expected to mature within the year are defined as bills, those that mature within ten years of being issued are known as notes, and those that are expected to mature ten to twenty years after their issue are known simply as bonds. The more conventional name for all three categories of government-issued bonds is treasuries. It is not uncommon to hear them all being referred to as treasury bills, treasury notes, and treasury bonds respectively.

Local governments issue bonds to raise money for certain development projects. Because these bonds are unfamiliar and investors are often unsure whether the issuer can actually pay up, the coupon income is often specified as being tax-free in a bid to attract more investors.

## Comparison with Stocks

The main difference between bonds and stocks is that stocks represent a stake in the business while a bond is essentially a credit service an investor extends to the company or the government. The only reason corporate entities and governments issue bonds is to raise money while stocks may also be issued to comply with government regulations. While the money raised during an IPO goes a long way to boost the company's operations, it is often held as liquid assets because an IPO is simply a matter of a business going public to increase its legitimacy and boost public confidence in its products. An initial public offering is a statement that a company is past the start-upstage. A bond issue means nothing more than that a company needs money for operations and wishes to borrow.

Another area where stocks and bonds differ is in maturity. While bonds come with a pre-arranged maturity date, stocks are perpetual. One can hold on to a stock for as long as they wish, collecting dividends on their investment for as long as a whole century. The longest maturity time for a bond is about 30–50 years.

The way that investors make money from either a stock or a bond also differs. With a stock, the price appreciates over time, raising the purported value of an investment (the money a person would make if they sold their shares at this exact moment). This rise is determined by the laws of demand and supply, such that when the market perceives the company as being healthy financially, the price rises because there is greater demand. The opposite is true when the company is struggling financially and enjoys no confidence in the stock market.

From an investment perspective, stocks and bonds differ in one key area, and that is the perception of security for them both. A stock is viewed as a volatile investment because its price is likely to drop at any time. Even though the overall interest rate of publicly traded companies maintains the lower double digits levels, some perform very badly and often go into the negative for protracted periods of time. This volatility makes it extremely hard to predict the return that an investment will bring. For a bond, the interest rate is predetermined and mostly fixed, save for slight deviations up and down, depending on the state of the economy and interest rates. A bond is considered to be safe and conservative, bringing a stabilizing effect to an investment portfolio. Stocks, on the other hand, come with high risk and high reward and tend to make a portfolio substantially more unpredictable.

# Chapter 5

# Risk Measurement

## The Necessary Phase of Learning

The first phase in trading is to know your environment well and to master the tools that will be mobilized. The number of people rushing into the markets without controlling anything is simply staggering.

Before being able to conquer the markets, the trader must first master the rules of the game. He must know the stakeholders, the tools for decision-making, and the analysis methods that work best in his market (technical and technical analysis). / or fundamental analysis), well-mastering money management and risk management. This is an often exciting phase as the trader discovers a new field and tries to learn as much as possible. Enthusiasts will read all books available on the domain subscribe to stock market letters, attend seminars and whatnot.

At Jack Schwager's question, how did you learn to trade, Baldwin responds, "I started one lot at a time. I always had an opinion. All-day I stayed on the floor and I developed an opinion. When I saw that my opinion was working, I was reinforced in my approach even if I did not trade. I realized that by standing six hours a day, every day, most of the time I was right. I saw the same scenarios to develop recurrently. Some market patterns were repeated and market operators would make the same mistakes day after day. You just had to grab them."

This market initiation phase, therefore, should not be overlooked and is a prerequisite. Nevertheless, during this period novice traders will seek techniques to achieve a significant performance while the most important for a beginner is primarily to train and manage its risk to be ready when the time comes. The trader must learn to walk before running: the money management saves time to learn the ropes.

## Risk Management: An Imperative

Good risk Management enables the trader to ensure his survival and therefore to retain his most valuable work tool, namely his capital. A ruined trader no longer has the opportunity to exercise his activity. In addition, risk management allows it to focus primarily on the best opportunities. Indeed, there are multiple opportunities in the markets but the trader must first select those that offer the lowest risk for a high potential of gain.

A trader who manages his risk correctly controls the probabilities. Indeed, the biggest danger in trading is to think you have found the magic formula because it is easy to be intoxicated by success and to believe yourself infallible. If you follow Sun Tzu, a person who thinks he is infallible becomes extremely vulnerable. Therefore, the trader must manage his risk even more strictly after a series of winnings. Unfortunately, this situation often corresponds to a euphoric state of the trader who begins to have disproportionate confidence in his "instinct" and ends up making dramatic mistakes.

## Larry Hite Risk Management

For the best traders, it is important to respect the risk. The famous trader Larry Hite even considers respect for risk as one of the creeds of his hedge fund. According to him, before making money, the job of the trader is not to lose. L. Hite strictly controls his risk and applies these principles:

His system never positions itself against the dominant tendency. There is no exception and he always follows his system; the maximum risk on each position is limited to 1% of its total capital;

Diversification is taken seriously; volatility is monitored in each market to generate signals to liquidate or suspend trading in a market.

Always follow the trend and we never deviate from the method. The positions are all the same. There are bad bets and good bets. Many people think that a losing trade is a bad bet. That's wrong; you can lose money even on a good bet. If the probability of success is 50% and you expect a gain of two dollars for a dollar risk, then it is a good bet even if you lose

## The Art of Achieving One's Goals without Taking Risks

Contrary to a widespread belief, the best traders take a very little risk. They put risk management at the top of their trading plan. Performance is only the result of strict monitoring of the plan. When the title evolves against its original scenario, the trader must seek to get out of his position as soon as possible. He can, of course, wait for a rebound to come out with a lesser loss, but he must never drag on and go into hope mode.

Linda Bradford Raschke explains the importance of testing the markets: "In trading, part of the process involves testing the markets. If the timing of your entry is good enough, you will not lose much even when you are wrong."

In trading, you have to manage your risk and the profits will come naturally, the art of lasting is it not the key to success? The trader must identify situations where the risk is low (close stop) and the potential for high gain. He will have to avoid situations where the risk is too high even if the potential is interesting and wait only for the best opportunities.

One must always think about the consequences of one's actions. The ruin is the financial death of the trader. Indeed, it is difficult in this case to go back and rebuild its capital. The trader must above all aim for survival even when he is at the top of his game. Indeed, it is often at this moment that it is the most fragile.

## Sometimes Escape Is the Best Alternative

According to Paul Tudor Jones, "we must always favor defense to attack". If we have a losing position that places us in an uncomfortable situation, there is a simple rule: to get out of his position at any cost in order to regain his senses and wait for a new interesting entry point. It is always possible to come back, and a trader must convince himself that there is nothing better than a fresh start.

Bruce Kovner evokes the importance he gives to his stops, (a level that invalidates our scenario and must trigger an exit from our position): "Every time I open a position I have a predetermined stop. This is the only way for me to sleep. I know where I'm going before I get home. I always place my stop over a technical barrier. A technical barrier is a level that the market should not touch if our scenario is good. I organized my life so that my stops are followed religiously."

During doubtful phases, the trader should stay out of the markets. It is useless to position ourselves if the probabilities are not favorable to us. You do not have to be in the market all the time. This exhibition is vain and useless. The leak can be beneficial in trading. It is even, for P. Fayard, "the stratagem of the stratagems". Indeed, when a conflict cannot find a favorable outcome, the best choice is the leak because it means that the trader preserves his capital for better times, which will not fail to occur.

To summarize, the trader will have to survive on the markets first and foremost. Profits are only the natural result of the application of his "survival" plan.

## Know-How to Attack

As discussed in the section devoted to psychological analysis, when the dominant consensus is not confirmed by stock market movements, the market is probably turning around. This is a period when the convention dominant changes occur, and a trader who detects these changes can advantageously position itself. The trader must strive to wait for the best moment before positioning himself. Opportunities will come to him and will result from mistakes made by other competitors. Thus, the trader is essentially concerned with his defense and does not hesitate to seize opportunities as soon as they occur.

But a good defense should not mean inertia. Indeed, sometimes the best defense is the attack and if the general does not dare to attack, the enemy will update his fear and use it at his expense.

## The Psychological Problems That Arise When Opening a Position

The trader can encounter various psychological problems when opening a position: Decision made without real reflection: a trader is primarily a man subject to cognitive and emotional bias. Thus, a trader who identifies a familiar configuration that has earned him money in the past will base his decision on this information alone to position. He falsely conceals all the other data, whereas he should above all aim for perfect rationality, to act.

Impulsiveness: The trader is afraid of missing the opportunity of the century and rushes forgetting the rules set out in his trading plan. If the trader receives a signal but for one reason or another he misses the entry, he will have to wait for another favorable entry point before positioning himself. Rushing hastily on a title is a dangerous act. Often, certain emotions such as euphoria, the fear of missing a movement are at the origin of the rush of the trader and incite him to make decisions not thoughtful.

Inertia: the trader sees an opportunity but does nothing to seize it. The trader must dare to seize the opportunities that arise if he wants to achieve a positive and above all sustainable performance. The trader may wish to wait for other items that confirm his point of view. The information is never perfect but by doing this, the trader will position itself at a time when all the operators have already perceived this information and are therefore already positioned. The growth potential of the asset will be limited. The trader must, therefore, dare to enter at the very beginning of a movement if enough elements are going in this direction.

The rationality of traders is limited in the sense of Simon: instead of performing a thorough analysis, the trader will take into account one or two factors and neglect others. This low-quality analysis is of little use in the decision-making process. A good trader should not overlook any parameters before making his decision. All contingencies must be taken into account by the trader who must aim for perfect rationality even if this is impossible in fact. Indeed, it must base its decision on relevant and complete information. Nevertheless, markets are governed by uncertainty and the trader will never be able to obtain perfect information. He will have to be content with solid information putting the probabilities in his camp and make his decision knowingly, that is to say by not neglecting the risk and placing a stop.

## Attack When the Probabilities Are Favorable To Us

The object of the battle is to win the victory and not to satisfy his desire for revenge. The trader must not open a position in vain, and he must enter a title only if the potential advantage is much higher than the tolerated loss. The great traders are like the great generals: they do not engage if they are not convinced that victory is within their reach; they know how to save the strength of their troops and go on the offensive only if the interest is real.

## Applying the Risk / Reward Concept to Elliott Waves

The waves are used to define risk zones and therefore stop levels. They are also used by operators to determine targets. In this section, we will use Elliott's Fibonacci ratios and waves and show how these tools can be useful in determining the Risk / Reward ratio.

## Anticipation of a Wave 3

Playing a wave 3 is always very interesting in terms of Risk / Reward. Wave 3 is often a powerful wave with high potential and limited risk. In addition, we have seen in the chart analysis section that the standard retracement ratio of Wave 1 is 61.8%. In other words, wave 2, which corrects wave 1, will often trace 61.8% of the movement and sometimes even (in extreme cases) 100% of the movement.

After studying the market, if a trader believes that a stock is about to draw a bullish acceleration in wave 3, he may initiate a position on the retracement ratio at 50% Wave 1 and strengthen its position on the next ratio to 61.8%. From this perspective, it will be able to place a stop under the ratio at 76.4% or even under the 100% retracement, under the old low point.

The same reasoning can be applied to type 4 corrective waves. The standard retracement ratio of a wave 4 is 38.2% and it is possible for a trader to position himself around this level and place a stop under the ratio of 50% to play the impulsive wave named 5.

## Can We Determine The Optimal Size Of A Position?

We will seek to determine the share of capital that can be risky for a known probability of success and a payoff ratio. Stops are an important part of risk management, but they are just one aspect of money management. Money management, which focuses on the size of the position and not on the right timing, seeks to answer the question: what is the optimal size of the position?

We will attempt to answer this question by first examining a basic system that relies on a uniform risk for each position, and then we will elaborate on this approach using Kelly's formula.

## Uniform Risk per Trade

This approach recommends risking an identical amount for all positions initiated. The main advantage of this strategy is its simplicity even if it lacks flexibility. Thus, for each position initiated, the trader will risk an amount of € 1,000 for example. The main problem with this approach is that this amount may be too large if the trader suffers several successive losses, or too low if the trader records several successive gains. Many traders prefer the approach that risks a fixed percentage of capital.

## Fixed Share of Risk Capital

With this system, the trader limits his risk to a fixed proportion of the capital available to him. Thus, if the capital decreases, the risk will decrease proportionally. Similarly, if capital increases, because of realized gains, the tolerable risk per position will increase. The trader has a capital of one million euros and the fixed portion of the capital at risk is 1% per position. The risk tolerated by open position will, therefore, be € 10,000.

## Kelly's Formula

Many traders have relied on Kelly's formula (scientist working for Bell) to determine the optimal size of the position.

$K\% = W - ((1 - W) / R)$

- With K% = percentage of capital that can be risky on a position;

- W = probability of success of the system;
- R = historical payoff ratio.

This formula indicates that the optimal portion that can be risky will increase with the payoff ratio and the probability of success. The trader cannot change market conditions and therefore will have no influence on his probability of success or his payoff ratio. The only parameter he can modify and that he is able to control thanks to money management is the size of his position.

## Criticisms of Kelly's Formula

To criticize this formula, we will base ourselves on the people who exercise a day trading activity. Often, the probability of success is high, and the payoff ratio is equal to unity. Good day traders and scalpers often have a 70% probability of success and a payoff ratio of 1. Based on Kelly's formula, optimal exposure of Kelly should be 40%. But this figure leaves us perplexed: it means that if the trader loses three times in a row he is ruined.

The trader must for its tranquility reduce the risk taken for each position so that even losing several times in a row (let's take a series of 20 losses for example) it is not ruined. We even think that the rules must be even stricter than this: a day trader who loses 5/10% of his capital in one day must stop all activity and then return the next day fresh and available.

## Patience Is the Key

"Trading is very much like surfing. I try to take a wave or good time and if unfortunately, I miss it, I'm waiting for the next."

As explained Weinstein, like the cheetah, the trader must wait to be responsive to the real opportunities. The cheetah, though it is the fastest animal in the world, will wait to be absolutely sure to catch its prey before attacking. He can hide for a week, waiting for the right moment. The trader must always be extremely defensive and attack only when conditions are favorable. He cannot force the market to draw his favorite storyline and must simply bend to his will and wait for a perfect opportunity. He must then ask himself before the opening of his position: "Does this position deserve to be taken? Wouldn't it be better to wait for another opportunity? Patience is, therefore, the watchword for the army general as well as for the trader."

Formerly those who were experienced in the art of combat made themselves invincible, waited for the enemy to be vulnerable, and never engaged in wars that they foresaw not having to finish with advantage. Before undertaking them, they were sure of success. If the opportunity to go against the enemy was not favorable, they waited for happier times.

Thus, the trader can be defeated only by his own fault, and he can only be victorious through the fault of his enemies. Great traders know that there are times when you have to let others work for you. Novice traders do all the work and allow professionals to seize low-risk opportunities. It is important for the trader to be able to return at the right time and retire quickly when market conditions demand. According to Linda Bradford Rashke, it is important to enter the markets around the best possible levels. She considers that timing is crucial because it buys time and allows seeing how the market will react.

## Stay In Control in All Circumstances at All Times

For trader Marc Ritchie, the strategy is to capitalize on the panic of other operators: "A trader must be able to think clearly and act decisively when other operators panic. The irrational markets are those on which we find the best opportunities. Traditionally, in a volatile market, even veteran traders prefer to stay out of business while this situation represents an opportunity to make money. As the saying goes, if you can keep your cool when others lose their heads then you can make a fortune. The trader is able to position himself against the majority opinion. The good trader remains true to his ideas and closes his ears to interpretations of the crowd that does not take the same positions. You have to have the courage to face the crowd, make a decision and execute it. The ability to think clearly and to have the courage to make a decision when others panic is an indispensable element for the trader. This is possible by having a trading plan. I mentally prepare for the market by developing several strategies in advance and plan what I plan to do if the X or Y scenario occurs."

A good trader knows when to be defensive (unclear market potential of trade already achieved, etc.). If the trader is positioned to buy and the market still seems powerful to him, instead of taking his profits, he will probably have to increase his position in order to take advantage of the amplitude of the current movement.

A good trader is able to determine when it is wise to defend and when to attack. A good strategist does not hesitate to implement his strategy when he is convinced of his solidity. He took care to analyze everything and took into account the different elements.

The good strategist has another quality which is the ability to change strategy if he thinks he has gone astray or if something is missing in his diagnosis. He will not hesitate in this case to modify his plans if the conditions require it. The wars in Iraq or Vietnam are classic cases where the military (in this case the US President) has stubbornly stuck instead of adapting its strategy to the context.

## Play the Probabilities

Never engage in small actions that you are sure they will turn to your advantage, and still, do not do it if you are not forced to, but above all be careful to commit to a general action if you are not assured of a complete victory. It is very dangerous to have precipitation in similar cases; a risky, ill-timed battle can completely ruin you: the least that can happen to you, if the event is doubtful, or you only half succeed, is to see you frustrated by the greater part of your hopes, and not being able to reach your ends.

## Behind Every Position, There Must Always Be a Reason

The trader must avoid at all costs the positions taken in uncalculated anticipation and with the sole motive to occupy his time because they can have extremely negative and damaging consequences. On the markets, the trader is not remunerated by the number of trades and his performance will depend closely on the success of his trading system as well as the average gain-to-loss ratio. Any position must be open only based on specific criteria respecting the trading plan.

## Stay Away From Markets When Conditions Are Not Optimal

In extremely volatile markets, there is sometimes no logic and opportunities are few or difficult to grasp. Some traders are desperate and operate in a totally irrational way, which gives rise to movements on which the trader will struggle to capitalize.

After the publication of a large economic figure, the trader has every interest in waiting for the markets to calm down before settling. Indeed, stock prices are often erratic and the probability of anticipating a movement is minimal. The trader must avoid situations where the probabilities are not favorable to him.

The trader must determine in advance the best time to position and do not hesitate to go on the offensive when it occurs. Nevertheless, when markets are not predictable, the trader will have to avoid positioning himself and wait for the situation to clear up. He must have a clear view of the forces involved; as there is no point in exposing himself if so few favorable signals are present. Some traders explain that they simply want to test the markets by positioning themselves, but in truth, it is the market that tests them. Adapt to the situation

# Chapter 6
# Risk Considerations

In this chapter, we are going to take a quick look at some of the candlestick patterns that are important to you as a beginner. Understand that no individual pattern alone can give you all the clues you are looking for, so as I earlier mentioned, be sure to combine whatever information you deduce from a pattern with other information from other tools as well. The aim is to get a balanced perspective before jumping into conclusion. As a side note, it is not important that you cram the names of these patterns. What is most important is to know the appearances or the shapes of these patterns and what they mean.

## Bullish Patterns

This bullish pattern occurs on a stock chart when a hollow or white large candle engulfs a previous smaller filled or black candle; hence the name engulfing. The bullish engulfing pattern often occurs in a downtrend and when it does, there is a high chance of a reversal from the downtrend (bearish trend) to an uptrend (bullish trend). This pattern shows up to signify that active traders as well as investors have had a change of mind about the value of a stock and are beginning to be aggressive about it. This is what usually leads to a reversal in the stock's trend.

## Doji

This bullish pattern often shows hesitancy or indecisiveness in the minds of the traders. Usually, the stock price remains the same for the entire time frame after it opens. It closes almost at the same opening price. When this happens, there is likely to be a reversal of the trend in the opposite direction because traders are more than likely to doubt the price's dominant trend. In a dominant downward direction, the question in the traders' minds would be something along the lines of "why is the price not going down?" and this could possibly result in buying rushing to buy and causing prices to rise. There is no one single candlestick that has the entire messages you need to make your trading decision, but the Doji is a very significant candlestick you need to watch out for.

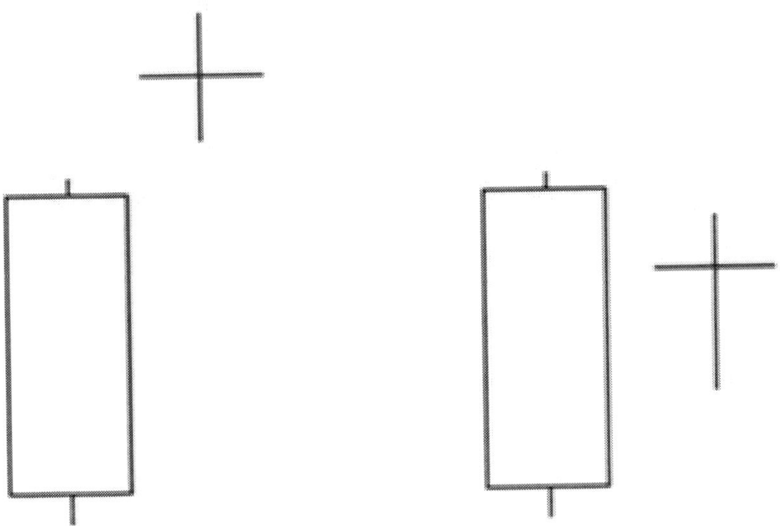

## Hammer

This occurs when traders begin to short-sell a stock after it opens. However, before closing, buyers force a reversal and the price closes at the top of the range. Sometimes hammer patterns show up when there have been considerable orders placed for a stop loss.

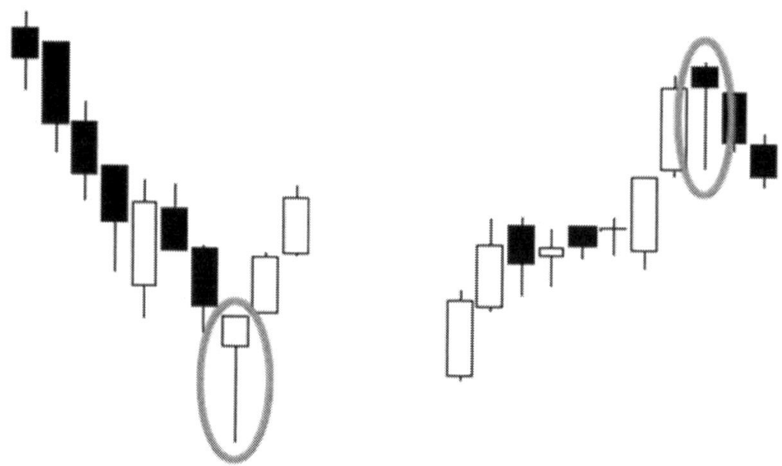

## Piercing

This pattern can also signify an imminent reversal. From a previous trading period, there usually is a wide range black candle which closes at the bottom of a range or near the bottom, signifying that sellers have the upper hand. But in the next trading period, a wide range white candle closes at a position that is somewhere halfway into the previous candle. Short sellers in the previous trading period are at a loss when this occurs.

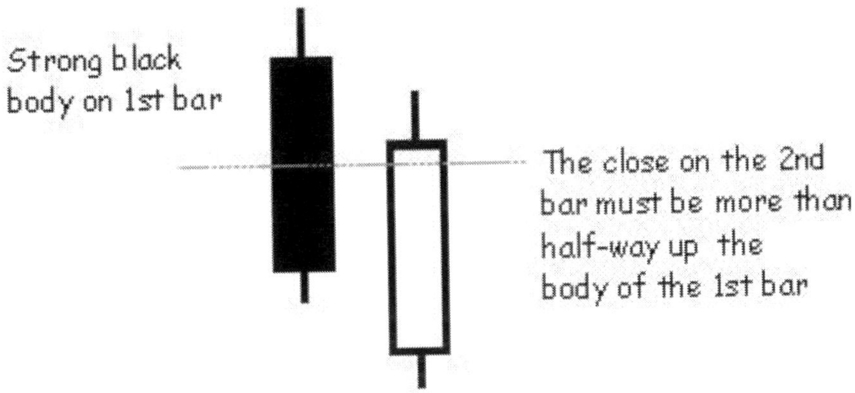


## Harami

Harami means pregnant in Japan; hence, the Harami pattern usually shows up as two candles with the smaller one nestled inside the larger one. It can easily be mistaken for the engulfing pattern, but there are not the same. The positions of the candles are opposite that of the engulfing pattern. Usually, this pattern signifies a stop in preceding momentum. From a previous trading period, there usually is a wide range black candle which closes at the bottom of a range or near the bottom, signifying that sellers have the upper hand. However, in the next trading period, a narrow range white candle closes the period.

## Bearish Patterns

This bearish pattern occurs on a stock chart when a filled or black candle engulfs a previous smaller hollow or white candle. The bearish engulfing pattern often occurs in an uptrend to signify a likely reversal to a bearish trend or downtrend.

## Doji Star

The Doji Star is a bearish pattern that is formed by the appearance of a white wide range candle on the first day and followed by a Doji on the second day that gaps above the first day. The wigs of the Doji are not very long. This also signifies a possible reversal from an upward to a downward trend.

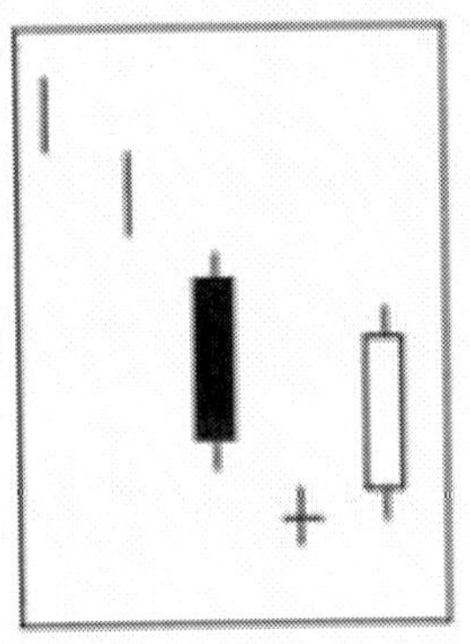

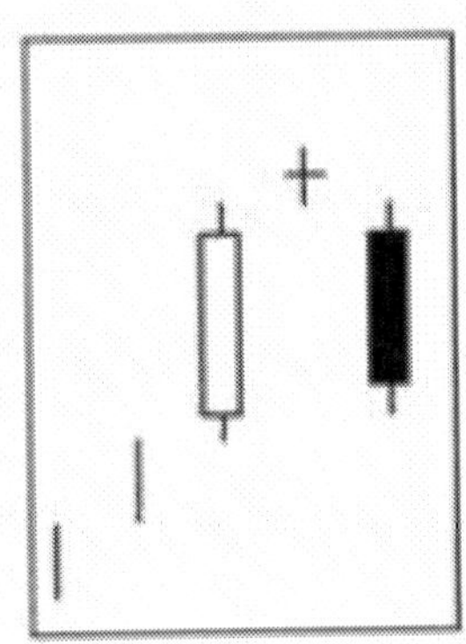

## Shooting Star

This bearish candle pattern looks like an inverted hammer pattern. It occurs when a stock's price goes above the opening price during the trading period, but at the closing, it came lower than the opening price. This bearish candle pattern is a good sign that an uptrend is losing steam; therefore it is a good idea to consider entering short trades when you see this pattern.

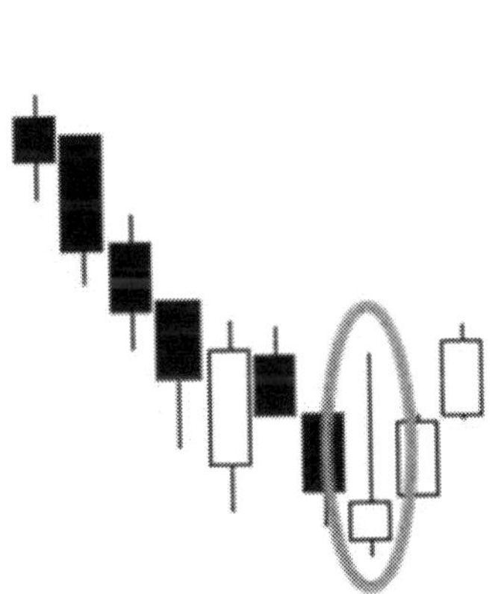

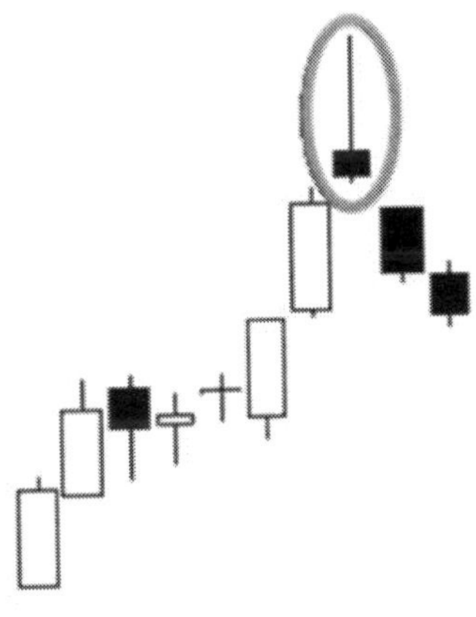

## Dark Cloud Cover

This bearish reversal pattern occurs when a filled (black) candle's opening price is above the closing price of a hollowed candle and is, at the same time, below the hollowed candle's midpoint.

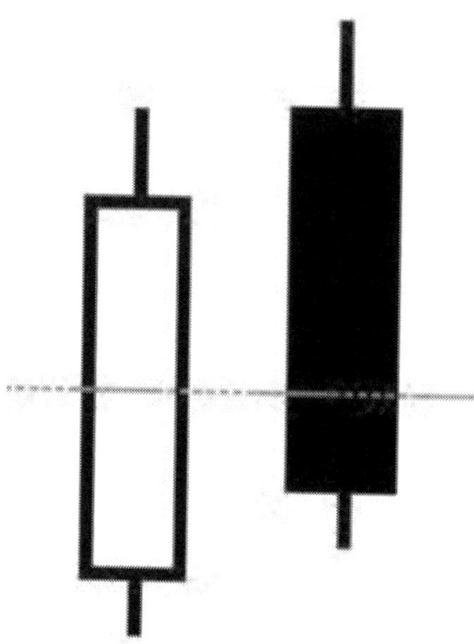

## Bearish Harami

This two-bar bearish candle pattern indicates a possible reversal to a downward trend. Obviously, an uptrend goes before a bearish Harami pattern occurs. Bearish Harami shows a hollow candle that is followed by a small filled candle. The opening price, as well as the closing price of the small filled (black) candle, has to be contained within the range of the hollow (white) candle.

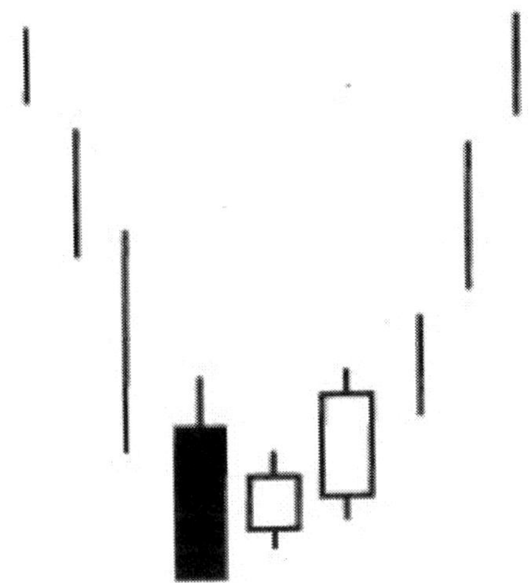

In summary:

- A wide range bullish candle signifies that buyers were actively buying and were therefore in charge of the trade during a larger part of the specified time frame.
- A wide range bearish candle means that sellers were vigorously selling and were more in charge of the trade for the most part of the trading duration.
- Narrow range candles show that neither buyers nor sellers were too passionate about the stock, therefore, creating a lesser impact on the opening price.
- A rather long tail at the bottom of a candle means that sellers were aggressive at the beginning of the time frame, however, before the close, buyers took the lead.
- A long tail at the top of a candle shows that buyers were tenaciously holding to their positions for a good part of the trading period. Nevertheless, sellers took over before the stock closed.
- When the body of a candle falls in between long upper and lower tails, it simply means that both buyers and sellers

had an almost equal impact on the price of the stock. So trading appears balanced.

By now you should be able to look at a stock chart and, using what you have learned so far, understand exactly what the candlesticks are telling you.

## Using Two or More Candlesticks

Basing your options trading decision solely on the message of only one candlestick may not be a wise way to use candlesticks. Even if you do not fuse candlestick messages or signs with other tools, you should at least combine two or more candlesticks before taking any action.

Now, let us piece all of the patterns and all of the information about charts, trends, stages, waves, etc., together into charts and learn how to read them effectively. You will not be able to succeed as a swing trader without knowing how to read charts. The vital information you need to know before letting your money go into any trade is all in the chart. The chart tells you if the risk is worth it.

In order to get yourself familiarized with reading stock charts, you need to do this. Look for stock charts online and print them out. Now look at each stock chart and try to determine the following:
What trend is the stock on the chart? Is it going up (uptrend) or is it going down (downtrend)? Is the stock price falling or is it rising? What is the current stage of the stock? Is it in the first, second, third, or fourth stage? Can you determine the support and resistance points? Are there any signs of a breach? Is the trend of the stock a strong one? When was the last breakout? Has

there been any pullback or rally? Is this the beginning, middle, or the end of the trend?

Practice with a good number of stock charts and you will definitely get better. With time, you wouldn't have to force yourself to remember these questions – they will occur to you as soon as you look at any chart and the answers will come to you as fast as you can think of the questions.

Let me break down what you should be looking for as you practice reading stock charts. Remember, in this beginners guide, we are using only the candlestick stock chart.

## Look for the Stock Trend or Chart Pattern

Firstly, train yourself to quickly identify the general stock direction (uptrend or downtrend) on the stock chart. I would suggest that you should adjust your daily chart to show the chart patterns dating back to about 7 to 8 months. The chart pattern for that time frame should show you clearly the trend, stages, and waves of the stock. When you have successfully identified a trend, you are ready to look for the next important thing on the stock chart.

## Look for the Price Pattern

Secondly, try to identify the price pattern of the stock. What you are looking for on a stock chart that you have identified as having an uptrend is a pullback. If you have identified the chart pattern as a downtrend, then what you are looking for is a rally. So, you've identified a chart pattern (stock trend) and you have found a pullback or rally depending on the direction of the trend. Now you will need to find one more piece to solve the puzzle.

## Look for the Candlestick Pattern

Lastly, look at what the candlesticks are saying. In an uptrend, if the pullback you observed in the price pattern is really a pullback, when the trend comes back around (returns to the dominant trend) the candlestick that should follow in an ideal situation would be a bullish candlestick such as the piercing, hammer, or an engulfing candlestick pattern. In a downtrend, if the rally you observed in the price pattern is really a rally, when the price movement returns to the dominant trend, the dark cloud cover, engulfing, or a shooting star are the likely bearish candlestick pattern that will follow the rally.

When you can effectively combine these three parts of a stock chart, you would have successfully learned one major aspect of reading stock charts.

## Technical Indicator: What It Is

The OHLC (open, high, low, and close) price of a stock over a period of time forms the price data of that stock or security. Now when the price data of a particular security is passed through a set of mathematical functions or formulas, a sequence of data points are created. This is what is known as a technical indicator. So to give it a proper definition: a technical indicator is a series or sequence of data points that are generated through the application of mathematical formulas to the price data of a particular security. Several other indices such as the volume of stock may also be included in the formula to generate the data points.

I am going to save you the headache of how the formula is applied to the price data and all the computations involved in coming up with a technical indicator. All you need to know as a beginner is that technical indicators are displayed graphically on top or below the chart of a security or stock. And it is there to aid you in your market analysis – to compare the stock's chart with the information on the technical indicator. The more in agreement they are, the better decision you can make.

Before you go hunting for the perfect technical indicator that will show you all the good trades, be aware that these indicators are not 100 percent accurate all of the time. They can signal a false buy or sell alert. So be warned.

## Functions and What You Get From Technical Indicators

Perhaps I should refresh your memory about moving averages. What did we say moving averages are used for? (Feel free to look back at chapter 4 to reacquaint yourself with moving averages.) We said the lines of a moving average indicate a stock's average price over a given period. So, they are basically indicators that show you the average price of a stock. Well, that's one thing you get from technical indicators.

While the stock chart shows you price action, technical indicators show you other information about the same stock from a different vantage point.

Anyone functions of technical indicators are summarized below:

- **For Confirmation:** Throughout this guide, I have advised that you should not base your trading decisions solely on one tool. A technical indicator can serve as a tool that you use in confirming whatever you deduce from price actions on a chart. For example, when you observe that a stock has broken a support level, you could look at the OBV to confirm if there is a low reading to indicate that there is an actual weakness. OBV means On Balance Volume; it is a technical indicator.

- **For Calling Attention:** Technical indicators can draw the trader's attention to study price actions more carefully. It can prompt you to a variety of alerts that can really save you from some serious financial damage. For example, you may be prompted to look out for a break in support level when momentum is declining.
- **For Predicting Price Direction:** A technical indicator can also serve as a tool for predicting what side future prices will lean towards – up or down.

## Proper Use of Technical Indicators

- **No One Size Fits All:** Different stocks may cause the same indicator to behave differently. In using technical indicators, it is important to know that different indicators tend to work well for different stocks. With continuous practice and application, you will come to discover which indicator will serve you best for your chosen stocks.
- **To Indicate:** There is no single tool that has all the trading answers! Have I said that enough times yet? That is because it is of vital importance to keep that in mind. In that sense, it is important to note that one proper way to use a technical indicator is to see them as tools that only point to the likelihood of an outcome. They must be used in combination with price action. A technical indicator does not directly represent price action; what it does is to present you with information about its own generated or computed results from price data. There are times when a technical indicator will signal you to buy or sell, yet they could be very wrong. If you do not verify each signal with

what the stock chart is telling you, it may lead to fatal trading mistakes. The bottom line is this: technical indicators aid you but they do not do the trading for you. Ultimately, you are the one who decides what and when to trade based on signals from indicators and other analysis.

- **Use Time Tested Indicators:** The proliferation of technical indicators seems to be on a constant rise. Some newer computer programs even provide users (traders) the choice of developing custom made indicators! But with all of the numerous new indicators available at our beck and call, it seems they do not offer anything too unique or new from others in existence before them. As a matter of fact, I would advise that as a beginner, you stick to time tested indicators to avoid being sent on a wild goose chase.
- **A Few Is Good Enough:** As mentioned above, there are several technical indicators available today. But you really do not need all of them. Heck! You do not even need more than three good technical indicators to succeed in a proper analysis. What matters is that you are well acquainted with the few you use. The fewer the number of indicators, the better you will learn and know how to use them.
- **A Few Complementary Indicators:** What would be the point of having three indicators that all function almost exactly the same way? That's a huge waste of time and resources. When you are picking out your few indicators, make sure that you select indicators that complement each other. That is to say, select indicators that perform functions that add to the functions of the other(s). If you decide to use only two indicators, for example, it doesn't make much sense to choose the Accumulation/Distribution Line and Chaikin Money Flow (CMF) as your only two technical indicators. Both of them perform the same function which is to show if money is

coming in or going out of stock by combining volume and price.

# Learning the Options Trading Strategy

## Develop Your Trading Strategy

There is no perfect trading strategy; so stop searching for one. Moreover, you do not need a perfect trading strategy to make money from trading stocks. Ultimately, your trading strategy will be unique to you. However, as a beginner, you may need to lean a bit on an existing strategy in order to get the hang of it. With time, you can tweak things around to fit your particular trading style or build yours completely from scratch.

Here is a general idea you can use to build your own trading strategy.

# Preparation

You could start preparing for your trade at the beginning of a new week. Find out what types of trade (short or long) you will want to focus on. You could use a technical indicator such as the moving averages to determine this. After that, take a look at a few financial columns or news, reports, etc. This will give you the general outlook of how stocks are performing and what the market is up to. Look at charts of various industries to see stock strengths and weaknesses, plus promising stocks. Be sure to write down 9whatever catches your attention in your trading notepad (you don't have one yet?), because in the heat of trading, most things you note mentally won't come to your mind.

## Finding Stocks

Begin to search for potential trades by looking for stocks that:

- Have a strong trend
- Have shown first pullbacks or rallies
- Are at a resistance or support level
- Are in the second or fourth stages
- Are repeatedly touching a support or resistance area

If you do not find a trade that you are comfortable with as a beginner, please do not trade. Remember, trading involves going long, short, or staying in cash. So, learn to stay in cash if there is nothing appealing for you to trade.

## Double-Check

After you have found a trade, verify that the company whose stock you are about to trade is not going to release its earnings reports anytime soon. Trading a company's stock just before their earnings report is released can lead to a massive loss for you. So be sure to double-check. Here's one way you could find out. Simply go to Yahoo Finance and type in the company's symbol. The date of the next earnings report will be shown.

## During Trades

All things checked and verified, start your trade. Do not give your attention to stock market news or other traders opinion during your own trades. Your attention needs to be only in one place: the stock chart. Ensure that you use trailing stops to closely follow your profits and that would be all you require during trades.

## Your Entry Strategy

Your money is at risk as soon as you enter a position to buy or sell a stock. So, you must be careful that you time your entry very well.

Your entry point should be at a swing point: a low swing point for buying, and a high swing point for selling.

A swing point is made up of three candles.

**Low Swing Point** (for entering a long position – buying)

- Candle one goes low
- Candle two goes lower than candle one (lower low)
- Candle three goes higher than candle two (higher low)

Candle three indicates that sellers are no more aggressive. This is a precursor for a trend reversal. This is your cue to enter a long position.

**High Swing Point** (for entering a short position – selling)

- Candle one goes high
- Candle two goes higher than candle one (higher high)
- Candle three goes lower than candle two (lower high)

Candle three indicates that buyers are no more aggressive. This is a precursor for a trend reversal. This is your cue to enter a short position.

## Successive Up Days or Down Days

Another way to enter a trade is to look for successive up days or down days. These are a lot easier to spot, but be sure that you are not entering the trade when the trend is about to end or reverse. Take a look at the chart below for a clearer understanding.

## Your Exit Strategy

You have read all the charts, and picked your stocks to trade and you have determined which market to trade on – in fact, you know exactly when to time your entry. But when do you exit a trade? When do you lock in profits? You see, as important as timing your entry is, if you neglect when to exit, you may not take any profits home after all.

You must plan well ahead of your entry how you intend to exit a trade. And remember that a plan is not a plan until it is written down. Following a plan in your head is the same as trading based on your emotions. It usually fails. Basically, there are three reasons why you should exit a trade, namely: when making profits, when losing money, and when you are not making or losing money.

Let us take a brief look at each of these reasons for exiting a trade.

## Taking Your Profits

Before you enter a trade, it is important to set a mechanism that tells you it is time to take your profits and exit the trade. Do not rely on some abstract feelings. Remember to be emotionally detached from your trade outcomes. That way, you will pay more attention to your previously set mechanism when it alerts you of an exit point. If you are greedy and wait too long, you may lose a substantial part of your profits. And if you are too fearful and quit too soon, you may equally lose a significant part of profits that should be yours. This boils down to emotional intelligence. The good news is that it can be developed. So if you intend to become a successful swing trader and you have determined that you do not have enough discipline to follow through with your plan, do not worry. You can learn how to do that as you take baby steps in options trading.

When you buy or sell a stock, ensure that you have a stop-loss point in mind. You can use that point to set a stop-loss order, or you can click buy or sell when prices get to that point.

## Ending Your Losses

Make up your mind long before you enter any trade that you are going to cut your losses early enough before it digs a hole in your account that will require a lot of money to mend. Again, you have to set up a prior mechanism for identifying when to cut your losses. I strongly suggest that you use the trailing stops to cut losses. Set your losses to somewhere around 3% (or less) of your capital. Make your losses are as small as possible so you don't get all emotional about the loss.

Be on the lookout for repeated price attempts to breach support or resistance. That is an indication of a possible breakout. Sticking to a losing position in the hope of it rebounding is abandoning your plans and listening to your emotions. In options trading, hope doesn't give you profits. Most often than not, hope has an ironic way of crippling your account.

## Freeing Up Your Capital

Whether you choose to quickly exit a trade that is neither making you money nor making you lose money, or you choose to watch it for a few days, both choices are okay. The important thing is that before you enter the trade, you should make up your mind about how long you are willing to watch a trade that is generally lukewarm. Remember that you are in a type of trade that is considered short-term. You don't have the whole month to wait for one position. If it is tying down your money, free up your capital and reinvest it in another stock or position.

## Trading Pullbacks and Rallies

As earlier discussed, pullbacks and rallies are great opportunities to buy and sell stocks (in case you missed it, you can check it out in chapter 3).

Usually, when stock prices begin to move in an upward direction (an uptrend), they tend to briefly pullback. This presents you a good opportunity to buy at low risk and increases your chances of selling at a higher price later. On the reverse side, when stock prices begin to move in a downward direction (downtrend), they tend to briefly rally and offer you an excellent opportunity for shorting.

Here is something for you to consider as a beginner in options trading. If all you do is simply stay in cash (that is, holding on to your money without trading) until you find excellent pullbacks and rallies, you will be making a wise beginner decision.

Think about it. It stands to reason that the best time to buy stocks at a great price is right after a recent occurrence of selling.

It equally shows better judgment to short sell right after the occurrence of buying.

The best time to trade pullbacks and rallies is the first time they appear on a chart after a significant trend. So the first time you notice a pullback after a trend line is breached or broken, seize the opportunity. Be on the lookout for a pullback that happens immediately following a wide range candle. Buy or sell at that point. When you see a breakout, be ready to trade the first pullback after it. When a new high is set, wait for the first pullback. When it comes up, go in for the kill.
Let us look at the chart below to get a clearer picture of the above. The first pullback after a significant downtrend offered those who were watchful an excellent opportunity to buy early.

## You Cannot Win All Trades

No, you can't. It doesn't matter what tools or magic formula you use. Remember that the stock market contains so many moving parts that are far beyond the control of any one individual or a body. Any of these moving parts could have a significant adverse effect on even the best technical indicators or analysis tools.

But you can win a lot of trades enough to make you good profits. The profits you make come from the ignorance or mistakes of other traders. In the stock market, you are either making mistakes or you are making profits. Unfortunately for most traders, they are making mistakes. Whether you will choose to make profits depends largely on if you will take your learning seriously to avoid the mistakes most novices make.

Some of these mistakes are depending 100% on technical analysis, being too afraid to lose, looking for a fail-proof system or trading magic formula, being emotional, etc. The truth is, not everyone is cut out to be a trader or a swing trader. However, a lot of people will give it a shot and eventually fail. It is from these failed attempts that you will make profits if you learn and apply what these other traders won't.

You will not win all your trades, but you will win a lot of your trades provided you do not buy and sell as the novices do. When do you time your buys? At the beginning of a pullback or when the crowd has said it is okay to buy? At what times do you sell? When you notice a rally or when major selling is almost over? You see, buying or selling too late is the hallmark of novices, which a lot of traders are, no matter how long they have spent trading. The number of years a trader spends trading the stock market does not necessarily make them experts. It is what you learn and applies that distinguishes you from the novices.

Stand apart by trading in the opposite direction of the crowd. Don't worry, expert and veteran traders don't usually trade in the direction of the crowd, so you are not making a mistake when you do so. But when the crowd is selling – the prices are a lot cheaper then. And of course, you know very well to sell when the crowd is buying, the price is a lot higher then because everyone wants to get the hot-selling stocks which you happen to have.

## Options Trading Is a Continuous Learning Process

There are challenges you will encounter as you trade. You do not improve if you quit or if you stop only at what you have learned so far. Becoming a swing trader means you are going to keep learning on a continuous basis in order to bring on your A-game.

It is important to recognize the dynamism of the market. The market doesn't stay still for too long. For you to be anything close to success in the art of options trading, you must be ready to continue adapting to changes in rules, regulations, and laws. Additionally, new and exciting vehicles of investments keep springing up. Stay up to speed with new information about the market.

There is money to be made from options trading, but you must be ready to do your part by continuously learning new ways to make money. You should see options trading as an art of improving your trading skills rather than a way of making money. The money part is a natural result of making good trades. You cannot flop on your trades out of ignorance and expect to make money. It is not out of line to assume that the amount of profit you generate from options trading is directly proportional to your options trading skill level. The more you improve, the more profits flood your account. And you certainly cannot improve without keeping yourself abreast of up-to-date information about stocks, prices, markets, etc.

As part of your learning, you will encounter situations that will teach you better than any book the art of accepting losses. You may follow every single detail in your well mapped out strategy or plan, yet you will still lose a trade. It is not time to argue with the losses or stubbornly hold on to the position. Accept it. You have lost. It happens. Now dust yourself up and try again this time, more intelligently.

Remember that you are a swing trader who is supposed to study the psychology of traders. You are supposed to leverage the emotional shortcomings of other traders and make profits. You cannot successfully do that if you have not mastered your own emotions. Continuing to trade with the aim of breaking even when you are losing is a gateway to financial disaster. Avoid it by all means.

I will not fail to add that you must shield yourself from the herd mentality. You must distinguish yourself from the trading crowd. Do not follow the crowd unless you have determined by yourself that they are towing the right direction (which is not a very common occurrence both in options trading and any other aspect of life). And the reason why herd mentality is not good for you is that the herds do not think for themselves. They depend on one person's or one organization's opinion. These opinions were thought of by human traders (even if they used computerized tools to draw their conclusions). You are capable of reaching your own opinions too. Herd mentality is generated from the internet, message board, and even so-called guru analysts.

Nevertheless, do not discard time-tested facts about the market in the guise of shielding yourself from the herd mentality. That is why I would recommend that you find reliable sources of information so that you can digest them and draw your own conclusions.

## Finally, Learn Some Basic Money Management

A lot of people win the lottery by chance (how else would you win a lottery if not by chance!), but they still become broke after a few weeks, months or a couple of years? Why is that so? They do not have basic money management skills. It doesn't matter how much money you make from the stock market (or from winning the lottery!), if you do not have money management skills, you are simply exposing yourself to trade like a gambler or someone buying a lottery ticket – you will begin trading in the hope that you will win (like a game of chance) because you are under pressure to make money you have previously lost due to bad money management policies.

## Contract

A contract allows portfolio managers and companies to hedge against random events.

For example, a French company that exports to the United States and bills in dollars may have an interest in blocking the selling price as of now. It will, therefore, ask its treasurer to sell future contracts for an amount equivalent to the exported goods, so as to block its selling price (which has many advantages, because the company knows now its costs, but also future cash inflows).

Suppose the price in it is the following: 1 $ = 1 €. The company planned to export $ 10 million worth of goods over the year. If the price of the euro falls to the level of $ 0.90, in the event that the company did not cover these sales, it would have lost one million euros (0.10 x 10 million).

The main advantage of futures is to allow hedging. For this, these markets must be liquid and speculators will represent the counterpart and therefore bear the risk. The liquidity of the futures markets is mainly due to the presence of many speculators in the electronic markets. Henceforth, the absence of intermediaries on the floors makes these instruments perfect vehicles for intraday speculation. In addition, brokerage fees, due to recent technological advances, have collapsed allowing an individual to become profitable from the first tick.

The most famous contracts with day traders are the E-mini Nasdaq 100 and the E-mini S & P 500, which are traded on the

Chicago Mercantile Exchange. Orders are placed electronically and executed almost automatically. More recently, we have seen the appearance of the mini-Dow. In Europe, the most traded contracts on stock market indices are Dax, Footsie, and CAC21.

The value of a CAC point is 10 euros and the minimum deposit is 2,250 euros (negotiable for intraday). The value of a Nasdaq E-mini point is $20, and the minimum deposit is $ 3,250 ($ 2,500 for intraday or even $ 500 / $ 300 with some brokers). The value of a E-mini S & P 500 is $50, and the minimum deposit is $ 3,500 ($ 500 for intraday).

These future contracts have many advantages:
- The trader follows only a few indices instead of following dozens of actions;
- These markets are extremely liquid, and it is, therefore, possible to get in and out very quickly of its positions. Moreover, thanks to the passage of electronic orders, orders are executed almost instantaneously.
- Leverage is important. It is usually 20 but can easily reach 100 with some brokers.

## The Hybrid Method

Some traders consider that the optimal system combines both approaches. Jesse Livermore's method is interesting in that it capitalizes on the concept "the trend is your ally". She considers that it is possible to miss several small movements, but we must never miss a strong trend because the bulk of the profits are made in this type of market. Nevertheless, it does not allow the trader to quickly take profits while this attitude should be favored when the market is without a trend.

We have developed a method taking into account the contributions of the two methods (the classical method and that of Livermore). If the trader has a strong conviction about a title, he can open the entire position at the very beginning and take his profits after an average boost (example: 10%) on half of the position and ride his stop. If the stock consolidates and offers a new interesting entry point then we can ride the stop under the previous support and increase our position.

This system takes the best of the other two. We secure profits when the stock moves in the expected direction and we continue to capitalize on the current trend with the profits made at the first momentum. The first movement will be a net winner and the second should be neutral if the position is stopped.

To summarize, rigorous risk management is necessary to survive in the markets, but it assumes that the trader strictly complies with the following points:

- He must only retain opportunities offering a Risk / Reward of at least 3 positions (therefore a potential gain three times greater than the tolerated loss);
- Diversification of investments for a swing trader. Any market operator can set romper on the evolution of the markets. Diversification reduces the risk of error by betting more uncorrelated contracts, rather than bet on one with the risk of suffering a consequential loss in the event of adverse movement;
- The specialization for the day trader and the scalper. The trader must avoid opening more than three positions at a time and focus on a few titles in order to be totally focused on the process. Diversification is not necessary because the positions are closed before the end of the day. The most important for the trader remains the perfect knowledge of the main technical levels

(supports, resistances, Fibonacci ratio ...) in order to operate in the most efficient way;
- Ideally, the tolerable loss on a position should never exceed 1 to 2% of the capital, but this percentage will also depend on the size of the capital and the strategy adopted.

## The Strategic Dimension of Trading

The strategy consists of developing an action plan, defined according to the strengths and weaknesses, taking into account the threats and opportunities observed by the protagonist. The strategy was first a war science, but soon found many other areas of application. The art of trading has many similarities with the art of war.
The armies that win are those whose general master the art of strategy. Likewise, the most successful investors are true strategists. "The market is an arena where other traders are opponents." – Martin Schwartz

Trading represents a fight between buyers (who want the market to rise) and sellers (whose main objective is to lower prices), whose ultimate objective is to grab the resources of the other party. There are many similarities between war and trading. According to Sun Tzu, the first objective of the war is not to humiliate and shed blood within the ranks of his opponent, but above all to ensure his survival and win by avoiding unnecessary deaths. Similarly, in terms of trading, the strategy aims essentially to achieve a pure monetary performance, while taking a little risk and ensuring that the results are not very volatile.

Sun Tzu has enunciated five principles of victory that apply in our opinion perfectly to the art of trading: knowing when it is appropriate to fight, and when it is appropriate to withdraw (defend); know how to use the little and the most according to the circumstances (save your resources and use them intelligently); to skillfully match his ranks (discipline); he who, prudent, prepares to face an enemy who is not yet; he himself will be victorious. To take advantage of its rusticity and not to foresee is the greatest crime; to be ready without any contingency is the greatest of virtues (to be perfectly prepared); to be safe from the interference of the sovereign in all that one can attempt for his service and the glory of his arms (to have an independence of mind)

To succeed in the markets, the trader must know himself perfectly and therefore understand the role played by emotions before, during and after the taking of a position: it is about his survival. Similarly, it will allow him to understand the behavior of other traders and capitalize on it.

Indeed, the trader operates in a very often virtual way and sometimes alone. It has real-time information flows and must position itself according to specific criteria. The precepts developed by authors like Sun Tzu provide extremely useful elements to help the trader to be totally focused on his task. What could be better than to think of yourself as the general of an army that must be led to victory? Nevertheless, this comparison is not only done in a motivational perspective, but it also provides valuable insights on the attitude to adopt in trading. The words developed in the art of war perfectly apply to the world of business and trading.

On a psychological level, the fact that a trader represents himself as a strategist can help him to increase his discipline. A positive personal image plays an important role in the success of the trader and this is all the more true as trading is a virtual world where competitors are not always known.

To illustrate this, let's take the example of a market that is falling sharply. The common traders will panic and seek to rush out of a position or sell. A good trader will first analyze the situation and coldly evaluate the interest of positioning. If the conditions look good then he will not hesitate to do so. Similarly, like the general who leads an army, the trader should not be stubborn and do not hesitate to retreat if it is the most favorable outcome, even if he returns to the battlefield by the following.

## The Main Categories of Investors

Behavioral finance (NTA) has highlighted three categories of investors:
The rational investor is the one who controls the fundamentals, but who also takes into account the reaction of other investors to market information. He acts as a strategist.

The fundamentalist investor relies essentially on fundamentals to position himself, in this sense; he is passive on the markets and is not a strategist.

Ignorant investors, or noise traders, have no strategy and only follow mass movements. Their expectations are formed in an unreasonable way. They will rely on weak signals (they ignore the probabilities and operate on instinct) to intervene and use popular models such as technical analysis to act.

For behavioral finance, an investor should be concerned about the views of other traders even when it differs from the fundamental value. Indeed, this opinion can considerably influence prices when it receives a sufficiently large membership. Thus, prices can shift in a sustainable and significant way compared to fundamentals solely due to sheep phenomena and other beliefs of ignorant investors. According to the behaviorists, the rational investor must take advantage of the behavior of ignorant investors.

# Chapter 7

# Risk & Money Management

## The Rhythmic and Cyclical Markets

Ralph Nelson Elliott has developed an approach to interpret wave market movements. His work focuses on hourly Dow Jones quotations and is released from 1938, arousing interest due to the emergence of fractals and chaotic movements.

This analysis considers an alternation between unpredictable periods and deterministic periods. Markets would not be governed by a random walk as Burton Malkiel mentioned. Mandelbrot develops this aspect in his book Fractals, chance, and finance. He considers that the evolution of prices is discontinuous, that prices can shift suddenly, and not in a gradual and continuous way, like good weather and bad weather in short: "If the markets were perfect, they would react instantly to all the news," he exclaimed. Now, they sometimes take time to integrate information and sometimes do so with exaggeration.

Elliott's research leads him to the following conclusion: the continual changes in the stock market reflected a fundamental harmony of nature. Thus, he notes that variations in the Dow Jones Industrial Average (DJIA) construct visible figures that return in the same forms, although they may vary in duration and amplitude.

These observations will allow him to develop a theory, known as Elliott's Wave Theory. It combines the psychological dimension borrowed from Charles Dow and the harmony of nature identified by the mathematician Fibonacci. It consists of a set of empirical rules to interpret the evolution of the main stock indices. This tool is powerful because the rules and principles stated by Elliott are supposed to contain all the action of the market. The main advantage of the Elliott Wave Method is to set up scenarios, set targets and has points of invalidation, the universe of possibilities being known.

This approach is very interesting because it allows one to consider the cyclicality of the financial markets. Indeed, stock prices evolve in a cyclical way: a rise or a fall will never appear in time and will be punctuated by movements of consolidation or correction. Elliott was one of the first writers to highlight the concept of action/reaction which posits that each impulsive movement must be followed by a corrective movement, the impulsive movement being more important in amplitude than the corrective movement.

For example, in an uptrend, the amplitude of impulsive (bullish) waves is generally stronger than that of corrective waves (downs) and vice versa.

During a marked trend, it seems obvious that the market can blow after an impulsive movement. This phenomenon can easily be explained by profit-taking. New entrants (buyers in an uptrend and sellers in a downtrend) are waiting for the presence of a low point to position themselves, which will allow the resumption of the dominant trend. The great strength of Elliott's waves is to be a complete method that emphasizes the two most important elements in trading that are price and time.

# Elliott Wave Decomposition

In various articles that were published in the Financial World in 1939, Elliott indicated that the market's bottom rate was a cycle of eight waves, containing five waves of the rise and three waves of decline. The three waves of decline are a correction of the five previous waves of increase.

For Elliott, every impulsive movement is followed by a corrective movement. An impulsive movement is composed of five waves of a lower degree of which three are impulsive and two are corrective. The corrective movement is composed of three waves, two of which are corrective, and one is impulsive.

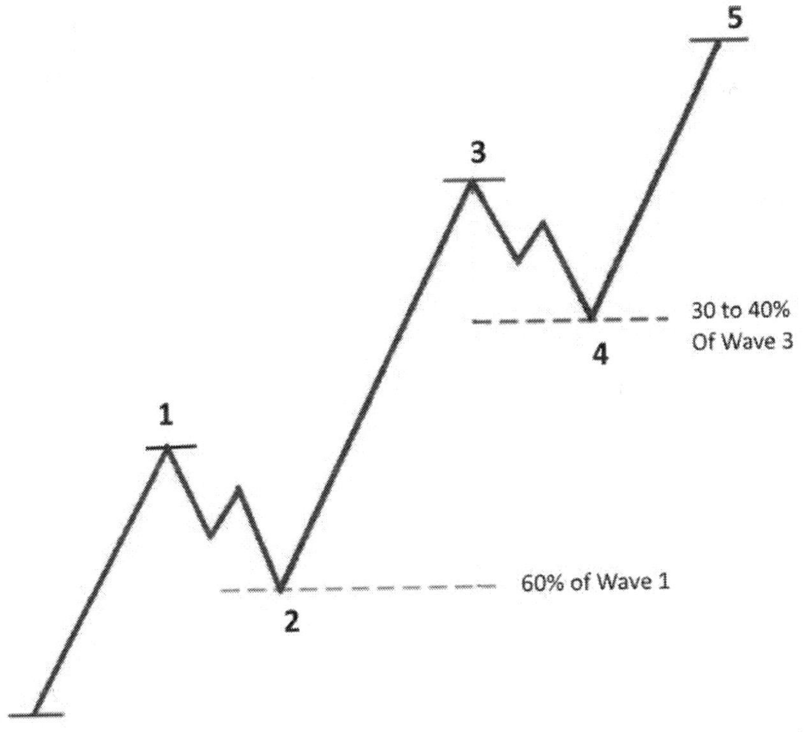

We will first describe the decomposition of the five waves contained in the impulsive movement:

The first wave represents the arrival of precursors on the markets. The latter anticipates the market turnaround and the imminence of an impulsive movement. They seek to return at the very beginning of the movement and correspond to the initiated investors mentioned by Charles Dow.

The second wave very often corresponds to a strong correction of the first impulsive movement. It represents the entry of contrarians who play the decline because they believe that the market remains in a bearish phase.
The third wave is usually that of followers and professional investors. The news is positive and the operators are rushing on the title, causing a strong upward acceleration. It's the most powerful impulsive wave, and it's never the shortest.

The fourth wave is profit-taking by operators who took advantage of the sharp rise in a wave. Nevertheless, the trend remains bullish and it is not questioned.

The fifth wave is the last impulsive wave of major impulsive movement. It corresponds to the entry of late followers, who have observed the rise without positioning themselves and who are eager to enjoy the movement like others. Generally, they are the first victims of the market downturn. This wave is also characterized by a depletion of the technical indicators which often draw a bearish divergence and point the breathlessness of the trend in progress and the imminence of a correction.

On many impulsive waves, it is not uncommon to note the presence of an "extension": it is a wave of impulse which is prolonged and which marks the power of the wave in question.

This extension usually takes shape on a single impulsive wave, which allows analysts to take the measure of other waves. Thus, if the first and third waves are of the same length, the fifth will certainly be an extension. The rules set out by Elliott are supposed to contain all the action of the market.

According to Elliott, this decomposition is found whatever the period is chosen. Some analysts do not hesitate to make a comparison with the theory of chaos, developed especially by Mandelbrot. According to this theory, there would be an order in apparent disorder, and images taken at different scales (short term, long term) may have striking similarities. They forget, however, that the principal concerned, Mandelbrot, does not take Elliott's waves seriously. But let us leave aside these sterile quarrels and interest us in the most important: this method is popular, it is followed (the trader must, therefore, integrate it into his arsenal) and it is even sometimes effective!

## Four Basic Principles and Five Rules

There are several principles governing Elliott's waves, which we will summarize into basic principles:

Action is followed by a reaction: markets never go up in a single time; the impulse waves, movements in the direction of the primary tendency, break down into five waves of a lower degree, and the corrective waves, movements against the primary trend (bullish or bearish), are decomposed into three waves of a lower degree;

When a movement in eight waves (five up and three down) ends, a complete cycle comes to an end, and this cycle becomes two subdivisions in the immediately higher degree wave; whatever the time horizon, the way of counting is the same because the market is moving at the same pace. The rules stated must imperatively be applied during a count and will be controlled over time.

## Corrective Waves

There are several types of corrective waves (zigzags, flats, etc.). In a 5-step movement, corrective waves always correct the previous upward movement. The following properties are the most commonly observed: wave 2 corrects wave 1 and wave 4 corrects wave 3. Elliott, along with several top-flight analysts, noted that corrective waves regularly corrected the impulsive movements of a certain percentage.

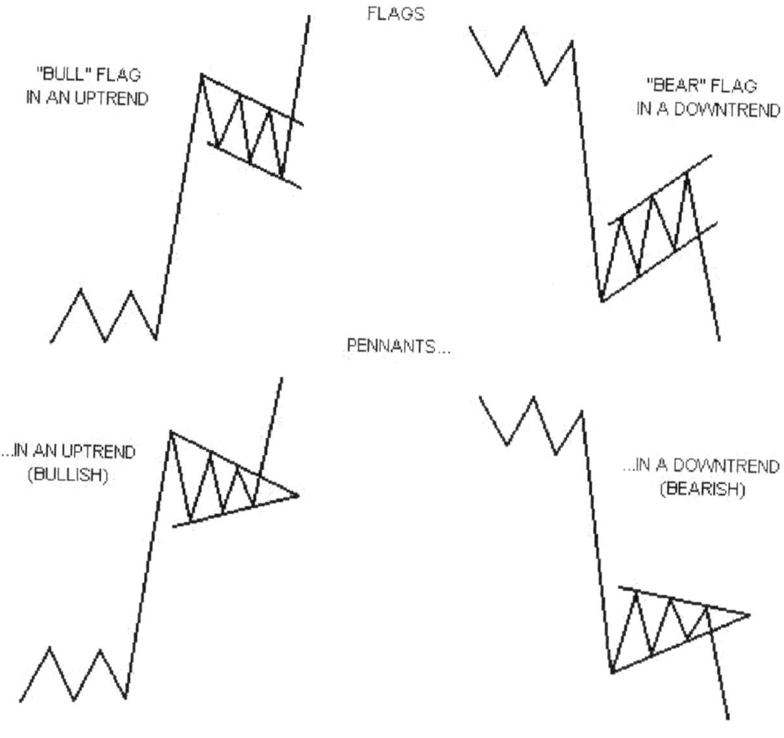

## Standard Wave Retracement Ratios 2

Wave 2 is often the strongest and corrects waves 1. It traces the previous move at a minimum of 38.2% to 50%, but the standard retracement is 61.8% and can go up to a maximum of 76.4%.

## Standard Wave Retracement Ratios 4

Wave 4 represents profit-taking. The correction is never strong and stands at least 23.6%, the standard is 38.2% and they never retrace more than 50%. If the correction is greater than 50% then it is probably necessary to question its count because it is probably a wave 1.

In summary, Wave 2 corrects strongly (61.8% is the standard ratio); while Wave 4 is profit-taking (the standard ratio is often 38.2%).

## Can We Distinguish A Corrective Wave From A True Reversal Of The Trend?

We have previously seen that an uptrend could be called into question when a lower precedent was depressed. A correction was then drawn, and the prices have depressed the two previous low points without that preventing the title from continuing its ascent. Indeed, this corrective movement corrects the entirety of the previous movement.

The corrective movement corresponds to a true reversal of the trend if and only if the corrective wave sinks the low point of the previous impulsive movement. If not, the current trend remains healthy and nothing comes to question it.

## The Rule of Alternation

This rule is a powerful principle of Elliott's waves. The principle is simple: if a wave 2 corrects strongly, then the correction in wave 4 will be weaker. Conversely, if wave 2 corrects weakly, expect an impulsive wave 3 but also a correction in wave 4 powerful.

The second property of alternation rules is based on the simplicity or complexity of the correction. At a wave 2 simple usually follows a complex wave 4. Conversely, if Wave 2 is complex then Wave 4 will be simple.

## Impulsive Waves

Impulsive waves are linked together by Fibonacci ratios. Thus, the objective of wave 3 is often obtained in the following way: we multiply the length of the wave 1 by 1.618 and we postpone the result obtained on the bottom of the wave 2. Often, wave 3 will go to hit this objective before correcting in wave 4. But during powerful movements in extension, the ratio will be higher than 1,618. The following ratios are usually taken: 2-2,618-3 and so on.

If wave 2 is weakly traced (less than 50%), expect a powerful wave 3 and project it with ratios above the standard of 1.618.

## Advantages

The main advantage of Elliott's method of waves is that it forces the analyst and the trader to imagine different counts, which is an excellent preparation to face the different eventualities.

A good "elliottist" is never closed, and he will always highlight in his analysis a favorite scenario (the one that has the best chance of unfolding) and an alternative (a scenario that would invalidate his ideal scenario).

## Disadvantages

The first disadvantage of Elliott waves is the learning time they require. Does the time devoted to training Elliott's waves necessarily find a justification?

I will answer that it may be interesting for a trader to know the basics of Elliott's waves and their fundamentals, but that the signals provided by this method do not seem sufficiently convincing to devote too much time.

The waves of Elliott fascinate many stakeholders, so much so that they become slaves. This method makes it possible to identify turning points with a confusing precision. Nevertheless, the trap of this method of analysis is to force the countdown in a situation where none seems apparent. The analyst then stubbornly searches for movements in five times where there are none.

This danger is well illustrated by the well-known Elliott Wave Advisor Prechter, who became famous in 1987 for predicting the stock market crash with this method. In the 1990s, his market diagnosis was extremely negative and he hammered in all the media that the US market was about to enter a prolonged bearish phase. This analyst was trapped by his method. He fell in love with it instead of considering it for what it really is: a simple analytical tool.

The moral of this story is two-fold: the markets are always right, and the trader who fights against this reality may pay very dearly.

## Graphical Analysis

Graphical analysis (also known as chart analysis) is a method that aims to identify the levels of media and resistances on a graph, as well as the current trend, through the tracing of trend lines and channels. This long-standing and well-known method owes its existence to operators and analysts who have studied the stock market charts and taken care to postpone in writing the recurring configurations, thus creating a directory of the most widespread configurations on the financial markets used by the vast majority of investors.

As with other methods of technical analysis, these figures can effectively capture the dominant sentiment in a market, even if their effectiveness is largely explained by the phenomenon of self-fulfilling prophecies. Indeed, these figures are known stakeholders, and their occurrence will often be the cause of a reaction that can be noted on the stock chart. Thus, resistance will not necessarily cause a downward reversal of the current trend but it can slow it down, even slightly. This reaction around key levels will need to be seriously analyzed by stakeholders.

Graphical analysis is an important tool in any trader's arsenal, but it is also risky and should be used with caution. The trader must avoid at all costs a too rigid reading. Indeed, a good trader's own strength is flexibility, and technical analysis should in no way be considered an exact science. From then, around support, the trader does not have to rush to buy. It must consider all the technical elements and the market context before making a decision. Similarly, when a support is broken, the trader must always ask if it is a break in front to be taken seriously or simply a false signal that he will have to ignore.

- What are the main graphic figures?

- How is a graphic figure validated?
- How to guard against false signals generated by these figures?

# Supports and Resistances

## Support (Media)

A medium can be defined as a level that supports the market and has been marketed many times in the past. Nevertheless, this definition is restrictive because round figures and Fibonacci retracements can also support the market without necessarily being affected before.

The strength of support can be explained by the following elements:

Around support, the buyers are more powerful than the sellers and manage to counter the progress of the bears; a support is an ideal level to position itself for the purchase for a trader whose market diagnosis is bullish, or for a profit-taking by an operator who is seller; bullish traders generally place their stops behind the main graphical media for an obvious reason: the breaking of the medium invalidates their bullish scenario and makes it possible to exit at a correct level; the importance of this graphic level is all the stronger as it is observed by most operators. The market often reacts around these levels, which makes some economists say that the reliability of technical analysis is primarily due to self-fulfilling beliefs.

Beware, in today's markets, many operators manipulate these levels in order to trigger stops. Media should, therefore, be used prudently by traders. Their reliability is fragile, and the trader will have to rely on other graphic and technical signals to support his scenario.

## Resistance

Resistance is a level against which the market has stumbled several times. Several elements explain the effectiveness of this level graph:

Around a resistance, sellers are more powerful than the buyers and manage to counter the bull's advances; this level attracts sellers short on the market because it is a good opportunity with a low risk: the stop is close and the bearish potential can be important; buyers, meanwhile, anticipate a consolidation, or even a correction of the title and take their profits or completely out of their positions;

As for the supports, the signals given by resistance can induce a trader in error. This level is observed by most operators; professional traders know this and voluntarily promote false signals (breaking resistance) in order to provoke the panic of the novices they know how to profit from.

Resistance will generally support the market when it is exceeded. Stakeholders remember this level and know that the bulls won the fight. They will, therefore, take advantage of this return on the support (old resistance) to initiate low-risk buying positions.

# Detailed Analysis of the Supports and the Resistances

This analysis is of great importance: the trader must get used to considering the different possible alternatives and must at all costs avoid the search for certainty. By having in mind the different possible reactions of the title around resistance or support, the trader will not be disappointed or surprised if his position results in a loss.

Around a significant resistance, the title can react in several ways and we have classified the possible reactions into four main categories:

1. The title breaks against resistance before drawing a major correction. This resistance indicates the presence of a high point and signifies a major reversal of the current trend;
2. The title draws a slight consolidation around the resistance before taking the path of the rise. This level could be used by traders positioned to buy to take their profits, but certainly not to sell. The current trend is not in question and the trader must strive to play this movement in all its amplitude;
3. After a slight hesitation, the title ends up breaking the resistance but does not manage to stay very long above this new support. It is downward refractory and is on a downward path. This is a typical case of false signal that can prove fatal for a poorly prepared trader.
4. This situation is generally delicate and frustrating for a trader. It is not common, but when it is formed, it can cause real damage. The trader, in this situation, is often "wandered" by the market and loses control of his emotions. It must, therefore, take the distance and always favor a convergence of signals before positioning.

## The Effectiveness of Supports and Resistances

Supports and resistances attract stakeholders for obvious reasons: these levels generally correspond to round figures or levels on which the market has been asked several times. They can represent a significant barrier that hinders bearish movements and blocks progress.

Their importance is even greater in situations where the market is without a marked tendency. Some traders have even specialized in buying media and selling resistors in this type of market.

Supports and resistors are areas around which many operators are positioned or are already positioned. It is for this reason that emotions are easily exacerbated around these levels. Many traders are trapped by their psychological bias (bias momentum, anchor bias, etc.) and their emotions quickly take over, whether in winning or losing position.

A trader who sees a title down thinks that the movement will continue and rushes to sell it. Similarly, a person who has sold security around support [a common occurrence when a person rushes to sell security] will panic when the security goes up and participate in the bullish move by seeking to close his position as soon as possible.

The strength of the supports and the resistance rests on the observation according to which these levels are observed by most of the operators, and it is for this reason that the stock prices mark most of the time a stop around these levels. Nevertheless, the break will be more or less marked according to the current trend and the importance of support or resistance. In a strong trend market, the break will be short and the market will irremediably continue its trend without really catching a breath.

To summarize, the importance of supports and resistances will depend on the configuration of the market:

- **In a bull market,** resistances will be levels used exclusively to take profits and certainly not to sell a security. The media will be privileged to position themselves for the purchase;
- **In a bear market,** the trader will have to adopt the opposite attitude. The supports will be used exclusively to take profits or to cut a short position. They will never be used to initiate a long position. On the other hand, resistances will be relevant levels to open a new short position or increase an existing short position;
- **In a market without trend,** the operators are undecided, and the market will hit the main support/resistance. In this market configuration, the supports and the resistances will be of crucial importance and will have to be taken into account.

## The Importance of Round Figures as Supports / Resistances

Many authors and practitioners have highlighted the importance of round figures as supports/resistances: they attract the attention of stakeholders and cause an accumulation of new orders and profit-taking; they do not require special skills in technical analysis. Anyone involved, regardless of their original training (technical analysis, fundamental analysis, etc.), will naturally take as references round figures for obvious reasons of convenience.

For these different reasons, most operators are positioning themselves around these levels, or at least monitoring them, because they know that other stakeholders are doing the same and that a reaction around them is likely.

## The Courses Have a Memory

The courses have a memory and that is the reason why a resistance or support remains valid even if they have not been touched for a long time. During the corrective phases, it is not uncommon for a stock to land on a medium that has not been touched for four or five years and stabilizes around before resuming the upward path.

# Chapter 8

# Position Analysis

Swing trading is an approach based on the observation that stock prices never evolve linearly. An increase never takes shape in some time, and it is often punctuated by corrective phases. As per the experts, the basic trading philosophy can be summarized as follows:

- The best opportunities lie in detecting low-risk entry points in the direction of the prevailing trend. Thus, in an uptrend, the trader will have to wait for a correction or consolidation before positioning himself for the purchase.

- Conversely, in a downward trend, the trader will have to position himself only after a rebound around a significant resistance.

In the 1980s, a hedge fund manager went in the same direction by making famous the concept of contraction/expansion. It highlights the NR7 (or smaller range of the last seven days) and specifies that a consolidating market should accelerate just after the appearance of NR7.

Wilder and Appel are the two most cited authors for technical indicators. They introduced mathematics in technical analysis through the development of some technical indicators, very popular in trading rooms.

These indicators are based on different mathematical formulas inspired by physics. The main thesis of these authors is that the speed of an object thrown in the air is reduced as and when its progression, to become zero on the tops. They argue that market movements can be anticipated through these indicators, whose main function is to take the pulse of the market and answer the question: "The current trend - Is it intact or exhausting?"

These first steps have been relayed in the financial world and are the cause of the emergence of technical analysis and many technical indicators of development. People have always been fascinated by the world of trading however with the risks involved, it can get to be a daunting task. Understanding the stock market and paying attention to the different kinds of trading options can be very stressful. This book will help you understand the basics of swing trading and how you can benefit from it.

## Diversification and the Choice of Markets

Diversification is a common-sense concept, which consists of not putting all your eggs in one basket. In our opinion, this approach applies mainly to traders who have a swing trading perspective (medium and long term) but does not seem suitable for short-term traders such as day traders and scalpers. The latter generally focus on a few titles or contracts that they master perfectly and on which they play low amplitude movements.

## The Importance of Diversification

The risk of high bankruptcy in trading requires any operator to aim first and foremost the protection of its capital, and in this perspective to ensure that the risks are limited. At any moment, an unexpected event can make him lose a big part of his capital. (Crash, warning on results, extremely negative news).

The concept of diversification is based on the idea that any market operator can be mistaken about the evolution of the markets. Diversification is a way to reduce the risk of error by betting on several uncorrelated contracts rather than relying on a single contract. Some opportunities seem more promising than others and will encourage traders to significantly increase their exposure. Should we increase its exposure excessively on this type of opportunity? Is it reasonable?

After determining the desired global exposure (10%, 5%, 2%), the trader will have to divide his capital in different positions. However, it is possible to allocate the same amount (in the capital and in maximum loss) for each position initiated. The main criticism of this approach is that it assumes that all operations present similar opportunities, which is rarely the case.

Finally, another important element is the correlation between the different securities in the portfolio. Two titles are positively correlated if their evolution is similar. Generally, securities in the same sector move in the same direction. A trader who has highly correlated securities in his portfolio is therefore exposed to significant risks that only diversification can mitigate by decreasing the volatility of the portfolio. In return, the trader will have to accept lower performance.

## Peer Trading

This technique is used by many hedge funds and traders in the trading room. It offers a way to reduce risk by taking two opposing positions on two positively correlated products (for example shares in the same sector). The purpose of this operation is to take advantage of the relative difference in the adjustment between the two financial products.

If a trader believes that Peugeot is undervalued compared to Renault, he can buy Peugeot and sell the Renault to take advantage of this temporary valuation gap. Here, the trader will not try to predict whether Peugeot will go up or down but is based primarily on the relative evolution of Peugeot compared to Renault. Both stocks may fall but this will have no impact on his performance since the gain on Renault (a title he sells) should be offset by the loss recorded on Peugeot (a title he buys). This transaction considers that the loss will be largely offset by the gain and will generate a profit. The purpose of the spread is to reduce the risk related to a forecast error and to base its decision on the valuation difference between two assets.

The advantage of this approach is that the trader is not a victim of market risk - an unexpected rise or fall in the market will have no impact on his position since the loss on an asset (linked to a random event) will be offset by the gain on the other asset assumed to move in the same direction. This technique requires significant funds and low brokerage fees, but it can lead to significant gains for those who control it.

## The Limits of Diversification

Diversification reduces the risk associated with trading but cannot completely eliminate it. Indeed, there is always a portfolio risk that cannot be eliminated despite diversification. In the same way, diversification diminishes the trader's attention and does not allow him to make the most of his positions. This strategy will depend heavily on the fund's philosophy and time horizon. We will privilege for the short term a specialization of the trader on some titles and for the swing traders a specialization on some sectors or markets.

## How to Select a Powerful Trading System?

According to J. Welles Wilder, most financial assets evolve in trend 30% of the time. The rest of the time, the markets evolve laterally, that is, no clear trend is detectable. The trader will have to adapt his method to the type of market as well as the current trend. The ideal for a trader is to work in a trending market. Indeed, it is difficult to make money in markets without trend because of brokerage fees and the need for the trader to be constantly in the markets. The trader will have to select first the markets offering the most beautiful configurations, and then make a ranking opportunity offering the best opportunities, according to an order of preference. However, this remark does not apply to traders who favor short-term techniques (day trading and scalping). Good traders will proceed as follows:

Firstly, they will identify several markets trend or about to enter the trend phase; select from those markets those with the highest potential and with little or no correlation with others.

Choose one with a high Sharpe ratio. William Sharpe has done a study on the performance of mutual funds in the United States. He put forward the idea that risk-adjusted portfolio return was a significant measure of performance. He created the ratio that bears his name: It goes without saying that it is better to have a smooth performance indicating the regularity of the trader and therefore the elimination of the random phenomena of his performance. A chaotic performance means that the investor is subject to significant risk, that its performance may be by chance and that the risk of ruin is high. A portfolio with a high return and extreme volatility is a danger.

The trader will have to select the trading system with the highest Sharpe ratio. For example, he will be able to analyze a system that he has used in the past and will rely on the history of his performance. He will also be able to evaluate a trading system (not yet used but derived from his research) thanks to the Sharpe ratio.

## A Powerful but Simple Trading System

The trader has every interest in opting for a simple system whose rules he rules, rather than for a more efficient system (on paper) but whose rules are complex.

Indeed, there is a good chance that the trader does not respect his plan, especially with a sophisticated trading system, because his emotions will quickly take over. On the markets, there is no room for hesitation and it is decisive for a trader to be convinced of the veracity of his system and especially to control it well. To be operational, a system will have to prove its effectiveness in the facts. A system will never be fixed or fixed once and for all, and the trader will proceed by trial and error at first. With experience, the trader can sophisticate his system.

We are convinced that it is preferable to have an imperfect but simple system rather than a system that is efficient on paper but complex and therefore difficult to implement: the financial markets have the power to destabilize traders and this deal will have to be imperative. Be taken into account when developing the trading system.

## Some Techniques to Improve Its Performance

In this part, we will study the swing trading system and we will see to what extent it is often successful. We will also study the classic system used by most novice traders and we will highlight its weaknesses.

The swing trading system means “in the direction of the dominant movement”. This system, often used by traders, allows testing the market before increasing its exposure. Indeed, if the market confirms the trader's initial scenario, it is because his reasoning is good, and he can, by crossing some pivotal points, strengthen his position. This system was successfully used by one of the greatest speculators of the last century and is described in his book.

# Conclusion

Thank you for making it through to the end of *Options Trading 2*, let's hope it was informative and able to provide you with all of the tools you need to achieve your goals whatever they may be.

You've now had a careful stroll through the key standards and ventures in options trading we feel are fundamental to progress as an options trader. You've figured out how the options markets function, the best trading strategies and why it's basic to pick the best possible fundamental assets for the procedures you need to utilize. You've additionally observed that great exit strategies are nearly as imperative as discovering great trades to enter, that focusing on the points of interest is basic, and that achievement is virtually inconceivable without a decent money-management plan—and the discipline to follow it.

At last, you've got lots of pages loaded with vital inquiries to consider in your search for the best online options broker. At the end of the day, it's a great opportunity to control up, plugin—and profit. You have all the data you have to appreciate 24-hour access to the options markets, fast and programmed execution of your orders and the most reduced commissions in the history of options trading. In any case, to share these advantages, you should confront the lot bigger individual duties that accompany coordinate access online trading.

You should have the discipline to do your very own research, screen your own positions and monitor every one of the points of interest you may leave to your full-benefit financial firm. You can never again depend on a broker to watch your positions and call with guidance or suggestions. You are currently an autonomous administrator — and, all things considered, must be absolutely in charge of your own behavior.

You should likewise be mindful and be prepared to react to both fast moves in everyday trading designs and consistently evolving longer-term economic situations.

A Dose of Reality to Induce Caution . . .
In case you think tolerating such difficulties and practicing such discipline is simple, think of one as a little preventative portion of the real world. An investigation—"Online Investors: Do the Slow Die First?" by Brad M. Barber and Terrance Odean, published in Economic Intuition,

Spring 2000—discovered that: "Online trading makes a deception of information that really gives traders less profit for their investments. While online-trader certainty ascends with extra data, exactness does not. Accordingly, traders are more averse to make a profit on every transaction—and will make less profit on successful transactions. Statistically, online traders:

- Trade 96 percent more as often as possible than telephone-based traders.
- Are twice as speculative online as they are with their disconnected trades.
- Produce overall returns that slack the market returns by 3.4 to 4.0 percent, notwithstanding when figuring in the lower commission costs. "In this manner, while full-benefit commissions can be costly, they're for the most part justified, in light of the additional experience and alert that brokers add to the trading procedure."

. . . A Final Dose of Reassurance

That is a calming bit of research, and way back 2000—and I concur that a specific level of caution is something to be thankful for. Notwithstanding, we stay persuaded that you can be an accomplisher as an options trader. For a thing, the investigation above depended on stock trading, not options trading—and the proficiency differential among online and stock trading is far, way lower than between electronic and conventional options trading.

The same is valid for commissions—which, not long ago, have been a lot higher on a percentage basis for options, than stocks. Immediate online access to prices, the accessibility of enhanced analytical tools, including screening programs, and the simplicity of utilizing stops and limit orders additionally have an altogether more positive effect on options traders than on stock buyers. As it were, the variations are substantial to the point that we'll utilize them as a reason to repeat the argument we made in the Introduction: "In the event that You Haven't Traded Options, You Haven't Really Traded." what's more, the stock traders overviewed by Barder and Odean didn't have the advantage of the abundance of data you've recently read.

Furthermore, we're not through yet! As a last note, I would like to ask for one more thing from you. That is a solid dedication on your part to observe the following five rules and regulations—rules we promise will significantly improve your chances of getting to be an accomplished online options trader, as well as an accomplished investor generally speaking.

They are:

1. **Give option trading a reasonable chance—no less than a whole year.** Regardless of whether your initial three or four trades result in losses, that is not an excuse

to surrender and cash in your chips. By then, despite everything, you're beginning to understand the complexities of the online system and honoring your market skills. If you encounter a couple of losses initially, simply reduce the extent of your trades—for example, stop ordering 10-contract positions and begin ordering single, three or five options. Keep your size low until the point when you begin to get few losers and more winners—at that point return to greater positions once more. In that manner, you'll save your underlying stake and allow yourself to make right an amateur's mistakes—or, to ride out your present losing streak if you're more of a veteran.

2. **Avoid spreading yourself too thin.** Rather than wanting to move from index to index, or stock to stock, looking for the "most blazing" option openings, monitor a limited number of basic stocks and just a single or two market indexes. Focus on following the news and financial numbers on your picked issues, and soon, you will realize what in general trigger price moves — and when they're probably to happen. At that point, you'll realize the best periods to start the suitable option trades.
3. **Are you brave enough to accept the loss?** Even the most accomplished option professionals don't make a profit on all trades, be ready to get out of a terrible position when you notice it. That is the initial phase in finding the next incredible chance. Furthermore, come what may occur in the market, NEVER move a stop so you won't be presented to a bigger loss. That is the initial phase in finishing your trading profession—and finishing it terribly.
4. **Try not to give achievement a chance to make you presumptuous—or far more terrible, selfish.** When you manufacture your account equity to a decent working dimension, begin moving a segment of your future profits

into less-speculative investments. For instance, if you begin with $20,000 or less, keep 100 percent of your profits working until the point when you manufacture your equity to $50,000. At that point begin moving no less than 25 percent of your trading profits into better secure investments, giving 75 percent a chance to keep working—until the point when you reach $100,000. At that point, put 50 percent of new profits aside for more conservative interests. If you feel constrained to keep 100 percent of your profits working constantly, you'll most likely end up being presented to risk more—which means one snappy string of awful trades could clear all your previous gains.

# Swing Trading

*A beginner's guide with proven strategies on how to trade with options, stocks, futures and make profits fast. Tools, time and money management, rules and routine of a trader.*

William L . Anderson

# Table of Contents

# Introduction

Dear reader!
If you have just left or are preparing to enter the stock exchange, if you have only heard about fundamental and technical analysis, if you have already heard and understand the word "action", and understand what it means not only in advertising, then the book you hold in your hands, was written especially for you.
In the professional jargon of traders, swing is the amount of time during which the position to buy or sell a volatile stock remains open. Common sense suggests that holders of long-term positions have the greatest chances to succeed in this since it is they who lose the least amount of money on the costs associated with trade: on various commissions and spreads. In this book, I tried to concentrate on methods that allow busy people to hold positions from one week to several months, leaving aside short-term market entry lasting several minutes or a couple of hours. I explain to you not only trading methods but also the principle of operation of new online tools, giving investors a chance to win in this challenging game with market professionals. This book is aimed at a wide audience of readers interested in trading in financial markets, that is, at private and institutional investors. It will be of interest to trustees and investment consultants, managers of pension funds and investment management departments of insurance companies, as well as bank employees and currency speculators who operate in financial markets.
Happy reading!

# Chapter 1

# Price Is Everything

Terry Bedford, a tenacious and experienced swing trader with over 20 years trading experience, works from his apartment located in a high-rise condominium in the suburbs of Toronto. He has an office in the business center of the city but he is rarely in it. Terry's work day is filled with a mass of events and noise. He watches CNBC with the sound turned off, tracks his stock on two flat-panel computer monitors, and when the market is dull, he launches alternative rock at full capacity—Bjork or the Clash. He does not object at all to the regular invasions of his three-year-old daughter, Zoya who radiates a mass of energy. Terry's clients, with whom he maintains constant communication in chat or e-mail, are accustomed to the kind of funny emoticons that are occasionally entered into messages with little hands.

Terry Bedford trades mainly on the accounts of his hedge fund Grayhawke Equity Partners. Hedge fund payments to its customers in 2000 amounted to 16 percent; in 2001, 42 percent; in 2002 by the month of June, it was already 25 percent per annum. He calculates weekly earnings, without betting on big winnings. Terry makes up to 30 transactions per day, working on both sides of the market. He buys stocks of companies that he hates and sells securities of enterprises that cause sympathy since he perceives shares only as certain symbols of commerce and not as real business. "When trading, falling in love with what and how the company makes is the shortest way to losses," he says. "If you are extremely attractive to a semiconductor equipment company, then you will most likely miss a dozen excellent opportunities to sell its shares. With swing trading, a surplus of fundamental market analysis can be dangerous—it dims your judgment. This is reality. Promotions are like playing cards, and it is in this quality that they should be perceived. "

In his spare time from trade, Terry enjoys painting. His style is reminiscent of the work of the Impressionists, which in a certain way correlates with the characteristics of trading. He holds positions on stocks from three to five days, treating them as the Parisian painters of the late 19th and early 20th centuries handled the brush, imposing juicy, fast and color-rich strokes on the canvas. When selecting tools for work, he descends from top to bottom, starting with sectors in which, according to his sources, there is a powerful accumulation of funds, and then focuses on 4-5 actions that, in his opinion, are capable of the most powerful movement. Before making a final decision, he considers a three-year chart of a security with weekly bars, and then includes an annual chart with daily bars, after which it reaches 10, 5 and one-day schedules for 10-minute bars, trying to identify intraday trends. After finding models that have proven themselves in the past (which will be discussed in more detail later), he starts the attack by buying or selling lots of 2,500 shares each until he forms an open position of 7,500 or 10,000 shares. Trading with such volumes allows Terry to recognize his mistakes and if necessary, immediately begin to minimize losses.

Terry was born in 1964 in Halifax (Halifax), located in the Canadian province of Nova Scotia (Nova Scotia). After his father, who had served his entire life in the navy, retired, the family moved to Brantford, Ontario, the home of legendary hockey player Wayne Gretzky. This city is also famous for the fact that it was there that the first officially registered telephone call on the device, invented by Alexander Graham Bell, rang.

Terry turned out to be involved early in the pool. Already at the age of fifteen, he worked in two places—washing dishes in a Chinese restaurant called Danny's Grin and in the steak Ponderosa. The teenager managed to save money, after which he decided to invest. Having found Richard Blair, a broker who had worked for McKay Ross, which had long since passed away, Terry received a list of books from him for reading and invested $3,000 in Alcan's securities, hoping to improve its performance in future. At the end of that summer, the demand for aluminum rose sharply. According to Terry, he felt like a genius, earning $ 1,500 in two months. After that, he spent a huge amount of time in the small office of this brokerage company, raising the bill to 15 thousand dollars, desperately risking and making "a lot of stupid bets." By the age of 18, he had acquired the first car from his long series of BMW models and entered the business course at McMaster University in Hamilton. Years of college were mainly devoted to the study of business periodicals in the search for trading ideas. By the time the course ended, his account was already about 100 thousand dollars. At first, Terry had serious intentions to practice law, but in the end, he made a choice in favor of a career as a stock broker. By the time the course ended, his account was already about 100 thousand dollars.
Terry worked as a broker in three companies until he realized that brokerage activity contributes to rapid aging. He was tired of the routine of placing client orders and decided that it was much better to manage his own money and not strangers. "It became clear to me that I prefer to be on the other end of the phone, placing orders rather than accepting them," he says. In 1992, at the age of 28, he completed a broker career. However, after a while, Terry "leaked" his own trading account to almost zero, after which it became clear to him that trading should be carried out with a full load; otherwise you will not survive in the market. Trying to cover the previous losses from self-trading, Terry began to sell his technical analysis results for individual stocks to the

institutionalists. He started with several portfolio managers in Toronto, gradually expanding the field of activity. In the end, he had at his disposal an extensive network of clients, including major American fund managers. He sleeps no more than five hours a day, constantly tracking markets around the world and studying charts of price movements.

Terry is convinced that the key to trading activity is the ability to constantly stay in the game. You have to keep your capital and you must endlessly evaluate and reassess possible risks and rewards. And, most importantly, you should concentrate on the reproduction of money, profit. You should wait for the profit on the transaction and get out of it in time for good, healthy. "Imagine that every day you send an army of your soldiers into battle with the task of capturing capital, more capital. Like all true generals, you want your soldiers back safe and sound after completing the mission," he says, "every time the soldiers return home with captive capital, your army's strength increases."

He does not care that frequent market entry leads to an increase in tax liabilities. He says: "A lot of people live on the sidewalks without worrying about taxes at all. But they have no money at all. Taxes are a payment for success. A much more important trading rule is profit withdrawal, if any."

Terry relies almost entirely on technical analysis when making trading decisions. He believes that a surplus of knowledge about the company and the state of affairs in the economy can serve a disservice. In his opinion, the most important statistical information on the stock is its value is the only right way to assess investor sentiment. According to Terry, the technical analysis is based on the assumption that the mood of investors determines the price to a greater extent than such fundamental factors as revenue and profitability. In other words, he is confident that all fundamental points of view on a share, all perceptions by investors of such points of view are naturally reflected in one informative unit of measurement—price.

The three most important principles illustrating his approach to swing trading are formulated as follows: first, price movements are not chaotic; secondly, the price foresees the perception of fundamental changes; thirdly, the relationship between price and time is linear.

Keeping in mind this "roadmap", you can begin to consider Terry's approach to swing trading. We will start with his basic views on the causes of trend price movements, then discuss the psychological aspect of support and resistance, deal with the most successful graphic reversal models, and then finish with Terry's favorite trend models.

## Price Is Not Chaotic

Professors who lecture on financial affairs try to convince us that price changes are fundamentally chaotic and random. But this is nonsense! If this were true, traders like Terry would simply not exist. Prices move in accordance with the ebb and flow of supply and demand, forming repetitive price patterns. The price consolidates when the demand for a stock is approximately balanced by its supply but the price drops sharply or rises when there is an imbalance between them.

## The Price Foresees Fundamental Changes

Fundamental changes during the night do not occur; they require more time. A new product or service that can fundamentally change the situation with the company's profit has been developed over the years. After the development is completed, the product or service is presented to distributors and retailers. Sellers, in turn, acquaint buyers with a novelty—in a private way or through a specially organized event. Then, as a rule, the new product undergoes refinement and is launched into mass production. During all this time, the company's shares continue to trade, and investors have no idea about the fateful new product. Although, to be completely honest, it should be recognized: some of the buyers and sellers of shares of a separate company are a little better informed than others. This is the so-called "smart money".

Sometimes "smart money" is wrong but mostly they use information hidden from the wide masses of speculators. In many cases, such information is a product of costly independent fundamental analysis but its source may also be personal contact with the management of the joint-stock company. This and there are those sales or purchases that anticipate the fundamental news and initiate a change in price trend that swing traders can track on charts.

Apparently, "smart money" has some advantage over the others. To a certain extent, this is true. People with great financial opportunities may well afford such a purchase. The swing trader should not forget about this, watching the price rise or fall in the absence of any public information.

## The Relationship between Price and Time Is Linear

One of the most difficult to understand about ideas concerning the market is the linear nature of the relationship between price and time. The longer the price behavior contradicts our forecasts, the stronger the temptation to make adjustments to their expectations.

The simplest example that vividly illustrates this phenomenon is our ability to take losses. Most investors do not like to lose money. When buying a "wrong" stock, they sometimes try to get out of the situation, closing the position without loss. But the days turn into weeks, weeks into months of waiting, and their perseverance begins to contradict common sense. The process of rationalization begins, the awareness of what has been experienced during a long stay in an unprofitable position, the opinion about the levels convenient for exiting gradually changes. In fact, no one wants to forever hold a long position on a loss-making stock. This is a linear relationship between price and time—the more stretched the time frame, the more elastic the price expectations become.

And once again for better mastering: it is also important for the swing trader to realize why certain price behavior patterns appear on the charts, as well as recognizing these very models. Speaking in a general sense, the emergence of models is a consequence of the fact that the "smart money" presented by successful managers of large funds is much better informed than the mass of ordinary investors. It is these managers that initiate price trends, from which the conclusion follows: a change in price precedes the development of the situation from a fundamental point of view. On the other hand, "stupid money" acts in accordance with the peculiarities of human psychology, seeking to minimize losses after shares are bought or sold at inappropriate levels. In the ideal case, investors would like to close positions without loss.

Now, when we better understand the behavior of the price, let's deal with another basic element of the practice of swing trading—support and resistance.

## Support and Resistance Levels

Support and resistance—the cornerstones of technical analysis. Their idea is quite simple. They are price values at which buyers and sellers show an increased desire to buy (in the case of support) or sell (in the case of resistance).

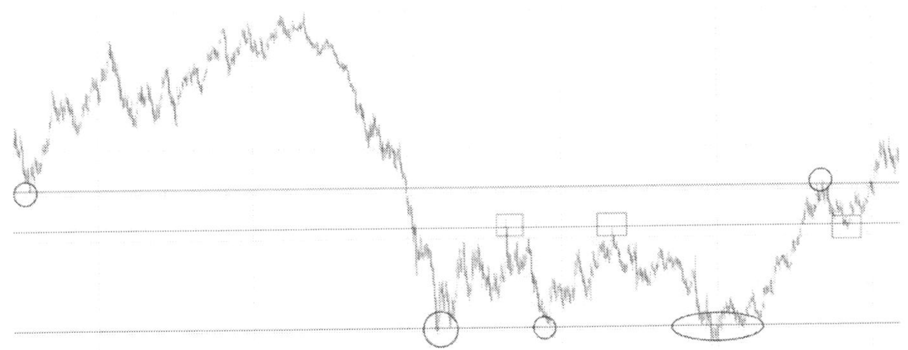

Such an explanation may seem rather simplistic but very often the direction and strength of price movements is determined by human emotions. We all happened to buy stocks for a moment before they began to fall. At such moments, the dominant feeling is the reluctance to sell until we can do it without loss for the account. If many investors buy at the same price, after which the moment of “buyer's repentance” immediately comes, then a similar situation forms a point of resistance on the chart. Such points of resistance are sometimes formed at the end of a long price climb after the release of any positive news. After the start of the sale of shares "smart money", many unhappy bulls are trapped. The lack of new buyers means the weakness of the security, and the price starts to fall. But every time, when the next price attempts to rise to the initial level, investors who have unsuccessfully bought shares will sell them. A similar concept leads to the formation of points of support.

If, after you purchase a stock, its immediate rise begins, it is not difficult to guess what thoughts will settle in your head regarding yourself and the purchase price. After taking profits and closing a long position, it is highly likely that you will try to buy this share again when the price goes down to the level of a recent purchase (if it worked once, then the second one will work). Thus, if a sufficient number of investors are ready to buy a share at a certain value of the price, then this level of price turns out to be support.

Understanding all the nuances associated with identifying levels of support and resistance is the most important component of a swing trader. And there are many nuances in this matter. Therefore, let's look at how support and resistance work with some typical technical models on an uptrend and downtrend as well as during price consolidation.

## Support and Resistance Levels in a Downtrend

I hope you remember that the relationship between price and time is linear. This means the desire of investors who unsuccessfully bought shares to close long positions "by zero." But as the days turn into weeks and weeks into months, the thought process of rationalization of what is happening is gaining momentum, as a result of which the investor decides to close the position at a loss for himself. Of course, the investor seeks to do this at the most favorable price possible. He carefully watches the stock, noting for himself the price level leading to purchases and the value of the price from which other players sell. Swing traders should be clearly aware that such price points are not random.

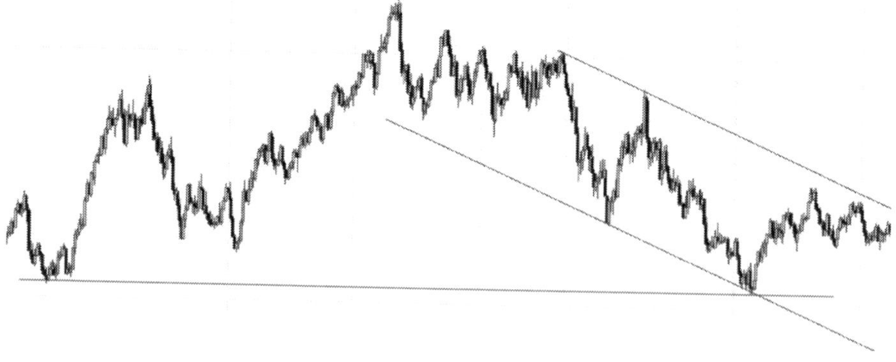

## Support and Resistance Levels in an Uptrend

Despite a completely different motivation, most of the circumstances contributing to the formation of a downtrend are also present in the formation of an upward price trend. Such models arise from the fact that investors are chasing strong stocks, coming to the conclusion that even a higher purchase price is not so bad if we take into account the strength of the trend. The higher the price is taken, the higher the likelihood of new purchases. Some will argue, and not without reason, that such rationalization is directly related to the expected changes in fundamental factors. And this often turns out to be true. Understanding the principles of technical analysis does not mean a refusal to take into account the fundamental component.

So, to summarize, it should be noted once again that the support and resistance lines are price areas where buyers or sellers express more than the usual willingness to buy or sell stocks. When pushing the support level, it transforms into a resistance level. After breaking through the resistance level, the latter turns into a support line. This is due to the fact that weak hands (uncertain traders) give way to a strong hand (those who believe). Support and resistance levels play a crucial role in determining the main trends of price change, creating stepped models of the levels at which buyers and sellers give each other a fight.

Now we have dealt with the second most important component of the theory. It is time to move on to the last basic concept—the volume of trades.

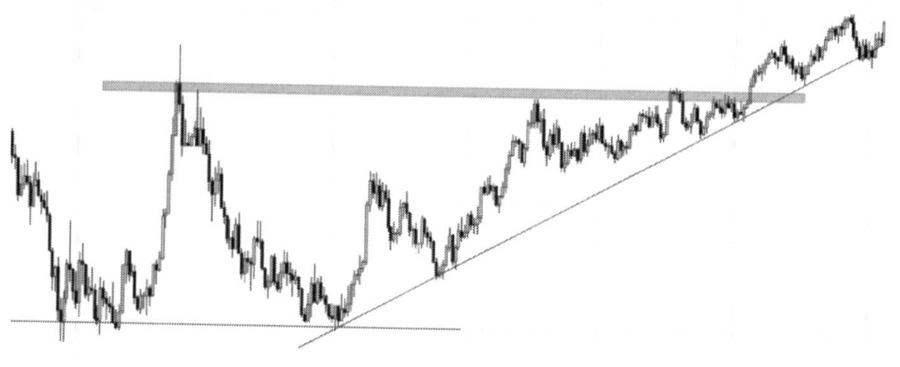

## The Importance of Trading Volumes

Let's start with the theory of common sense, which swing traders just need to own perfectly—volume should follow the trend. This means that during the bovine phases of the development of market cycles, the volume increases when the price rises and falls during corrective descents. Conversely, when the market is bearish, the volume increases with falling, shrinking during rises. That is the theory. Now we turn to common sense. For an uptrend, a steady increase in the number of buyers is required to absorb pressure. In the end, as the price rises, the likelihood that investors who bought at the lower levels of investors will want to close their lucrative positions by selling also increases. Therefore, for continued growth, it is necessary to absorb such sales by new buyers. If the price rises too fast, buyers can step aside, thereby contributing to the temporary weakening of the price. However, if the trend is really strong, such periods of kickbacks occur when the trading volumes fall.

When the stock is bogged down in a bearish trend and its prospects are bleak, the volumes increase during descents, as possible buyers are completely suppressed by the prevailing sellers. If the stock sinks too fast, some of the possible sellers may well abandon their plans to open short positions, preferring to expect a slight increase. Such a temporary lack of sellers leads to a rise in small volumes, after which investors enter, having not had time to close their long positions immediately after the beginning of the fall in prices—they sell. And again on large volumes the price is rolling down to the next record bottom.

## *Volume with Trend Movements*

Strong bullish trends and bearish trends are characterized by trend volumes that increase in the direction of major price changes. But what happens when a stock rises in price when the volumes, or when it falls, and the volumes increase? In theory, such events should not occur. But when this still happens to be, then such signs are always harbingers of a sharp reversal and, therefore, a perfect scenario for swing traders.

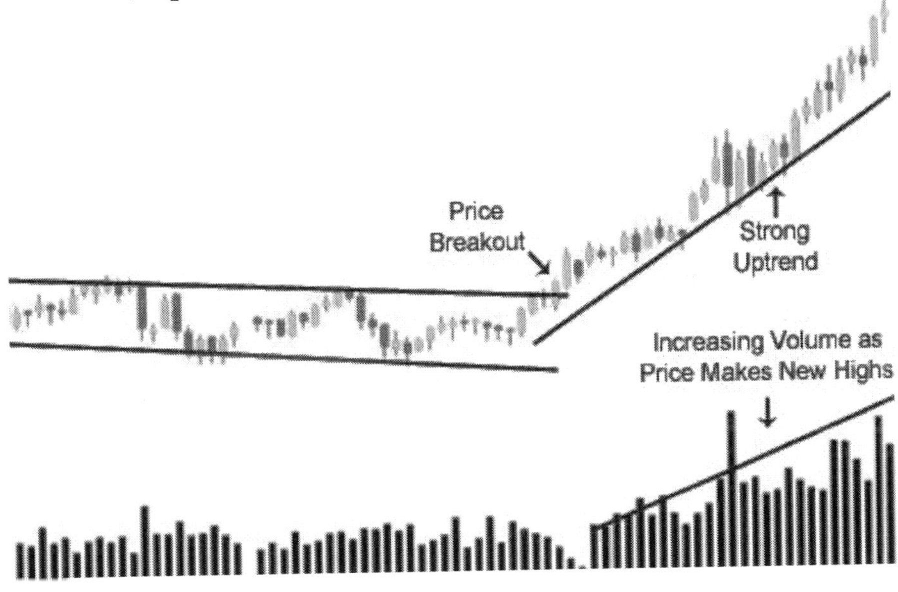

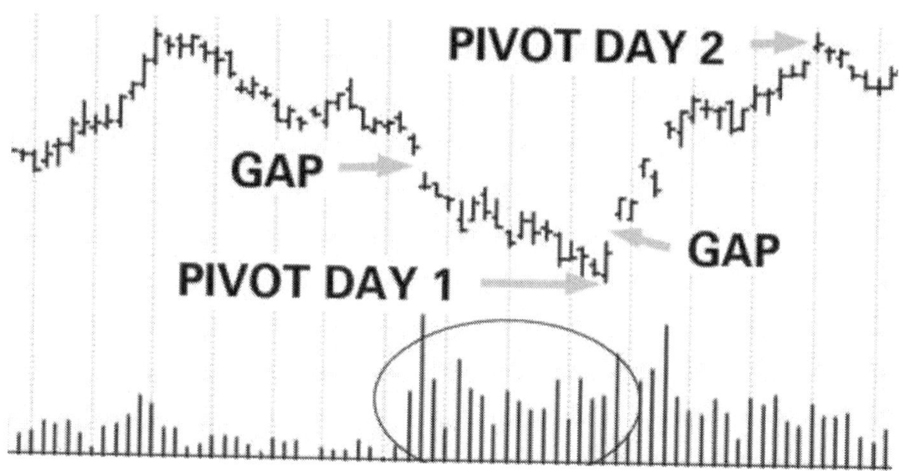


## *Volume during Consolidations*

One of the lessons that swing traders need to learn is that large-scale price changes often follow a significant fall. The reduction in volumes and a narrow range of trading are almost always a sign of the uncertainty of the intentions of some of the investors. When they are unable to agree on the objective value of a certain security, the volumes fall and the trading range shrinks. In such cases, most investors prefer to refrain from active actions and expect news. After the release of news that can lead investors to some consensus regarding the future of this company, the volume of trading grows, this, in turn, leads to a strong price movement. In such periods, the slowdown in volume growth is determined by technical analysts in most cases as a consolidation phase.

Consolidation patterns on daily charts can form over several days, weeks, or even months. As a rule, they have the form of a horizontal rectangle, although the question of the geometric shape in this case is not so important. The fact is that consolidation models are a consequence of the uncertainty of investors' mood. Almost always, they are followed by explosive price movements.

Price consolidation is an essential step in the development of all stocks. After the consolidation phase, a breakthrough comes, which can be considered the most tense and exciting moment in the life of a stock on the stock market. Consider the behavior of volumes with a similar breakthrough.

## *Breakthrough Volume*

In the classical sense, "breakout" is the period immediately following consolidation. In the time aspect, it should be considered the moment when investors reach a consensus—investors on the same side of the market are inferior under the pressure of opponents and switch to the "enemy" side. Market participants agree on the direction of price changes.

The consolidation period accounts for 70 percent of the life of the shares. The remaining 30 percent goes to dramatic breakthroughs, up or down, which are excellent trading opportunities. Traders are waiting for breakthroughs with impatience, since it is during such price movements that the chances of successful transactions increase.

### Breakthrough Up

The importance of the value of volume growth in the case of an upward breakout is quite simple: when a breakthrough, the trading volume must increase in order for such a movement to be taken seriously.

The situation with volumes in breakouts downside is more complicated and ambiguous, since large volumes are not necessary for a sharp fall. Unlike price increases, in which an increase in volumes helps to neutralize bearish pressure, during price collapses, stockholders demoralize so much that it is extremely negative for their activity. Of course, you can cite many examples of breakthroughs down, amid a significant increase in volumes. However, the growth of volumes, as a rule, occurs at the very end of the descent, marking the capitulation of the bulls. Thus, the longer the fall lasts, the more the volumes are transformed into bulls' allies. Traders should closely monitor the increase in volumes on a bear market, especially after long descents.

Having dealt with the basic questions, you can proceed to the most fascinating topic for swing traders: graphic models of turns.

# Chapter 2

# Graphic Reversal Patterns

Stocks are going up and stocks are getting cheaper. Swing traders are quite capable of mastering the ability to recognize reversal patterns in practice. Despite the fact that the fundamental and technical signs that imply a reversal in the direction of price movement are very different from each other, as a rule, reversals are the result of one of the following two processes: distribution or accumulation of shares.

In this section, I will explain the way Terry uses to determine distribution or accumulation patterns, as well as signs of an upcoming reversal.

## One-Day Spread

The starting point for most reversal patterns is called a One-Day Reversal. The stock with a gap goes up when a trading opens after a long rise, fixing a new peak after the release of positive news. During the trading session, volumes grow significantly. However, at the moment of closing the market, growth is no longer to be said—the price closes lower.

### *Why Is This Happening*

One-day reversals occur for the simple reason that, in order to close long positions, investors need high liquidity. They know for a fact that selling stocks after the release of positive news—when liquidity reaches maximum values—is to sell stocks immediately. That is why they are willing to sell on days when stocks record peaks and everyone is excited about the positive economic news. After that, investors and the press can only wonder how such good news could lead to a bearish closing of the day. After a few trading days, they will realize that they missed the best moment to sell stocks, and all subsequent jumps in prices will be untenable. In a few more weeks, the price will be far below the recent peaks.

## *How Are Technical Objectives Determined*

One-day turns are events of one day by definition and therefore, technical targets are not determined by them. But if you look at any large-scale reversal, you will immediately notice that, starting with a one-day reversal, they all lead to good opportunities for swing trading.

## *Key Features*

- One-day reversals occur due to the desire of investors to close their long positions at the peak of the price so a very important sign of this is an increase in volumes when the movement starts down.
- On the day of reversal, the closing price should be at the bottom of the daily range.
- Short positions open the next day after a one-day reversal if the opening price of the session is lower than the previous closing price by 12 percent. If the session opens with a bearish gap of five percent or more, this means that you have missed the deal. And if the price opens higher, then the reversal of the previous day is considered false. Place a protective stop order directly above the midpoint

of the trading range of the previous day. The mass liquidation of positions after the release of good news is an eternal topic of discussion when considering day-long reversals. Now that we have come to understand the general principles of a one-day reversal, let's proceed to the study of the so-called island reversal.

## Island Turn

Island reversal pattern is called isolated breaks (or gaps) price segments. After a long rise, the stock jumps upwards with a gap, which often means the price leaves the old trading range.

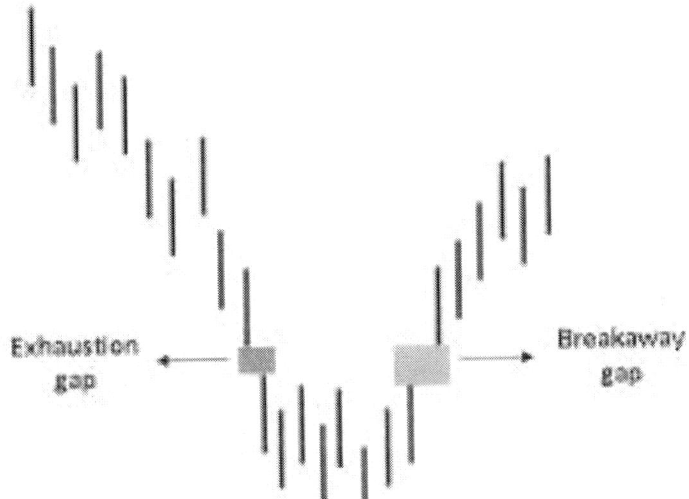

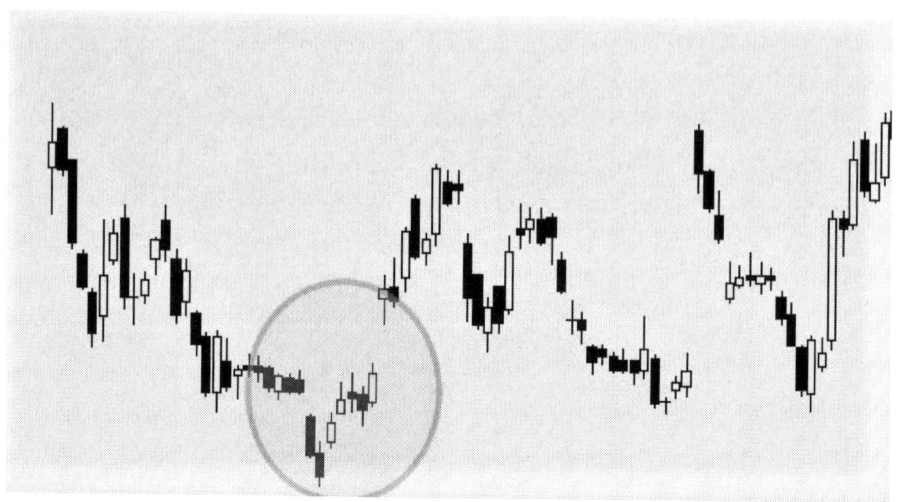

## *Why Is This Happening*

After a long rise, the action opens much higher, due to the release of good news. Such a breakthrough after consolidation is made on huge volumes and seems to be quite natural but over the next few sessions, the action fails to build on success. Investors who bought it recently are starting to worry, as sellers had to weaken their efforts after the recent breakthrough upward resistance level. Something is wrong here! A few days later another news comes out, inherently contradicting the previous one, in which the action went into an upward breakthrough. And now investors are caught in a real panic, which drives the price down at an accelerated pace. A few weeks later, recent peaks seem to be inaccessible.

## *How Are Technical Objectives Determined*

As with one-day turns, island turns usually mark the beginning of the formation of a larger-scale technical model. That is why the exact goals are not defined. However, such reversals lead to significantly lower prices.

### *Key Features*

- Island reversals occur on news when conflicting messages follow each other for a short time.
- Volumes should grow at the price return and the initial breakout.
- Island reversals disrupt the trends. As a rule, they lead to the formation of large-scale post-trend models.
- Short positions open the next day after the price is under the "island". The size of the gap is usually estimated at 5 percent or more. A protective stop order should be placed directly above the maximum price reached on the day of the second break.
- Now it is time to do some longer for the formation of reversal patterns.

## Double Top

The formation called the double top is a clear, easily readable model, which is characterized by a rise in price to a new peak, followed by a modest pullback and a second rise to the level of the recent peak. When re-raising sellers take over the buyers, after which the price falls off. In a few weeks, she is already testing new levels of support.

### *Why Is This Happening*

Being with stocks bought at the very top of the price chart is a very dubious pleasure. The double top is formed due to the fact that the majority of investors who bought paper at such a top refuse to exit the market until they close their positions “by zero”. Double tops appear after long rises, which led to new record prices. As the bull share is covered by a touch of magical attractiveness, an increasing number of investors are willing to pay a crazy price for it. But one fine day, they still come to the conclusion that the price is prohibitively high, and the stock begins to fall, forming top 1. This first peak it is enough to force many speculators to leave the market. As they sell shares, the price drops lower and lower but many market participants refuse to part with their securities, no matter how low the price falls since they have no desire to fix the loss. After several bear sessions (sometimes weeks), the price stabilizes and begins to move up. In most cases, such boosts are explained by the release of fundamental news that gives investors some hope, for example, analyst comments, earnings reports, and so on. As the price rises, volumes fall, and investors who have bought shares when forming the first peak, are preparing to close their positions. When the price approaches the first peak, the volumes begin to grow, and the newly converted bulls indulge in speculations about an excellent fundamental perspective. Just at this moment, investors who bought at the first peak, begin to close their long positions with sales. Volumes soar even higher, and the price falls, forming a peak two. On the chart there are two equally-level peaks—this is the "double top" figure. Very often, such a model leads to significant subsequent price reductions since two separate groups of investors are disappointed at the same price level.

## *How Are Technical Objectives Determined*

At double top, technical targets are calculated by subtracting the price difference between top one and the so-called reaction bottom (reaction low) from the price breakthrough of the bottom level. After the formation of the second peak, the price value of the reaction bottom becomes the breakthrough level. The "double top" model is considered to be incomplete, if it is not broken through this level, which is considered one of the best opportunities for a swing deal.

## *Key Features*

- During the formation of a double vertex, the volumes decrease significantly as the price moves upwards in an attempt to test the level of the first vertex, and during the subsequent descent it increases.
- A double top is not considered complete until the level of the reaction bottom has been broken.

- Breakthroughs downward often lead to a small fall in price (two to three percent), followed by a return of the price upwards and testing of the penetration level from below. If the price closes above the level that has already become the resistance level, then the model is considered failed.
- Transactions are initiated after penetration of the reaction bottom level. A protective stop should be placed directly above the reaction bottom. A more common tactic implies waiting for the retest of the level of the reaction bottom already below, after which a short position is opened. You can also sell when the price rises in the direction of the first peak with a protective stop order directly above it.

Now consider the "double bottom" figure.

## Double Bottom

The design of the double bottom pattern is similar to the image of a double top. After a long drop to the newest smallest values, the stock pushes off large volumes from the bottom, forming a slight rise. After a few days, sometimes weeks, the price goes down and tests the level of the recent bottom, after which a new rally begins.

### *Why Is This Happening*

Just as a double top is formed due to the process of distribution of shares, just as a double bottom owes its formation to the accumulation of shares. After a long time price descent, characterized by aggressive short sales, investors with a broad time horizon, value-oriented investors, begin to accumulate stocks. They understand that the only way to build a large position to buy attractive shares for them is to buy when sales dominate. It is their willingness to buy with bad news and leads to the formation of a level of support (bottom one). This first half of the reversal pattern is sufficient for many professional traders: they close their short positions. Such actions, together with long-term purchases of strategic investors, are encouraging to market participants who have bought a share at a higher price. Several bull speculators open up new buying positions.

Unfortunately, after several sessions, during which the price behaved positively, the pressure from the bulls dried out. An intermediate vertex is formed—a reaction to the formation of bottom 1, which is called a reaction peak by technical analysts. Sensing the smell of easy prey, lovers of short sales return, and bull speculators decide to take profits. As prices fall to the level of bottom one, the volumes become lighter, and sometimes on such small volumes the price slips below the recent bottom.

At such moments, the degree of pessimism is very high and there seems to be no reason to continue holding shares. New parties of fans of short sales open fresh positions. Lost hope bulls, convinced of the imminence of the descent to a new bottom, begin to give up. However, the fall does not materialize—the bearish pressure is drying up. Professional traders, who have short positions, feel the change of situation and begin to take profits. Long-term investors adjoin this process, continuing purchase of shares. All this leads to price stabilization. Bottom two begins to take on a graphic shape and the intensity of closing short positions increases. In the end, price growth begins. In many cases, a double bottom leads to powerful price rises, because it forms an important level of support.

## *How Are Technical Objectives Determined*

The technical goal for the "double bottom" figure is determined by adding the price difference between bottom one and the reaction peak with the breakout level of this peak. After the formation of bottom two, the reaction peak becomes the new breakout level. The formation of a double bottom cannot be considered complete until the breakout of the named resistance level has taken place.

## *Key Features*

- In the process of double bottom formation, volumes grow when prices fall towards the bottom one and two. Sometimes when the bottom forms one, the volumes are somewhat larger, since it is here that the value-oriented investors first come into business and open buy positions.

- Double bottom is not considered complete until the price breaks through the reaction peak.
- Breaking up the level of the reaction peak sometimes leads to a small-scale continuation of the movement (two to three percent), after which the price returns to the point of breakthrough. When the price closes below the breakthrough point, the model is considered failed.
- Definition of technical objectives is possible in principle but their meanings should not be regarded as dogma.
- Swing traders should enter the market above reaction peak two, placing a protective stop directly below it.
- We have completed the consideration of the figures "double bottom" and "double top", now we turn to similar structures, but of a triple nature.
-

## Triple Top

The model “triple top” is very similar to double top, the difference is only in the number of peaks. The triple top is formed after the price rises to a new peak, followed by a slight descent, a new growth in order to test the recent top. When forming the second peak, sellers gain the upper hand over buyers and the price drops again. All this is repeated for the third time, after which, in the end, the bulls surrender, the price falls and breaks through the support levels.

### *Why Is This Happening*

As in the case of double peaks, this happens mainly for two reasons. First, investors who bought stocks at the "right" levels use positive news to close their positions. In this sense, the triple top can be considered a stock distribution model, as smart bulls "attach" their shares. Secondly, investors who bought shares unreasonably high, refuse to close positions at a loss. The triple top appears after long rises to new peaks when the fundamental perception of the stock becomes extremely positive and investors are willing to pay a crazy price for it.

However, at some point in time, buyers holding profitable positions feel the desire to close them. Bearish pressure after the release of good news leads to the formation of resistance (top 1), after which the price begins to fall. For most speculators, the level of top 1 is enough to close positions. As they sell their shares, the price falls, but many market participants still refuse to part with their unprofitable long positions, not wanting to fix the losses. Over time, the price begins to stabilize, forming a reaction bottom, so-called technical analysts due to the fact that the downward movement turned out to be a reaction to the news while forming the top 1. Gradually, stocks begin to grow again. In most cases, this is due to the ongoing stream of positive news. With a secondary price increase, trading volumes decrease, investors remaining out of the game during the first rise are ready to sell stocks. When the price approaches the level of the recent peak, the volumes increase, the novice bulls begin to talk about a bright future, as the new record price values seem inevitable.

Right now, all speculators aimed at selling, are beginning to act. Trading volumes are increasing sharply, and the price rolls back down (top 2). Two peaks are beginning to stand out on the chart and recent buyers are beginning to realize how difficult this resistance level is to overcome. Bears again begin to dominate, the price falls on large volumes, and panic prevails in the market. In most cases, the price breaks down the level of the reactionary bottom, forming a double top. But, after breaking through this key support level, sales do not become more intense. Moreover, one more rise begins rather quickly, as traders with short positions start closing them. Due to the liquidation of these positions, accompanied by the release of positive news, the price is again approaching the top. Volumes are small.

After the price reaches the level of two recent peaks, volumes sharply grow. Vertex 3 is formed. Inability to break through this resistance level, depressing bulls and for the first time the fundamental value of a stock is questioned by the press. The stock price drops quickly as recent buyers sell it at any price. The price reaches the basin between peaks 2 and 3, pushing it. Triple top formed. In most cases, this is followed by a significant depreciation of the stock, since three different groups of investors were disappointed in it at different price levels - on the tops and on the reaction bottom. Now all these levels are serious levels of resistance.

## How Are Technical Objectives Determined

As in the case of double peaks, technical objectives for triple peaks are determined by subtracting the price difference between peak 1 and the reaction bottom from the value of the breakout level. After the third vertex is formed, the breakthrough level is considered to be the lowest point of the "saddle of the gorge" between peaks 2 and 3. The "triple top" model is not considered complete until the price breaks through that level.

## Key Features

- In the process of forming a triple top, volumes fall during ascents to peaks 2 and 3. As prices fall, volumes increase. Such changes in volumes confirm that when the price rises, the stock distribution model takes place.
- Sometimes the lowest prices reached between peaks 2 and 3 are lower than the reaction bottom. However, this condition is not considered mandatory in the formation of this model.
- A triple top is considered formed after the session closing price falls below the bottom of the valley between peaks 2 and 3.
- Sometimes the downward breaks are followed by the continuation of the downward movement, during which the stock becomes cheaper by two to three percent but then the price rises and tests the level of the recent breakthrough from below. When closing a trading session above this level, the model is considered invalid.
- Swing traders should sell when the price falls below the reactionary bottom after the formation of peak 3. Since you may have already suffered a loss on this stock after an unsuccessful attempt to form a double peak, another entry into the market requires additional courage. Place a

protective stop just above the reaction bottom. If there is a price gap on the chart directly below the reaction bottom, then a stop order is placed above such a gap.

Since the "triple top" figure refers to the stock distribution models, the triple bottom is related to their accumulation. Consider this figure.

## Triple Bottom

The triple bottom pattern like the triple top image. After a long price descent, the stock forms the bottom with large volumes of trades and begins a slight rise. It takes several days and sometimes weeks, and the price goes down again to test the level.

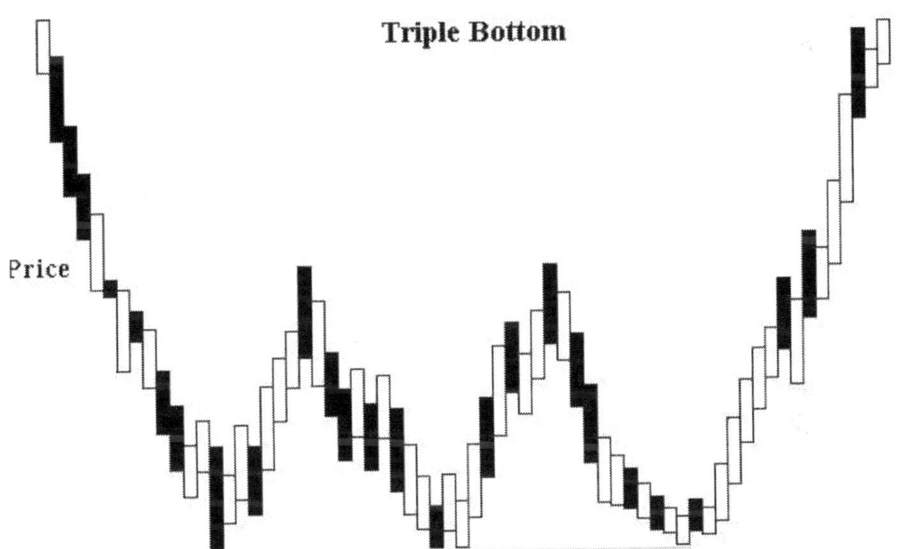

## Why Is This Happening

Triple bottom is related to the stock accumulation process. After a long fall in prices, accompanied by aggressive short sales and concerns of market participants about the fundamental value of the stock, long-term investors set about building their long positions. They are well aware that the best way to do this is to buy when prices fall. It is their willingness to buy amid bad news and leads to the formation of the first level of support (bottom 1). Such activity of large buyers, proceeding against the background of negative news, usually turns out to be sufficient reason to close short positions by many professional speculators, which, coupled with long-term purchases, has a reassuring effect on those unfortunate people who recently bought shares at a high price. They may even come to the conclusion that the worst is over, as the bulls come into action. But, alas, after a few days, the bullish pressure is drying up, and the price starts to decline again. The positive reaction after the formation of bottom 1 ends. Technical analysts call this peak a reaction peak. Bad news is heard again, short sales fans return to the market and the bulls decide to make a profit. As the price approaches bottom level 1, volumes remain low, very often it happens that on weak volumes the price slips even lower. At this stage, prevailing pessimism. It seems there is no reason to be in a long position. Young bears sell even more, and the depressed bulls, who bought higher, begin to give up, believing that a move to new, record-low levels is inevitable. However, long-term investors continue their bottom-line shopping policy. A new upswing begins, as the speculators who have opened short positions are forced to buy shares to close them. However, long-term investors continue their bottom-line shopping policy.

The formation of bottom 2 begins, the closing rates of short positions increase, and the stock quickly takes off towards the reactionary peak. Despite the steep nature of the rise, the volumes are small. At this stage, a new wave of unfavorable fundamental news covers the market. Bears feel the possibility of revenge and the price goes down to the bottom level of 1 and 2. At this point, the pessimistic mood reaches a peak. New short positions are opening bulls with unprofitable long positions capitulate. Volumes are growing but in some incomprehensible way the support at the bottom 1 and 2 remains safe and sound. Professional traders feel the change in the trading atmosphere, since the price is not going to fall further.

After the price stabilizes, bottom 3 becomes apparent. As if by a wave of a magic wand, the news is not so bad, the bears start to panic, and strong growth begins. The price rises above the peak between bottom 2 and 3. A triple bottom is formed on the chart. In many cases, after this, a significant price rise begins due to the fact that strong levels of support are formed, both at the bottom and at the reaction peaks.

## *How Are Technical Objectives Determined?*

The technical goal for a triple bottom is determined by adding the difference between bottom 1 and the reaction peak to a new breakthrough level. After the formation of the bottom 3, a new breakout level is considered to be a peak between bottom 2 and 3. The model is not considered complete until the price breaks through this level.

## *Key Features*

- In the process of forming a triple bottom, volumes increase during a price drop. Increasing volumes at the bottom is a sign of stock accumulation.

- The triple bottom is not considered complete until the reaction peak between bottom 2 and 3 is broken upwards
- At the close of the trading session below the breakthrough level, this model is considered false.
- Technical goals can be calculated but their values should not become a dogma.
- Swing traders open long positions when the price breaks through the level of the reaction peak after the formation of bottom 3. Since you could already lose after failing to form a double bottom, opening a new position requires some courage. Place a protective stop right below the reaction peak. In the case of pricing break above the reaction peak, put a stop order under the break.

# Chapter 3

# Reversible Models of a Complex Type

Now that you have become familiar with the main types of reversal patterns, let's proceed to the study of their more complex varieties. Let's start with the expanding vertex.

## Expanding Top

The broadening top appears on the charts after the price rises to a new peak, its subsequent descent to an intermediate support level; the second rise, forming a new record peak, and against the background of higher volumes. Then the price falls below the intermediate support level and then rises in high volumes to a new record peak, the third in a row. After that, in the end, the price falls down.

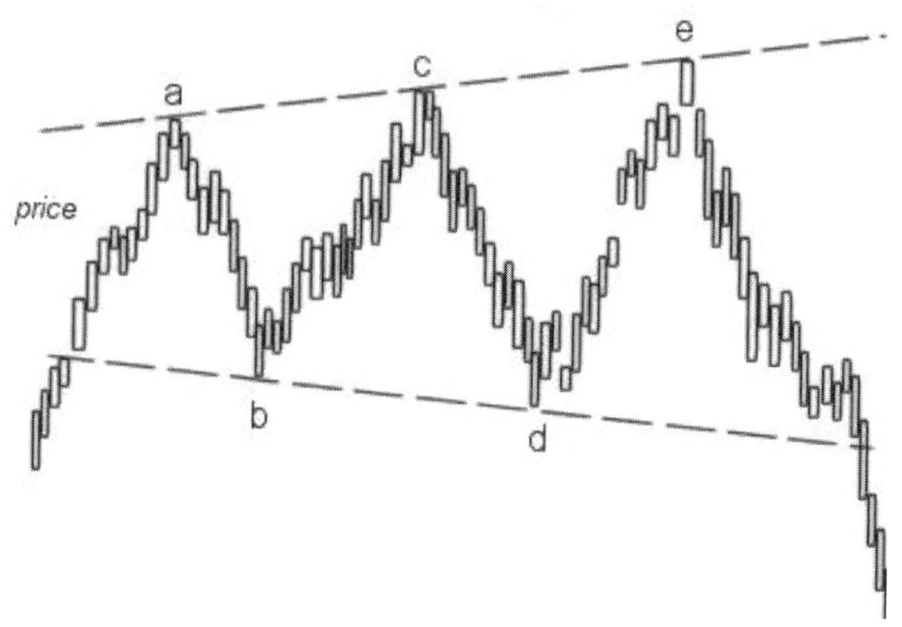


## *Why Is This Happening*

These models always reflect the indecision of market participants and excessive volatility. The external graphical similarity of the expanding vertex with the horn is striking. Price gives to the surface a whole series of higher peaks and lowering bottoms. In principle, as fundamental information is accumulated, investors tend to come to a consensus, which in turn leads to a decrease in volatility. However, in the case of the "expanding vertex" model this does not work. Each similar model can be divided into independent parts. The first of the three small peaks (vertex 1) appears as a result of an impressive price increase for large volumes. Usually this happens after the release of news about higher company revenues compared with the projected ones, about creating a new product, or about positive feedback from Wall Street analysts. But after the record prices have been reached, the bears enter the battle, and soon the price rolls back to the previous level of support (the "a" symbol on the chart).

After several relatively quiet sessions, a new batch of positive news again pushes the price upwards in large volumes (top 2). It is the increasing volumes that serve as a sign of a possible consensus between buyers and sellers. However, after only a few days, the price falls again, fixing the new value of the bottom (the "b" symbol on the chart). Despite the fact that the news continues to be positive, there are rumors about some insiders and institutionalists who began to close their long positions. Bulls are moving to active defense, Wall Street firms confirm their recommendations, providing them with new exorbitant goals. As a result of all these efforts, the price starts moving up again.

Sufficient but it is important that they are still inferior to the volumes during the previous rises. Price draws a new peak record (top 3). All news is positive and the future seems cloudless with a planned stock split. However, even the new record value of the price is not able to dispel a little cloud of skepticism fluttering among investors. Very soon, the price falls amid growing volumes but in the absence of news. Gradually, the fall is gaining momentum, calling into question the integrity of support, passing by the level of the recent bottom. It may well be rumors that some major shareholder decided to sell his stake. Bulls are very nervous, and after a few weeks the stock drops to a long-term level of support.

## *How Are Technical Objectives Determined*

Due to the fact that the expanding vertex is a very large reversal figure, the technical goals can be very significant. When determining the target level, one should subtract the height of the model from the value of the final breakthrough.

### *Key Features*

- Unlike most other consolidation models, the expanding top is characterized by an extremely wide price range and high volatility.
- As prices rise, trading volumes increase. This is a bull sign by definition. However, in this case, rises are short-term, followed by falls with a break through the current levels of support.
- Expanding figures are formed only when consecutively rising peaks are formed, since they are the result of unjustifiably high expectations of some investors.
- Downward breaks are often followed by small price descents (two to three percent), after which the penetration rate is tested from below. When closing a trading session above the resistance level, the model is considered failed.
- In swing trading, a sell position is opened after breaking down the trend line drawn on the reaction bottoms after vertices 1 and 2. A protective stop is placed directly above this level. If after the triggering of the protective stop the model continues its downward development and reacts poorly to the positive news, then you should try to open a short position again. If there is a price gap directly below the reaction bottom, place a protective stop order immediately above it.

## Bottom in the Form of a Head and Shoulders Model

From a technical point of view, the bottom in the form of a "head and shoulders" model is a price drop with the formation of a new bottom. Then a new rise to an intermediate resistance level follows a second price descent to a record low bottom and another rise to the resistance level, followed by a relatively small price fall. After that, the price rises, breaking up the resistance level.

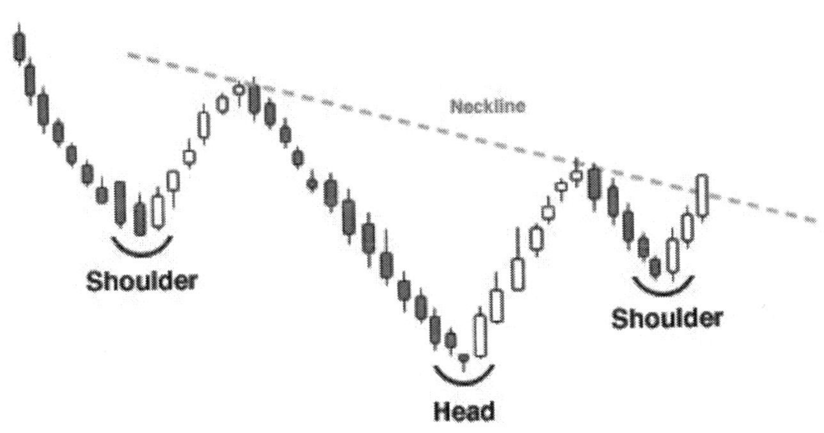


## Why Is This Happening

Because of their prevalence and reliability, the “head and shoulders” graphic models are among the most important in technical analysis. The bottom in the form of a “head and shoulders” model consists of three descents of price and its subsequent breakthrough upwards. This model is often called the “inverted head and shoulders” model since this is how it relates to the “head and shoulders” model. The left shoulder of the “head and shoulders” bottom is formed after a long fall as a result of which new low price levels are fixed. Against the background of extremely unfavorable fundamental indicators, the stock is cheaper, drawing one after another new bottoms and contributing to the spread of bearish sentiment among investors.

The first phase of the formation of this model is the reason for the release of extremely negative fundamental news.
Moreover, trading volumes are increasing all the time. However, despite the bad news, the price eventually stabilizes as long-term investors begin to open buy positions.
Already after a few sessions, the imbalance in the relationship between buyers and sellers leads to a sharp and rapid rise to an intermediate level of resistance. Technical analysts call such a peak reactionary, as it is in essence a reaction to a long price drop. This rise completes the formation of the left shoulder of the model. But since all the news continues to be negative, investors and analysts come to the conclusion that nothing prevents the stock from further falling, after which the price is again falling. A new bottom is being formed, however, the reduced volumes indicate that the bears are running out of steam.
New, even lower price levels and modest volumes provoke buyers to additional long positions. A new rise begins, as a result of which the price once again rises to the reactionary peak, which has now become the upper resistance level. This is how the head of the model is formed. After that, bears come to the fore, once again drawing confidence from the bad news. Such news may be a decrease in the company's rating analysts or negative events of corporate life. The main thing is that the stock starts to fall again, for the third time.
And once again, when the price falls, trading volumes decrease, new herds of bulls enter the battle, and the price makes a rise towards the reactionary peak. This completes the third phase of the model formation—the right shoulder. Wall Street analysts continue to pour negative comments but this time, the buyers are even more aggressive—the price breaks up the resistance level. A few weeks later, the stock rises even higher—to the long-term level of resistance.

## *How Are Technical Objectives Determined?*

The technical goals for the head and shoulders model are determined by adding the difference between the neckline and the top of the head to the value of the breakout level upwards.

## *Key Features*

- The symmetry of the model is important. The most reliable head and shoulder models are always symmetrical. This means that the formation of both shoulders takes approximately an equal number of days. It is better to avoid "crooked" models with a bias towards the right shoulder.
- It is important to note the decrease in volumes at each of the phases of model formation and their increase when the neckline is broken through. Weak volumes and falling price are clear signs of the stock accumulation process.
- The model cannot be considered complete until the close of the trading session above the neckline.
- Breakthroughs upward sometimes lead to a slight price increase (two to three percent), after which it rolls back to testing from the top of the recently broken level. When closing below this level, the model is considered failed.
- Swing traders should buy at the break of the neckline, keeping in mind the possibility of a pullback to a broken level before continuing growth. A protective stop is placed below the neckline.

Now consider the Top in the Form of a Head and Shoulders Model.

## Top in the Form of a Head and Shoulders Pattern

From a technical point of view, the head and shoulders top is formed by raising prices to a new peak, followed by a rollback to an intermediate support level. Then a second rise to a higher peak develops, followed by a descent to the support line. Finally, a third rise is formed, after which the price falls and breaks through the support level.

## Why Is This Happening

Because of its prevalence and reliability, the "head and shoulders" apex model is considered one of the most useful for the trader. The model consists of three climbs and a breakthrough down. It owes its name to the fact that the second upward price movement reaches its highest value, while the other rises are almost the same as the height.

The left shoulder is always formed after a long rise in price. Buyers do not stand behind the price, all the fundamental news, for example, income reports, are perceived positively. After one of these reports, the bulls raise the price to new heights with the help of increased volumes. However, after the withdrawal of profits, a natural reaction occurs—the price rolls down and a new reaction bottom is formed—resolute investors along with new recommendations from buyers! Analysts, consider such a retreat as a temporary one, explaining it to the normal process of withdrawing profits after a long rise. And they are partly right. These sales were really the withdrawal of profits but not so ordinary.

During the first pullback, investors who bought shares at lower levels began distributing their shares after the release of good news. They made money and now they want to take profits. As the price goes down, the bulls regroup their ranks and begin a new attack. Largely due to the fact that fundamental indicators are still positive, the new peak is reached easily. Everything would be fine if it were not for the volumes, which, despite the streams of bright analytical comments, were reduced compared with the first price increase. At the top of the chart there are sales of shares by investors. Soon, this lack of balance between buyers and sellers leads to a serious fall in prices. There are rumors that are unpleasant for the bulls that large institutionalists and insiders sell stocks.

After a few days, the price is already testing the level of the reaction bottom, near which, however, volumes are increasing. This is how the head of the model is formed. In the region of the reactionary bottom, a new batch of positive news comes from the news agencies "tapes, so buyers return and the third recovery begins, fueled by analysts" recommendations from Wall street, "Buy!".

Unfortunately, this third climb is weaker than the previous one. As the price rises, volumes fall, and it becomes clear to everyone that the process of distributing shares has ended. Very soon a fall begins towards support at the level of the reactionary bottom. In the spirit of the name of the model, this line is often called the neckline.

The third descent to this level completes the education of the right shoulder model. At this time, when approaching the support line, the market no longer responds to the positive speeches of experts, sellers outnumber buyers, volumes increase sharply and the price falls down.

## *How Are Technical Objectives Determined*

The technical goal for the head and shoulders top model is calculated by determining the difference between the level of the top of the head and the neckline, after which it is subtracted from the breakout level downwards.

### *Key Features*

- The symmetry of the model is crucial. The most reliable are the symmetric models of the "head and shoulders" tops, on which the right and left shoulders are formed for approximately the same number of days. Models with a hypertrophied right shoulder should not be trusted in any case.
- It is important to remember to reduce the volume during each of the three lifts. Weak volumes with rising prices are a good sign of the ongoing process of share distribution.
- A model cannot be considered formed if the trading session ends above the level of the neckline after it is broken.
- Breaks down often lead to a small-scale continuation of the movement (two to three percent), after which the price returns to test the breakthrough level from below. When closing a trading session above this level, the model is considered failed.
- Swing traders should sell below the neckline penetration, taking into account possible growth to the level of the recent breakdown. A protective stop is placed directly above the neckline.
- Now that we've finished our anatomy lesson, let's move on to a dynamic model called the diamond.
-

## Diamond

From a technical point of view, the diamond pattern is a price increase with the formation of a new peak, then a descent to an intermediate level of support. This is followed by another rise, as a result of which a new height is reached and a subsequent sharp drop with the support level breaking. Finally, it is the turn of a modest price increase and the subsequent collapse of prices with a breakdown of the long-term level of support.

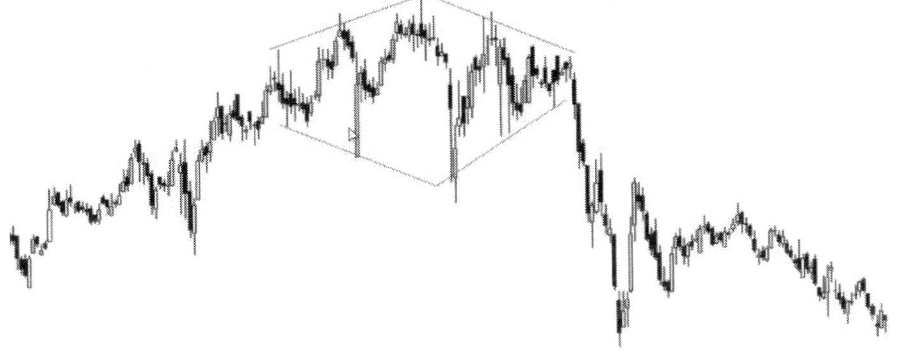

## *Why Is This Happening*

At first glance, the diamond model resembles a head and shoulders top with curved neckline but that's only half the story. In fact, the "diamond" has more similar to the "expanding top", since the latter, as a rule, changes the direction of the uptrend only. In this sense, both of these models relate exclusively to the process of distributing shares. The formation of the model occurs after the action of a strong company, known for its stable and powerful growth, rises to new heights and begins to consolidate after a long and fruitful rally. While the experts are busy discussing the fundamental advantages of the action, the price remains in indecision for several sessions. In the end, it all ends with a breakthrough price up.

After the news release, the price soars to new heights, accompanied by a serious increase in volumes. In fact, such a movement can hardly be called failed because it lasts several sessions and is marked by new record milestones. Then the price drops, and quite sharply. However, the volumes remain insignificant, no special news is observed. However, many bulls that buy at low levels decide to cover up their positions.

The stock continues to fall at relatively low volumes until the news comes that it turns out that the recent breakthrough upward does not reflect the real state of affairs in the company. Yes, things are not bad, but, nevertheless, investors realize that the current price still does not correspond to the present state of affairs and, therefore, contains a considerable share of risk. Sales continue amid increasing volumes. When the price returns below the level, the breaking of which upwards has so recently rejoiced the bulls, signs of panic appear. Analysts stubbornly stick to their buy recommendations but the price is still significantly lower than the recent consolidation area.

Panic moods gradually subside, which is a considerable merit of the company's management, which is making titanic efforts to create a positive fundamental background. Management is echoed by Wall Street analysts. All this leads to the formation of a reaction bottom on the graph, after which the price begins to rise slowly. In the following days, even more good news appears and investors suddenly dawns. Recent fears are groundless, the current price level is an ideal opportunity to open long positions. A new rally begins, but as it develops, the volume stubbornly remains at an average level. In the end, despite the next portion of the fundamental positive, the stock refuses to grow towards the recent peaks.

Worse, on the day of the release of good news, the close of the trading session turns out to be bearish, and the volumes are very large. Such signs are characteristic of the stock distribution process, that is, the recent bulls are selling on good news. Analysts and many investors are confused. Many of them are not able to understand how the action can be cheaper with such good news. However, holders of long positions use every price increase to sell their shares. Soon comes the collapse. A few weeks later, investors will learn about the deterioration of the company's fundamental state from the news program.

## How Are Technical Objectives Determined?

Due to the fact that "diamond" is a very large-scale graphic model, the determined values are sometimes adequately large. The technical goal is determined by subtracting from the level of the final breakthrough the difference between the record peak and the reaction bottom. The breakout level is determined using a trend line drawn through the reaction bottom and the first significant bottom on the right side of the model.

## Key Features

- It is considered a complex reversal pattern, as volume changes often imply stock accumulation. The highest volumes in the breakthroughs are up and down. However, all rallies to new peaks always end in one-day U-turns.
- Although the rise in prices from the reactionary bottom sometimes looks very steep, the willingness of shareholders to get rid of them at any price, and without any negative fundamental news, foreshadows lower price levels.
- "Diamond" is a large model so technical consequences are sometimes impressive. It is important to wait for the completion of the formation of the model, which implies the opening of short positions only after breaking down.
- Breakthroughs downward often lead to small price drops (two to three percent), followed by testing below the recent breakthrough rate. When closing the session above such a resistance line, the model is considered failed.

- Swing traders should sell three to five percent below the original uptrend line drawn through the reaction bottom and the subsequent significant bottom, above the reaction one. Swing traders should take into account the possible return movement of the price to this line. A protective stop is placed directly above the ascending trend line.

"Diamond" is considered to be a difficult model for trading as it often has ambiguous signals. Understanding the diamond model will definitely help to deal with the rounded apex.

## Rounded Top

From a technical point of view, the "rounding top pattern" model is formed by growing to a new record value of price, flowing with large volumes, followed by several weeks of more or less quiet trade with limited but still moving the price upwards. Then come a few weeks of quiet trading but with a bearish accent. In the end, it all ends in a sharp breakthrough down on large volumes.

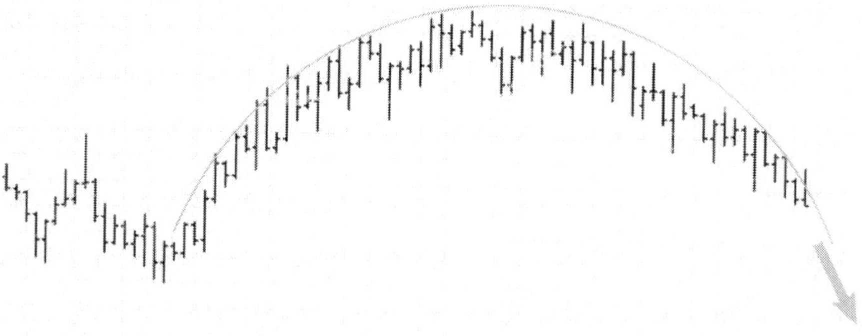

### *Why Is This Happening*

At first glance, and perhaps at the second, the "rounded top" model seems quite familiar, since its signs largely coincide with the "head and shoulders" top model. The rounded top appears on the graphs in many respects for the same reasons as the head and shoulders but often has several shoulders. This is its key difference. The first part of the model always formed as a result of a long rally to new heights. The flow of fundamental news is usually positive and buyers are still willing to pay a high price for shares. Following favorable news, the price fixes a new peak with large volumes but to the surprise of investors tuned in bull, there is suddenly a mass of people who want to sell this share.

After several sessions, the price begins to roll down with large volumes of trades. Investors and analysts explain this with a normal withdrawal of profits but the volume growth and price weakness are alarming. Long-term investors who have bought shares at lower levels now sell them. They use good news to distribute shares. The rise to new heights with the subsequent rollback to the nearby support level (reaction bottom) completes the formation of the first phase of the model.

Due to the fact that fundamental indicators continue to be positive, bulls soon return to the market and again drive up the price—testing recent peaks. The attempt is unsuccessful. The price is wrapped up by the bears and once again descends to the reactionary bottom, which now represents a key level of support. Encouraged by the new positives from Wall Street analysts and the company's management, the buyers are making another upturn in top resistance, this time to their joy; a new peak has been registered. The problem is that this time the volumes are much weaker. The bulls are starting to get nervous. With good news and new peaks, the price refuses to take off, and the bearish pressure is increasing. Rollback begins, but the situation stabilizes as it approaches a key support level.

With the help of another stream of positive news, buyers make two more attempts to break through the resistance level. Each time the volumes fall and the attack chokes. In the end, the bulls are beginning to doubt the feasibility of their efforts, since already as many as five attacks to the heights have failed. Just at that moment, the first batch of negative news appears. Immediately reviewed all the fundamental indicators, more recently, pulling the price up. Panic begins, and a key support level is forced under the pressure of the crowd. After a few weeks, the price drops to a long-term level of support.

## *How Are Technical Objectives Determined?*

In contrast to the "head and shoulders" model, the rounded top does not provide the ability to accurately define technical targets, due to the fuzzy-defined graphic pattern. In most cases, we can expect a descent to the long-term level of support followed by a break down.

## *Key Features*

- The symmetry of the model is important. The most reliable models of the rounded top have the strict outlines of a semicircle and resemble the head and shoulders top model with two left shoulders, a head, and two right shoulders. Beware of skew models.
- Volumes fall every time a price rises; weak volumes against a rising price are a sure sign of the stock distribution process.
- Breaks down often lead to small price drops (two to three percent), followed by testing from the bottom of the breakout point. When closing a session above the resistance level, the model is considered failed.
- Swing traders are advised to sell three to five percent below the breakout level of a key support level conducted on at least three reactionary bottoms. A protective stop is placed directly above the breakout line.

As you understand, the presence of a rounded top implies the existence of a "round bottom" model. Consider this model.

## Round Bottom

From a technical point of view, the "rounding bottom pattern" model is formed after descending to a new bottom on large volumes, then several weeks of trading on medium volumes with insignificant pressure on the bottoms. After that, a few weeks of trading in small volumes, but with an emphasis on resistance levels, followed by a sharp upward movement, accompanied by an increase in trading volumes.

### *Why Is This Happening*

Like the rounded top, the curving bottom is often confused with the head and shoulders model. These models have a lot in common: a series of peaks and hollows, decreasing volumes. The difference is that the rounded bottom has an increased number of shoulders. This model is formed in the process of transferring shares from nerve sellers into the hands of serious long-term investors, focused on the value of paper. Sellers are gradually getting rid of stocks as a result of a whole series of ups and downs.

The first part of the model is always formed as a result of a prolonged fall in prices to new lows. Against the background of extremely negative fundamental news, market participants agree to sell shares at increasingly lower prices. At some point, particularly unfavorable news, such as reporting on estimated profits or postponing the release of a new product, sends the price down with excessively swollen volumes. One by one, Wall Street analysts give out unfavorable comments and forecasts, which only contributes to the continuation of the free fall in prices.

# Chapter 4

# First Steps in Financial Trading

Are traders becoming or being born? There is no single answer to this question. Both innate abilities and acquired skills are important but the ratio of the two elements is different. There are geniuses who almost do not need to learn. On the other hand, there are gamblers and those who are not studying for nothing. Most, like us, are closer to the middle of the spectrum: we have certain abilities but we need to learn. The genius does not need a book—he has an amazing sense of the market. It will not help the gambler since he is too passionate about the process and is intoxicated with adrenaline. This following section is written for traders in the middle of the spectrum.

## Investor? A trader? Player?

Before the beginner, who came to the market, three trails are open. They lead to a thicket of ups and downs, of riches and dangers. The first trail—for investors—goes through the meadows. Most people who choose it reach the finish line, if not wealthy, then at least alive. The second trail—for traders—is led into the woods. Most disappear and get lost but to those who successfully come out, they make an impression of being successful people. The third trail—for gamblers—leads straight into the swamp.

Which path to choose? This should be well thought out so as not to be in a crowd of gambling players, especially since their path intersects with the paths of investors and traders.

## *Investor*

Investors make money by recognizing a new trend in the economy and investing in promising stocks before most people wake up and move in the same direction. An astute investor can make very high profits just by holding positions and not showing much activity.

What are the difficulties of investing? It requires tremendous patience and absolute self-confidence. To decide to purchase Chrysler shares after the company barely escaped bankruptcy or Internet search engine stocks when almost no one knew the meaning of these words, you need to be absolutely confident in your ability to recognize and track new trends in society and in the economy. We are all strong in hindsight but few have been given to anticipate events; and only units have the strength of mind, so that, having made their own forecast, put a large amount on it and patiently hold a position. Those who can do this over and over again are people like Warren Buffett or Peter Lynch who are the stars of the investment business.

## *Trader*

Traders earn on short-term price fluctuations. They buy stocks when the upward movement begins on the chart, and sell when the trend slows down, or vice versa. You can play short—sell when the analysis indicates a downtrend and then buy when a base begins to form on the chart. The idea is simple but it's not easy to implement.

A good analyst is difficult to become and a good trader is even harder. Beginners think they will get rich thanks to their ingenuity, computer literacy, and past business success. You can buy a powerful computer and even purchase a trading system tested on historical data, but putting money on these wonders of technology is like sitting on a stool, which has two of three legs broken off. These missing legs are psychological preparation and risk control.

Psychological preparation is as important as market analysis. Your emotions influence how you perceive reality, making them one of the main factors for success or failure. Reasonable risk control allows you to survive the inevitable periods of loss and create the conditions for long-term success. Psychology, market analysis and capital management are three essential success factors.

There are two main ways to benefit from crowd behavior. One is a speed, or dynamic, game (momentum trading): we buy when the crowd starts moving up and sell when the speed of its run decreases. Finding a new trend at an early stage is not an easy task. As the trend picks up speed and the crowd enlivens, joyful amateurs become more confident that they are right. Professionals remain calm and watch the pace of price changes. Noticing that the crowd returns to its usual drowsy state, they take profits without waiting for the trend to turn.

The second method is the game against the trend. Here we open positions when the price deviates from the average value, putting on the market return to normal. Traders who play against the trend open for a fall when the pace of growth slows down and close the position when the downtrend slows down. Beginners love to play against the trend ("Let me sell above. This market will not rise!") But most, like a stake, sit on peak prices that continue to rise. Anyone who likes to urinate against the wind should not complain that they often have to wash their pants. Professionals make money on the game against the trend only because of the willingness to run at the first sign of danger. Before you put on a trend reversal, you must clearly know under what conditions you will give up the position and how you will control the risk.

Both fans of high-speed game and those who play against the trend, earn on two opposite aspects of crowd behavior. Before you open a position, decide what exactly you intend to do: invest, play for speed or against the trend. Get out of the transaction strictly according to plan, do not change tactics halfway.

Beginners choose what to buy for a long time and professionals spend no less time thinking about how to close positions. In addition, they pay a lot of attention to money management, calculate the admissible position size, and decide whether to increase it, choose the moment to withdraw part of the profit, and so on. They also spend a lot of time counting deals.

## *Theory of Effective Market*

The trader strains the mind and puts the soul, trying to squeeze out profits from the market. And here comes the unpleasant news - the theory of an effective market. Its supporters, mostly teachers of economics, say that prices reflect all available market information. The actions of buyers and sellers depend on the amount of their knowledge, and the latest price reflects everything that is known about this market. From this quite reasonable observation, theorists of an effective market make an amazing conclusion: no one can win on the market. If the markets know everything, play them—how to try to beat the world chess champion. It is better not to spend time and money but simply to buy a stock portfolio that reflects the market as a whole (this is called indexing).

What about those traders who make money? From the point of view of an efficient market theory, their success is simply luck. At one time or another, everyone can hit the jackpot but the market very soon takes the win back. And what about those who make money in the markets year after year? Warren Buffett, one of the greatest investors of the twentieth century, says that playing in a market where people believe in efficiency is how to play poker with those who don't look at the cards.

I think this theory contains one of the most authentic views on the market. At the same time, I believe that this is one of the most delusional theories. She rightly points out that the markets reflect the knowledge of all participants. Its fatal miscalculation is that according to it, investors and traders are sensible people, seeking to maximize profits and minimize losses. This is an extremely idealized view of human nature.

It's easy to be calm and sober on Sunday when the markets are closed. Traders intelligently analyze charts, decide what and when to buy or sell, look for when they can make a profit, or where to place a stop order. But Monday is coming, markets are opening up, and carefully made plans are crumpled up in the sweaty palms of the traders.

People make decisions on the stock exchange partly with their head, and partly with emotions. They can buy or sell, even if it hurts them. The player, whose shares are growing, begins to show off and skips the signals for sale. The trader, beaten by the market, becomes so fearful that it costs the price of his share to fall a bit; he immediately sells, breaking his own rules. When his stock rises above the level where he planned to make a profit, he cannot accept the idea that he has missed a profitable deal and buys at an awkwardly high price. The rise stops, and the price begins to crawl while the poor fellow looks, first with hope, and then with horror, as his stock collapses. In the end, no longer able to endure, he sells at a loss just at the very bottom. What is this rational? Maybe the original plan to buy shares was reasonable,

Emotional traders think little about long-term interests. They are not up to this. They are either stunned for adrenaline or fettered by fear and think only about how to get their fingers out of a trap. Prices reflect how investors and traders behave and they reflect

mass hysteria. As the market becomes active, emotions soar. People who think soberly are in the minority among a crowd of players.
Markets are more efficient in trade corridors when people work more with their heads.
Efficiency decreases when prices accelerate and the emotional heat builds up. It is difficult to make money on small price fluctuations since your rivals are relatively calm. A cold-blooded opponent is more dangerous. In fast moving trends, it is easier to get hold of the money of traders who get excited. Emotional are primitive and more predictable. To win the stock game, you must remain calm, taking money from excited amateurs.
When a person is alone, he is more inclined to act rationally. In the crowd, his actions become more impulsive. His interest in a particular stock, currency or futures draws him into the mass of trading in the same instrument. The price moves up and down, and with each of its jumps, the heads of traders rise or fall. The market is hypnotizing traders, as an oriental fakir hypnotizes a snake rhythmically shaking a pipe. The faster the prices change, the hotter the emotions. The more emotional the market is, the less effective it is, and low efficiency enables cold-blooded and disciplined traders to make money.
A serious trader makes money on loyalty to their own rules. The crowd rushes for the growing action, and during a recession throws it out, screaming from fear. All this time the disciplined trader sticks to the plan. He can use a mechanical system or play according to the situation, tracking the market, and making buying and selling decisions. In any case, he is guided by clear principles, not emotions, and this is his advantage over the crowd. An experienced trader pulls money through a hole in the theory of an efficient market, according to which investors and traders are rational people. Most of them are not at all—this is typical only for the winners.

## *What Is The Price?*

Each exchange transaction is a contract between the buyer and the seller. The transaction can be concluded at a meeting, by phone or via the Internet, with the participation of a broker or without it. They buyers wants to get the lowest possible price while the seller, on the other hand, wants to sell in the highest possible price. Both are motivated by a crowd of traders around them who can intercept a bargain at any moment.

A stock exchange transaction occurs when the most greedy buyer, fearing a price increase, decides to offer a cent more. It can happen when the most fearful seller, fearing that the price of the goods will collapse, will offer to reduce the price by a cent. It happens that the seller, frightened by the market, delivers the goods at a bargain price to a cold-blooded and disciplined buyer, who calmly waited for the right moment for the transaction. All transactions reflect market crowd behavior that surrounds buyers and sellers. Each price on the quotation screen captures an instant agreement between market participants about the value of the product.

The fundamental value of companies and goods changes slowly but prices can fluctuate greatly because traders quickly change their opinions. One of my clients once said that price and value are interconnected by a kilometer-long rubber band. The market is swinging on it between overbought and oversold levels.

The typical behavior of the crowd is to make noise and stagnate. But sometimes the crowd gets excited and prices fall or soar. Rumors and news spur the crowd and it rushes from side to side, leaving traces on our quotation screens. Prices and indicators reflect changes in the psychological state of the crowd.

When thc market does not give clear signals to buy or to sell, many newcomers dig their eyes at the quotation screens and squint, trying to look for a good bargain. The truly valuable signal on the graph itself is striking, screaming about yourself - do not squint, it is impossible not to notice! It is better to wait for a signal than to try to force a deal when the market does not want to give it to you. Amateurs rush into battle, professionals wait for easy deals. Beginners intoxicate the process of the game, while experienced stockbrokers wait for signals for transactions with the highest chance of winning.

The best signals about deals come from active markets. When the crowd is engulfed in emotions, the prudent exchange trader makes money. When markets become sluggish, many knowledgeable traders leave the battlefield, leaving it to gamblers and brokers. As Jesse Livermore, one of the most famous stockbrokers of the twentieth century, said, “There is time to buy, time to sell, and time to go fishing.”

## *Player*

Most people, at least occasionally, participate in gambling. For many, this is entertainment, for some it is turns into mania, and some people manage to break out into professionals and start earning. The game serves as a source of income for the tiny minority and entertainment for the masses but a random player chasing a crazy dollar has no more chances for success than an ice exposed under the noonday sun in the tropics.

Some famous investors love to play at the hippodrome. Among them is Peter Lynch, the former manager of the famous Magellan Fund and Warren Buffett, who at one time issued a newsletter with forecasts of race results. My friend Lou, to whom I dedicated my first book, spent several years professionally engaged in horse racing and lived on these incomes. Later, having bought a spot on the stock exchange, he approached the analysis of financial markets with the same composure as the choice of race winners. There are card games in which everything depends only on chance (baccarat refers to such). Others (for example, blackjack)

are partially dependent on calculations and thus attract more savvy people.
For professionals, the game is work. They constantly calculate the probability of winning and act only if the potential profit exceeds the risk. Those who cannot wait to enter the game and make a bet, lose money no matter how much they change one ill-conceived approach to another.
If the game is entertainment for you, follow at least a few money management rules. First of all, determine the amount you are willing to risk. In those rare cases when friends drag me to the casino, I put as much money in my right pocket as I don't feel sorry for losing this evening. I'll put everything in my left pocket. I quit the game immediately, as the right pocket is empty, and I never get money from the left. Sometimes in the left pocket is more money than it was in the right, although it is not worth counting on it.

One of my buddies, who loves Las Vegas, is a successful businessman. Several times a year he flies there for the weekend with $ 5,000 in cash. Having lowered his "game fund", he bathes in the pool, dines in a good restaurant, and flies home on the next flight.
Just for entertainment, he spends around $5,000.00 but he doesn't lose more than his previously set amount. When, after lowering the cash, he stretches on a lounge chair at the pool's edge, it is strikingly different from the crowd of casino regulars who frantically withdraw money from credit cards to buy more gaming chips in the hope that luck will smile upon them. To a player who does not control the risk, failure is guaranteed.

# Chapter 5

# What Markets to Play?

Many people make the most important decisions in life without thinking too much. Their choice depends on a random combination of circumstances, with whom to live, where to work, in what markets to play. For many of us, the answers to these questions pop up randomly, without much thought. Is it any wonder that many people are so unhappy? You can choose the market offhand but it is better to stop and think about the better to speculate: stocks, futures, or options. Each tool has its pros and cons.

Successful traders think soberly. The one who completely focuses on money wins and the loser catches the buzz from the very process of the game—like a football player who is hitting the ball blindly. Another question is where this ball will go.

When choosing a market, keep in mind that any stock exchange instrument, whether it is stocks, futures or options, must meet two criteria: volatility and liquidity. Liquidity is dependent on the average daily volume—the bigger it is, the easier it is to enter and exit the market. You can build a profitable position on the illiquid stock, but get stuck at the exit and lose due to slippage when trying to make a profit. Volatility is the degree of mobility of your exchange instrument. The sharper its price changes, the wider the field of activity of the trader. For example, stocks of many utility companies are very liquid but it is difficult to trade them as they tend to be kept in narrow corridors. Some stocks with low trading volume and low volatility may be good for investment but not as tools for speculation. Remember that not all markets are suitable for the game just because you have good predictions. They must have high trading volumes and high volatility.

## Promotions

A promotion is a certificate of ownership of a part of a company. By acquiring 100 shares of a company that has issued 100 million shares, you will become the owner of one millionth part of this business. If someone else wants to get involved, his order to buy shares will push up the price.

## Your Package

When people believe that the company has good prospects, they seek to acquire its shares, and prices rise. If the prospects are unimportant, then the shares are thrown onto the market and prices go down. Joint-stock companies seek to maintain the price of their shares, as high quotes facilitate the issuance of additional shares or bonds. Awards to top managers are often tied to the stock price of their companies.

In a very long-term perspective, stock prices depend on fundamental parameters, primarily on the income of companies. But, as the great economist John Maynard Keynes, who was, by the way, an extraordinary exchange player, said, in the long run we all die. The markets are full of speculative stocks of questionable value (the so-called "cats and dogs"), issued by unprofitable companies. They may soar above all expectations. Promotions in fashion industries, such as biotechnology or the Internet, may jump in anticipation of future profits rather than actual results. Even lousy pooch is a holiday. Shares of profitable, well-managed companies can sit in the basement for a long time. The market reflects the sum of the knowledge of all participants, the course of their thoughts, and the attitude to a particular action. Falling prices mean that big holders get rid of the stock. One of the main rules of a trader: “It’s good to buy cheap but it’s bad to buy what is cheaper”. Do not buy stocks in a downtrend, even if the deal seems profitable. If you like the fundamental parameters of a stock, check with technical analysis whether its trend is growing.

Warren Buffett, one of the most successful investors of the twentieth century, chuckles: “By purchasing stocks, you become a partner of a manic-depressive subject called Mr. Market. Every day he resorts to you and offers to sell his stake or buy yours. These proposals are almost always better to ignore as they come from a madman. But from time to time Mr. Market falls into such a depression that it gives up shares practically for nothing, and then they should be bought. And sometimes in the manic phase, he offers such a mad price for your shares that it is worth selling them. ”

The idea of Buffett seems simple but to embody it is not easy. The mood of Mr. Market is contagious. Most want to buy when he is seized by mania and sell when he is depressed. We need to calmly determine objective criteria in order to decide which price reflects depression and which mania. Buffett relies on fundamental analysis and subtle intuition. Traders can rely on technical analysis.

By the way, about the intuition. This property is developed by investors and traders on the basis of many years of experience. What newcomers call intuition, or flair, is usually nothing but an itch to play. To lovers, I say: you have no right to intuition, it is not earned.

The stock market offers us a huge choice even if we sweep aside the less liquid and slow-moving shares. The pages of business newspapers are full of reports of ups and downs in stocks. I just want to jump into the last car of the departing train and buy stocks that the press writes about. But have we missed this train?

Maybe it is better to try to calculate tomorrow's leaders? Amateurs often start to fuss, trying to make such decisions. They disperse forces, rush from one stock to another instead of focusing on a small number of stocks. Newbies who cannot really trade stocks of one company are looking for computer programs that will allow them to scan thousands.

The shares have close relatives—mutual funds. Long-term investors often invest in large funds that include hundreds of stocks. Traders usually prefer industry funds that allow them to bet on a particular economic sector, country, or region. These funds allow you to select those sectors or countries that you like best and leave the selection of specific stocks to analysts of mutual funds.

Every trader needs a system for selecting promising stocks and mutual funds. It's more complicated than just nodding on party tips or reading newspaper headlines. The traders must look for market indicators based on fundamental or technical analysis, develop discipline and develop a competent risk control and capital management system.

## Futures

At first, futures seem like an insanely dangerous subject of speculation. During the first year, nine out of ten traders go bankrupt. Contrary to what others tend to believe, the risk does not lie in the futures but in the traders. Futures open up tremendous opportunities for traders but they put dangerous weapons into the hands of gamblers, with which they are close to the crossbow. A trader who has learned how to manage capital and keep risk under control should not be afraid of futures.

At one time, futures exchanges were called commodity, meaning the basic elements of the economy. There was a saying on the stock exchange: a commodity is something that will hurt if you drop it on your leg: for example, gold, sugar, wheat, a barrel of oil. Over the past decades, contracts for many financial instruments, such as currencies, bonds, stocks, stock indices, have begun to circulate in the market in the same way as contracts for goods. The concept of "futures" covers both traditional products and new financial instruments.

A futures contract is a contract in which you are obligated to deliver or purchase a commodity in a specific quantity by a certain date. The buyer and seller are bound in a futures contract. It is not the obligation of the buyers—it is his right—to take the delivery. If you have purchased a call or put option, you can opt out of it if you wish. Dealing with futures, you are deprived of such luxury. If the market situation turns against you, you will have to either replenish the margin or close the position with a loss.

Prices are more profitable for traders but between futures and options, futures are stricter. You become a co-owner of the company when you buy stocks. When you purchase a futures contract, you do not get anything and you do not own anything. Instead, you enter into a legal contract for the future purchase of goods of whatever nature—treasury bonds, grains, or wheat. Whoever sells you this contract is bounded by the obligation to deliver. The seller receives the money paid for the shares; in the case of futures, the security deposit, or margin, remains with the broker to secure your execution of the contract. The seller makes the same margin. Previously, it was called "honest money." When trading stocks, you pay interest on a brokerage loan; by trading futures, you yourself can earn interest on your security deposit.

For each futures contract there is a settlement period, and the price of goods varies depending on the month of delivery. Some professionals monitor the spread between different delivery months to predict trend reversals. Most futures traders do not wait for the delivery date, but close contracts earlier, fixing profits and losses in monetary terms. Nevertheless, the fact of having the date of delivery of goods leads people to action, tying them to reality. You can sit on unprofitable shares for ten years, comforting yourself with the thought that these losses are only on paper. In the world of futures, reality in the form of a settlement day dispels good dreams.

To understand the mechanism of futures, let's compare a futures deal with a cash transaction, when the goods are bought or sold "on the spot." Suppose now it is February and gold is sold at $400 per ounce. Our analysis shows that the price for a few weeks should rise to $420. With $40,000, you can buy a gold bar in the bank. If your computation and analysis are right, your gold could cost $42,000.00 in just a few weeks. You can make a $2,000.00 profit if you can sell it, which is 5% without commission. Not bad! Now let's see what happens if, on the basis of the same analysis, you decide to trade futures.

Since it is February next month, the supply of gold will be in April. One futures contract includes 100 ounces of gold, and its current value is $40,000. At the same time, the margin on this contract is only $1,000. In other words, with $ 1,000, you can control gold at $40,000. If your analysis is correct and gold really goes up by $20 per ounce, you will get about the same profit as buying 100 ounces of gold for cash, that is, $2,000. Only now your profit will be not 5% but 200% since the deposit was equal to $1,000. Futures give a much higher percentage profit!

Seeing this, many people embrace greed. A novice who has $40,000 calls a broker and orders 40 contracts to be purchased! He can earn $2,000.0 per contract if the price of gold reaches $420 and if his analysis and computation are right. In a few weeks, he can triple his money. You can be a millionaire by the end of the year once you repeat this operation several times. This is such an easy money. What is their mistake?

The problem is that the markets do not go straight. Charts are peppered with false breaks, false reversals, and sleepy shopping corridors. The price of gold may well rise from $400 to $420 per ounce but along the way, a temporary decline to $390 is not out of the question. To the one who acquired 100 ounces of gold for cash, such a failure of $ 10 would bring a nominal loss of $1,000, which he could well outweigh. The holder of a large number of futures contracts with a margin of $1,000 for each of this temporary price drop of $10 will simply ruin his chances. As he reaches this low point, the broker will give him a call, demanding the replenishment of the margin. He will forcibly close the position if the trader does not add additional funds.

Newcomers, sweating from greed, expect huge profits, climb to the margin by the ears, and the very first small price movement against them knocks them out of the game. Even if their long-term analysis is correct and gold eventually rises, as they had hoped for, newcomers are doomed because they open an exorbitantly large position and leave scanty reserves. Traders are not ruined by futures; they are ruined by the inability to manage capital.

Futures are a very attractive tool for those who can control risk. Futures can be much more profitable than stocks but require iron discipline. Starting the exchange game, do not rush immediately to the futures markets. It is better start with stocks where it is easier to control risk. Having gained experience in stocks, you can look at futures. If you are a disciplined person, then maybe futures are for you.

## Options

An option is a bet that the price of a specific stock, index, or futures reaches a specific level within a specific time. Now, reread the sentence. The word “specific” is repeated three times. You have to make the right action, make a prediction on how much and how fast its course will change. You have to make three decisions, and if you make a mistake in even one, you will lose money.

When you buy an option, you must slip through three hoops in one jump. You must choose the right stock; determine the level it will reach, and the speed of this movement. Remember the attraction in the amusement park where you have to throw the ball so that it flew through three suspended rings. Have you tried? This triple complexity makes buying options an extremely dangerous game.

“Options give a huge leverage—the ability to control large positions at low cost. By purchasing an option, you risk only the money that paid for it. Options allow the trader to make money quickly in cases where his predictions are correct; if the trend reverses, you can abandon the contract and just break it!” This standard brokerage propaganda seduces crowds of small traders. They don’t have enough money for stocks but do not want to break the bank. In fact, option buyers fall into the abyss themselves.

Professionals often sell options. This business is capital-intensive; to deal with it seriously, you need to have hundreds of thousands of dollars and the most successful stockbrokers operate with millions. And even their game is not without risk. A few years ago, my friend, who was considered one of the best financial managers in the United States, found himself on the front page of the Wall Street Journal after having suffered losses of more than $200 million on one extremely unsuccessful day, destroying its profits in 20 years and letting the company go with the wind and all thanks to the sale of “naked”, i.e. unsecured, put options. Option sellers are divided into two categories. Vendors of secured options buy shares and write options for them. Those who trade without coverage sell stock options that they do not have, guaranteeing their obligations in cash only. Selling unsecured options is how to make money out of nothing but make one wrong move and you are ruined. Options sale is serious and it can only be done by disciplined traders with a large capital. Markets are pumps that pump money from the pockets of a poorly informed majority to the pockets of a knowledgeable minority. Those who serve these pumps—brokers, information providers, officials in regulatory agencies, and even cleaners cleaning the floor in the sales area—earn money from the cash flow that flows through the markets. Markets take money from the majority, pay for the work of the servants, and give the rest to the savvy minority, who, by definition, must lose. Be sure: you should not act, think, and speak as most traders do, think, and speak. To succeed, you need to steer away from the crowd. Insightful traders are looking for situations in which the main mass moves in one direction and the financially secure minority in the opposite direction.

In the options market, most buy call options and, to a lesser extent, put options. Insiders (sensible minority) almost exclusively sell options. Professionals work with their head while greed and fear drive amateurs. In the options markets, these feelings are fully exploited.

Promotion of options is effective due to human greed. You are probably familiar with the advertising call: "Just a few dollars and you control a large block of shares!" Suppose a novice trader wants to play to raise $60 but he does not have $ 6,000 to buy 100 shares. He acquires an option.

A call with a strike price of $ 70, which expires after two months, for $500. If the stock price rises to $75, the intrinsic value of the option will increase by $500 while some of the time value will remain. In one month, the speculator will be able to double his money! The amateur buys a call option, relaxes and waits one hundred percent profit.

And then something strange begins to happen. Whenever a stock rises by two points, its option only rises by one but when the stock price drops or even just stops growing, the value of the call quickly drops. Soon instead of the expected doubling of capital from the hapless trader 50% of the potential loss. Meanwhile, the clock is ticking louder. The expiration date of his option is getting closer and, although stocks are now higher, the option has become cheaper. What to do is to sell an option in order to save at least some of your money, or to wait in the hope of a new takeoff of quotations?

Another powerful incentive to buy options is fear, especially in the case of futures options. Suppose a loser got burned several times on futures. His analysis was weak and he could not control the risk at all. He sees the possibility of a bargain but is afraid again to lose money. He hears brokerage propaganda "unlimited profit with limited risk" and buys an option on futures. Speculators buy options like poor people buy lottery tickets. The owner of a lottery ticket risks losing 100% of what he paid. In a situation where you risk losing 100%, it's strange to talk about "limited risk". It turns out that the risk is limited to 100%?! Most speculators do not take this ominous figure into account.

Option buyers have deplorable statistics. They can win a few dollars here and there, but I have not yet met a man who would make money by buying options. The odds in this game are so unfavorable that after several deals, the buyer is left with nothing. Options offer tremendous entertainment opportunities. They are considered as inexpensive tickets so that you can participate in the game, a cheap dream, such as a lottery ticket.

It is necessary to have at least an annual experience of successful trading in stocks or futures, before touching on options. If you're new, don't even think about using options instead of stocks. No matter how modest the amount in your account, select the appropriate stocks and learn how to trade them.

# Chapter 6

# First Steps

Gambling beckons us under the premise of freedom. You can work, you can play, and you can live wherever you want if you can gamble. You will no longer depend on everyday worries and do not obey anyone. Trading attracts smart people who love to play and are not afraid of risk. Before you dive into this exciting business, remember that other than enthusiasm, you have to understand the problems of the stock game.

Exchange game will create emotional stress. You need to have a healthy trader psychology if you want to survive and succeed.

Exchange game will require stress of mind. To beat competitors, you will need to master serious analytical methods.

The exchange game will test your knowledge of mathematics. Anyone who does not know how to count cannot control risk and will surely burn.

The psychology of the game, technical analysis, money management, if you master all of these, well, you can succeed. But let's start by considering the external obstacles to success.

Markets are designed so that the maximum number of people loses the maximum amount of money. Theft is being pursued but the markets give an advantage to the professionals putting lovers in a less advantageous position. Many traders have different barriers that prevent them from being successful. What are those and how can we reduce their height

## External Obstacles

You can become an investor from scratch by buying shares worth several thousand dollars. If you keep them long enough, the commissions and other expenses will be very small.

## Success or Failure Factor

For traders, the task is more complicated. At first glance, insignificant expenses can ruin them and the danger is greater, the smaller the funds in the account. Transaction costs often become an insurmountable barrier to success.

## Transaction Costs

Newbies do not think about them but for traders this is one of the main reasons for the defeat. If you can change your plans to reduce these costs, you will have an advantage over the market crowd.

Novice trader is like a lamb in a dense forest

It is likely to be eaten and the skin, the trading capital, will be divided into three by brokers, traders in the hall, and service providers. Everyone will try to grab a little more from the skin of the poor victim. Do not become that lamb. Do not forget about costs. They are of three types: commissions, slippage, and costs to ensure trading.

### *Commission*

It may seem that the commission is a small item of expenditure. Most traders do not take it seriously but if you add up all the paid commissions, it turns out that a broker took a large share of the profits. A brokerage firm can charge you about $20 for buying or selling up to 5,000 shares. If, having on account $20,000, you buy 200 shares at the price of $100 per share, the commission in the amount of $20 will be one-tenth percent. When you sell these shares and re-pay a commission, the cost of brokerage services for the entire transaction will be about two-tenths of a percent of your capital. Do this once a week and by the end of the month, your broker will earn an amount equal to one percent of your account, regardless of whether you made a profit or not. Keep up the good work and by the end of the year, the total amount of the commissions paid by you will increase to 12% of your capital. This is serious money! Professional financial managers are happy if they earn their clients 25% of their annual income. Such a result would be unattainable if they gave 12% per annum in the form of commission.

But that is not all

Imagine a small trader who can buy only one hundred $20 shares. Although the price of buying it is $2,000, the broker takes the same $20 in the form of a commission, eating a huge part of the trader's capital, which is 1% per trade. When he closes the position, again paying a commission, the loss on the broker will be another 2%. By repeating such deals once a week, by the end of the month, he will lose 10% of his bill on commissions, which is more than 100% per year. Great George Soros annually multiplies its capital by an average of 29%. He could never do that by jumping over the barrier of a 100 percent commission.

The more your capital, the lower the percentage will be eaten by commissions and the lower the barrier preventing victory. Large account is an advantage but in any case, do not show excessive activity. Each transaction and each seemingly insignificant commission raises the barrier to success. Develop an exchange game system where transactions are not very frequent.

If you have a five or six digit amount on your account and if you trade no more than a couple of times a week, do not waste time and money on illusory protection in the form of expensive brokerage services. Choose an inexpensive but reliable broker with whom you can easily contact online or by phone and start looking for promising deals.

## *Slippage*

Market slippage occurs when your trade does not open at the price you expected. In other words, you get either a small starting bonus in the form of profit, or a loss. But many traders see this as a loss, which does not correspond to reality.

Let's take an example. You send the broker an order to buy a stock at the price of $ 45 (your expectations). Order execution price can have three options:

Without slipping - Your buying order is a seller for $ 45.

Positive slippage - Your transaction opens at less than $ 45, say $ 44.50. In this case, you get a bonus of $ 0.50 per share. When is this possible? When a position is opened by a limit order from the support level.

Negative slippage - The order is executed above $ 45, which immediately takes a part of your possible profit. You probably know when such situations arise: when applying stop loss and market orders.

Brief conclusions: whenever your expectations for the price scatter with the reality of its execution, slippage occurs, which can bring you pleasant bonuses when using the correct orders.

Why does slippage occur?

The main question is: why do not we get the price we want and what does it depend on? To get the answer, we need to refer to the basics of trading.

For each seller there is a buyer. If you want to buy 100 shares at $ 45, then there must be a seller who offers at least 100 shares at $ 45. When an imbalance arises between market participants, the price begins to move toward the prevailing force. Why? To balance supply and demand.

Consider an example. A trader needs to buy 10,000 shares (100 lots) at a market price (market order) of $ 50. For this price, sellers offer only 3,000 shares, $ 50.01 - 2,000, $ 50.02 - no one sells at all, $ 50.03 - 500, $ 50.04 - 1,500, $ 50.05 - 3,000. Thus, the application will be processed gradually with an increase in the value of the share.

What does slippage depend on? As you already understood, the more papers are traded at each specific price, the less chance you have of slipping. In other words, you need to look for adequate daily trading volumes. For me personally, this is at least 300,000 shares per day.

Is it possible to control slippage?
No. But you can separate the positive and negative slippage using the correct orders. These include:
A limit order is used both for opening a position and closing (the so-called take profit), if it is, of course, profitable. You get either the price indicated in the application, or better. If the action does not meet these criteria, the order simply remains not executed.
Stop limit order - combines the advantages of stop and limit orders. In general, stop applications act as a trigger. That is, as soon as the price reaches the stop level, it turns into some other type of order. Stop limit order you can use for trading breakdowns of price levels.

## *Total Trading Costs*

Certain expenses are inevitable, especially at the initial stage: you will have to purchase books, buy a program, subscribe to a database, etc. It is important to keep all these expenses under control. Novice traders usually pay the costs of maintaining the game—computers, subscriptions, consultations—without withdrawing money from the trading account. This prevents them from seeing how much of the bill they spend on near-trading costs.

Amateurs think that their problems can be solved with money and they buy a lot of support services. Professionals spend on a near-trading cost only a small portion of the profits. They approach this in the same way as determining the size of positions. Experienced players increase the size of positions when they win and reduce when they lose money. Similarly, a successful trader allows himself to buy a new computer or program only after he has earned enough to pay for them.

Corporate traders can count on the support of managers and colleagues but private traders often feel completely isolated. Many of them become easy prey for sellers of all kinds of services that promise to become their guides in the dense forest. The higher the level of stress, the sooner the trader will fall for their advertising. Of the ten specialists in any field, whether lawyers, auto mechanics, or doctors, nine limp professionally. You are unlikely to trust the first oncoming mechanic or doctor but rather listen to the recommendations of those who opine respect. Majority of the private traders have no one to run to when they need some advice. They usually approach consultants with the most advertisements but these are rarely the best advisers in the stock game.

Some stock exchange tips are surprisingly valuable. You can buy a book containing the experience of a lifetime for a few dollars; a few hundred will be enough to subscribe to the newsletter, where you will get original and useful tips. But such pearls are a rarity and legions of smart traders expose goods for uncertain traders. I have two rules that allow weed out the worst of what is offered.

First, avoid services that you do not understand; secondly, avoid costly services.

If you do not understand what the consultant says, stay away from him. The exchange game attracts people with above-average intelligence; probably this applies to you. If you sincerely tried to understand what was said, but could not, the reason, most likely, is that you are intentionally confused. In choosing a book, I will never take the one that is written in bad language. Speech reflects thinking and if a person does not know how to write clearly and distinctly, then there is confusion in his thoughts.

Consultants and advisers who know the exchange business are usually modest and charge reasonable prices for their services. Obviously, the high price is a publicity stunt, which at the subconscious level suggests to the client that this service can work wonders. But miracles do not happen and such promises are impossible to fulfill. A relatively inexpensive service would be a profitable acquisition if it proves useful; otherwise you will lose a little.

Once Sigmund Freud was asked how, in his opinion, the patient should treat his doctor. "With benevolent skepticism," the great psychoanalyst replied. This is also good advice for traders. Keep healthy skepticism. If you encounter something incomprehensible, try to penetrate again. If you did not understand the second attempt, most likely, this is an unprofitable method. Run without regard to the people if they offer you the keys to the kingdom. Remember, limit your expenses and any information you get can be valuable only after you check it on your own data.

## Technical Equipment

A trader is like a fish swimming against a stream in a mountain river. Commissions, slippage, and expenses interfere with the

movement; they bring us down. You need to earn enough to overcome these thresholds before you can get a cent profit.
If, looking at the obstacles, you decide that the exchange game is too difficult and it is not for you, there is nothing shameful in this, as there is nothing shameful in the inability to dance or play the piano. Many beginners, without thinking twice, rush into the water and get financial and moral injuries. The exchange game is extremely interesting but if you decide to give it up, it is better to do it early.

## More is better

The outcome of your transactions on the exchange depends, in particular, on the size of your trading account. Two traders can conduct identical transactions, with one multiplying its capital and the other going through. How so, if they simultaneously buy and sell the same number of the same shares?
Imagine that you and I decided to spend an hour tossing a coin: if an eagle falls, your winnings, if the tail is mine. We both have $5 and we make the same bet on each roll, which is 25 cents. If we play fair, then in an hour we will both be in approximately equal position, that is, each will have about $5.
What if we continue the same game with the same coin, only now my initial capital will be $1 and yours still $ 5? Most likely, my money will move to your pocket. You will win thanks to the fact that capital provides vitality. To splurge, you have to lose 20 times in a row, four will be enough for me. The probability of four consecutive losses is much higher than twenty. The problem with a small account trader is that he does not have a reserve to survive even a short series of failures. Profitable trades always alternate with unprofitable ones, and after several losses, small traders drop out of the game.

Most newbies come to the stock exchange with insufficient capital. There is a lot of noise in the market—random fluctuations. A small trader who has fallen into a "noisy" period does not have a reserve to survive this lane. His long-term analysis may be correct, but the market will sink him, because he does not have the margin of safety to survive the period of failure. In 1980, being still a green newcomer, I went to a bank near the office and charged $5,000 from a credit card. This seemingly fabulous sum was necessary to me to replenish the margin. The mouse-eyed cashier called the manager and he demanded that I leave a fingerprint on the receipt. This operation jarred me but I received the money, and in a few months I let it go safely. I applied the right system but market noise ruined me. Only having accumulated close to a six-figure amount on my account, I began to work with a profit. If someone explained to me in those years why the size of the bill is so important!

A large account trader makes it easier to stay calm by making relatively small bets. A trader who has little money feels tense, knowing that any transaction can greatly affect his account. When stress builds up, the ability to make right decisions falls.

Some beginners have too much money but this is not good either. A newcomer with excessive capital starts chasing too many shares, loses caution, does not keep track of every position, and eventually incurs losses.

What is the amount to start trading? Note that we are talking about gaming capital. This does not include your personal savings, nor long-term investments, pension savings, or money set aside for Christmas presents. We consider only those funds that you intend to scroll through in the market, seeking to achieve a higher yield than treasury bills.

Do not even think about embarking on an exchange game if your capital is less than $20,000. This is a minimum and with an amount of $50,000, your flight will take place at a safer height, which will allow you to better diversify your portfolio and more efficiently control risks. At the same time, I would not recommend starting to play with a capital of over $100,000. This is way too much money on a newbie trading account that it weakens attention and often leads to carelessness in transactions. Professionals, of course, manage much larger amounts but while you are just learning how to trade on the stock exchange, $100,000 is your limit. Learn to fly on a single-engine plane, and only then change to a twin-engine one. To succeed, a trader needs to develop a habit of treating money carefully.

# Chapter 7

# Trading Strategy

What is trading? It is believed that it consists of three elements:

I. Trading strategy
II. Capital management
III. Psychology

A trading strategy is making decisions about where to open and close positions. Her tool is technical analysis. Capital management is associated with proper money making decisions. This is mainly stop loss and the choice of the right volume of positions. The focus of psychology, the impact of human emotions on trade.

Most newbies enter the world of trading with the wrong settings, their idea of what is important and what is secondary is turned upside down. Most of the time, novice traders devote to the study of the first element—technical analysis. They persevere in the interpretation of graphs and lose money until they realize that the answer lies not in graphs, but in money management and, finally, in psychology.

Why are priorities wrong from the start? This is due to several factors. First, starting to trade, a person naturally turns to books. The bulk of the books is devoted to only technical analysis. By volume, this topic occupies the main part in the books. Secondly, the trade itself begins with the opening position; this is the first decision that the trader makes. As a result, he concentrates on it, forgetting everything else. Thirdly, most of the software used to trade is not explicitly containing tools for managing capital or controlling losses because many brokerage companies are simply not interested. Trading platforms, which at least somehow implement the control of emotions, are practically absent.

In addition to incorrect prioritization, people, in principle, do not understand what trading is, or they are too naive to it, expecting to make millions quickly.

Entering into the world of trading, most people even have no idea how complicated this type of activity is and what they get involved in. The complexity of trading lies behind the apparent simplicity of the trading process. It would seem that it's difficult to buy and sell sitting at home with mouse clicks? But there is nothing more absurd than the assertion that money goes to traders easily. This can only be true if years of hard work, intense research, and the bitter experience of loss and disappointment are behind the trader's shoulders. Moving forward, the trader leaves behind the ashes of his own burned nerves. An area characterized by unlimited potential for material growth, a zero entry threshold and instant labor reward cannot be simple by definition. This is a highly competitive environment.

Trading is a subtle intellectual art that requires a special combination of personal qualities. This is a rather harsh reality in which inexperienced or weak people will certainly lose, and there is nothing unfair in this, because as long as a person is weak or inexperienced, but wants more, he must and will suffer, because he has not worked enough on himself. The market quickly puts a person in place, perhaps faster than in real life. In real life, imbalances can exist much longer. In this regard, the market, if you will, the ideal reality is that everyone gets what he deserves. There is no place for impulsive surface people who count on easy earnings. The market inevitably punishes those who objectively perceive reality and value themselves. The market is especially brutal with those who at the very beginning of the way accidentally caught a wave of luck but explains the success of

their personal qualities. Bitter disappointments await such traders. Fall from a recent pedestal is doubly painful. This is especially true today, when every second person, completely far from the market, becomes a crypto trader or a cryptoinvestor.
The main difficulty of trading lies in the fact that your main enemy in this game is you yourself. Here we have to deal with the manifestations of their own negative personal qualities. To achieve success in this field, to do it by chance and more than once is to overcome your human nature as much as possible, to jump above your head, that is, to do the almost impossible. If you are serious and ready to fight for a long time over your goal, I admire your courage and sincerely hope that my book will help you (however, if you have long been unsuccessfully fighting in this field for years like a fish against ice, then you can't exclude psychological incompatibility with such activities).
Prepare, however, for the path to be very, very difficult. Get ready for a long and exhausting marathon, in which everything is decided not by one day but by behavior over a long period. "We are what we repeatedly do. Excellence, then, is not an act, but a habit." These wonderful words of the American historian by the name of William Durant also means: "We are what we do systematically. Perfection is not a one-time action, but a habit. "
Try also to take care of the siding. In parallel with trading, build a career, acquire qualifications or develop a business. Do not make a bet your life alone.

## Trading Technique

For this section, I specifically chose a broader name than "technical analysis." I tried to include in it not only knowledge from the field of technical analysis. In any activity there is a set of basic rules, called technology, whether it is a tennis technique, a drawing technique, a sales technique, or a reading technique.

Having mastered the basic technique, anyone, regardless of the natural personal data, can become a good expert in any business. First of all, I would like to say at once: do not overestimate technical analysis. First, technical analysis is not an exact science. Here everyone can only share their vision. You will not find the exact rules in this book. Personally, in the interpretation of charts, I admit immense flexibility, considering that trading is an art. Anything can happen here at any time. Secondly, common sense dictates that the ability to find previous highs/lows on a chart or to draw support/resistance lines is not enough to earn serious money. Is it possible to read a dozen books on technical analysis and become a millionaire? Alas, it's not that simple. There is no perfect system. A system that seems perfect today can begin to show very mediocre results tomorrow. Market behavior changes over time. With the passage of time and with the growth of experience and capital, technical analysis has been assigned an ever smaller role and serious investment decisions are increasingly made on the basis of fundamental/macroeconomic analysis.

The task that I set, taking up the creation of this book, was not to describe the details and nuances of the technical inputs on the chart but to try to shape your mindset of a certain type and suggest a general approach to trading. Everyone should come to the trading system by himself. Many traders are looking for the "Grail," a wonderful entry and exit system that will take them to the financial pedestal. In my opinion, the Grail is not an exact entry and exit system but something broader and more general. In this book, I offer several of my options, or visions, of the "Grail".

I will not argue about whether it is possible to determine its future direction from past price movements. I personally answer this question positively. Although outwardly technical analysis is similar to fortune telling, I am convinced that many years of your own observations of price behavior may still provide a statistical

advantage in predicting movements. I specifically highlighted here the words "your own," because I believe that only uniqueness can lead to unique results. I had to read about 50 books on trading before I finally realized that it was better to go my own way and make my own observations.
Many who enter the path of trading often ask the question of whether there is a benefit in reading books on technical analysis. There is a benefit, but it consists, perhaps, only in the development of terms, and also in the fact that what you read can serve as a basis for reflection and creating your own systems. When reading these books, be careful. Instead of going by someone else's way, it's better to create a base of your own right from the start.

## *Experience*

To count on the fact that after reading a series of books on technical analysis, you will start earning is ridiculous because they describe someone else's experience that you have not tried out and that is available to many. What is available to the majority, has a small price.
This book was conceived as a base of own experience. Initially, it was a small textbook and I was not even going to publish it. Truly successful traders and managers rarely write books; they simply have no time for it. The money that can be earned on books is mere pennies compared to what can be earned in the market. Today on the bookshelves and in amazon.com, you can find a lot of books about speculation, investment, economics, and the psychology of success. Many of them have very beautiful names but inside is full of water. When reading them, there is a feeling that they were written by journalists specially employed for this. If you're lucky, you can only find one worthy book for 10 books ordered by Amazon. Useful knowledge has to be collected from

various sources only bit by bit. Sometimes I find more ideas for trading in books, which are completely unrelated to trading than in books that are entirely devoted to this issue. Gradually, my "training manual" has grown. I realized that I enjoy the process of working on a book. My book became for me the best teacher in trading: it made me think, to study materials on given topics from other sources more thoroughly. I even came to the conclusion that the book is probably the most important thing in my life at the moment.

What can your base of experience look like? If you have not created it yet, today, I recommend starting a simple notebook or creating a file in Word, which will be a collection of your observations. This may be a folder with graphs on the desktop, where you can record various market situations, your forecasts and how the market subsequently actually behaved. Personally, I am conducting a similar record of observations in electronic form for more than seven years. There are about 200 graphs in my folder with comments on the market behavior and a description of my own actions. Over time, the accumulated experience began to crystallize into a set of general rules, and then into a trading system, and this process continues to this day. It is necessary to fix not only the behavior of the market, but also your own actions, noting that you did the right thing and what was wrong. The faster you build a refined feedback mechanism, the faster you will come to the results.

Trading is also an art in the sense that it requires tremendous skill. In 2017, I came across the book How to Think and Draw Like Leonardo da Vinci. After examining the life and work of the great master, the author of the book Michael Gelb identified seven principles that permeated the life of Leonardo da Vinci and which can be used by any person to maximize their potential. I was surprised to find that all these seven universal principles can be applied in trading. Here they are:

1. **Inexhaustible curiosity**
   The life of Leonardo da Vinci was a constant search for answers about the nature of things and the structure of the world. Similarly, a trader should never stop exploring the market and new trading methods. The learning process should be permanent.

2. **The steady desire to check everything first hand**
   "You shouldn't imitate others," said Leonardo da Vinci once. His epoch and especially the dark time before the Renaissance were inundated with untested theories about nature that are dogmatic in nature. Independence of thinking, the habit of questioning conventional paradigms has allowed the great master to be closer to the truth than anyone.

Today, when the scope of trading is replete with repetitions of foreign repetitions and filled with unverified theses, this lesson for the trader is especially valuable.

3. **The severity of feelings**
   Like a truly creative person who is constantly improving the perception of the senses through the discovery of new flavors, sounds, tastes, tactile sensations, a trader needs to work not only on practical trading skills but also on the general development of his intellect.

4. **Willingness to accept uncertainty and ambiguity**
   As Leonardo learned more and more, he had even more questions. His creations are full of secrets and mysteries. One can only guess what lies behind the mystical smile and gaze of Mona Lisa. The trader must also be prepared to meet with the inexplicable. A trader's job is a job with uncertainty. At any time in the market can happen

unexpected. A good trader assumes that his ability to reason logically with respect to the market is limited and he will often be mistaken.

## 5. The balance between logic and imagination

It is known that the left brain is responsible for logic and analysis while the right one is for creative processes and imagination. Trading is not an exact science. The work of a great trader is akin to art. Trading within rigorous logic and rigorous systems can lead to good results, but will the results really be outstanding? Hardly.

## 6. Care of the body

Leonardo da Vinci was perfectly developed not only intellectually but also physically and took care of his health. The maestro walked a lot, swam, was an excellent rider, and swordsman. As they say, in a healthy body, a healthy mind. For the brain to work one hundred percent, a trader must sleep well, breathe fresh air, ensure that enough micronutrients enter the body, and maintain a good metabolism.

## 7. Understanding the relationship of things and system thinking

I think many have watched the film "Butterfly Effect." Can the flap of a butterfly wing in Tokyo affect the weather in New York? The trader, like anyone, must possess the ability to establish true cause-and-effect relationships even where seemingly there are none. Example: trade and your girlfriend's cousin. It would seem what the connection between them is? But imagine the situation:

Once, a woman's relative comes to your city from a province. It is a pleasant sunny day outside, and your girlfriend, who wants to introduce you, is having an outdoor meeting. You go on it and at this time in the market there is a situation that you miss. As a result, millions of profits are floating away from you. Here is another example. In between trade, you decide to go to the forum of traders and stumble upon a small interesting note. Later, you buy a book on the topic concerned and it completely turns your ideas about trading. Any minor event may entail a chain of significant consequences.

Leonardo da Vinci was a versatile person, a balanced personality. He managed to achieve outstanding success in completely different areas: in the humanities and natural sciences. In addition, he was a sporty, perfectly physically fit man. In my opinion, the chances of success in trading, like in no other type of activity, depend on how versatile a person has a mind.
By the way, Leonardo da Vinci devoted a lot of his time to studying the features of the "golden section." "Divine Proportion" was used by the master to create many works. The Fibonacci sequence, the logic of which reflects the "golden section", is one of the tools of technical analysis widely used today.

There are different approaches in technical analysis: classical technical analysis, computer indicators, candlesticks, Elliott waves, and others. Computer indicators in this book are not considered; they are repeatedly described in other books. And besides, in my opinion, they have little use. Computer indicators like RSI, all kinds of oscillators are only derived from the price, a workaround. The signals given by them depend on the settings. Change slightly the parameters of the indicator or change the dimension of the candles of the chart from 15-minute to 16-minute, and the signal of the indicator will be different. The performance of computer indicators essentially depends on the state market, trend or side. A fairly common mistake for newbies is using the overbought / oversold RSI indicator for a rebound game. This is too simple and naive. Judging the price movement by computer indicators is the same as, for example, judging an object thrown into the water, by divorce remaining on the surface of the water, or by an airplane flying across the sky, by a train that remains behind it.

## The Main and Corrective Movement

Be skeptical of everything that is available, light, and on the surface. Easy ways are often the most difficult.

The price movement in the market for any period of time will be called either the main (main trend) or corrective (correction). The alternation and combination of these movements forms a trend.

The main movement is always stronger and has a sharper slope than corrective. Corrections are less steep and take more time. These are horizontal sluggish, dull movements, or slight fluctuations within a certain range. As a rule, corrections occur in the absence of news or economic data. Often corrections happen before the release of important news. To understand which phase the price is currently moving in, it's enough to look at the current speed or the inclination of the movement and compare it with the inclination of the movement for a certain previous period.

At every moment in the market there is a contradiction, or "war," between trends. Thus, the long position is open at the point X. Therefore, almost no deal can be unambiguously called "right" or "wrong." A transaction may be "correct" with respect to a certain time period and at the same time "wrong" with respect to another time period. The universal principle "everything is relative" extends to market movements. From here you can make the first practical conclusions for trade. It is reasonable to forecast the future price movement for different time scales. Instead of one trading account, you can even have two corresponding to different time intervals of trading: for example, an account for intraday movements and another account for longer movements (several days or weeks). Often, movements on different time scales are oppositely directed. Admit the possibility of resuming the older trend, be on your guard, and think in different time scales. This will allow you to keep flexibility which is so necessary in the market. If your point of view about the direction of the market is “stiff”, you can easily become a hostage to your opinion and receive a margin call. In one book, I stumbled upon a good metaphor of flexibility, which is so necessary on the market in relation to the direction of movement. Imagine a lawnmower that rides across the lawn. Flexible young grass blades often remain uncut because they sag under the blade. Hard, ossified stems are cut off first.

Turn. If I remain flexible, I won’t break. When opening a position, you need to look back and see if you are up against a more senior trend. Do you open a position just where the probability of resumption of a major trend is very high? General and tactical directions should be the same. For example, in the “picture” above you enter the long at point X. Maybe tactically this is the right decision, but point X is at a level slightly above the recent maximum. Point X is re-high (new local maximum) in a downtrend, and often this area is reversal, i.e. from here comes the resumption of a higher trend.

## Impulses

Sometimes the main movement has the form of an impulse, a sharp powerful movement in a short period of time. Like a body set in motion, the price after a strong impulse most often moves in the same direction. This is a manifestation of the inertial nature of the market. I would like to give special attention to the impulses, since a decent trading system can be built on the basis of impulses alone.

In fact, the main task of the trader is to find a good point in the framework of the correction after the main movement (or after the impulse), calculated on the continuation of the trend. Ideally, this point is the exact moment when the correction ends and the main movement resumes.

In my opinion, with regard to technical analysis, this basic knowledge is already enough for profitable trading—particular, subtleties, choice and preferences of the trader. Detailed research in the field of technical analysis, the endless study of patterns, candlesticks, all sorts of laws bring the trader less additional feedback than the study of money management, psychology, and fundamental analysis, because the market is essentially just chaos, having, however, some spontaneous "trend." I do not know a better approach to trading for a private trader who trades hands than trading with the trend.

People form the views of each with their own speed and their own way; the opinion that the new information can be instantly processed is one of those ideas that are divorced from life and that correspond little to reality. This gradual assimilation of information by investors explains why the movement of markets is subject to trends. But there are times when investor reaction becomes more acute. There are points of accumulation on the charts, where prices fluctuate within narrow limits before moving in one direction or another. Charts resemble travelers at a train station crowded around a door. They spend a lot of time to get through a bottleneck in one direction or another, but as soon as they pass, they usually increase their speed.

The first thing a trader needs to do is work out trend thinking and suppress the thinking of the "counter-trend" type. For some reason, a huge part of novice traders tend to look for trend reversals while you need to bet that the current trend will continue. You should not open long positions on the new, just-appeared lows and you should not short on the newly-formed highs in the expectation of catching the correction. Playing against the trend in the hope of a “rebound” is a typical amateurish mistake. The rationale for such a game in the trader’s head usually looks like this: “Already too high/low. From here, the market will surely go back.” Such a game leads first to averaging, then eliminating stop-losses (the trader thinks that his stop-losses break down at the most unfavorable levels, after which the market will turn in his direction), and then when most of the capital is already lost and the trader begins to believe that it’s already pointless to set stop losses, a margin call comes in. Remember, if the thought “too high/low” flashed at you, especially the word “too”, then this is a reason to be wary: you are thinking in the wrong direction.

Playing against the movement often leads to a violation of the rules of risk management by the trader and forms the wrong habits. At that time, while the position is unprofitable (and this necessarily happens because the market is inert), fear is formed, which later, if the market turns in a favorable direction, forces the trader closing positions too soon. As a result, the trader begins to constantly take short take profits.

It is even more dangerous to play against impulses. Suppose, for example, that the price of an asset begins to fall sharply. On the screen, it looks like a long falling candle. Seeing hcr, a novice begins to buy, or "catch a knife." Still, “because the price is so low, everything will rebound now, you need to urgently buy it, otherwise, you will not be in time!” The logic that is absolutely failing to trade. A strong movement in the form of a huge long candle (especially in which the price does not immediately rebound but "sticks" and stays at the low/high of the candle for a long time) means some fundamental change: the market has just received very important information and now "embeds" it in the price. Most likely, the price momentum will continue its movement. And then, in a day or several days of correction, it will continue its movement even further in the direction of the initial impulse.

"What you don't have to do is catch the falling daggers. You must wait until they sink into the floor and stop trembling, then only then pick them up. This is the best lesson I have learned in many years, seeing how people lose money. "

Of course, there are times when the price literally immediately rebounds in the opposite direction. It happens that the received information is interpreted first erroneously or immediately afterwards new information appears. This, for example, happens when news agencies are mistaken with the interpretation of the statement of some politician or the head of the central bank. It also happens that the newly released data, which at first seemed positive, will not be so positive when viewed in more detail, but such cases are less common.

Returning to the talk about impulses, the first thing that needs to be understood is whether or not we have an impulse. This can only be understood some time after the completion of the "explosive" part of the movement. To open a position in the direction of the pulse immediately, at the moment of the most active movement, is unsafe. At this moment there is a struggle. If the momentum does not gain enough power, then the winning side at the beginning can in a matter of seconds collapse under the weight of its own stop losses. Therefore, it is necessary to wait for the outcome. Let the market decide on its future direction. In the foreign exchange market, the generated impulse can usually be judged in a few hours, better the next day or in a couple of days. Most often, impulses arise from decisions of central banks. The smaller the scale relative to the pulse, the stronger the signal is. And vice versa, the large scale of the correction raises doubts about whether we really have a full-fledged impulse.

Sometimes the correction after the impulse takes the form of a flat flag with a latitude of swing within 15–20 pips. This is a sure sign that the impulse is very strong and will follow further movement towards the impulse. There are also cases when the price is not even adjusted after the impulse, but slowly continues to creep further.

# Chapter 8

# What Extras Do I Need To Know?

## 1.Aggressive entry limit order

For aggressive, the input can use the area outside one of the extremes of the correction. Imagine that the market has not yet drawn the B-C movement and at the moment we are at point B. For this entry, you can pre-set a buy limit at a level just below the previous local minimum of correction (in the figure - below level A).

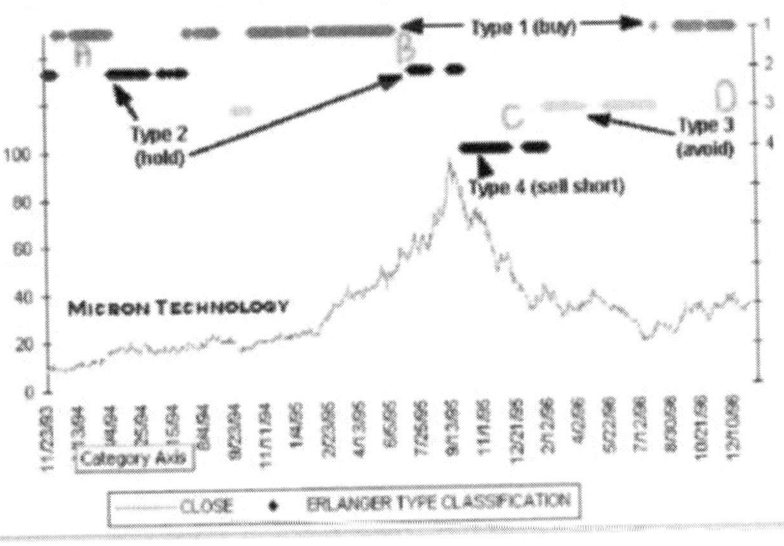


Such an entry is, of course, "running ahead," that is, premature in the sense that a position is being opened against a short-term corrective movement. It is not known how long the correction may last (and perhaps the price will subsequently drop completely to the base of the impulse and lower). The entry by the limit order in this case is not safe from the point of view of breaking the stop-loss, however it is at this point that the reversal often occurs, and the price rushes again in the direction of the initial impulse.

1. **Entrance after the formation of a candle with a long shadow**
   The next option is to enter immediately after the formation of a candle with a long shadow from below, which usually indicates the unwillingness of the price to go down. This input is more secure than the first option, but slightly less profitable. Stop, by the way, with such an entrance you can place a minimum of a long shadow.

2. **Entrance after confirming candles**
   After a candle with a long shadow is formed, you can open a position immediately or you can wait until another confirming candle closes (or two, depending on how aggressive the trade is). This is the third entry option. If this next candle does not "set" strongly on the shadow of the main candle, then the signal remains in effect.

3. **Entry with signs of acceleration within range**
   An even more secure, and perhaps more professional, option is to enter when there are signs of a resumption of the trend, or, as we shall agree to say, the main movement. If the price is somewhere in the middle of the trade corridor formed as part of the correction, and suddenly a candle appears with a clear bullish character (it is large relative to the last neighboring candles and closes at its

maximum, i.e. it does not have a tail on top), then it will be entrance of the fourth type.

4. **The entrance to the break through the channel**
   Often, local maxima and minima within the correction form an inclined channel. The next type of input is an input when the upper boundary of the correction channel is broken through.

5. **The input at the breakthrough of the maximum pulse**
   Behavior of the price in the area of point 6, many traders consider the key: if the price confidently consolidates above the level, then we should expect continued upward movement, and in the case of a false breakdown, a reversal will follow. According to my observations, in the case of a strong impulse, the rule of false breakdown rarely works: the price can fluctuate for a long time at the impulse maximum level, can dive back to the impulse maximum level, but usually continues upward after all. Sometimes the price so quickly flies through the maximum level that it is not possible to enter at point 6 in time.

6. **The entrance to the pullback after the penetration of the maximum pulse**
   After the initial overcoming of the maximum of the impulse (or some other important maximum), the price often returns to the level and again tests it, but from the top. This is an opportunity to increase or enter a position for those who did not have time to enter at point 6.

7. **Enter when prices return to the correction channel**
   Finally, the price can dive below the maximum pulse level. This should not embarrass you, and you should still bet on the continuation of the movement.

All options described above have the right to exist. The choice is yours. To guess exactly how the price will behave is extremely difficult. So, if you make a purchase after breaking through the maximum impulse (entry 6), the price after that can easily go back down for the level. At the same time, if you wait for this and plan to enter by entrances 7 or 8, the price can fly upwards immediately, without giving such an opportunity. It is quite reasonable to use the combined approach, creating a position in parts.

In what cases is it possible and justified to play on impulse against sharp jumps? I will describe two cases.

The first case is a sharp jump against the current trend, resulting from the release of secondary economic data or data that came out close to consensus. Against such "seemingly" impulses one can play immediately. Often jumps in the output of the secondary data is only 20-30 pips. As a rule, such jumps are quickly "extinguished", that is, they recoup back. Here, by the way, you can use limit orders, which are placed "under the output" of the data in advance. Example: Imagine that there is a strong uptrend in the euro against the dollar, and good data comes from retail sales in the United States. If the euro falls by 20-30 pips as a result, you can immediately make a purchase on such a move. Retail sales data is volatile and less important. Most likely, such a fall will be quickly bought out.

Secondary data is for professional managers and offers the opportunity to enter/increase position with the departing train.

Here is what Peter Pushkarev writes about secondary data and false breakdowns in the book "The Art of Being Meek":

“A possible false breakdown filter is a situation where an attempt to breakdown a level occurs after the release of insignificant, secondary information. Such events can cause a slight price twitch, and even sometimes spasmodic, which gives the impression of a decisive start. Except in rare cases, the breakdown during the release of secondary news is almost always false and the attempt fails. ”

Even data that is of paramount importance in a strong trend does not always change the overall picture and can easily recoup back. By the way, the price behavior in response to the output of statistical data can serve as an additional clue about the future direction of the market and be used as a separate indicator. If, for example, negative data for a currency comes out and the currency falls slightly for a short time and quickly bounces back, this is a sign of strength (strong price action).

# Chapter 9

# The Big Picture

This book is about trading and investing in financial markets. Its main goal is to help the reader create his own method. This goal is achieved by a critical analysis of various theories and the establishment of relationships between elements and practical observations. We hope that the book will help you transform the knowledge set into a plastic understanding of the markets. This, in turn, will allow you to save time on developing your shopping style as a whole and to make more effective such key elements as using information, finding your comfort zone, structuring your portfolio.

So that the reader can form his own expectations from the book, we have offered several short discussions about observing the goals that investors set when reading such books. Financial markets are a kind of informational jungle. The opinions of its participants are intertwined and changing in the most bizarre way, theories are built on the shaky ground of assumptions and are often misleading, and the information sometimes turns out to be incorrect or misinterpreted. In the financial market, as in the real jungle, in one case, you can be a winner, and in the other, a victim. The question of who you really are, a hunter or prey, will haunt you constantly. If such an entry did not scare you and did not cool your desire to succced in the investment market. Welcome to the ranks of the multi-million army of profit hunters! Do not be mistaken, dear reader: you are unlikely to be smarter, more talented, more educated or more successful than many other market participants. As a rule, it ultimately succeeds those in whom all these qualities are optimally combined. Those who are just embarking on this path face the task of simply surviving, although, to admit, in the information jungle, the chances of newcomers for survival are low. In the conditions of a growing market, a buyer can make a profit relatively easily and therefore sometimes he is filled with confidence in his talent, without drawing conclusions from the mistakes made. After the market "shaking" in 2014, everyone understands the consequences of wrong investment decisions!

Want to know how others earn money to learn how to do it yourself? Good idea, but who will you learn from? In the author's opinion, the well-known phrase “On Wall Street, everyone says they want ... no one listens to each other anyway” is not entirely true, since few market participants can really explain how he earned money; in most cases, people either boast about their successes, or pour out the soul to their interlocutor. Successful traders, as a rule, quite concisely describe the idea that became the basis of a successful transaction and it is difficult to draw any recommendations from their narration. The losers, on the contrary, tell in detail and emotionally about some “excellent” idea that came to their mind; on additional aspects taken into account when entering the transaction; about the subsequent "wrong" market behavior; About, that they were smarter than those who later realized their mistake or did not take into account any circumstances at all; and also about how they were unlucky. It is especially sad to hear the stories of losers, who claim that they took into account literally all aspects of the transaction. Does the fact of financial losses not convince such people that they managed to take into account not everything? However, the voluminous self-justification of the losers is equal to as well as short reports of the winners, which, as a rule, do not help the investor either to take his first steps on the market, or to improve the acquired skills.

Perhaps, a respected beginner or an experienced investor, sincerely believes that he manages to earn money thanks to a correctly made market forecast? I am sure that there are such. However, often an insider, even informed in advance of any important event for the market, subsequently discovers with surprise that he has missed one or several significant market movements.

You do not agree? In this case, let us cite as an example the history of the bankruptcy of the Long-Term Capital Management (LTCM) fund, which occurred in 1998. Ironically, two Nobel Prize winners worked in it! As one of the reasons for the collapse of the company, they cited, is the fact that they did not take into account the correlation of various markets, a factor that seemed to be existing for a long time and widely known. However, in this case, according to them, the market behavior exceeded all "reasonable" expectations. "Markets can remain irrational for a much longer time than investors can be liquid," Maynard Keynes once said of just such cases. A pessimistic conclusion suggests itself: it is impossible to take into account all factors, even if Nobel laureates are working in the company, which was confirmed by the history of the LTCM bankruptcy.

So, the book does not offer you knowledge in general as the key to success. It is aimed at sifting popular methodological messages in order to leave few more or less practically useful. However, the reader does this work himself with the help of various points of view selected in the book. This work, according to the author, should help the reader to create a suitable foundation for his own portfolio management style.

Why is independent critical work important? Own knowledge helps only when they are freed from the delusions imparted to us by popular theories and underlying market thinking. The point is not that these theories are wrong; they are often tested on a time interval that is several times longer than the average life expectancy of a trader. Sometimes these or other theories are recognized as wrong but in this case their authors are not responsible for your results!

In connection with the concept of “knowledge,” another question arises: is “big” knowledge a guarantee of success? To answer this question, we will give a story. Once upon a time, several professionals shared with the author their observations on the work of specialists in banking services sales and one story seemed very instructive to him. A certain bank has developed a new complex product. Of the two sales professionals trained in connection with its use, one perfectly understood the essence of the product and the specifics of its pricing and the second decided that this topic was too complicated for him to understand. The first expert to the question of customers about why the product is so “expensive” (buyers always resent its high cost, and sellers—cheap!) gave a lengthy description of the pricing process. The second was outraged by this question and answered, that he also needs to earn. The paradox of the situation was that in the next six months, the first specialist did not succeed in sales while the work of the second proved to be very effective.

Apparently, the reason for this state of affairs should be sought in the fact that for buyers, investors, and traders, the essence of the product was not important. By and large, they had a very vague idea of it. This begs the question: can these people be considered incompetent? Certainly not, because of the money they earned! The lack of understanding of the subject can be condemned by the teacher, and the result of the investor’s work only indirectly depends on his knowledge.

Therefore, the question of how much knowledge an investor should have is not entirely practical. More precisely, the question is what knowledge and other qualities one must possess in order to make money on the market. Although it is difficult to give an unequivocal answer, it seems that the personality of an investor and his own trading approach based on it, which consists of emphasis in analyzing the market and position management style, play a dominant role in achieving success. The author hopes that the book will help readers to reduce the number of their own mistakes on the way of developing such an approach.

This is the concluding part of the book. Much of what was said earlier refers to the first part of the book, which discusses the basic theories of finance, as well as technical analysis and liquidity analysis. The author seeks to show that theory and fundamental analysis are useful for a common understanding of financial markets but upon closer analysis, it turns out that they are useful to a private investor more for "pushing away", that is, as a kind of framework from which to build your approach, to understand how to work in the information environment. With a certain degree of confidence, it can be said that many readers can be encouraged to think about how to increase the efficiency of working with information. This part also discusses the concepts and assumptions that are behind the technical analysis. This is important in order to compare the effectiveness of fundamental and technical analysis. In addition, the concept of liquidity is discussed,

In the second part the book briefly highlighted the theory of behavioral finance. It is extremely important for investors, as it shows what subconscious motives guide us and what mistakes they lead to. This part may be too rich but it gives a good idea of how to optimize your internal decision-making mechanism.

The third part briefly summarizes the history of crises and general conclusions about their origins, which can be applied in the future. It is useful for investors to remember the feelings of their predecessors in order to be better morally prepared for activities during crises.

All in all, remember, in a single system, how, at different stages of the market, the interaction of information, liquidity and

psychology leads to an elusive change in market forces and a change in concepts such as risk.
Let us now dedicate this time in discussing one of the main skills vital for traders and investors—the ability to structure positions for survival and success in the market. The importance of this skill is not always clear to beginners, namely, it is a "magic wand" in a situation of increased volatility, such as during crises.

Now, the binding of investing with options with technical analysis is done. It is designed for those who are well aware of the basic strategies of options.
Note the following that happen mostly over a period of five years:

1. The role of governments in supporting markets will grow.
2. The role of regulators will grow.
3. The number of unexpected situations and sharp market fluctuations will increase.

Over the past few years, governments have, one after another, taken packages of measures that were supposed to stimulate a way out of the crisis or the entire industry, or individual companies. Let us recall, for example, the most well-known examples of the rescue by the US government—the deduction of the insurance giant AIG and the leader of the automotive industry General Motors in 2008 from bankruptcy. There were many such stories in Russia as well. Such events, on the one hand, increased stability in the economy, but, on the other hand, modified the concept of competition in the market: the probability of the disappearance of large inefficient players and the renewal of market participants has decreased. From the point of view of financial markets, the relationship between stocks and debt instruments was distorted: shareholders of companies receiving aid packages were "eroded", i.e., they lost their stake in the company, while bond investors had to restructure debt, i.e.

were able to get money back, although much later than they expected.

Governments worked together with regulators, who, on the one hand, supported the financial sustainability of financial systems by injecting liquidity, and on the other hand, streamlined markets and financial institutions. This is not the first example of such actions. Once, back in 1907, DP Morgan prevented a full-scale crisis by creating and financing a consortium of financial institutions, which offered money to key market players to fix the payments. Thus, a chain of bankruptcies was prevented that threatened the stability of the entire economy.

The success of this consortium served as one of the main reasons for creating the Federal Reserve System. And in the memorable days of the beginning of the crisis of 1929, she was able to raise the liquidity of the system, that is, to be as effective as the Morgan consortium. However, the Fed soon raised the stakes, strangling the economy and creating the prerequisites for the Great Depression. The reason for this was the desire of governments to avoid a crisis of overproduction by freeing the economy from unviable enterprises resulting from speculations of previous years of growth. "Eliminate labor resources, liquidate stocks, liquidate farmers, and liquidate real estate"—such advice was given by then Finance Minister Andrew Mellon to President Hoover.

An analysis of the sad experiences of this period and the preceding crises led economists to conclude that the best recipe for dealing with financial crises is a combination of setting low rates and providing liquidity.

It was this recipe that the Fed, the Central Bank of Japan, and the European Central Bank resorted to in the struggle against the 2008 crisis in the USA and the subsequent crisis phenomena in Europe.

These phenomena were largely unprecedented and the crisis of 2008 could be said to have surpassed the Great Depression in terms of destructiveness.

"The seriousness of the current crisis underlines the fact that the shocks of the American economy in the fall of 2008 were almost more than all the tests of the Great Depression," wrote Christina Romer, the former chairman of the Council of Economic Advisers to the Obama administration.

"The graph" compares three key indicators of both periods: a decline in household welfare and indicators of the reaction of the stock market and the credit market. In 1929, following the collapse of the stock market in October, a rapid recovery in stock prices followed. At the same time, housing prices fell slightly. As a result, the wealth index fell by only 3% between December 1928 and December 1929. In 2008, share prices fell by 24% in September-October, while housing prices fell by 9% during the year. In general, in the period from December 2007 to December 2008, the level of family well-being fell by 17%, exceeding more than five times the decrease in 1929.

This short analysis explains the reasons that prompted governments and regulators to large-scale intervention in the markets: they realized that they needed to support, change and strengthen the entire financial system as a key organ for blood supply to markets. Therefore, firstly, the central banks provided liquidity to the markets, which eased the burden of the 2008 crisis and continues to play a key role in the markets today.

However, central banks not only increased liquidity but also significantly tightened the requirements for the banking sector. Since 2012, new recommendations developed by the Basel Committee have become mandatory. One of the consequences of these changes was a sharp increase in capital requirements for the necessary trading operations in financial markets. As a result, these operations became unprofitable and were significantly reduced. The remaining dealer banks ("market makers") can no longer, as they did before, wait out the wrong position until the market recovers, absorbing market shocks. Under the new rules, they must "reserve" the capital for the transaction, which is very expensive. Therefore, they are limited to relatively small positions. Because of this, in moments of market fluctuations in the absence of banks, every major seller is able to "push through" prices, i.e., to cause them to collapse.

This trend is reinforced by new players—the algorithmic traders. They use robots, the automated trading systems capable of creating surges in the number of transactions, i.e., on the one hand, the number of one-stage peaks of trading activity has sharply increased, and on the other, the layer of dealers, which neutralized similar peaks, has been weakened. Thus, the amount of market liquidity has fallen, that is, not money available to the economy, which the central banks mean by the term "liquidity" but the possibility of exchanging securities for money and vice versa.

New requirements for banks and these new players in the market have led to an increasing sharp increase in market volatility. Take, for example, sigma—historical volatility indicators for the month (standard deviation of daily percentage market changes for the previous month is used as the value of volatility) of the US stock market (S & P 500), the Russian stock market (RTS index) and the foreign exchange market (USD/RUB). Movements of more than three sigma, according to statistics, should occur no more than three times a year.

In the past, such an abundance of sharp price movements was not observed. This is an obvious consequence of a decrease in market liquidity, but not only. Problems with the debts of southern European countries, geopolitical events in the Arab countries and Ukraine, the fall in oil prices, of course, were the initial catalysts for these changes.

The dynamics of recent years are forcing all traders and investors to develop tactics that will take into account the new inclination of the market to increase the number of very sharp movements. And the part of the book devoted to the structuring of positions will be important for those who are concerned about this problem.

Your style should also take into account your personal "big picture" outlook for the next few years. What awaits international markets in the coming years? Most likely, the role of regulators will at least not weaken, i.e., control over markets will increase simultaneously with the provision of liquidity to the economy. These trends will decline as structural reforms begin in Europe and Japan. For example, Europe needs a reform of labor legislation, which will increase the possibility of employers to dismiss, thereby facilitating the hiring of new workers. However, politicians have not yet gained courage to embark on reforms that will affect almost the entire population.

If you try to simply explain the impact of the governments of developed countries on the markets in the next few years, then we can say that they are searching for a new relationship between capital and society, or rather, entrepreneurs and bureaucrats. Most likely, until a certain balance is found, systemic growth will not begin. At the current stage, the capital lost the battle: taxes increased, financing became more complicated. But one day, voters will demand real jobs from governments. Governments, as always, will take the path of least resistance and create new agencies to accelerate the development of a particular area. As has already happened in Europe and the United States, these agencies are not likely to find projects that are ready for implementation, since bureaucrats will not be able to prepare them.

When the problem of unemployment reaches a critical size, they will elect those who will be ready for reforms and create conditions for returning to the capital scene. These complex transformations of the consciousness of society will require two or three electoral cycles, that is, another ten years. Until that time, unemployment will be compensated for by high social costs, and this will create a risk of inflation that can get out of control and cause heavy damage to the markets.

In recent years, in order to raise funds, the governments of the United States and Europe have resorted to the method used by their predecessors for thousands of years: they lower the purchasing power of money, devaluing along with them the size of the debt. In the past, this was achieved by reducing the content of the precious metal in coins. Today, they devalue savings by lowering interest rates on savings in the context of a simultaneous increase in the cost of public sector services. At the same time, a new euphemist "price increase" appeared: the universal appreciation is seen with the naked eye, but thanks to the cunning methods of calculation, "inflation" does not grow at the same time.

## Sophisticated (Monetary)

Politics are forcing older generations of voters, who once used the gifts of politicians, to quietly help current governments stabilize their economies. At the same time, the latter do not have the opportunity to create jobs for their children and in fact try to achieve some kind of stability for their grandchildren. Consciously or not, political consultants calculate which "piece of wealth" will get to which generation, at what point in their lives, because they decide which generation's votes are more important for them to win the next election.

But even this "scientific" process hardly fully takes into account the consequences of the current stage of labor productivity growth: today more and more highly paid jobs are Europeans and Americans losing to machines, and not cheap labor from Asia.

There is another factor of long-term instability – the rate of consumption of nations that have wealth. "Old money"—Americans and Europeans—as you know, helped the world economy through significant consumption. New Asian wealth owners are in no hurry to spend it. Moreover, as Asian economies continue to be export-oriented, the fear of weakening their main trading partners leads to even less propensity to spend. A certain historical relationship between capital and consumption has broken, and this affects the dynamics of business development, the credit cycle, and the creation of jobs around the world.

Thus, markets fear the worsening problems of unemployment and rising social tensions, uncontrolled inflation, destabilizing factors of the international division of labor and resources, etc. These clusters of problems will be confronted by readers, and their ability to properly understand them along with other problems of geopolitics will largely depend on the result of investing.

But a bunch of problems should not repel investors. Problems, the consequences of which were incomprehensible, have always existed, and investors have been successful in the most unusual circumstances. Recall the well-known recipe for success: to earn in the financial markets, you need to buy low and sell high. The mention of problems only emphasizes the meaning put by one emigrant in the following statement: “I moved to America because I heard that there was money lying on the road. Came - and the truth! Only now I have torn my back, trying to lift them. ” By analogy, we can say that in the financial markets money is also “lying around”, only in order to raise it, knowledge and good luck and hard work are required. The author hopes that this book will help you solve this difficult task and succeed!

# Conclusion

As mentioned earlier, swing trading is not a strategy but rather a way to trade. It is based on following the trend on the medium-term range (daily, maximum weekly timeframe). Transactions can have a duration of several hours or several days. They mostly open only in the presence of a pronounced trend. Sluggish market and periods of strong volatility are ignored.

Swing Trading involves maintaining positions for a short and medium time period (from two days to several weeks). The main goal is to catch the trend and take a trading position in the direction of the existing price movement. Swing trading has a wider range of price movements and therefore allows you to get a good risk/reward ratio compared to intraday trading and scalping. Swing trading can be conducted according to indicators as well as include a combination of technical and fundamental analysis.

Using swing trading gives us a relatively safe income with little effort. Working with the trend without the use of complex schemes or strategies, as well as the short duration of transactions help to achieve success. Following the crowd without a fight against the trend. In addition, the swing trading strategy has a flexible analysis system that helps to maximize the adaptation of trading to your preferences. However, it is worth noting that this method of trading does not suit every newbie—only having experience and understanding the situation helps to properly adjust your trading on it.

# Swing Trading with Options

*A Crash Course for Beginners to Highly Profitable Day and Swing Trade*
*Proven Strategies & Techniques to Trade Options, Stocks, Forex and Day Trading*

William L . Anderson

# Table of Contents

# Introduction

Congratulations on purchasing Swing Trading with Options: A Crash Course for Beginners to Highly Profitable Day and Swing Trade and thank you for doing so.

Welcome to the next step in trading: Swing Trading with options, forex, cryptocurrency, and even moving on to day trading. We'll start first with simple swing-trading strategies including long-options, long-option approaches, and short calls. Then we'll move on to synthetic options positions and iron-butterfly swing and day trading. Next we'll look at forex, or foreign exchange trading, and how it can be applied both in the swing and day trading, then pile on with a bit of cryptocurrency trading.

That's just the first half! Then you get a blow-by-blow playbook on how to become the best day trader you could ever be in just a few simple chapters. Learn how to choose a day trading broker, a trading platform, and a few key strategies that have been proven to be the most lucrative and successful time and time again. You'll learn how to create a stock watch list, use intraday scans, and how to plan a successful day that you can repeat again and again and again.

Finally we'll explore support and resistance levels, price action, candlestick and trade management, and how to understand the psychology of the trading masses and use it to your advantage.

We'll also hammer in throughout this book that successful swing and day trading isn't just about the strategy. It's about the skill. You'll need to practice, practice, practice and then practice some more before you really start to feel comfortable and develop your own trade style.

Swing and day trading aren't the easiest hobbies to get into. You're going to have to put in the work and effort. But we'll be by your side on your journey to become the best trader that you can be, and help you extract profits from the market that others won't.

Thank you so much for taking the time to check out this book. We know that the publishing world is flooded with books on how to "get rich quick" with day and swing trading, but we have put a lot of effort into making sure that this book is useful, practical, and doesn't hold false promises. We know that it took some work to find this, so thank you for your time and interest. Good luck!

# Chapter 1
# Delving Into Swing Trading Strategies

Want to start out with the best advantage swing trading can offer over long-term, position trading? The best place to start is with long-options, the most basic answer to that question. These are cheap, extremely leveraged, low risk assets that have easy entry points. There are a few dangers, including quick depreciation. According to recent statistics, long-options with expiration dates become void three-quarters of the time! However, that isn't prophecy. This doesn't actually mean they become worthless, but it's what a lot of investment writers claim to warn people off of long-options.

## Long-Option Approach

So what is the "75% rule"?

The quantity of long alternatives that end up worthless depends on holding the positions open until termination. While swing trading, you would once in a while, if at any time, do this. In any case, the measurement has prompted the fantasy that most choices lose profit. The choice of alternatives and timing of passage have everything to do with beneficial results or misfortunes. The task of a 75% misfortune proportion is wrong. The facts confirm that venders have explicit points of interest. They get cash as opposed to paying, so time decay can actually work in their favor. Choosing a short position enables you to profit from inversions. Likewise, with long choices however, there is less stress over time decay or price instability. Indeed, a short call may make you money, notwithstanding when the fundamental value averages everything out. This happens when price decay outpaces natural worth. So it's genuine that short-call traders have impressive favorable circumstances over long-choice brokers, yet they have many, many, many more risks that they're taking.

Among the dangers of short calls are the most evident: Extreme risk. Avoid risk by away taking little losses in order to maintain a strategic distance from greater ones later, moving forward, or covering uncovered positions. You can likewise maintain a strategic distance from these by limiting movement to secured calls. While this guarantees that you won't lose a ton (if the correct strike and termination are chosen), it doesn't ensure against conceivably serious drawback dangers. Secured calls additionally necessitate that you possess 100 offers for every choice you sell.

A long option or call, in correlation, controls 100 portions of stock and replaces by and large proprietorship at a little level of the expense. A 50 strike alternative may cost $250 or less, contingent upon strike ad termination. Owning 100 offers costs $5,000. This is the basic advantage to long-choice swing exchanging: influence and benefit potential.

All things considered, shouldn't something be said about that 75% measurement? Most prevailing logic and institutional knowledge claims that options are just unreasonably unsafe for purchasing since three out four become useless. In swing trading, however, you don't mean to hold options until termination. The perfect exchange will last somewhere in the range of three and five days— a swing trade— some of the time more and in some cases less.

The 75 percent rule is a deceptive end also. Actually, all things considered just 10 percent of all choices get practiced in a present cycle. In any case, this does not mean the other 90 percent lapse useless. Another 60 percent of options are shut before they expire. The staying 30 percent influence long-call merchants contrarily, yet keep in mind that is likewise influences short dealers decidedly. The staying 30 percent are liable to lapse useless, thus 30 percent—not 75 percent—is a number nearer to reality. This influences long-alternatives brokers contrarily, yet keep in mind that is additionally influences short merchants emphatically.

Before moving on, it's useful to have a passing familiarity with several definitions you'll see cropping up in this book and within the trade of swing-trading and day trading in general.

## Definition: What is a writer/ what is writing?

A writer (in some cases alluded to as a grantor) is the dealer of an option who opens a situation to gather an excellent installment from the purchaser. Writers can sell call or put choices that are secured or revealed. A revealed position is additionally alluded to as an exposed choice. For instance, the proprietor of 200 portions of stock can sell a call choice on those offers to gather a premium from the purchaser of the choice; the position is secured in light of the fact that the author possesses the stock that underlies the alternative and has consented to sell those offers at the strike cost of the agreement.

## Separating Writer

An alternative is revealed when the writer does not have a balancing position in the record. For instance, the creator of a put option, who consents to buy assets at an agreement's strike cost, is revealed if there is definitely not a comparing short position to counterbalance the danger of purchasing shares.

The essential goal for options writers is to create pay by gathering premiums when contracts are offered to open a position. The biggest additions happen when those that have been sold terminate out of the cash. For call writers, alternatives terminate out of the cash when the offer value closes beneath the strike cost of the agreement. Out-of-the-cash puts terminate when the cost of the underlying offers closes over the strike cost. In the two circumstances, the writer keeps the whole premium for the closeout of the agreements.

Secured writing is viewed as a traditionalist technique for creating salary. Revealed or stripped alternative composing is profoundly theoretical in light of the potential for boundless misfortunes.

## Call Writing

Secured call writing for the most part brings about one of three results. At the point when the choices lapse useless, the author keeps the whole premium and can compose alternatives again to produce salary. On the off chance that the choices terminate in the cash, the writer can either give the basic offers a chance to be summoned at the strike cost or purchase the alternative to close the position.

The results of composing revealed calls are commonly the equivalent with one key distinction. On the off chance that the offer value closes at a profit, the writer should either purchase stock on the open market to convey offers to the options purchaser or close the position. The misfortune is dictated by the expense of purchasing stock over the strike cost or shutting the alternative position, short the premium when the position was opened.

Put Writing

At the point when a put writer is short the fundamental stock, the position is secured if there is a comparing number of offers undercuts in the record. In the occasion the short alternative is growing in value, the short position counterbalances the loss of purchasing the offers. In a revealed position, the author should either purchase shares at the strike cost or purchase the situation to close. The misfortune is the contrast between the market estimation of the offers and the strike cost or the expense of shutting the position, short the underlying premium.

## What is a Long Position?

A long position—otherwise called just a "long"—is the purchasing of a stock, item, or cash with the desire that it will ascend in worth. Holding a long position is a bullish view.

Long positions and long calls are regularly utilized with regards to purchasing an options contract. The merchant can hold either a long call or a long put choice, contingent upon the standpoint for the basic resource of the choice contract.

A speculator who wants to profit by an upward value development in an advantage will "go long" on a call alternative. That option allows the purchaser the alternative to purchase the underlying for a predetermined and specific cost.

On the other hand, a financial specialist who anticipates that an underlying's cost should fall—are bearish—will be long on a put choice—and keep up the privilege to sell the benefit at a specific cost.

Remember: A long position is something contrary to a short position (short).

The Many Faces of Long

Long is one of those contributing terms that can have different implications, contingent upon where it is utilized. The most widely recognized importance of long is in the time allotment a venture is held. In any case, the term long has an alternate importance when utilized in choices and prospects contracts.

Key Points

A long—long position—alludes to the purchase of a stock or asset with the desire it will increment in worth—a bullish way to think.

A long position in options contracts demonstrates the holder claims the underlying.

A long position is something contrary to a short position.

In choices, being long can allude either to altogether responsibility for resource or being the holder of an alternative on the benefit.

Being long on a stock or bond speculation is an estimation of time.

Long Holding Investment

Going long on a stock or security is putting practice in the capital markets. With a long-position venture, the financial specialist buys an asset and claims it with the desire that the cost is going to rise. This speculator ordinarily has no arrangement to sell the security soon. In reference to holding values, long alludes to an estimation of time.

The purchase and hold system saves the financial specialist the requirement for consistent market-watching or market-timing, and enables time to deal with3r the inescapable high points and low points. Furthermore, history is one's ally, as the securities exchange definitely acknowledges, after some time.

Obviously, that doesn't mean there can't be sharp, portfolio-destroying drops en route, which can be deadly on the off chance that one happens directly previously, state, a financial specialist was intending to resign—or expected to sell property for reasons unknown. A delayed bear market can likewise be inconvenient, as it regularly supports short-dealers and those wagering on decays.

At long last, going long in the inside and out possession sense implies a decent measure of capital is tied up, which could bring about passing up different chances.

Long Position Options Contracts

In the realm of alternatives puts, the term long has nothing to do with the estimation of time yet rather addresses the owning of a basic resource. The long position holder is one who as of now holds the resource in their portfolio.

At the point when a dealer purchases or holds a call options contract from a choices writer they are long, because of the power they hold in having the option to purchase the benefit. A financial specialist who is long a call choice is one who purchases a call with the desire that the basic security will increment in worth. The long position call holder accepts the benefit's worth is rising and may choose to practice their choice to get it by the lapse date.

Be that as it may, few out of every odd broker who holds a long position accepts the product's worth will increment. The merchant who claims the asset in their portfolio and accepts the worth will fall can purchase a put option contract. Regardless they have a long position since they can sell the fundamental resource they hold in their portfolio. The holder of a long position put accepts the cost of an advantage will fall. They hold the choice with the expectation that they will almost certainly sell the fundamental resource at a profitable cost by the expiry.

Along these lines, as you see, the long position for an options contract can express either a bullish or bearish estimation relying upon whether the long contract is a put or a call.

Conversely, the short position on an alternatives contract does not claim the stock or other hidden resource but rather acquires it with the desire for selling it and after that repurchasing it at a lower cost.

Long Futures Contracts

Speculators and organizations can likewise go into a long forward or prospects contract to support against antagonistic value developments. An organization can utilize a long fence to secure a price tag for an item that is required later on. Prospects vary from options in that the holder is committed to purchase or sell the product. They don't get the opportunity to pick however, and should finish these activities.

Assume a manufacturer accepts the cost of gold is ready to turn upwards for the time being. The firm can go into a long futures deal with its gold provider to buy gold in a half a year from the provider at $2,000. In half a year, regardless of whether the cost is above or underneath $2,000, the business that has a long position on gold prospects is committed to buy the gold from the provider at the concurred contract cost of $2,000. The provider, thus, is committed to convey the physical item when the agreement lapses.

Theorists additionally go long on prospects when they accept the costs will go up. They don't really need the physical ware, as they are just keen on gaining by the value development. Prior to expiry, an examiner holding a long prospects contract can sell the agreement in the market.

Upsides and downsides of a Long Position

<u>Upsides</u>
Secures a cost

Points of confined risk

Works together with smart market execution

Downsides

Endures in sudden value changes/momentary moves

May terminate before preferred position is figured it out

True Examples of Long Positions

For instance, suppose Jane expects Amazon (AMZN) to increment in cost and buys 50 portions of it. Jane is consequently said to "be long" 50 portions of AMZN.

Presently, we should consider a December 17 call choice on Amazon (AMZN) with a $100 strike cost and $1.50 premium. In the event that Jane is as yet bullish on the stock, she may choose to buy or go long one AMZN call alternative—one choice compares to 50 offers—rather than obtaining the offers inside and out as he did in the past model. At expiry, if MSFT is exchanging above $100, Jim will practice his entitlement to purchase on his long choice to buy 50 portions of AMZN at $100. The writer of the contract—the short position—that Jim purchased must sell him the 50 offers at the 100 dollars cost.

Taking a long position does not constantly imply that a financial specialist hopes to pick up from an upward development in the cost of the benefit or security. On account of a put choice, a descending direction in the cost of the security is gainful for the financial specialist.

Suppose another financial specialist, Jax as of now has a long position in AMZN for 100 offers in her portfolio yet is presently bearish on it. She takes a long position on one put choice. The put choice is exchanging for $1.30 and has a strike cost of $100 set to lapse December 17. At the season of expiry, if AMZN dips under

$100 Jane will practice the long put choice to sell her AMZN shares at the strike cost of $100. For this situation, the choice writer must purchase Jane's offers at the settled upon $100 cost, regardless of whether the offers are exchanging at less on the open market.

## Long/Short-Call Strategy, Uncovered Short Style

First off, let's define what a short-call is now. You may have intuitively guessed that it's the opposite of a long-call, where the trader believes that the asset will increase above the price purchased.

## What Is a Short Call?

A short call alternative position where the writer does not claim an equal position in the underlying asset spoken to by their choice contracts. Making a short call is an option exchanging methodology which the broker is wagering that the cost of the benefit on which they are setting the choice is going to drop.

## How Does a Short Call Work?

A short call system is one of two basic ways choices dealers can take bearish positions. It includes selling call alternatives, or calls. Considers give the holder of the alternative the privilege to purchase a hidden security at a predefined cost.

On the off chance that the cost of the fundamental security falls, a short call procedure benefits. In the event that the value ascends, there's boundless introduction during the period of time the alternative is reasonable, which is known as a stripped short call. To constrain misfortunes, a few dealers will practice a short call while owning the basic security, which is known as a secured call.

## Certifiable Example of a Short Call

Cotton Candy Company chooses to sell approaches portions of Lollipop Ventures to Microsoft. The stock is exchanging close $200 an offer and is in a solid upturn. Nonetheless, Microsoft trusts that the valuation of Lollipop Ventures is exaggerated, and dependent on a blend of key and specialized reasons, they trust it in the long run will tumble to $50 an offer. Cotton Candy Company consents to sell 500 calls at $140 an offer. This gives Microsoft the privilege to buy Lollipop shares at that particular cost.

Selling the call choice enables Cotton Candy to gather a premium forthright; that is, Microsoft pays up right away. In the event that the stock heads lower after some time, as the Cotton Candy suspects, Cotton Candy benefits on the distinction between what they got and the cost of the stock. If Lollipop stock drops to $50, then Cotton Candy still makes a profit.

Things can go amiss, be that as it may, if Lollipop offers keep on climbing, making boundless risk for Cotton Candy. For instance, say the offers proceed their upswing and go to $300 inside a couple of months. In the event that Cotton Candy makes a stripped call, Microsoft can execute the alternative and buy stock worth $30,000 for $12,000, coming about in an $18,000 exchanging misfortune for Cotton Candy.

In the event that the stock were to ascend to $350 before the choice lapses, Microsoft r could buy stock worth $35,000 for the equivalent $12,000, coming about in a $23,000 misfortune for Cotton Candy.

## Short Calls Versus Long Puts

As recently referenced, a short call system is one of two regular bearish exchanging methodologies. The other is purchasing put choices or puts. Put choices give the holder the privilege to sell a security at a specific cost inside a particular time allotment. Going long on puts, as dealer's state, is likewise a wagered that costs will fall, yet the procedure works in an unexpected way.

Cotton Candy Company still trusts Lollipop stock is set out toward a fall, yet it selects to purchase 200 $200 Lollipop puts. To do as such, the Cotton Candy Co. gathering must set up the $40,000 ($200 x 200) in real money for the choice. Cotton Candy presently has the privilege to power Microsoft, who is on the opposite side of the arrangement, to purchase the stock at this cost – regardless of whether Lollipop offers drop to Liquid's anticipated $75 an offer. In the event that they do, Cotton Candy has made a clean benefit – $18,000.

As it were, it's accomplishing a similar objective, directly through the contrary course. Obviously, the long put requires that Liquid shell out assets forthright. The bit of leeway is that not normal for the short call, the most Cotton Candy can lose is $11,000, or the absolute cost of the choice.

Key points

A short call is a procedure including a call choice, giving a merchant the right, however not the commitment, to sell a security.

A short call is a bearish exchanging technique, mirroring a wager that the security hidden the choice will fall in cost.

A short call includes more hazard however requires less forthright cash than a long put, another bearish exchanging technique.

.

Strategy 3: Naked Call Strategy

What is a Naked Call?

A bare call is a choices methodology wherein a speculator composes (sells) call choices on the open market without owning the fundamental security. This stands rather than a secured call technique, where the speculator possesses the fundamental security on which the call alternatives are composed. This system is here and there alluded to as a "revealed call" or a "short call."

Understanding Naked Call

A naked call enables a speculator to create income without really possessing the hidden security. Basically, the premium got is the sole thought process recorded as a hard copy a revealed call option. It is innately dangerous as there is constrained upside benefit potential and, in principle, boundless drawback misfortune potential.

The most extreme addition is the top notch that the choice writer gets forthright, which is generally credited to their record. Thus, the objective for the writer is to have the choice lapse useless.

The most extreme misfortune is hypothetically boundless on the grounds that there is no top on how high the cost of the fundamental security can rise. Notwithstanding, in increasingly functional terms, the dealer of the choices will probably repurchase them a long time before the cost of the fundamental ascents too far over the strike cost, in view of his/her hazard resistance and stop-misfortune settings.

The breakeven point for the writer is determined by including the premium got and the strike cost for the bare call.

An ascent in suggested unpredictability isn't alluring to the writer as the likelihood of the choice being in-the-cash, and accordingly being worked out, likewise increments.

Since the choice author needs the exposed get to lapse out-of-the-cash, the progression of time, or time rot, will positively affect this system.

Edge prerequisites, justifiably, will in general be very steep given the boundless hazard capability of this procedure.

Because of the hazard included, just experienced financial specialists who firmly accept that the cost of the hidden security will fall or stay level ought to attempt this propelled system. The edge prerequisites are regularly extremely high for this methodology because of the inclination for open-finished misfortunes, and the financial specialist might be compelled to buy shares on the open market preceding termination if edge edges are ruptured. The upside to the methodology is that the financial specialist could get salary as premiums without setting up a great deal of beginning capital.

Key points

A stripped call is an alternatives procedure where the speculator composes (sells) call choices without owning the fundamental security.

A stripped call has restricted upside benefit potential and, in principle, boundless drawback misfortune potential.

An exposed call's breakeven point for the author is its strike cost in addition to the premium got.

Utilizing Naked Calls

Once more, there is noteworthy danger of misfortune with composing revealed calls. Be that as it may, financial specialists who emphatically accept the cost for the basic security, for the most part a stock, will fall or remain the equivalent can compose call alternatives to acquire the premium. On the off chance that the stock remains underneath the strike cost between the time the choices are composed and their lapse date, at that point the alternatives writer keeps the whole premium less commissions.

On the off chance that the cost of the stock transcends the strike cost by the alternatives lapse date then the purchaser of the choices can request the dealer to convey portions of the basic stock. The alternatives merchant will at that point need to go beyond any confining influence market and purchase those offers at the market cost to offer them to the choices purchaser at the choices strike cost. On the off chance that, for instance, the strike cost is $60 and the open market cost for the stock is $65 at the time the choices contract is worked out, the choices vender will bring about lost $5 per portion of stock less the premium got.

The premium gathered will fairly counterbalance the misfortune on the stock yet the potential misfortune can at present be enormous. For instance, suppose a financial specialist felt that the solid bull keep running for Amazon.com (AMZN) was over when it at last leveled out in March 2017 close $852 per share. He/she composed a call alternative with a strike cost of $865 and a termination in May 2017. Be that as it may, after a short delay, the stock continued its rally and by the mid-May lapse, the stock came to $966. The potential obligation was the activity cost of $966 short the strike cost of $865, which came about in $101 per share. This is balanced by whatever premium was gathered toward the begin.

### Long/Short-Call Strategy Writing on the Short Side

One of the questions or suspicions you might have about writing or shorting options is that they're riskier than going long. A big misconception is that risk is limited to how much you invest in long calls, ultimately making them a safer choice. This is not always the case.

The short answer is "It depends".

Specifically, it ought to be evident that it relies upon the cost of the alternative.

Likewise with anything, if the cost is low enough it is smarter to purchase the choice than to sell it. In the event that you claim a choice and the cost is sufficiently high, it is smarter to sell the alternative than to keep it. In the event that you don't possess the alternative, you can in any case sell it, however observe the notice beneath.

Cautioning: There are exceptional perils recorded as a hard copy alternative. A portion of these risks are self-evident, however some are definitely not. A portion of these perils are reflected in standard likelihood hypothesis, yet some are most certainly not. These perils can be a lot more prominent when you are composing a choice than when you are simply selling an alternative you claim. Consequently, the examination of the market cost to the normal estimation of the alternative includes various issues in the two cases. Basic likelihood hypothesis with desires in dollar terms does not consider this distinction. A non-direct utility hypothesis that loads misfortunes not quite the same as additions is essential.

[Actually, all types of choices can be hazardous in the event that you don't have a clue what you are doing. Then again, choices can be utilized to make supported places that really have fewer hazards than ordinary stock speculations. Be that as it may, this subject without anyone else's input could fill an entire book. Since it isn't straightforwardly important to the essential issue of contrasting composition alternatives with getting them, I won't endeavor to cover this subject here, aside from one little bit of general guidance. You can constrain this potential peril by utilizing choices for just a little part of your portfolio.]

Thinking about dangers: A not really short answer

Purchasing choices include unexpected dangers in comparison to selling them. For a progressively complete correlation, we have to dissect these dangers independently.

Any value venture, with or without alternatives, has an essentially likelihood of a misfortune. Indeed, under any sensible model there is a non-zero likelihood that you will lose everything. Are choices more hazardous or more secure than stocks? Obviously, "it depends", yet in an unexpected sense in comparison to in the short answer. Truth be told, the danger of a similar exchange can be altogether different relying upon your point of view and how it fits into your general speculation technique.

Examination of purchasing alternatives

First think about purchasing alternatives (either puts or calls) and contrast that and purchasing or selling the basic stock. The numerical examination is equal for either puts or calls, however the discourse will easier in the event that we contrast purchasing calls with purchasing the stock. There are two different ways to set up the examination that have inverse outcomes as far as near hazard.

Assume we contrast purchasing 100 portions of stock and getting one approach 100 portions of stock. In the event that the stock goes up, and the choice is at or in the cash, the dollar gain from the choice is equivalent to the increase in estimation of the stock short the sum paid for the choice. On the off chance that the stock goes down, the misfortune on the stock is the cost of the stock, yet the greatest misfortune on the choice is just the cost paid for the alternative, which is less. Therefore, purchasing an approach a similar number of offers has less most pessimistic scenario hazard that purchasing the stock. Be that as it may, purchasing the alternative consistently has a fairly higher likelihood of misfortune. Any expansion in the stock cost makes an addition for the stock buy, however for the call the stock must go up enough to cover the time premium for the exchange to get the opportunity to earn back the original investment.

Assume rather we look at making a similar dollar interest in the stock or in approaches the stock. The most pessimistic scenario misfortune for each situation is the entire dollar estimation of the speculation. In any case, on account of the stock buy, this most pessimistic scenario possibly occurs if the cost of the stock goes to zero, however on account of the call alternative this most pessimistic scenario occurs if the cost of the stock is beneath the strike cost at the termination of the choice. This most extreme misfortune has an a lot higher likelihood for the call choice than for the stock buy. This more noteworthy likelihood of misfortune is repaid by the way that, if the stock goes up over the earn back the original investment point, the increase is a lot more prominent for the call alternative since it speaks to a lot more offers. There is a sensitive exercise in careful control between the bigger likelihood of misfortune and the shot of an a lot bigger addition. Rudimentary likelihood hypothesis accurately figures this parity and the net anticipated worth (that is, the probabilistic normal of the additions and misfortunes) for the situation wherein misfortunes and increases are weighted regarding their dollar esteem. On the off chance that you are chance loath, you should weight the misfortunes all the more vigorously, which requires the non-direct utility investigation referenced previously. On the off chance that your absolute interest in choices is little enough that the misfortune won't trouble you, than you don't should be hazard disinclined, and you can accept direct utility.

Investigation of selling alternatives

The investigation of hazard is totally unique for selling choices (either puts or calls) than for purchasing. When purchasing choices the greatest misfortune is the measure of the venture. When composing choices, the misfortune might be a lot more prominent than the underlying speculation. The most extreme addition is the value you get for the choice. Then again, you make an increase regardless of whether the stock cost moves the negative way, as long and the change is stock cost is not exactly the time-esteem premium you got. On the off chance that the adjustment in the stock cost is little enough, both composed puts and composed calls may make gains.

Once more, the examination requires adjusting increases and misfortunes of contrasting sizes and of varying probabilities. Under rudimentary likelihood hypothesis the normal benefit of composing a choice is only the negative of the normal benefit of getting it, disregarding exchange costs. Be that as it may, the hazard investigation isn't only the negative or turn around of the hazard from purchasing. Composing a put alternative for a given number of offers, the most extreme misfortune is never again a fixed number that is considerably less than the cost of the stock. The misfortune from a composed put alternative is equivalent to owning the stock, with the exception of the cost got for the choice. The most extreme misfortune from composing a call is equivalent to for undercutting the stock, at the end of the day, it is boundless. Once more, basic likelihood hypothesis will adjust these probabilistic increases and misfortunes dependent on a direct utility in dollar terms. On the off chance that your interest in alternatives is little enough for your utility to be straight, at that point you ought to compose choices when the market cost is over the normal return and you should purchase choices when the market cost is underneath the normal return. You ought to do each in precisely the contrary circumstances from the ones wherein you would do the other.

In any case, for the vast majority, the negative impact of a misfortune is more prominent per dollar than the constructive outcome of an addition, particularly as the measure of the misfortune gets more noteworthy. This is the undeniable threat from composing choices that was referenced previously.

Some more subtle perils emerge from certainty that the investigation may under gauge the likelihood of outrageous occasions. For stocks, the increases from good sudden occasions make up for the potential misfortunes from troublesome occasions. For purchasing alternatives, the potential increases are a lot more noteworthy than the most pessimistic scenario misfortunes, so a symmetric dispersion of sudden occasions really implies that the assessed expected estimation of the choice is not as much as its actual worth.

Be that as it may, for composed choices the potential increases are constrained yet the misfortunes are definitely not. With a symmetric conveyance of surprising occasions, the increases and misfortunes don't adjust. This is an inconspicuous point on the grounds that, by definition, these unforeseen occasions are outside the standard hypothetical model. In any case, that does not imply that the impact is irrelevant. Doing affectability investigation with sensible suppositions, this impact is regularly enough to make an apparently good exchange into an entirely negative one. That is a shrouded risk recorded as hard copy alternatives. When purchasing choices, this awry affectability just creates an unforeseen bonus, so it doesn't change an ideal exchange into an ominous one.

In synopsis, alternative contributing can be dangerous. Appropriate examination of hazard requires demonstrating the non-direct utility of every individual speculator. Straight utility should possibly be accepted if the sum in danger is little contrasted with the abundance of the person. Composing choices has a lower likelihood of misfortune, yet this qualities shroud the reality than composing alternatives includes extra types of hazard.

A short increasingly useful answer, in view of general propensities

The short answer was that the net expected estimation of any alternative relies upon the present market cost of the choice. That leaves open the inquiry, are alternatives for the most part over evaluated or under estimated with respect to anticipated worth?

It would be nothing unexpected if the market cost were in every case near the normal worth. That would be the consequence of an effective market. In any case, the choices market isn't productive in this sense. Rather, alternative evaluating is ruled by the open door for dynamic exchange reflected in Black-Scholes-Merton investigation and its elaborations and upgrades. This subject would require an any longer discourse, so think about just a single acknowledgment of the issue, to be specific influence.

Alternatives make the chance to make ventures with generous influence. Moreover, a wide scope of various influence esteems is conceivable just from the alternatives accessible on a solitary fundamental stock. There are numerous elements that influence the estimation of a choice, yet the impact of influence without anyone else's input is scientifically extremely basic. For a specific likelihood circulation at the cost of the fundamental stock, the normal estimation of two subsidiary ventures that vary just in influence is that the normal worth is increased by the measure of influence. Do choice costs mirror this scientific relationship? No they don't. The likelihood of dynamic exchange prompts a totally extraordinary relationship among the costs.

# Synthetic Option Positions Strategy

Synthetics are places that copy the hazard/remunerate profile of another position, commonly utilizing a blend of stock and alternatives. Understanding synthetics gave those floor dealers a solid establishment and profound information of choices. I need to enable you to pick up a similar knowledge into choices methodologies by disclosing how to utilize and translate synthetics.

Once upon a time, floor dealers utilized manufactured positions for exchange, which is an exchanging technique that looks to secure a hazard free benefit by getting one venture and all the while selling a comparative or related speculation at an alternate cost. This exchange was accessible in the good old days to choices merchants on the floors of the trades. In any case, today, with the expansion in figuring power and splendid PhDs coding algorithmic exchanging systems, these exchange openings are hard to stop by for the rest of the floor merchants and for retail dealers exchanging from their screens.

In any case, understanding synthetics still offers the alternatives broker a few potential advantages:

- They can help lower exchange costs
- They can help with proficient value revelation
- They can give increasingly proficient utilization of capital and adaptability

## The Skinny on Synthetics

Before we dive into the subtleties of how these advantages work, how about we pause for a moment to relate synthetics to plain-vanilla alternatives methodologies. This is actually very straightforward. Customary choices techniques with a similar strike cost and lapse month all have engineered counterparts. Also, as a result of the connection between calls, puts, and their particular fundamental stocks, synthetics have benefit/misfortune and hazard profiles that are like normal alternatives.

## Less Transaction Costs

In light of these connections, synthetics can be utilized to express altering suppositions about the course of the market without finishing off a current plain-vanilla exchange. By executing fewer exchanges, brokers can conceivably save money on exchange costs. How about we stroll through certain guides to see where the investment funds may originate from.

Assume a merchant is as of now long a put, yet he supposes the market may go higher and needs to get bullish, as well. He could sell the put and purchase a call, which would cause two commission expenses. Or on the other hand, he could purchase the hidden stock and clutch the put. That is only one commission. This works on the grounds that a long stock + long put on a similar strike and month is comparable to a long call.

Here's another situation. Assume a merchant is long a call and chooses to get short the market. Rather than selling the call and purchasing a put, it may be less expensive to short the stock and hold the call. A long call + short stock on a similar strike and month is identical to a long put.

Imagine a scenario in which a merchant is uncertain about heading, however needs to express an assessment about evolving unpredictability.

State the dealer is long two calls. She's uncertain about what direction the stock may move, however she supposes it could be a major move in a brief span period. Possibly there's a profit declaration, court case, or some other twofold occasion coming up. She could enter a long straddle to conceivably benefit from an expansion in unpredictability. Rather than purchasing two puts, she could short the stock, since short stock + long two calls is equal to a long straddle.

Assume a dealer is short two calls and is uncertain about course, however he supposes the stock may encounter a little move for the time being. He needs to enter a short straddle. Rather than shorting two puts, he could purchase the stock. Long stock + short two calls is identical to a short straddle.

All reasonable yet? Synthetics can appear to be confounding, yet they're extremely simply various methods for taking a gander at—or perhaps exchanging—a situation with a similar benefit/misfortune and hazard profile. We've perceived how synthetics can conceivably offer less exchange costs as opposed to exchanging typical choices. In Part 2, we'll take a gander at how synthetics can offer a couple more advantages: productive value revelation and proficient utilization of capital.

Spreads, Straddles, and other different leg choice techniques can involve generous exchange costs, including numerous commissions, which may affect any potential return. These are propelled choice methodologies and frequently include more serious hazard, and progressively complex hazard, than essential alternatives exchanges.

## Expanded Iron Butterfly Swing Trading

The iron butterfly approach, can be a strategy for trading with restricted loss, restricted profit options. It takes its name from the wingspreads recognized as a class of options. This method is established through the combination of spreading a called bear and a bull spreading group.

To accomplish the iron butterfly, you must ensure that both have the same expiry times that meet at mid-strike. When drawn, this setup looks like a butterfly, hence the name!

Iron butterfly approach includes: A–Call purchasing and purging, and options for putting.

B–Includes 4 contract alternatives.

C–With the same expiry date, all alternatives have the same underlying asset.

D–Three equidistant strikes are involved.

Result:

When the fundamental stock is though to not be unpredictable, an Iron Butterfly procedure has more likelihood of producing a constrained benefit. On the off chance that the instability expands, the misfortune is restricted. Therefore, this is a restricted misfortune, and, constrained benefit procedure.

Inspiration:

This methodology should be used only when the broker thinks that the unpredictability should be lessened. The thought behind this procedure is to gain however much premium as could reasonably be expected on choices that have been sold. As time continues to progress, choice premiums rot; and, henceforth the best time to execute this methodology would be in any event a few days before the expiry; for week after week alternatives – this is definitely not a severe principle however; and, the merchant needs to think about the instability.Make sure to only use this procedure when dealing with a high-liquidity asset, while the merchant risks task on gone alternatives.

Exhibit One:
Assume that asset ABC has been valued and trading for sixty dollars in August. Those who trade in options would make an iron butterfly by laying out the following:
1 – Purchasing an August 60 Call for $80

2 – Selling an August 50 Call for $400

3 – Selling an August 50 Put for $400

4 – Purchasing an August 40 Put for $80

# Chapter 2

## How to Swing Trade Forex

Lets take a thorough review of FOREX or foreign exchange (currency). This shortened name can also refer to the "foreign exchange market." Foreign exchange trading means that you're trading within currency markets across the globe. Today, forex trading is done 100 percent on the internet and through virtual platforms. Dealers in currency are an extended limb of substantial financial centers all over the world. This global aspect is a critical part of understanding forex, since you're trading in multiple different currencies of multiple countries around the world.

Forex started to gain momentum in the early 1970s. Why? Because universal fixed exchange rates no longer became necessary, allowing currency values and exchange rates to fluctuate violently within the intra-day. Forex is currently the world's biggest trading market and brokers, including your own, get their quotes all from the same place. This

Forex exchanging, which includes trading one cash for another on the outside trade showcase, isn't for the swoon of heart or the unpracticed.

No speculation is without hazard, yet forex tips the hazard meter further with its fast exchanging pace and high influence, which means speculators can rapidly lose more than their underlying ventures. Obviously, that implies you can likewise benefit at a similar speed, which — joined with liquidity — is the thing that draws in financial specialists to cash exchanging.

When choosing your forex dealer, you ought to think about exchanging stages and apparatuses; the quantity of money sets offered, influence maximums, client administration and, obviously, costs. In any case, looking at expenses is dubious in forex exchanging: While a few agents charge a commission, many publicize no commissions, procuring cash in the offer ask spread — the contrast between the value a merchant or seller is paying for the money (the offer) and the cost at which an intermediary or vendor is selling a money (the inquire). Intermediaries basically fold their expenses into that spread, broadening it and stashing the overabundance.

That is only one motivation behind why the quest for the best forex merchant is mind boggling. Another is that there is an assortment of merchants, a considerable lot of them unregulated or controlled in nations outside of the U.S. For our rundown of best cash exchanging merchants, we considered just those that are directed by the National Futures Association and the Commodity Futures Trading Commission.

# Chapter 3
# Introduction to Day Trading

So you're thinking about making the jump from swing trading to day trading. You've had relative success with swing trading for a while, and you want to cash in on working the market full time. But the important question is: Can you make a living off of day trading? And further: Can it be sustainable, despite market fluctuations?

There are a lot of informal investors and swing brokers out there, a large number of them taking part in the securities exchange at various levels. A few people use day exchanging professionally, time others simply exchange for a couple of hours daily to get some additional salary. One of the inquiries I get posed to a ton is, "when is the perfect time to make the jump to full-time day exchanging?"

Obviously, there is no general response to this inquiry, anyway there are a couple of contemplations that become an integral factor. It ought to be noticed that day exchanging isn't as impressive as it is frequently depicted to be. Exchanging stocks isn't tied in with "making bank" or carrying on with an extraordinary way of life. For full-time informal investors, exchanging stocks is a profession. This implies it requires work – work that involves sitting by the PC for quite a long time multi day gazing at screens. You are not ensured to make a huge number of dollars. Hell, you're not ensured to get paid. Day exchanging is one of only a handful couple of vocation decisions where you are not ensured a check, and you may even lose cash in the wake of contributing hours of your time.

Disheartened at this point? Try not to be. This isn't expected to scrutinize day exchanging as a profession. I exchange each day and I cherish it. This post is proposed to be a rude awakening that enables you to set reasonable desires that will enable you to find a way to accomplish your objectives. It's likewise imperative to take note of that this post is focused towards individuals who need to realize how to begin day exchanging full-time (which means you are leaving your other activity to seek after day exchanging full-time). A portion of these focuses won't be applicable to the individuals who exchange as an extracurricular movement.

Day Trading for a Living - A Few Necessary Pre-Requisites

Preparing – Before you significantly consider taking the jump towards turning into a full-time stock broker, you should ensure you are appropriately prepared. You wouldn't leave your place of employment to turn into an architect with no appropriate preparing, isn't that so? What are your of odds of succeeding? A similar rationale applies to exchanging. Begin building up the correct ability before considering a vocation in day exchanging. We have an assortment of free and paid assets to kick you off on your voyage.

Experience – You can peruse 1000 books on exchanging hypothesis and still get squashed by the business sectors. Hypothesis and practice are two distinctive ranges of abilities. Most brokers need to invest some energy really exchanging before they can get a genuine vibe for the business sectors.

Consistency – If you are notwithstanding thinking about turning into a full-time dealer, ensure you are exchanging reliably. This will enable you to set sensible desires for what's to come. Consistency is evidence that you have really built up a pertinent range of abilities. For another merchant, there's increasingly long haul an incentive in making $5,000/month for a year than making $200,000 your first month and $0 the remainder of the year. Certainly, one gives a higher transient fiscal worth, be that as it may, it is less economical over the long haul.

There is no "enchantment number" with regards to computing the measure of experience required. Various dealers will learn at various paces. One merchant might almost certainly wind up reliable in a year, while others may take a couple of years. It's critical to consider these next couple of contemplations.

Step by step instructions to Become a Day Trader Full-Time

Both day exchanging and increasingly traditional profession ways have their advantages. A traditional activity promises you a pay (and, some of the time, benefits), though day exchanging has higher hypothetical versatility and enables you to work for yourself. For most full-time informal investors, the greatest advantage is that you get the opportunity to do what you cherish at a vocation that reliably challenges you. Sound engaging? Consider the accompanying:

As a full-time informal investor, you will have less soundness, particularly as you begin. You will have great months, terrible months, extraordinary months, and rationally debilitating months. While this crazy ride of feelings is a piece of what makes day exchanging energizing, it can likewise be unpleasant whenever drawn closer inappropriately.

Monetary Considerations

Record for Your Day Trader Salary and Build a Safety Net

Exiting your profession means leaving your ensured salary stream. An informal investor's compensation is never ensured. Indeed, exiting your profession implies you get the opportunity to get away from the dullness of a 9-to-5, however in the event that you need to day exchange professionally, you should be set up for what pursues. Make a monetary arrangement.

You should set aside up enough cash to cover your costs for a long time. This will remove a portion of the worry from exchanging. In case you're not exchanging to pay the lease, you can settle on a lot more brilliant choices. Obviously, this methodology depends vigorously on your capacity to precisely compute this number. It's smarter to overestimate than disparage.

Make a point to represent everything, including:

Lease

Utilities

Sustenance

Toiletries

PDA bills

Protection

Excitement

And so forth

Try not to undercut yourself here. It might be anything but difficult to state, "I can live without excitement for a long time" until you are 2 months into gazing at the screens for 12 hours every day. Be practical, be exact, and plan appropriately.

On the off chance that your determined spending plan is $3000/month, set aside $72,000 and adhere to your financial limit. In the event that you can live off of $2000/month, set aside $48,000 for costs. This spending will differ impressively by individual yet the ultimate objective is the equivalent. You are covering your costs for the following couple of years with the goal that you can withdraw yourself from money related pressure and have the absolute best at progress.

Your Stock Trading Account

We talked about the significance of setting aside up enough cash to cover your costs. You will likewise need the money to support a record. By and by, the measure of cash vital will fluctuate by individual. You will require in any event $25,000 to day exchange routinely (in view of the Pattern Day Trader rule), anyway you can swing exchange with less. Pick a number and arrangement the records.

Picking a number is tied in with giving yourself the most obvious opportunity. Evaluating a record too soon before learning consistency is just going to put yourself at the danger of losing all the quicker. Beginning little cutoff points what you can do yet in addition restricts your hazard versus beginning bigger.

Remember, that your business ledger and money market fund are totally independent. You shouldn't need to destroy from your business ledger to take care of your exchanging expenses and you shouldn't need to dismantle from your exchanging record to cover costs.

## Different Considerations

### Opportunity Cost

As yet, we examined the money related arranging associated with taking a jump into full-time exchanging. It's likewise essential to concentrate on the open door cost of the jump. What are you surrendering by making the change?

For instance, on the off chance that you are making $100,000/year + benefits at your other activity, you are leaving a strong compensation and entering a vocation with an erratic pay. Will you have the option to find a comparable line of work following 2 years if exchanging doesn't go as arranged? Perhaps indeed, perhaps no. Make a point to represent this before focusing on the jump.

### Character Traits

When you become a full-time broker, you enter a universe of 100% responsibility. No one is causing you to get up each morning and nobody is instructing all of you day. You are the driver of your own salary and you are the one in particular who considerations enough to produce it. Ensure you have the control and legitimate hierarchical aptitudes important to capitalize on this procedure. Is it accurate to say that you are somebody who appreciates the self-rule of working for yourself or do you lean toward being determined what to do? It is safe to say that you are ready to hold yourself under tight restraints and adhere to a calendar or do you veer off and do your own thing? Do you need solidness or does hazard keep the business sectors energizing? Be set up for the way of life change similarly as you are set up for the money related changes.

Day exchanging stocks is an inconceivably remunerating profession way with a considerable rundown of advantages and advantages. This post was intended to help individuals get ready for the progress. The prizes of day exchanging professionally can be energizing, making a few people overlook the work associated with arriving. Give this present to you a chance to practical and help you adopt a sensible strategy to the change. Arrangement is critical. You can arrive on the off chance that you make the essential strides.

Most significant is to appreciate doing it, for the cash as well as to discover some new information regular and not to feel debilitated by absence of learning or age.

Progressions in innovation have guaranteed anybody with a working web association can begin day exchanging professionally. Be that as it may, while it may be conceivable, how simple is it and how on earth do you approach doing it? This page will take a gander at the advantages of day exchanging professionally, what and where individuals are exchanging, in addition to offer you some significant hints.

Is Day Trading For A Living Possible?

The principal thing to note is indeed, bringing home the bacon on day exchanging is a superbly reasonable vocation, yet it's not really simpler or less work than an ordinary daytime work.

The advantages are fairly that you work for yourself, and can design your work hours any way you need. Exchanging on a workstation likewise implies you can do it anyplace, whenever.

Be careful – there are numerous out there who guarantee to make a fortune on day exchanging, however generally these individuals are attempting to sell you something. Try not to accept the promotion or that there is such a mind-bending concept as "pain free income".

There are approaches to make it simpler however – for instance, you don't have to make to such an extent on the off chance that you live in (or move to) a minimal effort, low-charge nation. Eliminating living expenses can likewise have a major effect, as "bringing home the bacon" on something generally implies that pay spreads costs.

Advantages versus Drawbacks

Regardless of the trouble, there are some undeniable advantages to day exchanging professionally. To give some examples:

No supervisor – You're your own manager. No all the more pandering to the necessities of requesting and outlandish managers. You can work decisively the manner in which you need.

Hours – You set your own working hours. In this day and age there is consistently a market open. In this way, you can pick when you need to work and for to what extent, fitting it around different duties. In the event that you need a multi week occasion, there's no HR division to explore first.

Overheads – No progressively costly train ticket to get the chance to work. No more petroleum and stopping costs. Not any more expensive suits. You essentially need a PC, a web association and some funding to get moving.

Solace – Whilst every other person is pressing their shirt for the day ahead, you can slip into some comfortable garments and start your 15-foot drive to your work area, with a crisp mug of espresso. Not any more stuffy office or diverting partners to manage. You work from the solace of your own home.

Downsides

In spite of the conspicuous appeals, remarks about day exchanging professionally likewise feature a few drawbacks. The most predominant of which are:

Lone way of life – Your associates may have driven you up the divider now and again, however now and then it's consoling to have individuals around. Day exchanging professionally can get forlorn. On the off chance that you don't care for being individually, reconsider.

Conflicting pay – Your pay will vacillate enormously. You may make $3,000 one day and after that lose $2,500 the following. You likely won't have a steady compensation to depend on. What's more, in the event that you take a vacation day work you, you won't get paid a penny.

Profession movement – The main thing that can improve is your takings. You may likewise think that it's difficult to get again into the business world. Some time or another exchanging professionally discussions have proposed you'll be less employable by the end.

The fight against bots – Algorithms, computerized frameworks, and bots are on the whole assuming control over the market. They are presently in charge of a gigantic 60% of all market volume. While, there will consistently be a spot for people in the market, you'll have to discover better approaches to adjust and advance in the event that you need to keep up an edge.

## What Are People Day Trading?

One of the most significant choices you'll make is the thing that to begin day exchanging professionally. What are the well known protections and markets at that point, among the individuals who day exchange professionally?

- Stocks
- Penny stocks
- Forex
- Cryptographic forms of money
- Prospects
- Eminis
- CFDs

- Goods
- Gold
- Options

Regardless of whether you're day exchanging penny stocks professionally or monetary forms, the unpredictability and volume in your picked market will truly affect your potential benefits. The digital currency advertises, for instance, is profoundly unpredictable, empowering some to bring home the bacon.

While, day exchanging stocks professionally might be all the more testing. It is as of now an immersed market. What's more, a generally high measure of introductory capital is required and misfortunes could be all the more monetarily wrecking.

Once more, day exchanging items or prospects professionally will show its own difficulties. All of which focuses to the requirement for successful

**Provincial Differences**

Regardless of whether you make it day exchanging as a living will likewise rely upon where you live, and the market you decide on. Day exchanging professionally in India, Indonesia or South Africa, offers unstable markets, yet you likewise have a minimal effort of living, bringing home the bacon an increasingly doable.

Day exchanging professionally in the UK, US, Canada, or Singapore still offers a lot of chances, yet you have a plenitude of rivalry to fight with, in addition to mind-boggling expenses of living. You won't be shy of instability or volume, yet you have to plunk down and figure the amount you should make by and large every week or month, to in reality live.

The most effective method to Make A Living

Bringing home the bacon day exchanging is no simple accomplishment. You'll have various possibly costly impediments to survive. Beneath the top tips have been examined, to help keep you immovably operating at a profit.

Arrangement

The inquiry on many hopeful dealers lips is, how to begin day exchanging professionally? The appropriate response is you need only a couple of basics. Get those basics right and you'll be in the most grounded position to make a liberal compensation.

Equipment – You need at any rate a mid-run PC and web association. Any equipment or web accidents could cost you beyond a reasonable doubt. Many propose having two screens going, just if there should be an occurrence of crises.

Dealer – Make sure you pick a facilitate that suits your needs. They have to offer aggressive costs, dependable client support, and a simple to explore stage.

System – You need a procedure that suits your exchanging style. It needs to depend on outlines, examples, and specialized pointers. It needs to empower you to make regular benefits on high volume, low-esteem exchanges.

## Exchanging Office

Area is a significant theme. Will you have an office at home or attempt and exchange an assortment of areas on a workstation? You may have seen the pictures of a solitary broker sat behind 6 or even 9 screens monitoring a wide range of information – yet is it vital? One option in contrast to attempting to devote some space at home to exchanging is to utilize leased work area space.

There is additionally an administration that makes things a stride further. ETrading HQ offer rented work area and office space, yet additionally day exchanging information and cooperation. Similarly invested merchants can trade thoughts and techniques eye to eye. The idea is blasting in both London and New York and may make day exchanging professionally considerably more practical for those worried about business sectors information, isolation and office space.

## Capital

One of the primary inquiries out of hopeful brokers lips, is 'how much capital do you need?' The one necessity of day exchanging from home professionally is capital. Move back the bones a couple of years and you required at least $25,000 to begin day exchanging the US. That, however you generally needed to keep up at any rate that sum in your record.

These extreme guidelines implied the for most of individuals, exchanging professionally was basically not monetarily attainable. In any case, globalization of the money related industry has enabled various stages to create outside of US guideline. Today then you can begin with as meager as a $1,000 in your record.

How much capital you will need will rely upon what it is you need to begin exchanging.

Instruction

In the event that you need the best odds of prevailing at day exchanging professionally you have to use a wide scope of assets. Luckily, you would now be able to discover free, instructive devices with only a couple of snaps of the mouse. Probably the best assets worth considering are:

- Digital books – for example 'new exchanging professionally digital book', by Alexander Elder (bother free download)
- Book recordings
- Online journals
- PDFs
- Instructional exercise recordings
- Gatherings – perfect for those hoping to begin bringing home the bacon day exchanging stocks, fates, forex, and cryptographic forms of money.

- Study guides
- Web recordings and MP3s
- Flipkart

You'll discover counsel from experienced brokers on discussions, online journals, and chatrooms. You'll profit by point by point procedure models from books, PDFs and instructional exercise recordings. A great deal of the day exchanging professionally digital books, epubs, and PDFs are accessible for nothing downloads as well and can be gotten to through Kindle.

In case you're searching for explicit direction on the most proficient method to bring home the bacon day exchanging forex, consider the forex page. On the other hand, see the stocks page in case you're keen on exchanging stocks from home professionally.

## Risk Management

In case you're seeing how to do day exchanging professionally, one of the fundamental parts is the manner by which you oversee hazard. As Larry Hite appropriately declared, "All through my monetary vocation, I have persistently seen instances of other individuals that I have known being demolished by an inability to regard chance. On the off chance that you don't go out on a limb a hard take a gander in danger, it will take you."

You need a framework that guarantees you have enough to make moves, while holding enough capital that you don't need to return to the normal everyday employment.

A decent framework spins around stop-misfortunes and take-benefits. These enable you to prepare and forestall increased feelings assuming responsibility for choices.

Stop-misfortune – This is basically the cost at which you will sell a stock and assume the misfortune. It will kill you hanging on with the expectation that 'it will return.

Take-benefit – This is the time when you will sell a stock and take the benefit. This will enable you to hold that benefit, by empowering you to sell before a time of solidification kicks in.

In case you're exchanging professionally, steady and stable benefits are the objective, which will require a reliably restrained personality. It might sound clear now, however when you have $2,500 hanging in the balance and you've been gazing eagerly and rigidly at the screen throughout the previous six hours, well keeping apprehension under control isn't so natural. A successful method to restrict your passionate risk is to utilize however much specialized assistance as could be expected.

Holding your feelings within proper limits will take practice, a ton of missteps and afterward considerably more slip-ups. Notwithstanding, a perfect trap that encourages numerous brokers is to concentrate on the exchange, not the cash. Take it from experienced broker Alexander Elder, "The objective of a fruitful merchant is to make the best exchanges. Cash is optional."

The quantity of individuals day exchanging professionally since 2014 has flooded. Is it reasonable however? The appropriate response is, it depends altogether on your desire and duty. It won't be a simple ride. Be that as it may, on the off chance that it suits your working style, you pick the correct market and you use the tips referenced, at that point you could be one of only a handful not many that triumph.

# Chapter 4

# Essential Day Trading Tools

Before getting started as a day trader, there are a few more tools that you'll need to add to your tool belt. When beginning to swing trade, you probably learned what brokers worked for you, how to use a trading platform, and probably even how to take advantage of that trading platform's demo tools. Day trading isn't much different – there's just a more in-depth set of conditions that you have to take into account when making sure you're set up for it.

## Choosing a Broker

The first step to really getting started with day trading is choosing a broker. These online services should offer access to quick trades (and have a simple, easy-to-use platform). While you are probably transitioning from swing trading to day trading and might want to keep your broker, what works for swing trading might not always work for day trading. Here's a list of some of the top brokers to consider for the day trade.

- Interactive Brokers: This platform is best for professional day traders, institutions, forex traders, and traders who are active frequently and delve into many different types of orders. The actual platform Interactive Brokers uses is called Trader Workstation, and it's not as user-friendly as some others. Interactive Brokers has low rates and low commissions per share up to one thousand shares. There's also no account minimum, which makes it incredibly popular. A large con, however, is that the platform charges account fees of all different types, including annual, transfer, closing and fees for inactivity.

- Lightspeed: Also ideal for a professional trader. Ideally, to make the use of Lightspeed worth it, you're making more than 250 traders of stocks or more than 500 purchases/sales of options contracts per month. To do the math, that's at least 8 stock trades per day or more than 16 options contract purchases per month. However, you'll never be surprised or hurt by commissions: they're $4.50 fixed rate. Account minimums are steep, though: $10,000 for the mobile or web trader platform, and $25,000 for the actual Lightspeed platform itself. To trade on a margin account, you'll need a whopping $175,000 to play with at least. The options here a bit more limited, too. Tradable securities include stocks, ETFs, options, and futures. A big drawback for non-professionals is that there are no commission-free ETFS, nor are there any offers of no-transaction mutual funds.
- TradeStation: This platform is focused more towards the non-professional, or at least towards the newer trader looking to break in. Account minimums are $500, the platform is much more user friendly, commissions are low, and there is a ton of research at your fingertips on this platform.

We won't go into every single broker and what they offer here, but the following are a few other brokers to consider researching on your own and seeing if they fit what you're looking for in your trading scheme.

- TD Ameritrade
- Tastyworks
- thinkorswim

Review of swing trading tools that are useful to carry over to the day trade

The first, most powerful tool in your tool belt as a trader, regardless of whether you're a "swing," or "day" trader is knowing how to stop losses. After trading for a while, you probably came to the realization that knowing how to stop losses is more important than anything else, despite the fact that it seems like you're putting the cart before the horse. The key to developing as a day trader is objectivity, or removing emotion from your trading equation. The best way to stop loss is by using hard stops, plain and simple. The following are four rules that you'll need to adhere to in order to protect yourself from loss.

1. Never buy or sell without choosing your initial stop beforehand.
2. Place your order as soon as you choose your position.
3. Decide whether your stop will move or if you'll have one stop left, after you move on your position/purchase.
4. Last but not least, put your stops on the opposite end of the support and resistance

The one problem would be if you become so risk averse that every trade ends in a hard stop. That wouldn't be any fun, and you wouldn't be able to make any money. Just keep an eye on your positions and remember the bigger picture.

If hard stops are your go-to tool to stop loss, and you haven't used a hard stop on a particular position in a while, then that likely means that it's working in your favor. Don't let it completely bust apart by using stops so heavily that you can't profit. It's probably going to happen to you, and it's definitely going to hurt when you watch a stock, option or any other financial product rise in value when you sold it off and "stopped your loss."

The final and simple end goal of day trading is going to by making money off of buying/moving on the long and selling on the short for the majority of your trades.

# Chapter 5

# Building Your Trade Watch list

## Which Stocks to Watch and How to Find Them

A stock watch rundown resembles as almost like a menu: It plans out your entire trading day. Your watchlist needs to have dynamic stocks prepared to exchange dependent on specialized or major news impetus. A broker can have a few watch records, notwithstanding, there ought to be two quite certain watch records, the general and dynamic watch list. Your overall stock watch list will probably have several stocks made out of stocks the dealer knows about and has exchanged the past. To whittle down your watchlist to something practical and usable, each broker should set up a their watchlist before the trading day even opens, perhaps even the evening before as they're wrapping up that day of trading. A trader will generally keep the assets that he or she has been following the past days up to a month that is ready for a specialized movement. The trader knows that it is significant not to put too many assets on their watch list rundown, inevitably spreading yourself excessively flimsy. Each broker needs to have many assets/stocks they are happy with exchanging. A center bushel of stocks ought to be added to the watch list when they are dynamic.

## What Makes a "Good" Stock watch list?

Any stock on your dynamic watch rundown should be one that you are content with trading. It should contain a blend of focus trading stocks and new gaper and dumper stocks. It can similarly contain companion stocks to the gapper dumpers. This general watch once-over can be kept on a market minder or articulation cross section. Assets that are prepared to trade can be put on the dynamic watch list, which shouldn't be more than then stocks. It is optimal to have by and large traded focus stocks in different divisions.

The best stocks to exchange have high volume, liquidity and above all development. This is the reason energy stocks get the most activity and volume. Stocks that have a crisp news impetus will in general produce the most noteworthy volumes every day. The most affecting news things are income reports, direction and admonitions. At the point when the news makes a value hole up, called a gapper, or a value hole down, called a dumper, it tends to be a watch list up-and-comer. Notwithstanding, in the event that it is a new stock, it is ideal to look for the initial 30 minutes. Numerous gappers wind up being difficult to exchange because of the more slender liquidity, which makes for wide spreads and an excessive amount of slippage for the individuals who are not accustomed to it's exchanging conduct.

## Checking out Assets

Most delegates have monitoring or stock screening platforms on their stages. The dynamic stocks and gapper and dumpers are the essential stocks to search for adding to the day's dynamic watch list. To use a screener to look for more for more stocks, especially during the day, vendors can support a working stock screener add-on from your delegate organization or a pariah dealer. The central stage scanners should have a screen for most unique stocks, driving worth/rate stock gainers and decliners and greatest volume stocks. A base typical consistently volume of 1 million offers should be a channel for liquidity purposes. The greater the volume, the more prominent liquidity there will all in all be.

## Outsider Stock Scanners

Watch out for the untouchable extra separating undertakings available through your agent arrange first, since breaking points may apply.

Most scanners have different pre-set screens including unequivocal model scanners that yield for excellent models like triangles, 1-2-3 plans, flame guides to moving typical and vitality pointer crossovers. Each of these can be added to each other to deliver revamp continuous yields like 'Critical up move more noticeable than 2% in 15-minutes'. It also gives brilliant vitality scanners that will find stocks aggregate with pre-organized model screens similarly as the ability to use your own one of a kind channel.

Finviz.com offers free screening services that customers can in like manner set express parameters and moreover search for stocks meeting select model criteria like wedges, triangles, head and shoulders plans. Stocks reaching the new highs and lows of the day are up-and-comers necessitating review.

## Entanglements of Stock Scanners

Stock scanners are not the end all. Dealers should be mindful so as not to take the outputs truly and jump directly into an exchange. Scanners create potential exchanging competitors yet at the same time require the merchant to deliberately break down the set-up and qualify if the exchange is ideal. Scanners can regularly produce results after the set-up has been played out so it's significant not to pursue the sections.

With scanners, the quantity of exchanging competitors can extend multi-overlay to a point where it's anything but difficult to spread yourself excessively slim among approach to numerous stocks. The absence of center can frequently bring about overtrading. Dissatisfaction can result in considerably more overtrading and pursuing sections. It's significant that merchants comprehend that scanners just give proposals and order must be controlled in being specific even among the most impenetrable sifted examines. Generally when an example triggers, it will produce a large number of stock possibility to deal with. Since timing is significant, one needs to develop the range of abilities to deal with these rapidly and altogether. Begin with the most natural names and be specific and possibly draw in when the set-up meets your criteria and time the sections appropriately.

## Building Your Trading Watch List

Turning into an effective broker requires a consistent procedure of refinement. With regards to the exercises of an informal investor, it's greatly critical to build up a well-characterized day by day schedule that can be effectively rehashed each day prior to the market opens. In this one article, we would like to impart to you ours.

Yet, before going into that, we would like to call attention to the three primary properties that each stock watch-list needs:

Reasonability: The quantity of stocks pre-chosen for the game time should be an inside a scope of names that can be really plausible to pursue once the market opens. To us, observing in excess of five stocks it's not practical in light of the fact that it basically a lot of data to be handled without a moment's delay. Our optimal watch-list contains one to three names. This is the thing that we are open to dealing with.

Selectiveness: The watch-list must be your own. While we generally predicate about the significance of being a piece of a learned network like Warrior Trading, it's fundamental for every one to develop their very own watch-list and don't depend on any other individual with regards to a nitty gritty arrangement. In this way, in the event that you truly like another person plan, simply make that your very own however don't reflect any other individual. Rather, we should comprehend what's in the background of each choice taken and be prepared to execute the arrangement all alone.

## Stock in Play

What does it mean when a stock is in play?

A stock is in play when it is broadly accepted to be a takeover target. A takeover target is a decent possibility for a purchase by an acquirer.

How it functions/Example:

How about we expect Company ABC has built up an energizing new gadget. A few organizations might be keen on acquiring Company ABC to keep Company ABC's innovation restrictive, thus Company ABC may turn into a takeover target.

Why it makes a difference:

It's not in every case simple to tell which organizations are great takeover targets, however on the off chance that an organization is battling, or on the off chance that it has a lot of money on its accounting report, all things considered, different organizations consider the organization as a takeover target.

Some potential acquirers will make the following stride of obtaining shares. On the off chance that the objective is an open organization, and if the potential acquirer buys over five percent of those offers, the purchaser must report the buy to the Securities and Exchange Commission (SEC). This regularly triggers a whirlwind of exchanging action the objective's stock.

How it functions/Example:

Suppose Company ABC has a huge amount of money on its accounting report, and extremist financial specialists have been influencing it for nine months to sell. Organization ABC at long last concludes that it is available to be purchased, and declares that it is investigating "key associations" with intrigued financial specialists.

Organization ABC stock is in play.

Why it makes a difference:

At the point when a stock is in play, it can keep running up rapidly. That is on the grounds that the possible purchaser is probably going to pay a premium over the present stock cost so as to initiate the investors to sell the organization and to destroy any contending bidders. Thus, a few brokers are keen on stocks that are in play, and maybe increasingly significant, stocks that could end up in play soon.

Float and Market Cap

Market cap depends on the complete estimation of every one of the organization's portions of stock. Buoy is the quantity of extraordinary offers for exchanging by the overall population. The free-drift technique for figuring business sector top avoids secured shares, for example, those held by organization officials and governments.

Confined and Float

When you look somewhat nearer at the statements for an organization's stock there might be some dark terms you've never experienced. For example, limited offers allude to an organization's issued stock that can't be purchased or sold without exceptional authorization by the SEC. Regularly, this sort of stock is given to insiders as a component of their compensations or as extra advantages. Another term you may experience is drift. This alludes to an organization's offers that are openly purchased and sold without confinements by people in general. Meaning the best extent of stocks exchanging on the trades, the buoy comprises of standard offers that a considerable lot of us will hear or find out about in the news.

Approved Shares

Approved offers allude to the biggest number of offers that a solitary company can issue. The quantity of approved offers per organization is surveyed at the organization's creation and must be expanded or diminished through a vote by the investors. In the event that at the season of joining the archives express that one hundred offers are approved, at that point just one hundred offers can be issued.

Be that as it may, in light of the fact that an organization can issue a specific number of offers doesn't mean it will issue every one of them to general society. Ordinarily, organizations will, for some, reasons, keep a segment of the offers in their very own treasury. For instance, organization DEF may choose to keep up a controlling enthusiasm inside the treasury just to avert any threatening takeover offers. Then again, the organization may have shares convenient on the off chance that it needs to sell them for abundance money (as opposed to acquiring). This propensity of an organization to hold a portion of its approved offers drives us to the following significant and related term: exceptional offers.

Remarkable Shares

Not to be mistaken for approved offers, remarkable offers allude to the quantity of stocks that an organization really has issued. This number speaks to every one of the offers that can be purchased and sold by the general population, just as all the confined offers that require uncommon consent before being executed. As we previously clarified, shares that can be unreservedly purchased and sold by open financial specialists are known as the buoy. This worth changes relying upon whether the organization wishes to repurchase shares from the market or sell out a greater amount of its approved offers from inside its treasury.

How about we glance back at our organization ABC. From the past model, we realize that this organization has one thousand approved offers. On the off chance that it offered three hundred offers in an initial public offering, offered one hundred and fifty to the administrators and held five hundred and fifty in the treasury, at that point the quantity of offers exceptional would be four hundred and fifty offers (three hundred buoy shares plus one hundred confined offers). On the off chance that following several years ABC was doing amazingly well and needed to repurchase one hundred offers from the market, the quantity of exceptional offers would tumble to three hundred and fifty, the quantity of treasury offers would increment to six hundred and the buoy would tumble to two hundred offers since the buyback was done through the market (three hundred to one hundred).

The quantity of extraordinary offers can vary in different ways too. Notwithstanding the stocks they issue to speculators and administrators, numerous organizations offer investment opportunities and warrants. These are instruments that give the holder a privilege to buy increasingly stock from the organization's treasury. Each time one of these instruments is enacted, the buoy and offers extraordinary increment while the quantity of treasury stocks diminishes. For instance, assume ABC issues one hundred warrants. On the off chance that every one of these warrants are enacted, at that point ABC should offer one hundred offers from its treasury to the warrant holders. In this way, by following the latest model, where the quantity of extraordinary offers is three hundred and fifty and treasury offers absolute six hundred and fifty, practicing every one of the warrants would change the numbers to four hundred and fifty and five hundred and fifty, separately, and the buoy would increment to three hundred. This impact is known as weakening.

The Bottom Line

Since the contrast between the quantity of approved and extraordinary offers can be so huge, it's imperative to acknowledge what they are and which figures the organization is utilizing. Various proportions may utilize the essential number of exceptional offers while others may utilize the weakened rendition. This can influence the numbers altogether and perhaps change your frame of mind toward a specific speculation. Besides, by distinguishing the quantity of limited offers versus the quantity of offers in the buoy, speculators can measure the degree of possession and independence that insiders have inside the organization. Every one of these situations is significant for financial specialists to comprehend before they settle on a choice to purchase or sell.

In free buoy advertise capitalization, the estimation of the organization is determined by barring offers held by the advertisers. These barred offers are the free buoy shares. For model if an organization has issued 10 lakh portions of assumed worth Rs 10, yet of these, four lakh offers is possessed by the advertiser, at that point the free buoy showcase capitalization is Rs 60 lakh.

3. How does free buoy showcase capitalization vary from absolute market capitalization?

Free buoy advertise capitalization is lower than all out market capitalization as offers held by advertisers or those that are secured are avoided. For example, Coal IndiaNSE - 2.59 % has complete market capitalization of Rs 1.8 lakh crore however the free buoy showcase capitalization is about Rs 35,600 crore in light of the administration's high holding.

4. How can it influence exchanging of offers?

Stocks that have little free buoy are probably going to consider higher to be instability as it takes less exchanges to move the offer cost. Then again, on account of a bigger free buoy, unpredictability is lower. In stocks with an enormous free buoy, the quantity of individuals purchasing and selling the offers is higher thus; a modest quantity of exchanging does not influence the cost fundamentally.

How does free buoy philosophy help in record figuring?

Both NSE and the BSE utilize the free buoy advertise capitalization strategy to ascertain their benchmark lists Nifty and Sensex separately and relegating weight to stocks in the file. So an organization with a higher free buoy has a higher weightage on the lists. A free buoy file reflects market patterns better as it mulls over just those offers which are accessible for exchanging.

**Gap and Go Strategy**

The following is the most significant in exchanging the Gap/Go system

Throughout pre-showcase hours, trading indices like the S&P 500 and New York Stock Exchange open up for exchanging assets. Very often the exchanging magnitude is decreased right now. In any case, there are special cases, similar to the first pre-showcase period after income declarations.

Exchanging the Gap and Go system means that you'll be taking action when the market is ready for business or closing for that

particular day; but you'll never be acting before the market opens for the day. That period of time during the pre-advertise hours is just expected to keep an eye on what the costs are doing.
Why? Since a hole means that it is characterized in terms of value distinction between the main passages of customary exchanging time connection to the final passage of the past exchanging period inside the normal exchanging window.

Often it so happens that there will be an immense hole appeared in the pre-advertise, however once the market opens the hole isn't there any longer.

It doesn't make a difference how high the pre-advertise volume is during the pre-showcase exchanging time. However, when markets open for the day the trading gets hot and heavy. Remember to stick to your guns.

Therefore you need – no, it is *essential* -- to have an excellent securities exchange scanner like Trade Ideas. It is difficult to screen a great many stocks every day physically.

Indeed, even the best representative stage can't work admirably here. Exchange Ideas examines the entire market with a large number of stocks for each exchanging example you characterize. Also, they have characterized checks too.

Hole and Go – The name clarifies what the procedure implies

On the off chance that the market holes up, we are searching for a long exchange (purchasing the stock).

On the off chance that the market holes in a downward pattern, we are searching high and low to find a short exchange (getting rid of an asset that we don't is not in our possession right now).

Now having said that, the trader is searching to try and continue that energy that the asset increased medium-term. The Gap and Go system isn't an inversion procedure, it is a momentum-building technique.

You might be wondering at this point if it really even makes a difference what the reason is if the stock holes up or down when the markets open for business?

A very common, run-of-the-mill explanation behind a hole on particular assets is news in regards to income declarations and friends news, while general market news can affect the entire money related market.

If the trader is searching for a Gap and Go system with a very elevated momentum/continuance of the force of the hole heading, then they need to know the reason behind why the asset holes. On the off chance that there is just broad commerce updates or an obscure rationale, the trader has to remain calm and refrain from any purchase or sale request.

The trader needs to realize the motivation to have the option to assess if the news has the power and capacity to proceed with value development. Keep in mind, it is constantly about free market activity.

You need to abstain from being the last individual in the line before costs alter course.

What's more, it would be ideal if you recall. News causes development. Not specialized arrangements itself. Numerous informal investors basically exchange an exhausting breakout or breakdown. However, on the off chance that there is no news behind it, at that point the move will end quick or the business sectors will simply go sideways.

The key point is the value development ought to be bolstered by significant news. Checking for news is simple with the power of Google or Yahoo! Finance. Event industry magazines can provide you with enough information to make better decisions that your emotions can.

Most different news destinations have deferred news information which is useless when exchanging ongoing. The news consistently precedes the Gap and Go value development, not the other way around.

Step by step instructions for day trading with the Gap and Go technique

Beneath, you will locate some exemplary approaches to exchange the Gap and Go technique. The majority of the section procedures depend on specialized examination, even if news updates and market fluctuations causing the move depends on key news.

Those techniques ought to be exchanged distinctly during the initial 30 to an hour of the ordinary exchanging hours. I for the most part exchange this procedure just with NASDAQ and NYSE recorded stocks.

On the off chance that you need to exchange different markets, you ought to investigate common value developments first to assess if the methodologies can be connected. Day exchanging penny stocks with the hole and go system is conceivable if the volume around the market open is sufficiently high to put your exchange.

All of those methodologies can be exchanged the reflected path on the short side also. However, recollect, shorting stocks is more hazardous than just exchanging long. Moreover, few out of every odd intermediary gives you the capacity to short stocks.

## Real Time Intraday Scans

Online Subscription-Based Scanners

Numerous prevalent membership based checking administrations accelerate the procedure by giving pre-chosen filter criteria that does the math on their servers and just streams the outcomes on the web. While these can be redone, most clients depend on the pre-set outputs. On the off chance that the appropriation base of clients is enormous enough, the aftereffects of the sweeps can produce much intrigue and have an inevitable outcome impact guaranteeing a swarming of exchanges on the most well known output set-ups. Nonetheless, with time, the impact can reverse discharge once the straightforwardness turns out to be excessively evident as dealers hope to blur the outcomes. In this way, it is basic that the output outcomes are approved as well as affirmed to be from the get-go in the example. You would prefer not to be cautioned of a competitor long after it has finished where you may end of pursuing a dispersed chance.

Remember, with online scanners; you aren't the just a single aware of the sweep results. The exchange openings can become busy rapidly. Dealers can get injured rapidly from bouncing straight into whatever springs up on an output.

The practicality of the output outcomes is a top for intra-day scanners, where seconds and minutes can have the effect between ready or lost chance. End-of-day scanners that create results after the market close are valuable for producing thoughts to exchange the following day and for swing merchants.

## Kinds of Stock Scanners

There are two essential capacities and quest periods for stock scanners, major and specialized dependent on end-of-day or ongoing intraday information. You should choose what kind of investigation is most appropriate for the sort of exchanges you plan on making exchanges and the style of exchange you intend to make. For longer-term Investment and swing exchanging purposes, a central scanner is perfect. For exchanging openings intra-day or transient swing exchanging, a specialized scanner is generally appropriate.

### Crucial

These are the richest kinds of "free" scanners accessible on the web and on most representative stages. They are custom fitted to long haul financial specialists and basics based dealers. These scanners are valuable for discovering stocks that are underestimated or exaggerated. These are additionally extraordinary for contrasting stocks against their industry, part, companions and benchmark lists. A basic worth output could have criteria like: Annual Earnings Growth greater than 20%, Annual Sales Growth greater than 25%, P/E less than 20, Price/Book less than 2, Priced somewhere in the range of $5 and $50. A profound worth sweep where an organization is exchanging under money would include a channel like Cash Per Share greater than Share cost. The blend of inquiry channels and criteria is boundless.

## Specialized

These scanners look for explicit value designs (IE: banner, triangles, breakouts, breakdowns, twofold help/obstruction) and triggers including explicit candle arrangements (IE: hammers, doji, falling stars), marker triggers (moving midpoints, stochastic, MACD, RSI) and value cautions (IE: new highs and lows, %Price change). Specialized investigation outputs require more customization on the program level or more exertion on the assessment procedure after applicants are recognized for the best effectiveness and ideal use.

## End-of-Day/Post-Market

These scanners yield example or central based outcomes. Merchants ought to be in no rush to venture into an exchange when utilizing a finish of-day (EOD) scanner. These sweeps are intended to aid the examination procedure to get ready for the following day's exchanging session. Since the outcomes are figured dependent on shutting costs, there is no quick need or chance to exchange the stocks.

## Constant/Intraday

These scanners work to spot stocks during business sector hours. These are exceptionally time touchy outcomes that expect you to have the option to investigate results on the fly and rapidly decide whether an exchange ought to be taken. Intraday examples can create and grow dim quickly. Informal investors get the most profit by these kinds of stock scanners.

## Step by step instructions to Use Stock Market Scanners

The best possible utilization of a stock scanner relies upon what you are utilizing it for. Keep in mind that a scanner is an instrument that gives potential possibility to exchange. You should in any case apply your own triggers once the competitors are approved and you know about the stock. Be mindful so as to abstain from hopping in head first to any stock that springs up in an output. You would prefer not to hop directly into the profound finish of the pool without realizing how to swim.

Building a Watch List

Stock scanners that quest the general markets for competitors are an incredible method to acquaint you with new stocks, which can be added to the watch list. Remember those new stocks ought to be checked first to get adjusted to the pace of the value activity, spread, volume and liquidity. By changing the channels to examine for just stocks that meet your value range and least volume necessities, you can limit the field drastically.

Intraday Alerts

The snugness of your channels will be the way to producing precise outcomes. Ensure the parameters are appropriately set. On the off chance that you are filtering for example set ups, make a point to approve how exact the outcomes are. For instance, examines for mallet candles may produce results with a flame that gives off an impression of being a sledge independent from anyone else, yet comes up short on the first three back to back red candles that make it a successful inversion mallet light. On the off chance that the sweep is a pre-set one, at that point know about the imperfection. On the off chance that the sweep can be tweaked, at that point it is judicious to get familiar with the fundamental programming so as to create the required outcomes. As the model delineates, scanners are not instinctive. They regularly miss the setting that affects the viability of the example during outputs.

## Criteria for Good Scan Results

To achieve strong sweep results, you should distinguish what precisely you are searching for early. What you info will represent the deciding moment your outputs. Know that tweaking will be required en route so as to create the most exact competitors. The exactness of the sweeps will be founded on your sifting criteria. Precise outcomes help to accelerate the time it takes to physically investigate the set-up, affirm triggers and put on an exchange.

## Parameter and Trigger Settings

Fundamental criteria ought to incorporate the structure parameters at the stock including cost run (for example, twenty to fifty dollars), least normal exchanging volume (for example, one million offers daily), least buoy (for example, one hundred million offers) and trades This is to stay away from outputs for slight, illiquid stale and penny stocks. For example based criteria, make sure to concentrate on the careful trigger that would provoke an exchange (IE: two hundred-period moving normal breakout with stochastic hybrid up through 20-40 band on more noteworthy than two times relative volume). This sets the channels to affirm a trigger first at that point enables you to affirm and choose snappier whether to put an exchange.

Eventually, it is tied in with expanding the proficiency by streamlining the procedure from possibility to exchange the timeliest way so as to have sufficient opportunity to exploit an exchanging opportunity.

## Quality Over Quantity

The reason for a stock scanner is to computerize the hunt and channel procedure to distinguish stocks that meet your criteria. You are utilizing innovation to do the dull legwork of checking the market or a watch rundown of stocks for your sake. Outputs ought to be particular and separating in creating results. Quality is estimated by the practicality, exactness and legitimacy of the outcomes in gathering your criteria.

Consider utilizing a stock scanner like employing a corporate talent scout to look the business sectors for qualified applicants. The talent scout goes about as the watchman that ought to qualify just the top enlisted people to pass on to you. Your main responsibility is to "talk with" them for the "work", break down them for potential exchanges. The stricter the capability procedure, the simpler it is to contract and put on the exchange.

Section Custom Scans to Your Niche

The more tweaked your outputs are, the more precise your outcomes ought to be. Concentrate on altering to your specialty exchanging set-ups and stocks. The key here is commonality compares to less personal time adapting to the stock before setting an exchange. Main concern, it brings about a less slippage and enables you to hit the ground "running" not long after an applicant triggers on the scanner.

Sweep for Stocks With Significant Price Movements

This may appear glaringly evident, however to guarantee proficiency it is judicious to ensure that your intra-day checked stocks have a channel set up to yield stocks with critical value moves. So as to benefit from unpredictability, there must be instability. Above all, there should be different members in guarantee liquidity. The best up-and-comers will be the ones with the most eyeballs. Eyeballs are attracted to stocks producing huge value moves.

## Using Scanners to Find Your Trade

What is a stock scanner?

A stock scanner is a screening device that searches the business sectors to discover stocks that meet a lot of client chose criteria and measurements for exchanging and contributing. Scanners can be adjusted to locate the most reasonable up-and-comers that meet your particular channels. Innovation has streamlined the tedious assignment of attempting to discover new exchanging chances to make it progressively advantageous and proficient for the end client. The speed and comfort of stock scanners make them a fundamental device for all merchants and financial specialists.

Commotion Reduction and Pitfalls

At the point when utilized accurately, scanners can enable the client to slice through the commotion in the business sectors to channel the emphasis on the most qualified applicants. Nonetheless, it critical to understand that output outcomes are implied distinctly as a channel. You will in any case need to deliberately dissect the tradability and affirm the set-ups before thinking about an exchange. Not all scanners are precise or solid, particularly example based scanners. At the point when utilized inappropriately, scanners can spread a broker excessively slim among competitors and make more chances to lose cash faster. A merchant ought to be knowledgeable in the criteria and test how well a scanner really screens to measure how solid it is.

## Stage Based and Desktop Scanners

Most exchanging stages have a type of an examining apparatus. These apparatuses can be as essential as an intraday new high/low output or as unpredictable as a symphonious example based sweeps. The more mind boggling the output channels are, the harder it tends to be to achieve exact and convenient outcomes. Stage based scanners can look through the whole markets or a select gathering of stocks. It is imperative to recognize whether the scanner is utilizing your PC's assets or the information supplier's servers to perform checks. The calculating can be a noteworthy asset hoard that can hinder your framework execution. Contingent upon how explicit your criteria is, you can decide whether you should some programming preparing to guarantee progressively exact outcomes.

## Work area Scanner Software

Downloadable work area based examining programming can deliver faster outcomes however can significantly deplete your PC's assets and hinder different capacities. Clients should confine the sweeps to gatherings of stocks like watch records or parts, as opposed to the entire market to guarantee appropriate usefulness and counterbalance execution delayed down. With a littler example size, these projects can be tweaked to alarm potential example triggers a lot speedier than a cloud-based scanner. They will require programming information and familiarity with the criteria determination procedure to modify the sweeps.

These are more involved projects that can be tedious to set-up for the client particularly if programming learning is required, however the exactness of the outputs are the most elevated. For instance, suppose you need to set-up an output to discover stocks that are shaping a 20-band stochastic hybrid joined with a rising 5 and 15-period straightforward moving normal on a 15-minute time span that is evaluated between $20-$30 on more prominent than 1.5 occasions relative volume with a base normal day by day volume of 1 million offers. Having the scanner screen your 100 stocks continuously contrasted with more than 6,000 stocks has a major effect. Notwithstanding depleting more assets and the practicality of results, you will likewise need to battle with possibly much more possibility to break down. Your redid work area scanner may release 3 competitors close to qualifying while an online scanner may release 50 up-and-comers close to qualifying. With your watch rundown examine, you should as of now be comfortable with the stocks and their tradability, while huge numbers of the stocks on the all inclusive sweep might be totally unfamiliar to you.

Unavoidably, you should rapidly break down and affirm the set-up before choosing to take the exchange. By being increasingly specific with the output channels and test size, you can pinpoint the accurate set-up with stocks you are as of now acquainted with and consequently can venture into the exchange inside seconds. Contrast that with filtering through the 50 results to locate the few up-and-comers that you know about and after that affirming the set-up precision before narrowing down which ones are legitimate to think about exchanging. This may take anyplace from minutes to 60 minutes. By then, the example may have finished as you pass up on the fateful opening due to the extra legwork expected to approve the outcomes. Which approach appears to be increasingly proficient for you?

Obviously, the output criteria could be tightened much more tightly if the project permits. In any case, the bigger the example size, the less perplexing the criteria ought to be so as to achieve opportune outcomes however that implies more legwork for the end client to approve results. The balance to this is either having an extremely incredible PC or potentially programming learning. This is the reason software engineers are in such high demand.re contributing your genuine capital.

## Day Trading Penny Stocks

Putting resources into stocks is generally connected with offers like AAPL, GOOGL, AMZN and different organizations from comparative gauge. In any case, truly, so as to profit, one ought not depend just on blue chips.

Truth be told, penny stocks uncover an entirely different universe of speculation openings. In the following couple of lines, you will get some answers concerning one of the not really prominent, yet profoundly potential pieces of the securities exchange – the universe of penny stocks.

How We Define Penny Stocks

As per the Securities Exchange Commission, penny stocks are portions of little organizations that exchanged under the five dollar cost mark.

These kinds of offers is generally exchanged over the counter, however penny stocks tend to be portions of available at certain trades too. Penny stocks are created and distributed and sold by organizations with that do not have a lot of capital.

All in all, penny stocks tend do be one of the highest-hazard/highest-remunerate investments. This is why an initial move step ought to exist to see if this kind of offers is an appropriate decision for accomplishing previously set venture objectives.

In all actuality they can help a fledgling financial specialist with little funding to develop the estimation of his portfolio rapidly. However, because of the high hazard, related with penny stocks exchanging, they have the ability to crash every one of your speculations too.

Day exchanging is related with an increasingly unique exchanging action, worked around making various exchanges every day. With regards to penny stocks, day exchanging for tenderfoots can be very testing. Also, no day exchanging procedure should be utilized for day exchanging penny stocks.

The reason is that the over the counter market for all of these types of offers generally needs liquidity. This implies in the event that you depend on exploiting value changes and profiting by the market force, you may wind up disillusioned.

Penny stocks may some of the time be very difficult to purchase and sell because of the absence of high exchanging volume. This makes force based exchanging procedures not all that suitable.

Penny stocks are progressively reasonable for long haul financial specialists. Since they speak to little or beginning period organizations that as a rule don't have the momentum or power or the assets in order to enhance rapidly, these might require significant investment until their stocks arrive at certain development levels.

However, putting resources into penny stocks may turn out entirely beneficial in the intermediate and the extended haul.

Independent ventures more often than not can possibly detonate in an incentive for only a couple of years, contingent upon the economic situations, the qualities of the business condition and the focused scene.

Consider it that way - a value hop from $1 to $1.5 per offer may in any case imply that the business is a long way from the top positions, however as a general rule, it is a half bounce in the estimation of your portfolio.

The most effective method to Scan for Penny Stocks minute-by-minute

Exchange Ideas is the main apparatus you have to filter for a wide range of penny stocks on any US stock trade. You can alter your inquiry dependent on up to five hundred distinct channels. Value, hole, development inside a particular time and exchanging volume are only four channels you can utilize.

What platforms it is possible to day trade penny stocks on

The way that most penny stocks are exchanged over the counter and implies traders are not able and cannot put resources into such instruments through every single specialist out there.

That is the reason on the off chance that a trader needs to exchange penny stocks, you should discover a rebate intermediary that has the greatest day exchanging stage. Picked probably the biggest player in the business as few out of every odd middle person out there offers such administrations.

Remember that some of them have account essentials of up to $1 000, which for financial specialists that arrangement on beginning little, may not be the best decision.

With regards to penny stock exchanging, the charges and the edges are much increasingly significant, when contrasted with high value and enormous top assets. This happens to be the reason it is a smart thought to think about no-exchanging charge arrangements.

Within the prominent exchanging application, RobinHood, is a decent alternative on the off chance that you need to keep away from expenses. The drawback in this situation happens to be the application is connected to trades and does not offer over the counter products, in this way giving a constrained measure of stocks for exchanging.

On the off chance that you need to exchange just the most famous and trade recorded penny stocks; at that point RobinHood might be your best choice. Apart from the organizations that they speak to, penny stocks vary from one another in another viewpoint too – the value they are exchanging at.

The overall rule that each offer exchanged at costs beneath five dollars is a penny stock is not really illustrating the entire, total situation. Penny stocks also can be additionally separated by their value run.

Here are probably the most well known penny stocks estimating classes:

Penny Stocks less than five dollars

These are typically the "major leagues of penny stocks". They are frequently favored because of the incredible upside potential that they have. For instance – Bank of America's offers were exchanging at five dollars several years ago in2011.

Right now, their cost is above twenty seven dollars an offer! There are a lot of different models, yet the fundamental thought of this kind of stocks is one and the equivalent – they have the ability to detonate in worth.

A lot of these penny stocks are recorded on the major market exchanges. This is a reward as there will be greater liquidity which can enable you to purchase and sell quickly and gain by market energy.

Penny Stocks less than one dollar

A level beneath, the offers exchanging under one dollar are another appropriate investible instrument that can even now be found on major market exchanges. Most of these stocks are sold over the counter.

The vast majority making up the offers beneath one dollar speak to organizations at their all around beginning periods or with extremely little tasks and capital. With regards to development potential, they are a superior speculation decision contrasted with the past class.

By the by, the related hazard is route higher as a portion of these organizations can't satisfy their economic possibilities and bomb in that initial time they are offered.

Penny Stocks less than one cent

As unusual as it might sound, in actuality, a few stocks are exchanging at costs underneath one penny. They as a rule speak to battling organizations or dangerous endeavors. The New York Stock Exchange, for instance, has a strategy of delisting organizations with an offer cost beneath 10 pennies.

Once delisted, these offers are exchanged over the counter. On the off chance that we investigate a free stock posting site we will discover that these penny stocks can possibly detonate with over three hundred percent in under multi day.

There are a great many penny stocks exchanging around the world. To explore the way toward finding the most proper exchanging instrument, one of the principal elements to consider is their exchanging volume.

Penny stocks, as their name recommends, are worth practically nothing. On the off chance that you have critical exposures to certain low-estimated offers and they experience an unexpected value drop, you ought to have the option to sell and exit as quickly as time permits, to limit your misfortunes.

When all is said in done, each stock that is exchanged at beneath 10 000 offers for every day is viewed as a low-volume one. Most penny stocks fall inside this classification. The absence of liquidity makes it harder for speculators to purchase and sell at the best minute. It likewise causes different issues, for example,

Value dangers

The lower the exchanging volume is, the simpler it is for market members with bigger positions at specific stocks to cause a value development.

Envision that an individual financial specialist has 10 000 portions of the organization XYZ and the normal exchanging volume for the given stock is 1 000 every day.

In the event that he attempts to sell every one of his benefits on the double, this will mean a selling weight that is multiple times higher than the normal exchanging volume which can possibly further diminish the cost.

Bolted benefits

In the event that an individual financial specialist purchased 1 000 offers at a cost of $5.00 each a couple of years prior and they are presently exchanging at $7.00, he might need to have a go at selling and catching the acknowledged increases.

Be that as it may, if the every day exchanging volume is low (100 – 200 offers per day, for instance) it might take him over seven days to sell every one of his stocks. This keeps the financial specialist from the opportunity to catch his 40% benefit.

How to discover Penny Stocks worth day exchanging?

You can discover a lot of sites offering "a definitive penny stock picking bulletins" or proposals about the "most blazing penny stocks". Make a point to think about all that while taking other factors into consideration.

Commonly, the creators of such bulletins are proprietors in specific stocks, themselves. By attempting to pull in potential speculators, they might look for impact the cost of a specific instrument for their own advantage.

Focus on starting investigation and track the recorded setting of each instrument that you mean to place assets into.

Daytrading.com can offer many bulletins for you to peruse, as well as Investopedia. There are plenty of websites out there to find penny stocks. Even come reddit.com threads can be beneficial to finding these over the counter products.

Generously complete your work and find anyway much as could be normal about the supervisory gathering and whether they rely upon issuing stocks to raise capital, what are their whole deal plans, how centered the particular division is, etc.

Keep in mind that a couple of divisions, tend to be progressively customary for finding penny stocks. Keep in mind that the risk related with penny stocks is way higher when appeared differently in relation to other similar instruments.

Day trading strategies like the opening and go framework can work out charmingly with penny stocks if low trading sizes reflect the high peril.

# Chapter 6

# Understanding Support and Resistance Levels

What are Support and Resistance Levels?

The ideas of support and resistance are without a doubt two of the most exceptionally talked about qualities of specialized examination. Some portion of breaking down graph designs, these terms are utilized by brokers to allude to value levels on outlines that will in general go about as obstructions, keeping the cost of an advantage from getting pushed in a specific bearing. From the start, the clarification and thought behind distinguishing these levels appear to be simple, yet as you'll discover, backing and opposition can come in different structures, and the idea is more hard to ace than it initially shows up.

Characterizing Support, Resistance

Backing is a value level where a downtrend can be required to delay because of a centralization of interest. As the cost of advantages or protections drops, interest for the offers expands, accordingly framing the help line. Then, obstruction zones emerge because of an auction when costs increment.

When a territory or "zone" of help or obstruction has been recognized, it gives significant potential exchange passage or leave focuses. This is on the grounds that, as a value arrives at a point of help or opposition, it will complete one of two things—bob move in an opposite direction from the help or obstruction level, or abuse the value level and proceed toward its—until it hits the following help or obstruction level.

Most types of exchanges depend on the conviction that help and obstruction zones won't be broken. Regardless of whether the cost is stopped by the help or obstruction level, or it gets through, brokers can "wager" on the heading and can rapidly decide whether they are right. On the off chance that the value moves off course, the position can be shut at a little misfortune. In the event that the value moves the correct way, in any case, the move might be considerable.

Key Takeaways

Specialized investigators use backing and opposition levels to distinguish value focuses on a diagram where the probabilities support a respite, or inversion, of an overall pattern.

Backing happens where a downtrend is relied upon to delay, because of a grouping of interest.

Obstruction happens where an upturn is relied upon to delay incidentally, because of a centralization of supply.

Market brain research assumes a noteworthy job as brokers and speculators recall the past and respond to changing conditions to foresee future market development.

The Basics

Most experienced brokers will probably recount to numerous tales about how certain value levels will in general keep merchants from pushing the cost of a fundamental resource in a specific heading. For instance, accept that Jane was holding a situation in stock among March and November and that he was anticipating that the estimation of the offers should increment.

How about we envision that Jane sees that the value neglects to get above $39 a few times more than a while, despite the fact that it has gotten near moving over that level. For this situation, dealers would call the value level close $39 a degree of obstruction. As should be obvious from the graph beneath, opposition levels are additionally viewed as a roof in light of the fact that these value levels keep the market from moving costs upward.

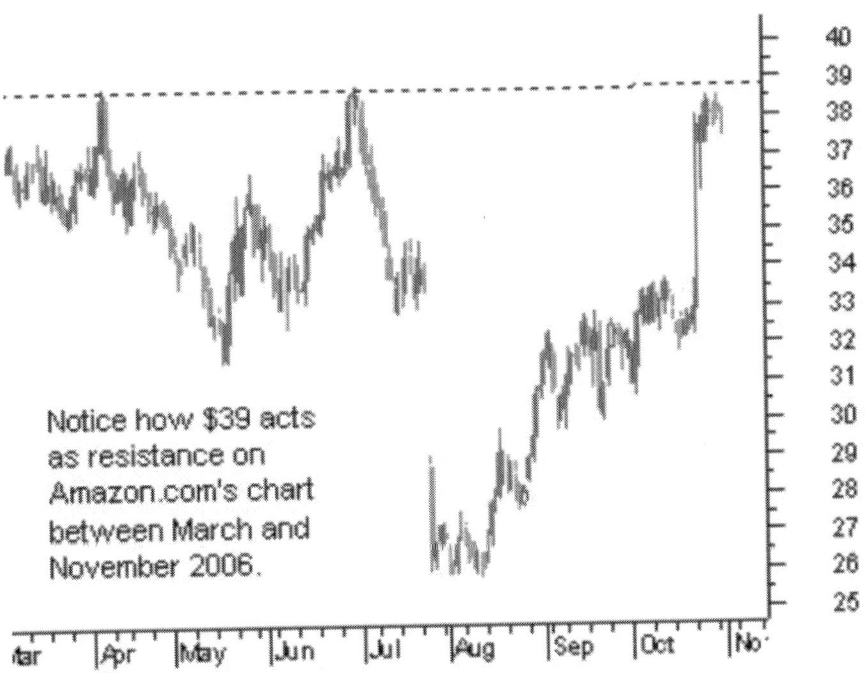

## Pattern Lines

The models above demonstrate a consistent level keeps an advantage's cost from moving higher or lower. This static boundary is one of the most well known types of help/opposition, yet the cost of budgetary resources for the most part slants upward or descending, so it isn't extraordinary to see these value boundaries change after some time. This is the reason understanding the ideas of inclining and trendlines is significant when finding out about help and opposition.

At the point when the market is drifting to the upside, obstruction levels are shaped as the value activity eases back and begins to draw back toward the trendline. This happens because of benefit taking or close term vulnerability for a specific issue or division. The subsequent value activity experiences a "level" impact, or a slight drop-off in stock cost, making a transient top.

Numerous dealers will give close consideration to the cost of a security as it falls toward the more extensive help of the trendline in light of the fact that verifiably this has been a territory that has kept the cost of the advantage from moving generously lower. For instance, as should be obvious from the Newmont Mining Corp (NEM) graph beneath, a trendline can offer help for a benefit for quite a long while. For this situation, see how the trendline propped up the cost of Newmont's offers for an all-encompassing timeframe.

Then again, when the market is drifting to the drawback, merchants will look for a progression of declining tops and will endeavor to associate these pinnacles together with a trendline. At the point when the value approaches the trendline, most dealers will look for the resource for experience selling weight and may consider entering a short position since this is a zone that has pushed the cost descending previously.

The help/opposition of a distinguished level, regardless of whether found with a trendline or through some other strategy, is esteemed to be more grounded the more occasions that the cost has verifiably been not able move past it. Numerous specialized brokers will utilize their distinguished help and obstruction levels to pick key section/leave focuses in light of the fact that these regions frequently speak to the costs that are the most persuasive to a benefit's course. Most merchants are sure at these levels in the fundamental estimation of the advantage, so the volume by and large expands more than expected, making it significantly more hard for dealers to keep driving the value higher or lower.

Not at all like the sound monetary on-screen characters depicted by budgetary models, genuine human dealers and financial specialists are passionate, make intellectual blunders, and fall back on heuristics or alternate routes. In the event that individuals were judicious, backing and obstruction levels wouldn't work by and by!

## Round Numbers

Another regular normal for help/opposition is that an advantage's cost may have a troublesome time moving past a round-figure value level, for example, $50. Most unpracticed merchants will in general purchase or sell resources when the cost is at an entire number since they are bound to feel that a stock is genuinely esteemed at such levels. Most objective costs or stop requests set by either retail speculators or huge venture banks are set at round value levels as opposed to at costs, for example, $50.06. Since such a large number of requests are set at a similar level, these round numbers will in general go about as solid value boundaries. On the off chance that every one of the customers of a speculation bank put in sell orders at a recommended objective of, for instance, $55, it would take an extraordinary number of buys to assimilate these deals and, in this manner, a degree of opposition would be made.

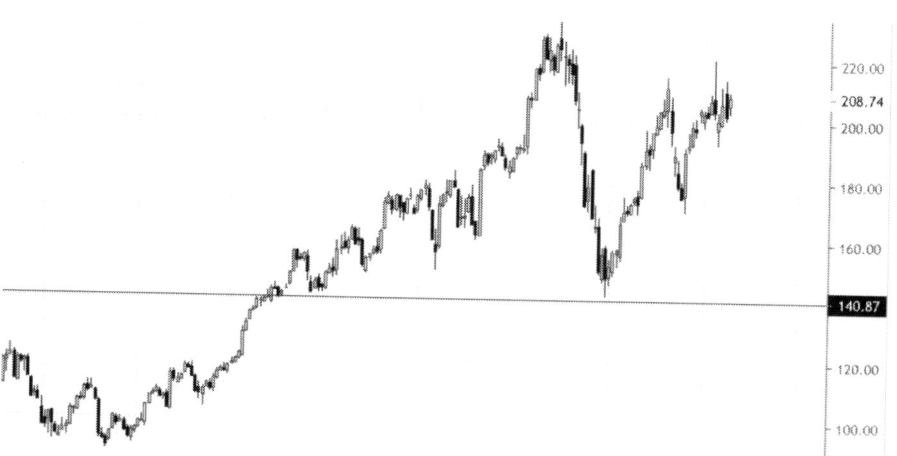


Moving Averages

Most specialized merchants consolidate the intensity of different specialized markers, for example, moving midpoints, to help in foreseeing future transient force, yet these brokers never completely understand the capacity these apparatuses have for recognizing levels of help and opposition. As should be obvious from the outline beneath, a moving normal is a continually changing line that smooths out past value information while likewise enabling the dealer to recognize backing and opposition. Notice how the cost of the advantage discovers support at the moving normal when the pattern is up, and how it goes about as opposition when the pattern is down.

Merchants can utilize moving midpoints in an assortment of ways, for example, to envision moves to the upside, when value lines cross over a key moving normal, or to leave exchanges, when the value dips under a moving normal. Despite how the moving normal is utilized, it frequently makes "programmed" backing and obstruction levels. Most merchants will try different things with various timespans in their moving midpoints so they can locate the one that works best for this particular undertaking.

Different Indicators

In specialized investigation, numerous markers have been created to recognize hindrances to future value activity. These markers appear to be confused from the start, and it regularly takes practice and experience to utilize them viably. Notwithstanding a pointer's intricacy, be that as it may, the elucidation of the recognized hindrance ought to be steady to those accomplished through less complex strategies.

For instance, the Fibonacci retracement device is a most loved among some momentary merchants since it unmistakably recognizes levels of potential help/opposition. The thinking behind how this pointer ascertains the different degrees of help and opposition is past the extent of this article; however see in Figure 5 how the recognized levels (specked lines) are boundaries to the transient bearing of the cost.

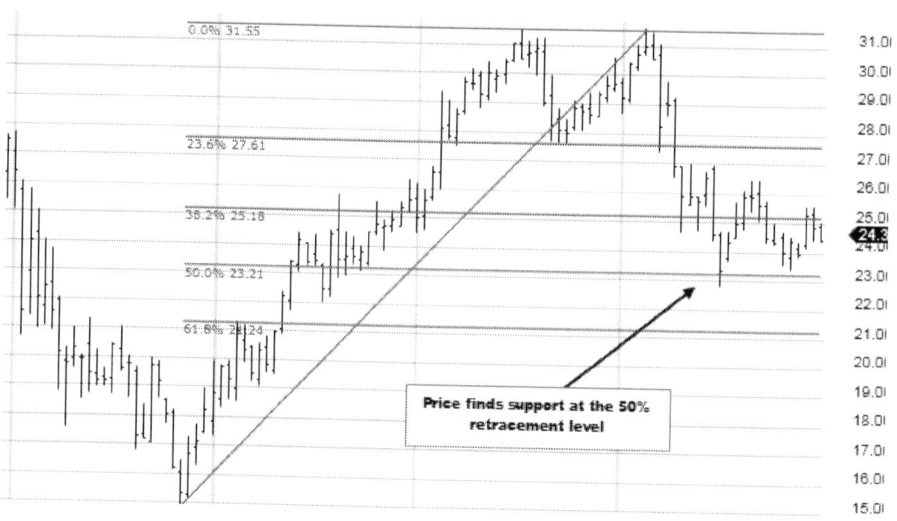


## Estimating the Significance of Zones

Keep in mind how we utilized the expressions "floor" for help and "roof" for obstruction? Proceeding with the house similarity, the security is the means by which an elastic ball that bobs in a room will hit the floor (backing) and after that bounce back off the roof (opposition). A ball that keeps on ricocheting between the floor and the roof is like an exchanging instrument that is encountering value union among help and obstruction zones. Presently envision that the ball, in mid-flight, changes to a bowling ball. This additional power, whenever connected in transit up, will push the ball through the opposition level; in transit down, it will push the ball through the help level. In any case, additional power, or energy from either the bulls or bears, is expected to get through the help or opposition.

Regularly, a help level will inevitably turn into an obstruction level when the value endeavors to move back up, and then again, an opposition level will turn into a help level as the value briefly falls back. Value outlines enable merchants and speculators to outwardly distinguish territories of help and obstruction, and they give hints with respect to the essentialness of these value levels. All the more explicitly, they take a gander at:

Number of Touches. The more occasions the value tests a help or obstruction territory, the more noteworthy the level moves toward becoming. At the point when costs continue ricocheting off a help or opposition level, more purchasers and dealers see and will put together exchanging choices with respect to these levels.

Going before Price Move. Backing and obstruction zones are probably going to be increasingly critical when they are gone before by soak advances or decreases. For instance, a quick, soak advance or upturn will be met with more challenge and energy and might be stopped by a more critical opposition level than a moderate, unfaltering development. A moderate development may not pull in as much consideration. This is a genuine case of how market brain science drives specialized pointers.

Volume at Certain Price Levels. The all the more purchasing and selling that has happened at a specific value level, the more grounded the help or obstruction level is probably going to be. This is on the grounds that dealers and financial specialists recall these value levels and are able to utilize them once more. At the point when solid action happens under high volume and the value drops, a ton of selling will probably happen when value comes back to that level, since individuals are unmistakably progressively happy with finishing off an exchange at the breakeven point as opposed to at a misfortune.

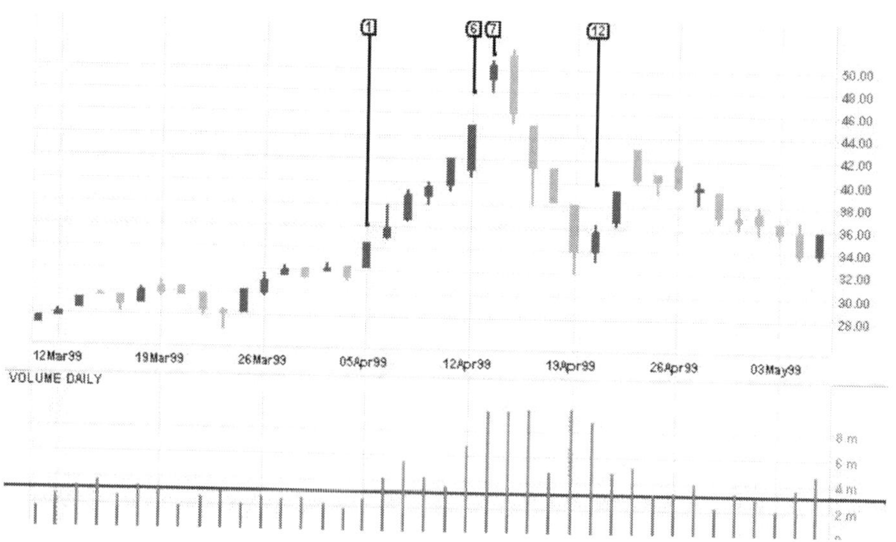


Time. Backing and obstruction zones become progressively noteworthy if the levels have been tried normally over an all-encompassing timeframe.

The Bottom Line

Backing and obstruction levels are one of the key ideas utilized by specialized examiners and structure the premise of a wide assortment of specialized examination apparatuses. The essentials of help and obstruction comprise of a help level, which can be thought of as the floor under exchanging costs, and an opposition level, which can be thought of as the roof. Costs fall and test the help level, which will either "hold," and the cost will ricochet back up, or the help level will be damaged, and the cost will drop through the help and likely proceed with lower to the following help level.

Deciding future degrees of help can definitely improve the profits of a momentary contributing technique since it gives brokers an exact picture of what value levels should prop up the cost of a given security in case of an amendment. Alternately, anticipating a degree of opposition can be profitable on the grounds that this is a value level that could possibly hurt a long position, connoting a territory where financial specialists have a high eagerness to sell the security. As referenced above, there are a few distinct techniques to pick when hoping to recognize support/obstruction, however paying little heed to the strategy, the understanding continues as before—it averts the cost of a hidden resource from moving in a specific heading.

## Price Action, Candlestick and Trade Management

- Price Action and Group Psychology in Forex Trading

Any traditionally prepared financial expert will guarantee that cost is the balance of free market activity. At the point when that reality stays to be valid in Economics 101, as a general rule cost is the aggregate agreement among market members. Development of cost then again mirrors their joined assumption about the directional inclination. In any case, in money related market we regularly observe nonsensical value conduct. The nonsensicalness gets from a mass mental occasion which states regularly value development is really the consequence of its earlier observational development.

## Mass Psychology and Crowd Behavior in Forex Trading

Separately, advertise members can utilize natural incentive by investigating different financial or frequently specialized pointers, for example, CPI, Inflation or MACD. In any case, as a gathering, frequently Forex merchants stress without anyone else crowd attitude to purchase or sell monetary standards which we call following the pattern.

The pattern following or group attitude can be seen in silly value development, for example, spikes during news discharges, working of help and obstruction zones where greater part of brokers respond to value activity and transforms those nonexistent lines on their diagrams into unavoidable outcomes. Indeed, frequently we see during a pattern value regards antiquated prime numbers, Fibonacci proportions and other extravagant numbers. These specialized instruments now and then work on the grounds that the Mass Psychology of the Forex Market or the crowd pays attention to those numbers and devices. For instance, pattern lines work since brokers use pattern lines! In the event that enough dealers wind up utilizing some sort of bend lines, those will likewise wind up having all the earmarks of being working!

There is really a faction in the money related market who turned out to be effective by recognizing how mass brain research functions at that point indiscriminately following the crowd. Richard Driehaus advanced that purchasing high, contrasted with purchasing low can be increasingly gainful contrasted with the customary venture worldview which supporters purchasing low and selling high! Purchasing low and selling high is an idea best executed by world's noticeable speculators like Warren Buffett. Notwithstanding, Mr. Driehaus wound up fruitful by essentially following the mass brain science of the market and purchasing high and selling at much more expensive rate, and reformed the hypothetical idea of all momentary financial specialists, merchants and examiners for the great.

Maybe the best demonstration of back this mass brain research based exchanging approach originated from one of unmistakable British financial expert of the twentieth century, John Maynard Keynes, who stated: "The market can remain nonsensical longer than you can remain dissolvable."

What he implied by this adage was that attempting to justify market or cost and exchanging against the "pattern" or crowd mindset can demolish your record. In any case, on the off chance that we can switch our mental molding and pursue Mr. Richard Driehaus' recommendation then in spite of agonizing over our dissolvability, we can make a decent measure of benefit by basically following the silly market.

There is a great deal of specialized exchanging methods that pursues this kind of hypothetical idea. For instance, "breakouts" are probably the best technique to pursue swarm attitude of the market. At the point when the value closes above or underneath a fanciful exchanging range, since key market members watch this, they participate and push the cost much higher once there is a breakout on the upside and the other way around.

Utilizing mass brain science to increase tremendous benefit has its traps too. One of the key parts of utilizing crowd attitude is figuring out how to deal with the innate hazard related with utilizing such system. Effective Forex dealers comprehend that when nonsensical value development can make inclines, these wonders can likewise change the pattern and wipe their record in all respects rapidly, if the hazard isn't overseen appropriately.

The Spinning Top candle example structures some portion of the huge Japanese candle collection with its own particular highlights. Frequently connected with hesitation in the market, Spinning Top candles can give profitable supporting data to an exchanging methodology. The fundamental arguments of this article are:

What is the Spinning Top candle design?

How is the Spinning candle framed?

Instructions to exchange the Spinning Top light

Become familiar with exchanging with candles

Exactly what is a spinning top candle pattern?

A Spinning Top example includes a solitary light demonstrating vulnerability in the market. The candle itself is characterized by a short body encompassed by long wicks (roughly a similar length) on either side. The Spinning Top can be either bullish or bearish at the light close. This candle example is frequently situated inside an upturn, downtrend or potentially solidification (sideways development) implying potential inversions.

How is the spinning top candle made?

The value development inside the Spinning Top light speaks to purchasers and merchants repealing each other bringing about a comparable open and close value level. The benefit of joining the Spinning Top candle design inside an exchanging methodology is that it is anything but difficult to relate to insignificant suggested time speculation.

The rationale behind the uncertainty appeared in the market during the development of a Spinning Top is basic - while the flame was shaping, brokers moved costs both higher and lower all through the graph time frame. This brought about the end value returning/extremely near the opening cost.

The Spinning Top example pursues a similar essential structure and rationale as the Doji be that as it may, the Spinning Top shows a more extensive light body which demonstrates an increasingly significant development in cost during the flame time frame.

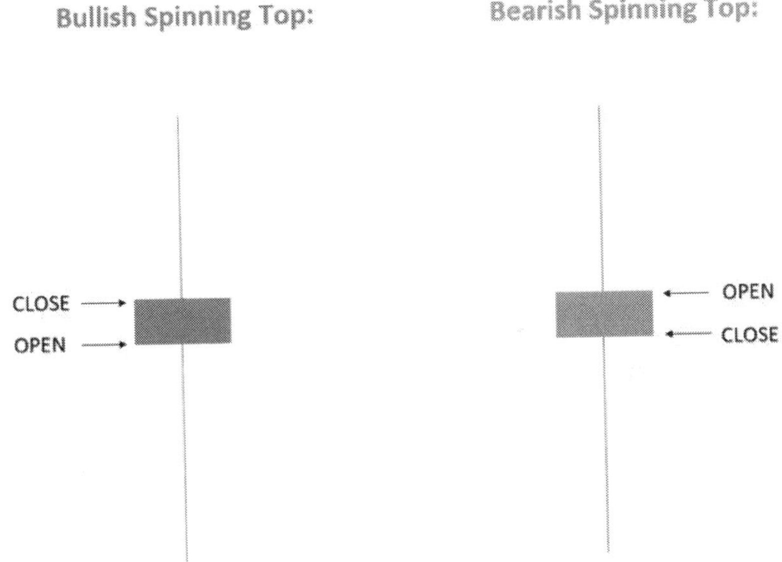


Instructions to trade the spinning top candle

Exchanging with the Spinning Top light includes seeing how it is framed and where it sits in connection to the general market pattern. The model beneath experiences distinguishing proof, affirmation and execution of a commonsense forex exchange utilizing the Spinning Top.

EUR/NZD turning top candle

In the EUR/NZD graph over, the Spinning Top flame (bearish) shows up at the highest point of an upturn – featured by the gold pattern line. The hesitation from purchasers and merchants is evident and prompts an inversion in pattern heading.

Live merchants ought not hope to enter an exchange following the Spinning Top has framed, yet rather defer the exchange to sit tight for affirmation. Affirmation can emerge out of specialized pointers, principal components or oscillators as observed utilizing a stochastic oscillator. The stochastic re-affirms a short section as demonstrated by the blue circle.

The most widely recognized technique utilized by specialized dealers to affirm a pattern inversion is sitting tight for the arrangement of the succeeding flame. Utilizing the model over, the succeeding light should close lower than the wick of the Spinning Top. Without this affirmation, the sign of pattern inversion may not be built up, and vulnerability stays in the market.

Key takeaways for exchanging the Spinning Top candle design:

Find light with a short body and long wicks on the two sides

Recognize market pattern by utilizing pattern lines or specialized pointers

Hang tight for affirmation preceding entering exchange

Whenever affirmed, place exchange wanted heading

All in all, the Spinning Top flame delineates advertise hesitation among purchasers and venders which could show value inversions. It is essential to perceive the situating of the Spinning Top inside the market – inside a pattern or at key value levels of help and opposition. The Spinning Top candle example is best at these specific focuscs.

Other indecision patterns:

The Doji Pattern

Doji Candlestick - Finance BrokerageDoji design, an uncertainty design that structures at whatever point both purchasing and selling weight is in balance. There are two different ways to perceive a Doji design. One, the open and close of the flame are around the center of the range. Two, lower and upper shadows are short. Both are about a similar length.

Despite the fact that Doji is a hesitation design, there is diverse significance. There are two sorts of Doji design.

Dragonfly Doji

Disparate with the standard Doji in which opens and shutting close the center of the range. Dragonfly Doji opens and closes close the highs of the range with long lower shadow.

Dragonfly Doji happens at whatever point there's a dismissal of lower costs while purchasing weight ventures in to push the market to a higher opening cost.

Unique with the ordinary Doji, Gravestone Doji closes open and closes close the lows of the range having a long upper shadow. Headstone Doji shows a refusal of more expensive rates while selling weight ventures in pushing the market lower to the opening cost.

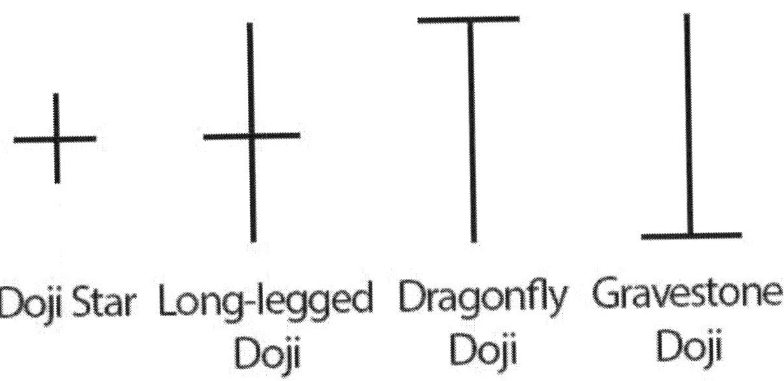


The Continuation Candlestick Pattern

Continuation example demonstrates that the market is going to keep exchanging a similar heading. As an accomplished merchant, a continuation example is the best open door in the market. Moreover, there are four sorts of continuation design.

Rising Three Method Pattern

Rising three techniques is a bullish pattern continuation example showing that the market is to keep exchanging higher. There are three different ways to perceive a rising three technique design. One, the principal light demonstrates a huge bullish flame. Two, the accompanying three candles have a littler body and range. Three, the last flame have an enormous body shutting beneath the lows of the main light.

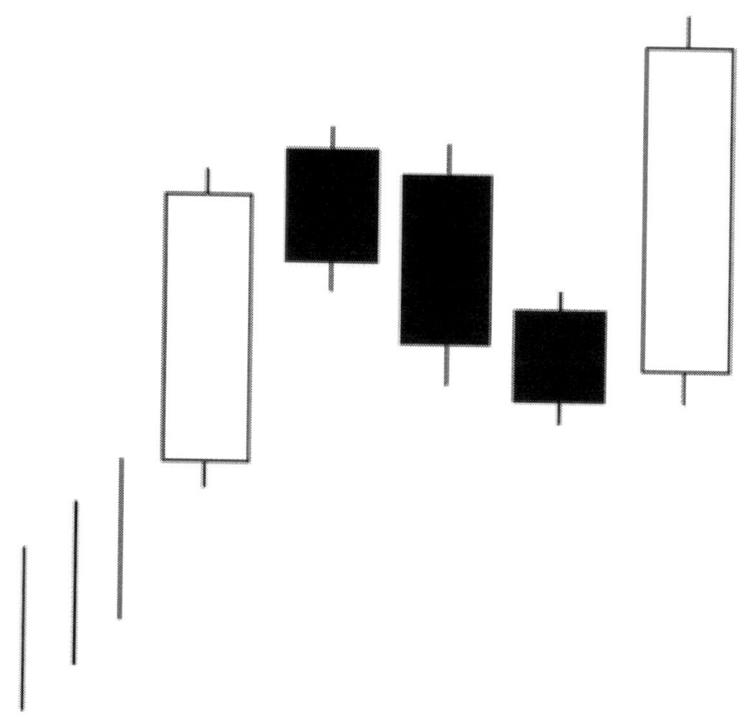

Falling Three Method Pattern

Falling Three Method Pattern - Finance Brokerage Falling three strategies demonstrates three things. Right off the bat, the main light tells that the dealers are in charge as they close the session emphatically lower. Also, the accompanying three candles demonstrate that the merchants are picking up benefits prompting a slight progressed. Be that as it may, it was anything but a solid rally on the grounds that there are new venders entering short. Ultimately, the fifth flame demonstrates that the vender's increase control pushing cost to new lows.

The Bullish Harami

Bullish Harami Pattern - Finance Brokerage The bullish harami functions admirably as a continuation design inside the upswing. It demonstrates that the purchasers are taking a break and the cost is to exchange higher. There are two different ways to demonstrate a bullish harami. One, the principal flame is bullish and greater than the subsequent light. Two, the following light have a littler range and body.

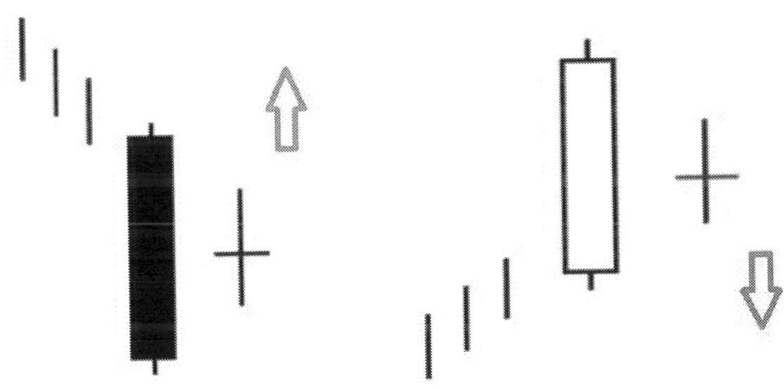

**Bullish and Bearish Harami Cross**

A Bullish harami example shows two things. Initially, the primary flame demonstrating the purchasing weight while the light bullishly closes. Besides, the subsequent light shows hesitation while both purchasing and selling weight seems to be similar.

The Bearish Harami

Bearish Harami Pattern - Finance Brokerage Bearish harami works best inside a continuation design inside the downtrend. It demonstrates that the venders enjoy a reprieve. Simultaneously, the sum is going to exchange lower.

There are two different ways to demonstrate a bearish harami. One, the primary flame is bigger and bearish contrast and the subsequent one. Two, the accompanying light have a little range and body.

Bearish harami shows two things. Initially, the principal light shows solid selling weight while the flame closes bearishly. Furthermore, the uncertainty from both (purchasing and selling) weight is indistinguishable.

Pattern Continuation Setups

To further comprehend the continuation arrangements, (Rising Three Method, Falling Three Method, Bullish Harami, Bearish Harami) how about we take a gander at them on an example market outline.

Here's the manner by which to do it. Right off the bat, at whatever point the market is in a range, sit tight for its breakout over the obstruction. Besides, when the market breaks out the opposition, hang tight for it to frame a continuation candle design. Thirdly, at whatever point the market makes a continuation candle, go long on the breaks the highs.

# Chapter 7

# Advanced Day Trading Strategies

Some intraday stock dealers state that on the off chance that they could pick just a single specialized pointer it would be the VWAP.

I find that VWAP isn't really a sacred goal and dealers can't help contradicting the most ideal approach to utilize it. In the remainder of this article, I test two exceptionally straightforward VWAP exchanging frameworks and present the outcomes.

What is VWAP?

In all respects just, VWAP represents volume weighted normal cost and it gives a thought at the normal cost that financial specialists have paid for a stock over the exchanging day.

It along these lines gives a thought for how different financial specialists are situated.

Another purpose behind its ubiquity is that it's frequently utilized by algos and institutional brokers to scale into positions. Utilizing VWAP, an algo can separate its position size into squares in order to limit its effect available.

In spite of the fact that speculators normally exchange with various thought processes and time spans the rationale of how VWAP is utilized can prompt different kinds of exchanging frameworks.

1. Purchase When Price Moves Above VWAP

As per a few merchants, the best time to purchase a stock is when value crosses above VWAP. This is on the grounds that it demonstrates that purchasers are in charge.

In the event that cost is above VWAP, at that point one might say that most of intraday positions are in benefit though if cost is underneath VWAP it proposes that financial specialists are likely losing cash on their exchanges.

I needed to test this out. Along these lines, the accompanying technique goes long when value crosses above VWAP on the 15-minute graph and sells when value crosses under VWAP. All sections and exits are made on the following bar open after the VWAP signal.

Following is a case of the exchange we are searching for in SPY:

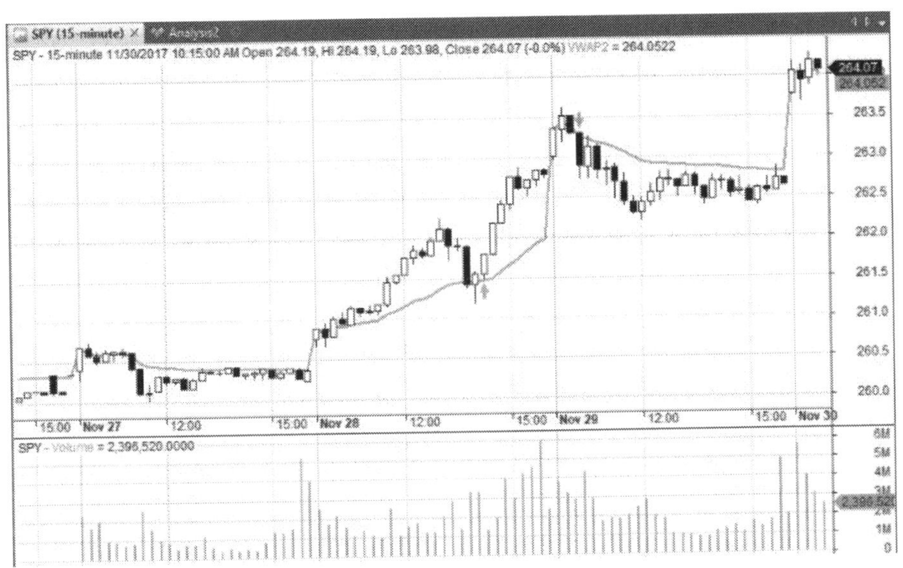


You can see SPY closes over the VWAP at 14:00 on Nov 28 so we go long on the following bar open at 14:15 (green bolt).

SPY closes underneath VWAP at 10 AM the following morning so we close our situation on the following bar at 10:15 (red bolt). This gives us a 0.67% benefit.

Some brokers use VWAP in the turn around way and search for a stock to dip under the VWAP line.

These merchants see VWAP as a manual for worth and feel that when a stock exchanges under VWAP then it demonstrates great worth and ought to be purchased.

The accompanying procedure, along these lines, goes long when value crosses beneath VWAP on the 5-minute diagram and it sells when value crosses back above VWAP.

Since there are numerous algos that utilization VWAP to scale in exchanges this appears as though it could be a strong exchanging thought so how about we test it out.

Following is a case of the exchange arrangement:

Well, it's clear that VWAP is not a holy grail in this simple form but it is capable of some good results.

Using VWAP to trade momentum worked great for Amazon giving us a 20.45% annualized return on the 15-minute chart despite only a quarter of trades being winners.

It worked even better on the 2-hour chart with half of the 20 stocks showing a profit.

Conversely, using VWAP for mean reversion worked well for KRFT giving an annualized return of 33% on the 15-minute chart with minimum drawdown. However, 6 assets were actually seen as moneymaking throughout this time.

In general inertia is most beneficial for VWAP; the more extensive two-hour strategy turns out to be the most positive and profitable.

The majority of day traders, contrary to popular belief, search for potential stocks during even smaller amounts of time than two hours. Best outcomes come from or reflect the results of arrangement fees during less amounts of time.

Our results reveal a similar conclusion.

Using VWAP on longer term charts works better because it reduces the impact of costs.

## The Key to Really Getting Better and Making Profit: Skill over Strategy

It's important to remember that overall, having a bunch of strategies in your arsenal isn't going to help you all that much. It's important to develop the skills that go along with that strategy; that's what makes a successful day trader. You can read all of the day trading books on the market, but if you don't practice, review, and adapt your techniques, then you won't get any better.

When the trader is trying to find data and benefitting as quick as could be permitted, most new casual financial specialists skirt ta majority of noteworthy walks in finding efficiency and consistency, which is called... practice!

At the point when a vendor knows how to place orders, how to figure the ideal position size, direct peril, and understands a fundamental procedure to seek after, the proportion of time spent on books, articles, and enlightening chronicles should drop essentially. Time should then be spent on practicing these capacities, so the aptitudes can be called upon for making split-second move in speedy moving day trading conditions.

The essential system casual financial specialists need to learn is the methods by which to practice.

In order to improve, you'll need to practice. Examining articles or watching videos isn't satisfactory. You need to practice what you are understanding, a lot before it will twist up ingrained enough to be useful in choosing trading decisions reliably changing monetary circumstances. Many different day trading platform offer “demo” options, where you can practice your strategies with fake money but with real-time data. Use these, and use them often. The trader that does will enter the market with an advantage.

Practice isn't just putting in hours. Basically putting in hours won't improve a vendor. It's possible to day trade for a significant long time, basically putting in hours, and never watch improvement since it's definitely not a purposeful and express development. To practice satisfactorily, chip away at something a little bit at a time. This is the spot the trading plan comes in. A trading plan is a report that unequivocally follows how, why and when an agent will enter and leave trades, how they will control risk and what their position size will be.

It furthermore nuances which markets will be traded and when. The word to look for here is "unequivocal." Rehearsal incorporates following a course of action with the objective that progression can be pursued. If it so happens that the occasion that trades are taken subject to self-assertive factors or mental driving forces, by then the trading results will take on the comparable erratic and unpredictable nature.

Practice day trading one piece of the trading plan without a moment's delay, in a demo account, until the procedure ends up being normal. Take this example: A trader might experience diagrams and pick section centers for their system. Do this until you can see all the segment centers that your strategy gives. Day trading requires quick, anyway deliberate, intuitive decision-making. Rehearse keeping in mind that your objective that segments happen decisively when they should, in light of the framework.
At that point proceed onward to putting the stop misfortune accurately. At that point, work on putting the benefit targets effectively. It could take two or three weeks to two or three months to excel and become proficient at component of the procedure. As you get the hang of setting your entrance, stop misfortune levels and benefit targets dependent on your exchanging plan, at that point begin to consolidate different components of the exchanging plan.

This might sound fairly odd or out of the ordinary, but this whole time you are in like manner practicing what NOT to do. Your goal isn't simply to seek after your technique and take all of the trades it guides you to take (when the state of the market is great, established on your trading plan) anyway you are also chipping away at "fail to move" when your framework isn't educating you to a take a trade. Trading is as much about the trades you take for what is value about those you don't. In case your method doesn't give a trading opportunity, by then sit inactive. The diligence required to keep things under control for an authentic trade sign

requires a lot of practice...and is an ability most new intermediaries need.
Work on being quiet, yet jumping when a substantial exchange opportunity emerges.

What exactly degree you practice each segment of your trading plan for will contrast by the trader. Normally, tackle each segment of the trading plan for ten to twenty or so days. When you have aced one part, incorporate another, and after that preparation those two segments for 10 to 20 days, and so on. After around a half year the seller using this technique will have a not too bad handle of their trading plan, will have practiced their framework for around 120 trading days, and will have a brilliant idea of how to utilize it in every single financial circumstance.

Over a multi month time range, the vendor will most likely have seen temperamental days, quiet days, floating days, running days, up days and down days. Practicing in one kind of market isn't adequate. A seller needs to deal with trading and not trading (when no sign are accessible) in a wide scope of business divisions conditions. Subsequently, chip away at realizing the focal points of the trading for at any rate a half year before utilizing real capital.

Assessing Your Day Trades

When you practice and seek after a specific game plan, you are gaining deliberate ground toward your target of transforming into a dependably profitable trader...even if the principal course of action is certainly not a better than average one. The show of following a course of action gathers control and resistance, two key attributes casual financial specialists need. The study methodology is the spot you find the opportunity to examine both your ability to seek after the course of action (what you need to tackle) and the plan itself (what changes the game plan may require).

"Self-overview" should be finished an ordinary timetable, while a "trading plan review" should be done on seven days after week and month to month premise.

Starting a Day Trading Business

Now it may seem like a ways off before you're even thinking about starting a day trading business, but traders who have lofty end goals, or at least something to aspire to, can keep their motivations up no matter what market changes do to them. It will help you weather through rough patches and stormy months.

The first thing to keep in mind whether or not you're thinking about starting a business is taxes. Unfortunately, you have to pay them, and there's no true way to avoid it. Ensure you prop that as a primary concern before up off to burn through the majority of your rewards!

So how would you make sense of what duties to pay on your exchanges? Your personal assessment will depend whereupon class you fall into, that is in case you're exchanging or contributing. Tragically, as an IRS agent rose, that the inquiry is self-evident, yet the suitable reaction is without a doubt not. In this way, you'll need to seek after take a look at the 70,000 (yep, that's four zeroes) page expense code and think about decisions in significant case law.

Financial specialist charges: If you're not qualified as a merchant (which is somewhat discretionary by Internal Revenue Service rules, yet for the reasons for this book, speculators are not swing or informal investors). Financial specialists should manage a quite steep assessment rate, particularly in the United States. This is typically represented on structure 8949 or a Schedule D. On that structure, there's a space for "random separated derivations." That's the place you'll put your costs.

To the extent what you can qualify as costs, you won't most likely case you home office. Any product or other hardware that you use in your exchanging devalues.

On a Schedule A, costs brought about while contributing are converged with different costs like the expenses to set up your charges (no, extremely, this tallies!). Exploit this. Yet, remember that just two percent of your salary.

Expense Categories: Where do you fall similarly as assessment orders go? Shockingly there's no unmistakable refinement, yet there is a ton of point of reference, which this following segment depends on. The two financial specialists and brokers manage stocks and resources, yet they're not the equivalent according to the IRS. To the Internal Revenue Service, financial specialists aren't really viewed as full-time dealers of protections.

Financial specialist increases are gotten from capital additions, profits and enthusiasm for the benefits they've been exchanging.

Page 1 conclusions are what you have to make sense of whether you reserve an option to or not. Don't worry about it Schedule A findings. In any case, there's a distinction, and that distinction is whether you do exchanging low maintenance, or your exchanging is a business. Regardless of the way that the IRS's expense code is 70,000 pages in length, obviously there's no spot where both of these two terms "exchange" and "business" are clarified, nor is there any obvious method for making sense of how the Internal

Revenue Service chooses they're unique in relation to one another.

Or maybe, there's fortunately point of reference as case law, since a great many merchants before you have confronted this comparable trouble. We'll investigate the distinctions beneath.

A great deal of the contrasts between the meanings of "Merchant" and "speculator" comes down to time. On the off chance that you go through the majority of your day behind a PC, acquiring and exchanging protections, at that point 99% of the time you will be viewed as a dealer. Since you purchased this book, you'll likely not fall under this classification, so we won't really expound. In any case, on the off chance that you advance further in your investing and exchanging vocation, it's valuable to have some foundation.

Don't stress, you don't need to recollect that. What you do need to recollect is that there are two fundamental things that characterize dealers: Your exchanging was noteworthy and huge, and that your objective was to pick up from day by day showcase changes, rather than holding and benefitting off of ventures over a more drawn out timeframe.

A Legal Trading Business

The best way to guarantee you are accepting a similar expense treatment as a certified merchant is to make a different corporate substance to exchange through. By making a restricted risk organization (LLC) or constrained association, you can get no different duty treatment as a certified broker without qualifying. The lawful element ordinarily gets less investigation by the IRS in light of the fact that the supposition that is nobody would experience the inconvenience and cost of framing the element except if they were focused on exchanging as a business adventure. It is amazingly hard for people to change a race, for example, MTM, when it has been picked. With the organization, if there is a preferred position to changing bookkeeping techniques or the legitimate structure, the element can essentially be broken down and re-shaped in like manner.

For very fruitful merchants, a few counselors will recommend structures that incorporate various elements to boost the duty and assurance benefits. Despite the fact that the genuine structure is dictated by a person's money related objectives, it for the most part incorporates a C company, which exists to be the general accomplice or overseeing individual from a few restricted obligation organizations. Along these lines, additional pay can be moved to the corporate substance (as a rule up to 30% of income) through a contracted administration charge to exploit the extra assessment methodologies accessible.

For instance, to finance school costs or to give kids cash tax-exempt, relatives can move toward becoming representatives. The enterprise would then be able to exploit deductible compensations and instruction costs, while building Social Security and Medicare accounts. Medicinal repayment plans can be made to subsidize a wide range of elective human services and therapeutic protection premium. Retirement records, for example, IRAs and 401(k) can be moved into a 401a. Since the partnership settles regulatory obligations on total compensation, the objective is to pay however many costs as could be allowed with pretax dollars and to limit assessable salary.

This kind of business structure likewise gives superb resource assurance since it isolates the business from the person. Long haul resources can be held by other constrained risk organizations that can utilize bookkeeping strategies more qualified for ventures. All advantages are shielded from loan bosses and the lawful liabilities of the individual since they are held by isolated legitimate elements. The measure of lawful assurance is dictated by state law. Numerous counsels propose framing these substances in states that won't permit the puncturing of the lawful structure. Most lean toward Nevada in view of its absence of corporate deals charge, adaptability to charge arranges as a sole cure by loan bosses, the obscurity of not posting investors, and the assignment of corporate officials.

In spite of the fact that exchanging through a complex lawful structure has clear advantages, it additionally can include a lot of unpredictability to one's close to home issues. For brokers who have been reliably beneficial yet can't or don't have any desire to meet all requirements for dealer status, exchanging through a straightforward business is fundamental. In the event that you wish to set up an annuity reserve to concede charges, pay compensations to friends and family or recover huge restorative costs tax-exempt, at that point the additional multifaceted nature is a better than average exchange off to pick up the advantages of a compound structure. In any case, to get the best assessment treatment and lawful insurance, talk with guides who comprehend the development and activity of these elements for brokers.

Assemble a marketable strategy. Would you go into a bank and request an advance to begin a café with no marketable strategy? Most likely not! Your exchanging should be a similar way.

What is your framework for hazard the executives?

What arrangements will you center around?

Assembling a far reaching plan will give you zones to concentrate on when you're exchanging on the test system, as reenacting without center isn't genuine practice. When you practice, it should be purposeful and copy genuine conditions.

3. Test it out! As you most likely are aware, what looks great on paper regularly doesn't bode well, all things considered, conditions, so take fastidious notes on what necessities to change in your field-tested strategy as you are reenacting your system.

It will respond to certain inquiries for you: does your technique blend well with your work routine? Does it profit? Does it suit your character, and so on. What it will likewise do–this is significant is keep a log of your exchanges to give you a thought of your inclinations. What are your qualities and shortcomings? What are your best arrangements?

Recognizing what you're great at and afterward rehearsing it again and again will enable you to construct aptitude in these arrangements. You need a large number of redundancies to truly begin to consider all to be edges as a merchant and to manufacture that ability that begins here!

# Chapter 8

# Risk and Account Management

Professional informal investors utilize a hazard the executive strategy called the 1-percent hazard rule, or change it marginally to accommodate their exchanging strategies. Adherence to the standard downplays capital misfortunes when a dealer has an off day or encounters unforgiving economic situations, while as yet taking into account incredible month to month returns or salary. The 1-percent hazard principle bodes well for some reasons, and you can profit by comprehension and utilizing it as a feature of your exchanging system.

The 1-Percent Risk Rule

Following the standard methods you never hazard more than 1 percent of your record an incentive on a solitary exchange. That doesn't imply that on the off chance that you have a $30,000 exchanging account, you can just purchase $300 worth of stock, which would be 1 percent of $30,000.

You can utilize the majority of your capital on a solitary exchange, or much more in the event that you use influence. Actualizing the 1-percent hazard principle implies you make chance administration strides with the goal that you counteract misfortunes of more than 1 percent on any single exchange.

Nobody wins each exchange, and the 1-percent hazard standard shields a broker's capital from declining fundamentally in horrible circumstances. In the event that you chance 1 percent of your present record balance on each exchange, you would need to lose 100 exchanges a line to crash your record. On the off chance that learner brokers pursued the 1-percent rule, a lot a greater amount of them would make it effectively through their first exchanging year.

Gambling 1 percent or less per exchange may appear to be a modest quantity to certain individuals, however it can in any case give extraordinary returns. In the event that you hazard 1 percent, you should likewise set your benefit objective or desire on each effective exchange to 1.5 percent to 2 percent or more. When making a few exchanges every day, picking up a couple of rate focuses for you every day is totally conceivable, regardless of whether you just win half of your exchanges.

Applying the Rule

By gambling 1 percent of your record on a solitary exchange, you can make an exchange which gives you a 2-percent return for you, despite the fact that the market just moved a small amount of a percent. Also, you can chance 1 percent of your record regardless of whether the value normally moves 5 percent or 0.5 percent. You can accomplish this by utilizing targets and stop-misfortune orders.

You can utilize the standard to day exchange stocks or different markets, for example, prospects or forex. Expect you need to purchase a stock at $15, and you have a $30,000 account. You take a gander at the outline and see the value as of late put in a transient swing low at $14.90.

You put in a stop-misfortune request at $14.89, one penny beneath the ongoing low cost. When you have recognized your stop-misfortune area, you can figure what number of offers to purchase while taking a chance with close to 1 percent of your record.

Your record hazard likens to 1 percent of $30,000, or $300. Your exchange hazard approaches $0.11, determined as the distinction between your stock purchase cost and stop misfortune cost.

Separation your record hazard by your exchange hazard to get the best possible position size: $300/$0.11 = 2,727 offers. Round this down to 2,700 and this shows what number of offers you can purchase in this exchange without presenting yourself to misfortunes of more than 1 percent of your record. Note that 2,700 offers at $15 cost $40,500, which surpasses the estimation of your $30,000 record balance. Thusly, you need influence of in any event 2:1 to make this exchange.

On the off chance that the stock value hits your stop-misfortune, you will lose around 1 percent of your capital or near $300 for this situation. In any case, if the value moves higher and you sell your offers at $15.22, you make right around 2 percent on your cash, or near $600 (less commissions). This is on the grounds that your position is aligned to make or lose just about 1 percent at each $0.11 the cost moves. In the event that you exit at $15.33, you make very nearly 3 percent on the exchange, despite the fact that the value just moved around 2 percent.

This strategy enables you to adjust exchanges to a wide range of economic situations, regardless of whether unpredictable or quiet and still profit. The strategy likewise applies to all business sectors. Prior to exchanging, you ought to know about slippage where you can't get out at the stop misfortune cost and could assume a greater misfortune than anticipated.

## Rate Variations

Merchants with exchanging records of under $100,000 ordinarily utilize the 1 percent standard. While 1 percent offers more security, when you're reliably gainful, a few merchants utilize a 2 percent hazard rule, gambling 2 percent of their record esteem per exchange. A center ground would be just gambling 1.5 percent or some other rate underneath 2 percent.

For records over $100,000, numerous merchants hazard under 1 percent. For instance, they may hazard as meager as 0.5 percent or even 0.1 percent on a huge record. While momentary exchanging, it winds up hard to hazard even 1 percent in light of the fact that the position sizes get so enormous. Every broker finds a rate they feel great with and that suits the liquidity of the market wherein they exchange. Whichever rate you pick, keep it beneath 2 percent.

## Withstanding Losses

The 1-percent principle can be changed to suit every merchant's record size and market. Set a rate you feel great gambling, and afterward compute your position size for each exchange as per the section cost and stop misfortune.

Following the 1-percent guideline implies you can withstand a long series of misfortunes. Expecting you have bigger winning exchanges than failures, you'll locate your capital doesn't drop in all respects rapidly however can rise rather rapidly. Before taking a chance with any cash—even 1 percent—practice your procedure in a demo record and work to make steady benefits before contributing your genuine capital.

## What should your position size be?

Not gambling an excessive amount of cash on some random exchange is fundamental for any informal investor. Tragically, when a great many people begin exchanging, they don't consider the hazard that they are taking – just about the potential prizes.

Each exchanging methodology must think about the most extreme level of the all out exchanging capital that ought to be gambled in any one exchange. Truth be told, a broker's capacity to confine his misfortunes is similarly as significant (or much increasingly significant) as his accomplishment in overseeing winning positions.

Consider it. On the off chance that a merchant misfortunes a modest quantity on each exchange, won't he remain in the game much more? Taking immense misfortunes is one of the essential reasons why such a large number of dealers don't make due around here. For what reason do brokers submit money related suicide along these lines, you may inquire? In the event that every single enormous misfortune begin little, shouldn't it be anything but difficult to keep a little misfortune from getting to be unmanageable? The appropriate response is a resonating "YES."

Restricting misfortunes in day exchanging includes a great deal of good judgment. In the first place, I don't figure any merchant should hazard more than 2 to 5% of his exchanging capital on some random exchange. Why? In the event that a dealer adheres to a 1% to 2% most extreme misfortune rule, his odds of remaining in the game are incredibly expanded in light of the fact that it will take numerous continuous misfortunes to clear him out and he will have more cash making openings accessible to him.

In the event that a merchant will deal with a $10,000 account, he ought not lose more than $100 to $200 (1% to 2%) on each position taken. Utilizing a similar thinking, on the off chance that we are managing an exchanging account that is $100,000 in size, the most extreme suitable misfortune can be expanded to $1,000 or $2,000 per exchange. In light of these rates and on the sum the cost can move against the broker (decided from the graphs), he can compute the most extreme size his position ought to have. This turns out to be much more clear with a numerical model:

Position Sizing Example utilizing Currencies (to get familiar with monetary standards, read this segment)

Accept that a financial specialist can exchange a ton of one hundred thousand United States Dollars starting out with a nest of two thousand dollars (that's a fifty against one influence) and that the trader has ten thousand dollars in a record. With this record size, he can exchange a limit of five parcels (2000 dollars per five parcels in his edge store = ten thousand) at any given moment – however is this a savvy activity? We should investigate this somewhat further.

Suppose that dependent on his approach, the dealer breaks down the graph and discovers that with the end goal for him to take a long position with a potential reward of $800 per part, he should be happy to lose $200 per parcel. He understands that on the off chance that he takes a 5-parcel position and all goes well, he could have an increase of $4000 or 40% (five segments per eight hundred dollars per parcel equals a whopping four thousand dollars) on his $10k account. Your size positive of five individual parcels means therefore that he will lose out on one thousand dollars (five segments for two hundred dollars per parcel equal one thousand dollars). Would it be a good idea for him to take the exchange? Perhaps, however not with 5 parts!!!

Lost $1,000 speaks to 10% of his exchanging capital!!! To what extent will anybody be ready to go after a couple of back to back ten percent loses? In this model, the trader's most extreme size of position should just be one part. With one part, the trader will try and chance two hundred dollars (two percent of his record size) to make eight hundred dollars (or an eight percent return). He might them want to try and attempt to make the four thousand dollars on one exchange, but most investing experts would advise that this is not a savvy activity. Exchanging is about your likelihood of survival. To endure, you can't hazard beyond what you can manage. Gambling an excess of isn't savvy cash the board.

Take for example, this scenario of position sizing: utilizing assets (remember that in today's market, to legally be considered a day trader in the United States of America, you are required to have a minimum of $25,000 in your record by law. For the purposes of this example, we'll use a balance size of $35,000 in the example following.

Expect that a financial specialist has a $35,000 record to effectively exchange assets. He needs to exchange Canopy Growth (CGN) stock, which is at $32 an offer.

In light of his procedure, he verifies that the stock can acknowledge $1.00 an offer during the day, yet to exploit the thankfulness, he should chance $0.50. His advantage in the day trade twenty five percent (four to one influence) he can take a

$140,000 most extreme position in CGN with his $35,000 (4 x 35,000 = 140,000). Would it be a good idea for him to do it? How about we do the numbers.

With $230,000, the dealer can purchase nearly three thousand eight hundred portions of CGN. On the off chance that CGN climbs 1 point, the merchant gains $7,400. On the off chance that it the stock decreases to $1.00 per share (his stop misfortune), the trader will miss out on less than four thousand. A four thousand dollar misfortune speaks to 13.4 percent of his exchanging funds – excessively enormous a hazard for him to take. Thusly, a four thousand-share CGN trade is unreasonably enormous for his record size. In view of a one percent ($600) great loss, the informal investor ought not purchase more than twelve hundred (1200) shares of CGM (1200/1.00 = twelve hundred shares). In light of a two percent ($1200) hazard, the most extreme exchange size ends up twelve hundred offers.

Hazard in day exchanging (or in some other type of hypothesis) must be controlled. One compelling method for overseeing danger is by not taking on a position bigger than a record of a given size can deal with. While a few creators and "specialists" have convoluted methods for deciding position size, these strategies will in general confound dealers and moderate them down. The one to two percent rule is easier to use as I would like to think. It is good judgment more than everything else. Try not to turn into another exchanging measurement by using stop orders as a defensive measurement; you can really mitigate your losses. Peruse further stop options by considering this tactic.

# Conclusion

Thank you for making it through to the end of *Swing Trading with Options: A Crash Course for Beginners to Highly Profitable Day and Swing Trade*. Let's hope it was informative and able to provide you with all of the tools you need to achieve your goals whatever they may be.

It's important to remember that this book is not meant to stand in for the role of a financial adviser, nor is it meant to provide investment or tax advice. We are proving this information as a resource for you to consider when making your own financial investment decisions.

Past performance does not indicate future outcomes, nor does its analysis prevent risk of loss. Investing, whether long-term, swing, or day trade, requires risk taking and always involved the potential loss of assets/capital.

Last but not least, like always, make a plan and stick to it. Day trading more than any other type of trading requires proper planning and diligence. Your trading plan is how you're going to make money. Deviate from it and you'll get lost in the weeds before you even realize it. Decide your position size, psychology, and handful of strategies before delving in full time. When the market decides to play a few tricks on you, you'll be glad that you were prepared.

Swing and day trading are the practices of getting the stock market to work for you. It does all of the heavy lifting, and you reap the benefits. The first step is to decide what type of trader you want to be, and what your style is. Then you can decide on the important things: your broker, your trading platform, the size of your positions, and your favorite strategy. We hope this book has given you advanced tips on swing trading and a base from which to start day trading. We've also tried to prepare you with the knowledge of how to pick strategies based on risk and reward, and how day trading strategies will change the way you schedule your life. You've also been taught how to evaluate risk, position size, and competition in day trading. We're confident that you're going to make some steps along the way to becoming an advanced swing trader or day trader. But that's the essential key. We can't teach you everything. If there's one thing that we hope this book does for you, is make you want to go out there and practice, practice, practice! That's the only way. As you learned early on in your trading days, separate your emotions from your trading, learn your lessons, and keep going.

Finally, if you found this book useful in any way, a review on Amazon is always appreciated!

- move pushup pic
- ✓ delete pic w/ dresses
- ✓ delete wedding pic ??
- move award pics down ↓
- move crazy pics
- move richardson down ↓
- move individual pics during #2
- delete some homecoming pics
- ✓ crop bathroom pic
- ✓ check squat pic
- move up flag pic
- ✓ 2nd bike pic

Made in the USA
Middletown, DE
17 May 2020

95370109R20459